Competing theories of the atonement jostle uncomfor+ ' side one
another in contemporary theology. McNall dra\~- church
history to creatively recraft each theolo~· ~eam-
lessly interlock. A portrait of the 1 he
is beautiful.

—N ɔɾessor
.ιy University

Joshua McNall has produced a reasor. ..able account of the atonement. He gets away from the defensive .ɔalism that the atonement is only
"this" or else that the atonement consists of a disparate number of images.
Instead he holds forth the cross of Christ in its biblical horizons and sets
it upon the rich tapestry of historical theology. McNall exposits important
themes related to substitution, triumph, transformation, and recapitulation.
Importantly, he shows that these are not competing ideas but pieces of a
mosaic that all fit together! This is an ideal primer for anyone wanting to
get a grip on the dense debates about the nature of the atonement.

—MICHAEL F. BIRD, academic dean and lecturer in
theology, Ridley College, Melbourne, Australia

A mosaic portrays an image but does so by means of the unseen bond
holding its many pieces in place. In *The Mosaic of the Atonement* McNall
gives us a clear image of the work of Christ, composed of careful interaction
with many of the figures and the topics that together make up this doctrine,
but does so in a way that draws attention to the bonds holding these pieces
together.

—ADAM JOHNSON, associate professor of theology,
Torrey Honors Institute, Biola University

In this well-informed and very readable volume, Josh McNall gives us a lively
and thorough treatment of the great Christian doctrine of the atonement.
While deeply committed to core theological convictions, McNall exhibits
catholicity of spirit and a concern for the proclamation of the gospel. The
result is a wide-ranging study and provocative proposal that will be of
interest to Christian ministers and students as well as scholars.

—THOMAS H. MCCALL, professor of biblical and systematic
theology, Trinity Evangelical Divinity School, and director,
Carl F. H. Henry Center for Theological Understanding

In this major new work on the doctrine of the atonement, Josh McNall presents a comprehensive and cogent approach, integrating the differing perspectives of recapitulation, substitution, victory, and moral influence. His judicious and balanced treatment rejects both the extreme that makes penal substitution the one and only model and the opposite extreme, which neglects the biblical theme of judgement. The scholarly command of the literature and clear argumentation make this a valuable resource for teachers, students, and pastors alike.

—THOMAS A. NOBLE, research professor of theology, Nazarene Theological Seminary

The atonement is a gloriously multifaceted accomplishment. But while much recent atonement theology champions the many-splendored nature of Christ's atoning work, Josh McNall argues that it's not enough to merely uphold the various images of atonement in a disconnected plurality. Rather, they must be integrated. By engaging with Scripture, church tradition, and an array of contemporary theologians, Josh McNall shows how the various images and models of atonement interlock and support one another, providing a fuller and more coherent understanding of the atonement. This book offers a unique contribution and advances the broader conversation that seeks to understand the meaning of the atonement by showing how the various images and models fit together, not as a puzzle but as a mosaic meant to inspire worship.

—JEREMY TREAT is pastor for preaching and vision at Reality LA, Los Angeles, California, adjunct professor of theology, Biola University, and author of *Seek First* and *The Crucified King*

McNall demonstrates the intimate relationship between the various models of the atonement, consistently refusing to condense the full meaning of the cross into any single theory. The doctrine of the atonement is carefully coordinated with other doctrines, especially the doctrine of the Trinity. Among other things, he helpfully distinguishes between the many historic versions of penal substitution, which he regards as an irreducible dimension of the multifaceted work of Christ. The author has achieved a difficult task: to provide a simple yet nuanced introduction to the church's reflection on the atonement, whilst making a constructive contribution to the state of "cross-talk."

—ADONIS VIDU, professor of theology, Gordon-Conwell Theological Seminary

THE MOSAIC
OF ATONEMENT

AN INTEGRATED APPROACH
TO CHRIST'S WORK

JOSHUA M. MCNALL

ZONDERVAN
ACADEMIC

ALSO BY JOSHUA M. MCNALL

Long Story Short: The Bible in Six Simple Movements

A Free Corrector: Colin Gunton and the Legacy of Augustine

ZONDERVAN ACADEMIC
The Mosaic of Atonement

Copyright © 2019 by Joshua M. McNall

ISBN 978-0-310-09764-8 (softcover)

ISBN 978-0-310-09765-5 (ebook)

Requests for information should be addressed to:
Zondervan, *3900 Sparks Dr. SE, Grand Rapids, Michigan 49546*

Cover design: Faceout Studio, Teff Miller
Interior design: Kait Lamphere

Printed in the United States of America

HB 02.17.2022

For Lucy, bright and brave.

Hoc est Corpus Meum

CONTENTS

ABBREVIATIONS

ANF   *The Ante-Nicene Fathers.* Edited by Alexander Roberts
            and James Donaldson. 1885–87. 10 vols. Repr.,
            Edinburgh: T&T Clark, 1989.
BECNT   Baker Exegetical Commentary on the New Testament
CD   *Church Dogmatics.* By Karl Barth. Edited by T. F.
            Torrance and G. W. Bromiley. Edinburgh: T&T Clark,
            1957–77.
Comm. Rom. *Commentary on the Epistle to the Romans.* By Peter
            Abelard. Translated by Steven Cartwright. Washington,
            DC: Catholic University Press, 2011.
EuroJTh   *European Journal of Theology*
Haer.   *Against Heresies.* By Irenaeus.
IJST   *International Journal of Systematic Theology*
Inst.   *Institutes of the Christian Religion.* By John Calvin.
            Edited by John T. McNeill. Translated by Ford Lewis
            Battles. Philadelphia: Westminster, 1960.
JETS   *Journal of the Evangelical Theological Society*
LCC   Library of Christian Classics
LCL   Loeb Classical Library
NICNT   New International Commentary on the New Testament
NIGTC   New International Greek Testament Commentary
NPNF[1]   *The Nicene and Post-Nicene Fathers,* Series 1. Edited
            by Philip Schaff. 1886–89. 14 vols. Repr., Peabody, MA:
            Hendrickson, 1994.
NPNF[2]   *The Nicene and Post-Nicene Fathers,* Series 2. Edited by
            Philip Schaff and Henry Wace. 1896–1900. 14 vols. Repr.,
            Peabody, MA: Hendrickson, 1994.

PG   Patrologia Graeca. Edited by J.-P. Migne. 162 vols. Paris, 1857–86.

SJT   *Scottish Journal of Theology*

WBC   Word Biblical Commentary

WJE   *The Works of Jonathan Edwards*. 26 vols. New Haven, CT: Yale, 1970–2008.

LAYING OUT
THE PIECES

Each year at Christmastime my wife's side of the family participates in a particular holiday tradition. While the fire glows red in the background and the children slowly grow bored with presents, several adults gather around and construct a massive jigsaw puzzle. The work takes hours. Caffeine is involved, and some have been known to stay up long into the night while working with the pieces. I do not participate.

At the risk of sounding antisocial, I confess that I have never liked puzzles. While some seem to find enjoyment in the tedium of assembling tiny pieces, the task has always seemed rather pointless to me. Why bother? If one wants to see the larger picture, there is a perfectly good version of it right there on the box. In fact, this cover image is often higher quality than the puzzle itself, for it lacks the curving crevasses that distinguish piece from piece and the annoying gap that is left when an elusive bit of cardboard slides off the table to be ingested by the family pet. Bah humbug.

Yet as I have now become a father, I have quickly learned that overseeing puzzle assembly is part of the parental job description. And I honestly don't mind it. My two young daughters love to play with puzzles, especially those involving copious amounts of pink and princesses, and I have found a certain joy in helping them. A father feels a sense of happiness when he watches his child recognize the way the pieces fit together.

But this does not mean the task is always easy. Because these puzzles are handled by children, there is the heightened possibility—or, one might say, the absolute certainty—that some pieces from one puzzle will end up in the wrong puzzle box. So not only are there gaps from missing pieces, but there are also pieces that do not fit anywhere, despite their presence in the box. What's more, I have found it quite possible for a three-year-old to switch the lids of two puzzle boxes so that even if the boxed-up pieces fit together, the guide for what one is working toward is entirely misleading. Such are the happy perils of parenting. But what has this to do with Jesus?

| FROM PUZZLES TO A ROMAN CROSS |

For many people, the atonement seems like a puzzle with pieces that do not fit while other crucial bits are missing. In response to this feeling, many now claim that some well-known pictures of redemption are the result of someone having "switched the lid" on Jesus's work, so that another agenda (whether ancient or modern) has been superimposed upon the biblical one.[1] If this happens, the traditions that shape us will also warp us and our notions of atonement.

Especially today, questions about Christ's work abound for both scholars and laypeople. For example, how does the life and ministry of a first-century Jew bring redemption here and now? How did Jesus do something *for us* that still reverberates? The Scriptures help us with these queries, yet even if one commits to believe every word of the Bible, it is not always easy to explain the "mechanism" (a very unspiritual word!) by which Christ's work results in salvation. Thus the question: How do the various pieces of the atonement picture fit together?

| FOUR FAMOUS PIECES |

In response, Christians have developed models, metaphors, and motifs that help articulate the meaning of redemption. These "pieces" of the picture represent imperfect attempts to imagine how Christ's work actually *works*. And in recent years, much ink has been spilled in the defense or destruction of particular accounts.[2] Though that history cannot be detailed now,

---

1. I first heard this analogy in a sermon by Brian McLaren, though I am using it differently.
2. There exists (in my usage at least) a kind of explanatory spectrum with regard to atonement terminology:

Images / Themes / Metaphors / Motifs————*Models*————*Theories*

First, and pictured to the left, are terms that point toward crucial aspects of the doctrine of atonement, but with less specificity as to the "how" of Christ's work. Second, on the opposite end of the explanatory spectrum, there resides the notion of a "theory" of atonement. Based on the scientific and rational connotations of this word, these approaches to the doctrine lean toward a more confident and comprehensive explanation of Christ's work. Finally, somewhere in between these poles sits the notion of a "model." In my use, models have the benefit of offering explanative suggestions (or mechanisms) to address the "how" of the atonement, but with a more cautious and measured acknowledgment of the limits of our understanding.

I will offer a brief snapshot (forgoing lengthy footnotes for the moment) to illustrate how the four most famous models of atonement have produced puzzling questions.

Penal Substitution: Can Punishment Result in Peace?

In its simplest form, the penal substitution model views Christ as having borne the penalty for human sin upon the cross. He was therefore our substitute because divine judgment was poured out on him instead of us. While debates about this paradigm are nothing new, going back at least to the Socinians of the sixteenth and seventeenth centuries, an increasing number of evangelicals, who have traditionally held the view, have also begun to question the merits of this model.

Penal substitution is accused of being historically deficient, logically incoherent, biblically bankrupt, and even morally repugnant. Some have argued that the model was a (mostly) modern invention, and a teaching that lacked precedent throughout most of Christian history. Then there is the logical critique: How exactly can an innocent person *justly* bear the punishment for guilty ones? Is that not the opposite of justice? If a criminal commits a serious offense—say, child molestation or defrauding the elderly—no judge would be commended for sentencing a blameless citizen in his place. Surely the basic principles of justice do not work in this irrational way, or so goes the critique.[3]

Others have claimed that penal substitution presents something primitive, akin to pagan sacrifice, whereby death and pain were required to appease bloodthirsty deities. Surely the Christian God is not like this. Does he not "desire mercy, not sacrifice" (Hos 6:6; Matt 9:13)? These issues have led some to argue that the Bible simply does not speak of sacrifice and wrath like penal substitution requires. Does this mean that the model is an example of someone having "switched the lid" to the atonement puzzle?

Christus Victor: Salvation via Triumph

A second famous piece of the atonement picture is often called the *Christus Victor* motif. Here Christ's work is seen as a triumph over Satan and evil powers. After all, the New Testament states that "the reason the Son of God appeared was to destroy the devil's work" (1 John 3:8).

---

3. The irrationality of the model was stressed by Immanuel Kant, *Religion within the Boundaries of Mere Reason*, in *Religion and Rational Philosophy*, ed. A. Wood and G. Di Giovanni, Cambridge Edition of the Works of Immanuel Kant (Cambridge: Cambridge University Press, 1996), 113.

But even proponents of this piece acknowledge that the victory is a strange one. As the past twenty centuries attest, evil and oppression continue largely unabated since the resurrection. If Jesus really crushed the head of Satan, why doesn't it look like it? The persistence of evil seems obvious with a glance at the headlines—or in the mirror.

Likewise, it seems rather strange to speak of victory at all, in the context of an execution. To be stripped naked and nailed to a Roman cross is, by all appearances, to be conquered in the most shameful way imaginable. How then is the cross a victory? In response, many would claim that while the crucifixion appears like a defeat, the resurrection proves it to be a triumph. Easter heralds *Christus Victor*. Yet even if one emphasizes the resurrection as the proof of Jesus's victory, it is not always clear how the victory carries over to God's people. Our caskets remain firmly closed upon our burials.

To speak of Christ as victorious is not to give any answer as to *how* that victory happened. Triumph is a result; it is not an explanation. For this reason, several theologians have noted recently that *Christus Victor* is not so much a *model* of atonement as it is a *picture* of atonement's upshot.[4] The victory must therefore stand upon some explanatory foundation if it is to elucidate the logic of redemption. Several early theologians did offer suggestions regarding how the victory came. In their view it involved the freeing of captives by way of a ransom, paid either to God or to Satan. Part of Christ's stated mission, after all, was to give his life "as a ransom for the many" (Mark 10:45).

Yet these ransom models raised even more questions. On the one hand, if the price was paid to God, then there were questions of *coherence* and of *character*. In terms of coherence, what kind of being pays a ransom to himself? Is this not like switching money from one hand to the other and claiming a transaction has occurred? And in terms of character, what kind of God is both captor and liberator? If the rescuers who storm the stronghold are discovered to be in league with the kidnappers, then it seems more difficult to claim that they are the good guys. On the other hand, if the devil receives the ransom, it seems even odder that God would bargain with him. Deals with devils are generally frowned upon. Hence, Anselm of Canterbury (1033–1109) argued that the only thing that God ever owed Satan was punishment.[5]

---

4. See Kathryn Tanner, *Christ the Key* (Cambridge: Cambridge University Press, 2010), 253. Likewise, Oliver D. Crisp, "Is Ransom Enough?," *Journal of Analytic Theology* 3 (May 2015): 1–16.

5. Anselm, *Cur Deus Homo?*, in *Proslogium; Monologium; an Appendix in Behalf of the Fool by Gaunilon; and Cur Deus Homo?*, trans. Sidney Norton Deane (repr., Chicago: Open Court, 1926), 2.19.

In another early explanation of the *Christus Victor* piece, triumph came not by paying the devil but by deceiving him. Here Satan was assumed to possess certain rights over humans because we chose to follow him, even though as a creature Satan was believed to lack omniscience. Therefore, by a "divine deception," God used the devil's ignorance and greed against him. Satan, in his appetite to seize upon the flesh of Christ, failed to notice the "hook" of divinity, disguised beneath the surface. In this way, the devil overreached; he took that which he did not own, and he thereby forfeited his human captives.

The tale is colorful. However, this version of the *Christus Victor* motif has not gained much support within more recent centuries. The questions, like the demons duped by Jesus, are legion. For starters, is it acceptable to view God as actively deceiving anyone? Is this not contrary to the very nature of the one who is truth? In addition, many have felt the argument grants Satan too much authority over God's creation, since the devil too is but a creature. Finally, the Gospels themselves seem to indicate that the demons were the one group that actually understood Christ's true identity. They were not fooled. For as one proclaims: "I know who you are—the Holy One of God!" (Luke 4:34).

If all these versions of the *Christus Victor* explanation are as crude as they appear, how exactly is Christ's triumph secured, at least beyond the straightforward answers of cross and resurrection? In light of these questions, the triumph emphasis (while clearly biblical) may also appear like an important puzzle piece with a few rough edges.

Moral Influence: The Power of Transforming Love

In a third approach to the atonement, Christ's work is seen as exerting a powerful and loving moral influence upon humanity. Here, Jesus's gracious and self-sacrificing ministry reveals to us the true nature of God: "God is love" (1 John 4:8). And when we look to the cross, we see how far Love was willing to go in order to redeem us.

According to the moral influence model of atonement, the incarnate demonstration of God's love serves to enkindle our thankful and obedient response.[6] Jesus is therefore the exemplar for how we should live. Like Jesus, we are called to love our enemies and sacrifice for the good of others.

---

6. This word is used most famously by Peter Abelard, *Commentary on the Epistle to the Romans*, on 2:26, in *A Scholastic Miscellany: Anselm to Ockham*, trans. and ed. E. R. Fairweather, vol. 10, LCC (London: SCM, 1956), 283. As I will note later (ch. 11), it is false to claim that Abelard was merely an "exemplarist" as has long been alleged.

To some who have been repulsed by the penal substitution or *Christus Victor* models, this version of the atonement sounds quite beautiful, especially to a modern world in which the power of love is more appealing than the logic of necessary punishment and wrath outpoured.

But there are questions too. If the purpose of the cross is *merely* to reveal divine love, then how does Jesus do something for us that others cannot? Many loving people have laid down their lives for others. How was Jesus's death different? Furthermore, if Christ did not need to die for God to forgive—as some who advocate this model argue—then wasn't his excruciating suffering unnecessary?

What's more, if one goal of the atonement is to *imitate* Christ's pattern of self-sacrifice, then one might ask whether the moral influence theory actually enables abuse. In particular, some who work closely with the targets of violence and oppression have questioned whether certain versions of atonement theology (usually penal substitution and some moral influence paradigms) might further unimpeded abuse while victims "live like Jesus" in patiently refusing to resist their torment. Might some views of the cross really perpetuate the cycle of violence?

Recapitulation: Christ and Adam

In a fourth and final piece of redemptive imagery, some look to the Scriptures and to the early church in order to speak of Christ as a kind of "second Adam," who *recapitulates* (or relives) the entire human story on our behalf. While the concept of recapitulation may sound foreign to the average person, the notion focuses upon the biblical idea that Jesus stands in a position similar to Adam as the representative of the entire human race.

In Romans, Paul claims that both sin and death entered the world "through one man" (5:12). Yet while "the many died" by Adam's sin, "the grace of the one man, Jesus Christ," overflowed much more "to the many!" (5:15). In similar fashion, Paul elsewhere speaks of Jesus as "the last Adam" (1 Cor 15:45), for just as Adam's failure redounded to his offspring, so too Jesus's faithfulness has redemptive significance for all who share in the humanity that he assumed.

While this *recapitulative* way of speaking has precedent in the Scriptures (e.g., Eph 1:10),[7] some massive questions arise within our modern context. Can intelligent people continue to speak of a literal Adam in the age of modern science? While Paul has been read as referring to the "one man"

---

7. English translations of the passage do not normally use the word *recapitulation* here, but the Greek term (*anakephalaiosasthai*) may be rendered as such.

who was the father of us all, recent science has challenged this view of human origins. Genetic evidence has now been taken to show that humanity did not emerge from a single primal pair—an "Adam and Eve" as one might call them. Instead, many scientists argue that there was no singular father from whom God "made all the nations" (Acts 17:26).[8]

In response to this debate, a 2011 cover story of *Christianity Today* concluded with a statement from a leading evangelical pastor: "If Adam doesn't exist, Paul's whole argument—that both sin and grace work 'covenantally'—falls apart."[9] Is this so? Given the rate of scientific discovery, even 2011 may seem like distant history. Recent publications show that evangelical academics hold to a diversity of perspectives on evolution and the historical Adam while remaining steadfast on their views of God as the creator and Scripture as authoritative. Regarding recapitulation, then, the question is clear: Is there a way to take seriously *both* science and the Scriptures on this Adam-focused view of the atonement?

| HOW THIS BOOK IS DIFFERENT |

The coming chapters will attempt what may seem like a tall order. Despite questions and critiques swirling around each of these four approaches, my goal is to show that these "pieces" of atonement actually *do* belong together. Each piece belongs in the box of Christian theology not just because each one is biblical but because each piece interlocks with the others in particular ways.[10] This approach, however, is notably different from many other works on the atonement.

Against Defensive Hierarchy

In particular, I will move to reject—or at least balance—two of the most common tendencies when exploring models of Christ's work. On the one hand, Jeremy Treat rightly highlights a slide toward "reductionism" (or what I'll call *defensive hierarchy*) in many interpretations of redemption.[11]

---

8. Evidence for this claim has been set forth by the findings of the Human Genome Project, led by Francis S. Collins, a professing evangelical. See ch. 2.

9. Pastor Timothy Keller, as cited in Richard N. Ostling, "The Search for the Historical Adam," *Christianity Today*, June 3, 2011, 8.

10. By choosing these four models of atonement, I do not mean to suggest that these are the only viable understandings of Christ's work. Still, these are four of the most famous models, and if one can integrate them both biblically and logically, then this integration will provide a significant benefit to the theological conversation.

11. See Jeremy R. Treat, *The Crucified King: Atonement and Kingdom in Biblical and Systematic Theology* (Grand Rapids: Zondervan, 2014), 177–81.

Whether intended or not, defensive hierarchy reduces the multifaceted nature of the atonement by elevating a single model as somehow most important. In so doing, all other models tend to become subservient to a single central theory. I will argue against this mindset.

To be fair to the proponents of hierarchal models of atonement, there is no logical reason that prevents one view of redemption from being superior. And it is understandable for Christians to stress the model that makes most sense to them. Not every articulation of atonement is equally valid. Surely, false interpretations of the cross should be rejected. Nonetheless, my own argument is that reductionism fails to account for the plurality of metaphors within the biblical canon and for the fact that Scripture gives no obvious reason for ranking one of these pieces as most important. There is no one "ring" to rule them all amongst these models. Hence defensive hierarchies should be avoided.

Against Disconnected Plurality

Neither will it do simply to scatter the pieces on the table, proclaim them all important, and leave them unconnected. This error is reductionism's opposite, and it represents the popular swing toward *relativism* (that is, disconnected plurality) with regard to models of atonement.[12] The claim here is that the Bible gives a "kaleidoscope" of themes that should not be arranged or ordered in any particular way.[13] For example, Stephen Holmes argues that in the Bible "a lot of different pictures are piled on top of one another with no real shape or order."[14] Likewise, Scot McKnight uses the analogy of a golf bag in which each club represents a particular model of atonement. Just like on the golf course, the important thing is to pull out the club that best addresses a current need or situation.[15]

The truth within these claims is that the Bible *does* use many images to describe the riches of Christ's work. And no single image is valued above the others. For these reasons, the "kaleidoscopic" viewpoint marks a praiseworthy corrective to a polemical reductionism. Yet it fails to note that the Scriptures themselves may give reasons to relate these different models of atonement in *particular* ways.

---

12. To be clear, this is not to be confused with the kind of relativism that proclaims all truth claims equally valid.

13. See Joel B. Green, "Kaleidoscopic View," in *The Nature of Atonement: Four Views*, ed. James Beilby and Paul R. Eddy (Downers Grove, IL: IVP Academic, 2006), ch. 4.

14. Stephen Holmes, *The Wondrous Cross: Atonement and Penal Substitution in the Bible and History* (Bletchley, UK: Paternoster, 2007), 78.

15. See Scot McKnight, *A Community Called Atonement: Living Theology* (Nashville: Abingdon, 2010), xiii.

Two Popular Extremes

Reductionism ◄─────────────────────────► Relativism
(Defensive hierarchy) *(Disconnected plurality)*

My claim is that there is another option alongside ranked reductionism and relativistic disorder when dealing with these pieces. Theologians need not embrace either defensive hierarchy or disconnected plurality with regard to models of atonement. Indeed, we shouldn't.[16] While multiple models are necessary, it is also important to understand how these models interlock and support one another—like pieces in a puzzle. And to this end we may benefit from considering a different metaphor.

| FROM PUZZLE TO MOSAIC |

At the end of the day, the atonement is not a puzzle to be solved. Nor is it a problem to be figured out or a riddle that demands human cleverness. While the cross will always appear as folly by the world's standards—"A stumbling block to Jews and foolishness to Gentiles" (1 Cor 1:22–23)—the apostle Paul goes on to marvel that God's perceived "weakness and foolishness" is in truth both strong and wise when viewed through eyes of faith (1:25). The proper response to the atonement is not a confident attempt to figure it out; the proper response is *worship*.

Beneath the Plaster

In the great cathedrals of the church, one sometimes finds another medium in which "pieces" play a part: the mosaic. Like a puzzle, the pieces of mosaic artwork remain visible upon completion. Unlike a photograph, whose tiny pixels present a seamless blend of color and shape, both puzzles and mosaics show us *how* the pieces fit together while also allowing each piece to retain a recognizable particularity. (For a beautiful example of this reality, take a moment to glance at the mosaic image on the cover of this book.) If one stands close, one can identify the individual squares of glass or tile that compose the greater picture. And if one steps back, one can admire the larger image. Yet when presented with the great mosaics of

---

16. Treat says, "The emphasis in upholding diversity has often come at the cost of unity, particularly the task of integrating and ordering the different dimensions of atonement." Treat, *Crucified King*, 182.

age-old Christian churches, viewers are meant not to *construct* the image but to appreciate it. The goal is worship.

The Turkish cathedral known as the Hagia Sophia contains one such piece of artwork. For nearly a thousand years, this church of "holy wisdom" (*hagia sophia*) was the world's largest house of worship, sometimes functioning as the center of global Christianity. Yet in the fifteenth century, Constantinople was conquered by the Ottomans, and the building was converted into a mosque. The massive mosaics were either taken down or covered over with a thick layer of plaster. Minarets were added, and the Hagia Sophia functioned exclusively as a mosque until the twentieth century.

Then the unexpected happened. In 1931, the building was closed to the public as it underwent extensive renovations to reopen as a museum. During this time, remarkable discoveries were made. Under thick layers of paint and plaster, workers uncovered the remnants of spectacular mosaics, the most famous depicting Jesus himself. Although some of the mosaics had been damaged, in some cases the plaster actually protected the images from centuries of wear. The renovation produced stunning results. Here was Jesus, after centuries of hiddenness, looking straight at the viewer with a piercing gaze.

This book attempts a similar (yet more modest) excavation. My guiding metaphor suggests that various models of atonement may be viewed as the oversized pieces of a Christ-shaped mosaic. "This is my body," Jesus proclaims, "given for you" (Luke 22:19). While I must spend time probing aspects of Christian history and addressing contemporary questions and critiques, the crux of the work—to use a fitting word—comes in understanding how these pieces of atonement *fit together*. In my view, it is high time we moved beyond defensive hierarchies and disconnected images of the biblical kaleidoscope. My single mantra therefore reads as follows: Neither reductionism nor relativism; rather, reintegration.

The Mosaic at a Distance

The book is divided into four parts, each devoted to a single piece of the mosaic:

1. THE FEET: Recapitulation
2. THE HEART: Penal substitution (and vicarious judgment)
3. THE HEAD: *Christus Victor*
4. THE HANDS: Moral influence

In part 1, I will identify a particular account of recapitulation as it highlights the ground and the foundation for the other models of atonement. The concept is therefore represented by the *feet* of the crucified and risen Christ. Though planted in the dust of fallen creation, Christ's recapitulative identity as the true human provides the foundation not only for the crushing of the serpent's head (Gen 3:15) but also for the other three models. In short, by viewing Jesus as Paul did—as both the true Adam and the true Israel—one sees *how* Christ is able to act on behalf of all humanity. Christ's work is rooted in his personhood. For as Gregory of Nazianzus famously proclaimed, "The unassumed is the unhealed."[17] It is for this reason that Jesus's recapitulative identity (fully human and divine) as the true Adam and the true *imago Dei* is foundational.[18]

In part 2, I will identify a properly nuanced account of penal substitution—or more broadly, vicarious judgment—as the *heart* of the Christ-shaped figure. Because Jesus is the new and true Adam (as recapitulation argues), he is therefore fit to serve as the representative, and even as the substitute, who willingly accepts the penalty for sin on behalf of humanity. Although this is a controversial claim, I will argue that a careful account of penal substitution is an inescapable reality of the scriptural witness, even if mangled, overzealous, and simplistic presentations of the view have sometimes caused problems. Just as recapitulation provides the logical and covenantal foundation for penal substitution, so too Christ's vicarious judgment on behalf of humanity reveals the "crucial" means by which he conquers. In the end, it is not *Christus Victor* or penal substitution, or even (merely) *Christus Victor* and penal substitution. Rather, Christ's victory comes by way of penal substitution, as a chorus of scholars now suggest.

In part 3, I will locate an account of triumph as the telos of atonement. In this way, the God-glorifying victory of Christ is the result of Jesus's ministry. The *Christus Victor* piece is pictured as the crowned *head* of my mosaic figure. The claim here is that atonement is ultimately about the glory of God; it is theocentric in the end. Yet this God-exalting victory comes about through Christ's recapitulative obedience and vicarious judgment. Here, too, the pieces fit together in a certain way. The God-glorifying victory may be the culmination of the atonement, but it depends upon the

---

17. Gregory of Nazianzus, *Epistle* 101.5 (*NPNF²* 7:439).
18. My claim is not that recapitulation *per se* provides a foundational presupposition for the other atonement models, but rather that a uniquely Irenaean version of recapitulation (centered on Christ's identity as the archetypal *imago Dei*) makes this particular account of recapitulation foundational.

other models in significant ways. "The head cannot say to the [other parts], I don't need you" (1 Cor 12:21).

Finally, part 4 will locate two forms of moral influence reasoning as the two outstretched *hands* of Christ, one beckoning and one restraining. Just as *Christus Victor* is the outcome of Christ's recapitulative vocation and his substitutionary death, so too is a Spirit-empowered account of moral influence necessary to show how humans are enfolded in Christ's triumph. Peter Abelard and René Girard have both made valuable contributions, even if we cannot agree with them on everything.

One reason for saving the moral influence piece till last becomes apparent in looking at Romans 16:20. Here, despite Christ's prior victory in the cross, resurrection, and ascension, we are told that a future triumph still remains. God's victory is a "staged" one—composed of an "already" and a "not yet." To illustrate this truth, Paul reaches all the way back to the recapitulative insight of Genesis 3:15: "The God of peace will soon crush Satan under *your* feet" (italics added). The *your* is crucial, though unexpected. For Paul, the church—the transformed body of Christ on earth—must participate in the present and future crushing of the serpent's head, despite our continued existence as cracked vessels in desperate need of grace.

Herein lies the link to moral influence. *Through* the grace-and-Spirit-driven transformation of sinners into saints, God continues to bring victory and healing to a groaning creation. And make no mistake, all of creation must ultimately be swept up by the Spirit into the God-glorifying drama of redemption (see Rev 21:5). For this reason, the ongoing, loving *influence* of atonement (Christ's outstretched arms, both beckoning and restraining at certain points) should be seen as yet another means by which the *head* is crowned.

| CONCLUSION |

Feet. Heart. Head. Hands. Though these entities make up my governing metaphor, two concluding caveats should be noted. First, despite the mosaic metaphor of Christ, I make no claim to present the full picture of the atonement. No theologian can do that. The riches of Christ's work are inexhaustible, and our little models are but paltry efforts to proclaim how wide and long and high and deep is God's love. Therefore, just as a human body is made up of much more than feet, heart, head, and hands, so too are there many facets of the atonement that are not "pictured" in this study.

Christ's work is always greater than the human attempts to describe it, and theologians must not make graven images of our portraits of atonement.

Second, at no point in my study will one part of Christ's mosaic body be played off against another. Once again, the head cannot say to the feet, "I have no need of you!" (1 Cor 12:21). This too has sometimes been a weakness in both reductionist and relativized (or disconnected) treatments of Christ's work. The overarching claim to be made in this book is therefore that particular pieces of atonement theology *do* fit together, not as a puzzle, but as a mosaic icon meant to guide our worship.

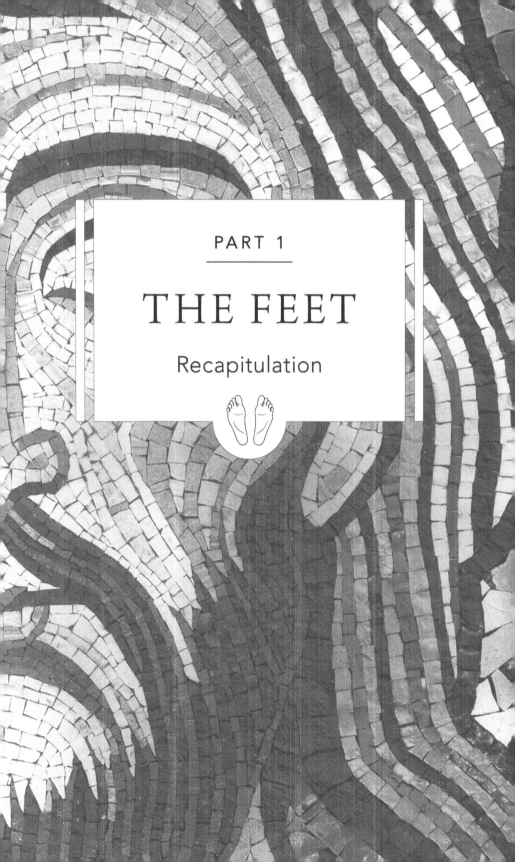

PART 1

THE FEET

Recapitulation

CHAPTER 1

EARLY WILL I SEEK THEE

IRENAEUS ON JESUS AS THE TRUE ADAM

What's past is prologue.
Shakespeare, *The Tempest*

B egin at the beginning" is common counsel for those launching long and complicated stories. According to the Bible, the human story begins with Adam. Likewise, in church history, one of the earliest understandings of Christ's work viewed Jesus as a kind of "second Adam" who *recapitulated* the human drama to bring about redemption. Thus, while the introduction sought only to spread out the pieces of this mosaic of atonement, part 1 will focus on the particular piece that forms a foundation for the other models: atonement as recapitulation.

In my Christ-shaped mosaic, this understanding of Christ's work will be identified with the feet of the crucified and risen Jesus. Admittedly, the feet are not normally seen as the noblest appendages. The head is higher, the heart pumps lifeblood, and the arms can embrace or restrain others. We keep our feet happily hidden beneath socks and shoes. We are not, on the whole, particularly proud of them. But in the words of Thomas à Kempis: "The highest does not stand without the lowest."[1] And in this mosaic, the feet form the foundation for everything else.

Part 1 will show that by reliving, retelling, and reconstituting the human

---

1. Thomas à Kempis, *On the Imitation of Christ*, trans. William Benham (Overland Park, KS: Digireads, 2016), 2.11 (p. 62). To be clear, this statement is not intended to place recapitulation lower on a scale of value. In my metaphor, recapitulation is "below" the other

story as the true Adam and true Israel, Jesus may be understood to bear the penalty for sin, secure the victory over evil, and set forth a loving example that compels us to follow. Therefore, Christ's recapitulative identity as the God-man and the true *imago Dei* provides a basis for these other models of atonement. In this way, my focus upon the foundational qualities of recapitulation aims to provide a theological "foot washing," both honoring and beautifying this dusty and oft-ignored part of the atonement. How beautiful are the feet that bring good news!

In the present chapter, I will explore the meaning of the model by virtue of one of the earliest (and too often neglected) theologians of Christian history, Irenaeus of Lyons.[2] In chapter 2, I will turn to a potential problem for the Christ-Adam connection in the form of genomic (and evolutionary) science. And in chapter 3, I will return to the mosaic metaphor to show how recapitulation fits together with some other pieces of atonement doctrine.

I will begin with a basic inquiry: What is recapitulation? And how does Jesus's identity as the true Adam help one understand atonement?

| INTRODUCING IRENAEUS |

Near the beginning of the Christian tradition stands Irenaeus of Lyons (ca. 140–202). As a youth in Smyrna (on the western edge of modern Turkey), Irenaeus likely heard the gospel from the lips of Polycarp, the Christian martyr (d. 155),[3] who was reportedly a disciple of the apostle John.[4] Thus it was with proximity to the time of the New Testament that Irenaeus became the first great theologian of the Christian faith.[5]

Like many writers, Irenaeus's work was defined (at least in part) by his opponents, the so-called Gnostics, whom he countered with his sprawling work, *Against Heresies*. While the Gnostic movement was diverse,[6]

---

models merely as a foundation is below the rest of the house. This does not, however, make it less important.

2. Support for the claim that Irenaeus has often been neglected in the subsequent tradition may be found in John Behr, *Irenaeus of Lyons: Identifying Christianity* (Oxford: Oxford University Press, 2013), 13.

3. See *Haer.* 3.3.4 (*ANF* 1:416); Eusebius, *Ecclesiastical History*, 5.20 (LCL 153), quoting Irenaeus's letter to Florinus.

4. This is affirmed in various places by Irenaeus, Tertullian, Eusebius, and Jerome. For a recent defense of the likely historicity of the relationship, see Behr, *Irenaeus*, 57–66.

5. For support on this judgment, see Denis Minns, "Irenaeus," in *Early Christian Thinkers: The Lives and Legacies of Twelve Key Figures*, ed. Paul Foster (Downers Grove, IL: IVP Academic, 2010), 44.

6. Given the movement's diversity, recent scholars urge caution against even using the term *Gnosticism*, which did not come into popularity until the seventeenth century. See K. L. King, *What Is Gnosticism* (Cambridge, MA: Belknap, 2003).

its various branches all emphasized the renewal of the human spirit through a secret form of knowledge (*gnosis*). For the Gnostics, the human plight involved the entanglement of spirit with the inferior realm of matter, time, and physicality. Such a world could not be the good creation of the true God but must be the shoddy workmanship of a lesser deity, the Demiurge. In short, creation coincided with the fall. And because materiality was part of the problem, redemption must be accomplished *not* by a God who took on flesh but by the reception of a higher spiritual knowledge that offered the opportunity to "un-world" the human soul.[7] It was this so-called knowledge that Irenaeus sought to smash with a biblical theology of creation and incarnation.[8]

| CREATION AND INCARNATION |

Concerning creation, Irenaeus often referred to the Son and Holy Spirit as the "two hands of God" at work within the world: "It was not angels . . . who made us, nor who formed us . . . nor anyone else, except the Word of the Lord. . . . For God did not stand in need of these [beings] . . . as if He did not possess His own hands . . . the Son and the Spirit, by whom and in whom, freely and spontaneously, He made all things."[9] To speak of God's two hands was to say that the Son and the Spirit *are* the divine presence within the created order. They reveal that the good Creator is not detached from this messy and magnificent world. Christians worship a "hands-on" God who is closely involved within the material realm. In the well-framed words of Katherine Sonderegger, "Deity is not repugnant to the cosmos, nor paradoxical to it. . . . Rather . . . God has a 'positive' relation to the world. The thornbush burns with divine fire, and the bush is not consumed."[10]

At the same time, Irenaeus also argued that the Creator is not to be confused with the creation. God is *other* than the world, despite his personal presence within it. As the analogy of the two hands illustrates, while a man may cradle a piece of pottery in his palms, the object and the man

---

7. This phrase is that of David Bentley Hart, *The Beauty of the Infinite: The Aesthetics of Christian Truth* (Grand Rapids: Eerdmans, 2003), 22. For an introduction to various Gnostic theologies, see Robert M. Grant, *Irenaeus of Lyons* (London: Routledge, 1997), chs. 2–3.

8. "So-called knowledge" was Irenaeus's own designation for these teachings, as evidenced by the original title of the work now known as *Against Heresies*. Irenaeus referred to the composition as *Refutation and Overturning of the Knowledge Falsely So Called*.

9. *Haer.* 4.20.1 (*ANF* 1:487).

10. Katherine Sonderegger, *Systematic Theology*, vol. 1, *The Doctrine of God* (Minneapolis: Fortress, 2015), xix–xx.

are nonetheless distinct. Similarly, it is by the Word and Spirit that the Father holds the world close without collapsing into it.[11]

Irenaeus moved easily from creation to incarnation since the linkage of these two themes was crucial in refuting Gnostic errors. In a winsome passage, he writes that "this Hand of God which formed us in the beginning, and which does form us in the womb, has in the last times sought us out who were lost, winning back his own, and taking up the lost sheep upon his shoulders, and with joy restoring it to the fold of life."[12] Irenaeus also made much of the fact that just as God formed Adam from the earth, so too Jesus chose to heal by mixing saliva with the dust (John 9:6).[13] This was "not without purpose or by chance, but that he might show forth the Hand of God that had at the beginning molded the human being."[14]

| THE DIVINE ECONOMY |

Whereas Irenaeus's opponents focused upon ethereal and complex theories, Irenaeus emphasized the divine economy (*oikonomia*). The word referred to the careful and purposeful ordering of one's household (*oikos*), but in literary contexts it also described an author's purposeful arrangement of the episodes within a story.[15] The fact that *Romeo and Juliet* involves five acts is not an accident of history but a mark of authorial intent.

With these domestic and literary contexts in mind, Irenaeus used the word *economy* to refer to God's purposeful actions within the drama of redemption. Because of this, he saw acts within the divine economy as the source of one's knowledge of God. History is the theater of divine activity. One knows God not by arcane philosophies but by what he has *done* within space and time. If the good Creator has united himself with matter in the incarnation, then materiality cannot be denigrated. If the Word became flesh (John 1:14), then physicality must not be seen as loathsome. And if Christ rose bodily from the grave and ascended bodily to heaven, then the human body must not be viewed as something to be happily cast off forever.

---

11. In recent years, perhaps the most passionate champion of a neo-Irenaean doctrine of creation was the late Colin Gunton. See, for instance, Gunton, *The Triune Creator: A Historical and Systematic Study* (Grand Rapids: Eerdmans, 1998), ch. 3.

12. *Haer.* 5.15.2. This translation is that of Behr, *Irenaeus*, 163.

13. For Irenaeus, the saliva—as with water throughout his writings—is connected to the Spirit. Thus we see again that both "hands" continue to work together within the incarnation.

14. *Haer.* 5.15.2; translation by Behr, *Irenaeus*, 162.

15. See Behr, *Irenaeus*, 125.

| THE RULE OF TRUTH |

For Irenaeus, the rule (or rod) of truth affirmed all these realities.[16] This measuring stick (or *canon*) formed the standard by which all theological claims were to be judged. But what exactly was this rule? Irenaeus gave no clear-cut definition. It was not, strictly speaking, Christian Scripture. In these early years, the canon of authoritative books had yet to be fully defined, despite the fact that Irenaeus quotes repeatedly from these inspired texts.

Likewise, the rule was somewhat different from the *creeds* of later centuries. When speaking of the rule, Irenaeus was not quoting from a formal doctrinal statement, like those produced by later councils. In contrast, the canon of truth remained more flexible in wording.[17] Nor was the rule to be identified straightforwardly with something as broad as church tradition—although this too, like the concepts of Scripture and creed, appears to be related to it. So what exactly was this rule of faith?

A careful reading of Irenaeus makes clear that this measuring rod was to be recognized *within* a straightforward and Spirit-led reading of the Scriptures. This straightforwardness did not negate the cryptic or typological nature of some biblical texts, but the accessibility of the canon was apparent in the way that even unschooled "barbarians" could easily grasp the gospel, while the more educated, elitist, and intensely speculative Gnostics distorted the plain sense of the biblical narrative.[18] Likewise, this same standard was to be recognized *within* the unified tradition that had been handed down from Christ, to the apostles, and through the unbroken succession of church leaders. While the rule was less rigid than a creed, it involved certain immovable components. In the first place, there is one God, the good Creator of all things. Likewise, there is one Christ, the Messiah, who came in the flesh for the purpose of redemption.

When laid against this basic standard of the faith, the claims of so-called Gnostics fell short on numerous accounts, yet none more obvious than in what is now called the doctrine of atonement.

| CHRIST AND ADAM |

Like Paul before him, Irenaeus pictured Jesus as a kind of "last Adam" (1 Cor 15:45). And in this role, the connections between Christ and Adam

---

16. Also referred to as the "rule of faith."
17. See Behr, *Irenaeus*, 112.
18. See Behr, *Irenaeus*, 126.

were seen to be important. For Irenaeus, both Christ and Adam came from "untilled soil," which meant that both were formed materially but apart from male intervention.[19] Just as Adam came from virgin earth, so Jesus came by virgin birth.[20] And because Mary was a descendant of Adam, Christ's flesh was of the same stock as Adam's flesh.[21] He was truly "one of us," despite his sinlessness.

The Christ-Adam relationship also continued by way of contrast. While Adam succumbed to the devil's call to eat in disobedience, Christ fasted in the face of his wilderness temptation.[22] And just as Adam's sin involved a tree, so too transgression was undone by the "tree" of the cross.[23] In all this, Irenaeus emphasized the fitting parallels between Christ and Adam.

| BEAUTY AS A SIGN OF TRUTH |

Irenaeus's emphasis on a fitting correspondence is sometimes referred to as the "aesthetic criterion." That is, the suggested links between the Old and New Testaments were seen as valid partly on the grounds of poetic justice and thematic symmetry.[24] In some instances, this aesthetic criterion led to undue speculation. For example, Irenaeus confidently asserted that Adam's sin took place on a Friday, for we know that Good Friday was the day of Christ's crucifixion.[25] Likewise, he was certain that Jesus was crucified as an "old man" of around fifty. The theological justification for this belief resides in Christ's identification with all humanity: since he came to save persons of all ages, it was deemed appropriate that he should pass through every stage of life.[26]

---

19. *Haer.* 3.21.10 (*ANF* 1:454).

20. This phrase is that of Thomas Holsinger-Friesen, *Irenaeus and Genesis: A Study of Competition in Early Christian Hermeneutics* (Winona Lake, IN: Eisenbraus, 2009), 7.

21. *Haer.* 3.19.3 (*ANF* 1:446).

22. *Haer.* 5.21.2 (*ANF* 1:549).

23. Irenaeus, *Demonstration of Apostolic Preaching*, trans. A. Robinson (New York: MacMillan, 1920), 33.

24. See Eric Osborn, *Irenaeus of Lyons* (Cambridge: Cambridge University Press, 2001), 18–24.

25. *Haer.* 5.19.1 (*ANF* 1:547). As with other early Christian understandings of the creation narratives, this "day" in Gen 1 was not to be viewed as a literal twenty-four-hour period of time. For Jews, Friday was the sixth day, and for Irenaeus, this sixth day (in Gen 1) was a reference to the present and ongoing age of imperfection, to be eventually followed by the Millennium of Christ's perfect earthly reign. Thus there was more going on in the references to "Friday" than mere aesthetic sensibilities.

26. *Haer.* 2.22.2 (*ANF* 1:390). In fairness, Irenaeus also bases this conclusion, in part, upon John 8:57 in which certain Jews remark that Jesus is "not yet fifty years old." For Irenaeus, this implies that Jesus was approaching his fiftieth year, which was the year that many teachers were recognized as being a "master" in their craft. See Behr, *Irenaeus*, 170n70.

While arguments like this seem unconvincing today, the purpose was praiseworthy. Irenaeus was attempting to counter false teachings with a story that was superior not only in logical coherence and biblical attestation but in beauty and poetic justice. The gospel was not only truer than Gnostic mythology; it was more winsome. In the divine economy, the reflection of God's goodness was to be encountered not merely in the rationality of the immaterial mind but in the physicality of a fallen but majestic world. To cite the American novelist Marilynne Robinson, we catch glimpses of this truth from time to time: "As though the Lord breathes on this poor gray ember of Creation and it turns to radiance."[27] For Irenaeus, the splendor of the aesthetic criterion was leveraged (however imperfectly) to show that God's acts within creation reveal the marks of providence just as beauty has the ring of truth. In this way, connections between the first and second Adam were seen to give more credence to the Christian faith.

Nearly two millennia later, an analogous judgment on aesthetics would lead a young physicist named Albert Einstein to gauge the veracity of certain theoretical equations on the grounds that "God" could not have passed up such an elegant solution. In the theory of general relativity ($E=MC^2$), this aesthetic sense would prove justified, while in others, as in Einstein's attempts at a unified theory of everything, it would not.[28] For Irenaeus, the logic—and the mixed results—were comparable.

| THE IMAGE |

The symmetry between Christ and Adam is also apparent in Irenaeus's view of the *imago Dei*. Though the image of God may seem somewhat removed from the cross and resurrection, Irenaeus's account of the *imago Dei* is crucial for his explanation of how Jesus saves. Genesis teaches that humans were fashioned from earth in the image and likeness of God (1:26), yet the meaning of this claim brought great debate throughout church history. While there have been numerous suggestions on the content of the *imago Dei*, a great many interpretations may be placed within one of three categories.

First, substantive views see the image as something that humans innately possess, perhaps in reason or free will. Second, functional views see the image as something humans are called to do, perhaps in stewarding

---

27. Marilynne Robinson, *Gilead* (New York: Picador, 2004), 245.
28. For more on Einstein's use of a so-called aesthetic criterion, see Walter Isaacson, *Einstein: His Life and Universe* (New York: Simon & Schuster, 2007).

creation or reflecting the Creator. Third, relational views see the image as something humans experience in the encounter between the human and God or the human and the human. Once more, the options are

1. something we *have*;
2. something we *do*; or
3. something we *experience* via relationship.

At the risk of oversimplification, many interpretations of the image of God are connected to at least one of these three approaches.[29]

What of Irenaeus? In some ways, he fits most naturally within the substantive camp because for him the image is something that humans innately possess. Irenaeus believed that the likeness of God was (temporarily) lost because of sin but that the image remains a fundamental part of our identity.[30] And while other theologians tended to focus more *exclusively* on immaterial qualities—like human reason[31]—Irenaeus's emphasis on incarnation led him in a different direction. He began with those New Testament passages that identified Christ as the image of God (Col 1:15; 2 Cor 4:4). Irenaeus then formulated an account of the image that linked Christ and Adam in a way unlike most other theologians since. In the words of Denis Minns, Irenaeus argued that "when God fashioned the earth creature from mud he did so after the pattern of the *body* of Christ."[32]

While Jesus of Nazareth had (quite obviously) not yet been born at the time of Adam's making, Irenaeus believed that the Creator had consciously constructed humans in conformity to the incarnate Son. For this reason, Christ served as the archetype, or pattern, of the entire human race. Jesus was the mold for Adam's making. In the words of Irenaeus, "[God] made man in the image of God; and the image of God is the Son, after whose image man was made: and for this cause He [Jesus] appeared in the end of the times that He might show the image (to be) like unto Himself."[33]

---

29. See Millard Erickson, *Christian Theology*, 2nd ed. (Grand Rapids: Baker, 1998), 520–28.
30. See *Haer.* 3.18.1 (*ANF* 1:445–46); 5.1.3 (*ANF* 1:527).
31. See, for instance, my treatment of the contrast between Augustine and Irenaeus at this point. Joshua McNall, *A Free Corrector: Colin Gunton and the Legacy of Augustine* (Minneapolis: Fortress, 2015), chs. 4 and 9.
32. Minns, "Irenaeus," 60, italics added; cf. *Haer.* 5.16.2 (*ANF* 1:544).
33. Irenaeus, *Demonstration*, 22.

Following the New Testament, Irenaeus argued that the incarnate Christ simply *is* the image of the invisible God.[34] Thus when one speaks of the divine image within the human, one ought not to begin with discussions of immaterial entities (whether reason or free will) but with the physical person of the Messiah.[35]

| THE BODY AND THE IMAGE |

This allowed Irenaeus to do something virtually unparalleled throughout much of church history: he included the human body within his understanding of the divine image. In his view, the physical body was linked to the divine image because the true image (Jesus) had a body, which served as the pattern after which Adam was fashioned. The whole human was "modelled after [God's] Son," for while "soul and the spirit are certainly a part of the human," they are not the whole. "The perfect human consists in the . . . union of the soul receiving the spirit of the Father, and the admixture of that fleshly nature which was moulded after the image of God."[36]

This holistic account of the image allowed Irenaeus to blast opponents who disdained human physicality. And it also fits quite well with recent biblical scholarship. As J. Richard Middleton argues, *tselem* (or image) in the ancient Near East was used to describe a "localized, visible, corporeal representation of the divine."[37] In pagan cultures this was invariably an idol or a king, but in every case, the image was a visible and bodily thing. As *embodied beings* the first humans represent God's rule on earth, and as an embodied being Jesus Christ shows forth the perfect image of God in his work of recapitulation.

| DEFINING RECAPITULATION |

Before diving into Irenaeus's view of recapitulation, I should first define this rather loaded word. In the Greek language shared by Irenaeus and the writers of the New Testament, the term is *anakephalaiōsis*. And while

---

34. In the words of Irenaeus, "The Father is the invisible of the Son, but the Son is the visible of the Father." *Haer.* 4.6.6 (*ANF* 1:469).

35. See Anders-Christian Jacobsen, "The Importance of Genesis 1–3 in the Theology of Irenaeus," *Zeitschrift für Antikes Christentum* 2 (2004): 305–6.

36. *Haer.* 5.6.1 (*ANF* 1:531–32). Here I have replaced *man* with *human*.

37. J. Richard Middleton, *The Liberating Image: The Imago Dei in Genesis 1* (Grand Rapids: Brazos, 2005), 25.

the pronunciation may seem daunting, finding a satisfying definition can be even more so.

The term is present in the Scriptures. In Ephesians 1:10, the church is told that it has redemption and forgiveness because God purposed to *recapitulate* "all things in heaven and on earth under Christ." In some translations, the word is rendered "sum up," as when a speaker or author brings a long story to an appropriate summation. In this sense, it has a similar meaning as when one briefly recaps a lengthy narrative. Jesus is therefore seen as the "concise Word," who succinctly illustrates what the long narrative of the Old Testament had been saying all along.[38]

Unfortunately, this definition is not particularly helpful in explaining how Jesus saves. A concise rearticulation of the Old Testament would indeed be helpful, but it would not necessarily explicate the atonement. Thankfully, recapitulation means more than just "recapping." The word for "head" (*kephalē* in the Greek; *caput* in Latin) appears within both Greek and Latin versions of the term. Hence one might refer to recapitulation as the process of "reheadshipping." To press the language just a bit, one might say that when humanity "capitulated" to sin (via Adam), we found ourselves "decapitated." Hence what was needed was no mere repentance, but a full-scale reheadshipping of the entire human family.[39]

The relation to headship also explains why Irenaeus connects the term so readily to Adam, the supposed head of the entire human race.[40] Likewise, it also explains why Ephesians speaks of recapitulation as bringing all things under Christ (1:10), who is the head of the church (5:23).

| ROOTS AND BRANCHES |

One way to understand Irenaeus's recapitulative logic is to picture humanity as a single tree. By this imagery, even today, in maternity wards and dirt-floored huts throughout the world, new shoots of life are sprouting upward from the forked branches that support us all. In this sense, we are all connected. And according to the biblical story, at the root of this expanding family tree—and deep in the ground from which he was formed—is Adam.

---

38. See Behr, *Irenaeus*, 124–28. Rom 13:9 seems to use *recapitulated* (or *summed up*; Gk. *anakephalao*) in this sense.

39. Holsinger-Friesen, *Irenaeus and Genesis*, 128.

40. While Irenaeus himself does not refer to Adam explicitly as the "head" of the human race, the etymology of *anakephalaiosis* (with *kephale* meaning head) shows that the notion is not antithetical to his thought.

In the Bible, Adam is the head of the entire human race. And in Scripture, what happens to the head has repercussions for others. The actions of a family's head often carry over to the offspring, just as the actions of the anointed ruler have implications for the nation as a whole. Thus, while David fights and bears the insults of Goliath, the Israelite people reap the victory because they have a portion in him. In the Bible, the head may act for the whole.[41]

To cite a negative example, Paul claims that the sin of Adam has unleashed catastrophic consequences. "Sin entered the world through one man, and death through sin" (Rom 5:12). If one is to continue the family tree analogy, Paul views the Adamic root as being rotten with a malady that affects us all.[42] Thankfully, however, the apostle also locates the Messiah in a position of redemptive contrast (and excess!) when compared to Adam's failure: "The gift is not like the trespass. For if the many died by the trespass of the one man, how much more did . . . the grace of the one man, Jesus Christ, overflow to the many!" (Rom 5:15). In this way, Christ and Adam are clearly linked, for "as in Adam all die, so in Christ all will be made alive" (1 Cor 15:22).

In all of this, Irenaeus followed Scripture when he connected Christ and Adam in a mysterious but genuine continuity.[43] In doing so, however, he was not simply repeating the words of Paul; he was developing them. By expanding upon the New Testament understanding of Christ and Adam, Irenaeus attempted to provide a partial picture of *how* atonement works. Here again, the *imago Dei* is paramount. As I have argued, Irenaeus viewed Adam as having been fashioned after the pattern of the (yet-to-be) incarnate Christ. Jesus was the "cast," or "mold," for Adam's making, just as the ring of a ruler provides an imprint in wax to leave behind his image. Thus Christ is not merely the offspring of Adam but also his archetype and the true head of God's whole family.[44]

In related fashion, Scripture proclaims that the Messiah is both the

---

41. For a related account of how participatory notions of incarnation and atonement connect to kingship, see Joshua W. Jipp, *Christ Is King: Paul's Royal Ideology* (Minneapolis: Fortress, 2015).

42. For one treatment of precisely how human sinfulness (or fallenness) spreads from Adam to humanity at large from the perspective of biblical theology, see Mark Biddle, *Missing the Mark: Sin and Its Consequences in Biblical Theology* (Nashville: Abingdon, 2005).

43. Beyond the Pauline corpus, Luke's genealogy also traces the link between Christ and Adam.

44. For a recent endorsement of something like this christological account of the *imago Dei*, see Oliver Crisp, *The Word Enfleshed: Exploring the Person and Work of Christ* (Grand Rapids: Baker Academic, 2016), ch. 4.

"root" and the "descendant" of David (Rev 22:16; cf. Isa 11). Christ is not merely a son but also the *source* of humanity at large and of Israel in particular. Because of this, and by the biblical logic, the Messiah may act on behalf of the whole because he is the rightful head.[45] To return to the biblical analogy, at the deepest root of this expanding family tree—deeper even than Adam himself—is the Son, the Word, the *Logos*. Christ is the true image of God and the archetype of human identity.

| IRENAEUS ON RECAPITULATION |

All this provides the context for Irenaeus's most famous expression of recapitulative logic.

> Not despising or evading any condition of humanity . . . he came to save all through means of himself—all, I say, who through him are born again to God. . . . He therefore passed through every age, becoming an infant for infants, thus sanctifying infants; a child for children, thus sanctifying those who are of this age. . . . So likewise he was an old man for old men, that he might be a perfect master for all. . . . Then, at last, he came even to death itself, that he might be "the first-born from the dead, that in all things he might have the pre-eminence," the prince of life, existing before all, and going before all.[46]

In this passage Irenaeus viewed Jesus as reliving the entire human story on behalf of his people. At each stage and under all conditions of human experience, Jesus is obedient and victorious. At every point, his holiness spills over ("sanctifying those of this age"). The reason that Christ's righteous acts may "stand in" for ours involves his identity as the archetype of the entire human race ("existing before all, and going before all"). Once again, the head may act for the whole. Christ's recapitulative personhood as the

---

45. To those who might object, saying that the preincarnate Christ could not be the mold for Adam's making based on chronological concerns, note the words of Robert W. Jenson: "Time, as we see it framing biblical narrative, is neither linear or cyclical but perhaps like a helix, and what it spirals around is the risen Christ." Jenson, "Scripture's Authority in the Church," in *The Art of Reading Scripture*, ed. Ellen F. Davis and Richard B. Hays (Grand Rapids: Eerdmans, 2003), 35. Likewise, as Chris Tilling notes, "Time does not always 'behave' around Jesus Christ for Paul; it is not business as usual." Tilling, "Paul, Christ, and Narrative Time," in *Christ and the Created Order: Perspectives from Theology, Philosophy, and Science*, ed. Andrew B. Torrance and Thomas H. McCall (Grand Rapids: Zondervan, 2018), 162.

46. *Haer.* 2.22.2 (*ANF* 1:390).

true *imago Dei* provides the biblical basis (and the logical foundation) for his unique ability to act *for* others. This explains why an Irenaean account of recapitulation provides the "footing" for other models of atonement.

Elsewhere, Irenaeus said that when the eternal Son became incarnate, "the Word" was "united to his workmanship." And in kind, "he commenced afresh [literally, 'recapitulated'] the long line of human beings, furnishing us with salvation; so that what we had lost in Adam—namely, to be according to the image and likeness of God—that we might recover in Christ Jesus."[47] Here again, the victorious obedience of Christ is contrasted with the failure of Adam. Thus "God recapitulated in himself the ancient formation of man, that he might kill sin, deprive death of its power, and vivify the human being."[48] In all of this, salvation is spoken of in the context of Jesus reliving (and recapitulating) the human story on our behalf.

| UNDERMINING INDIVIDUALISM |

In an individualistic culture, this concept may seem foreign and far-fetched. As Colin Gunton defines it, "Individualism is the view of the human person which holds that there is so much space between people that they can in no sense participate in each other's being."[49] Thus follows the modern maxim that

> I am the master of my fate,
> I am the captain of my soul.[50]

These sentiments can give a sense of control to our confusing lives. But they are also absurd. In a multitude of ways, I am *not* the master of my fate. My present options have been conditioned by the past. My genetic code was inherited, and the places and parents that shaped me were not my choice. In all of this, one sees the truth of Shakespeare's line about how history shapes the future: "What's past is prologue."[51]

Realizations like these need not lead to a knee-jerk embrace of fatalism

---

47. *Haer.* 3.18.1 (*ANF* 1:446).

48. *Haer.* 3.18.7 (*ANF* 1:448).

49. Colin Gunton, "Trinity, Ontology and Anthropology: Towards a Renewal of the Doctrine of the *Imago Dei*," in *Persons, Divine and Human: King's College Essays in Theological Anthropology*, ed. Christoph Schwöbel and Colin Gunton (Edinburgh: T&T Clark, 1991), 55.

50. William Ernest Henley, "Invictus," which first appeared in Henley's *Book of Verses* (New York: Scribner & Welford, 1888), 56–57.

51. Shakespeare, *The Tempest*, 2.1.

(Irenaeus, for his part, was a staunch defender of free will), but they do reveal that our freedoms have been impinged upon in profound ways. Both science and psychology now insist with growing certainty that the outcomes of our lives are greatly affected by the lower "branches" on this crooked family tree. If, however, this uniquely modern view of individualism is fatally flawed, then perhaps the logic of recapitulation may gain a fresh hearing.

| THE FORGOTTEN IRENAEUS |

Before coming to the contemporary relevance of Irenaeus's theology, I must first address what happened after his death. In the words of one scholar: "No early Christian writer has deserved better of the whole Church than Irenaeus."[52] While the claim may be overstated, the fact remains that Irenaeus was often overlooked by the subsequent tradition despite a period of initial acclaim.[53] Proof of this may be found in Erasmus of Rotterdam, when he finally republished *Against Heresies* in 1526. He was thrilled to have "restored to light a book that had been virtually forgotten for over a thousand years."[54] There are several reasons for the overshadowing of Irenaeus,[55] yet because my topic is atonement, I will briefly deal with just one change in subsequent tradition: the evolution of original sin.

Whereas Irenaeus had remained relatively silent on the mechanism by which Adam's disobedience affected his descendants, Augustine of Hippo (354–430) was more specific. According to Augustine, because (1) all fallen humans were literally "in" their ancestor Adam, and because (2) all "sinned" *in* him (as evidenced by his unfortunate Latin translation of Rom 5:12),[56] therefore, (3) all fallen humans inherit both the guilt of Adam's sin (*reatus*), and (4) the debilitating *concupiscence*—that is, the disordered nature of human desires—that follows from the primal failure.

---

52. This quote from H. B. Swete originally appears in the foreword to F. R. M. Hitchcock, *Irenaeus of Lyons: A Study of His Teaching* (Cambridge: Cambridge University Press, 1914).
53. Hans Urs von Balthasar notes that Tertullian, Eusebius, Theodoret, and Epiphanius all showered praise on Irenaeus as indisputably the greatest theologian of his century. See Irenaeus, *The Scandal of the Incarnation*, trans. John Saward (San Francisco: Ignatius, 1981), 8.
54. So says Minns, *Irenaeus*, viii; cf. 132–34.
55. See my treatment of "The Forgotten Irenaeus," in *A Free Corrector*, 251–56.
56. In his Latin Bible, Augustine read that "sin came into the world through one man, *in whom* all have sinned" (Rom 5:12). Most scholars now agree that this translation is erroneous. It would be better rendered as stating that death comes to all "*because* all sinned" (NRSV, italics added). For an assessment of the much-discussed interpretive options here, see Stanley Porter, "The Pauline Concept of Original Sin, in Light of Rabbinic Background," *Tyndale Bulletin* 41 (1990): 22–25. See also Biddle, *Missing the Mark*, 4–5.

Because Augustine believed these states were passed from parent to child, supposedly through the lust of the father,[57] even infants were seen as sinners worthy of damnation. After Augustine, the practice of infant baptism became crucial for washing away Adam's damning stain.[58]

| ORIGINAL IMMATURITY |

I mention Augustine's doctrine only to note some contrasts with Irenaeus. While Augustine emphasized a fall from primal perfection, Irenaeus emphasized the notion that Adam and Eve were created as "little ones" with a childlike *immaturity*; they were "unaccustomed to and unexercised in perfect conduct."[59]

For Irenaeus, the naiveté of Adam and Eve did not mean that their early state was manifestly flawed but that they had not yet reached the goal God intended.[60] Though they were "very good," they were nonetheless to grow up into the full likeness of Christ, just as a healthy toddler must mature into an adult. From this perspective, the fall represents an arrested development from a good beginning. By taking the fruit, humanity sought knowledge for which they were not ready, like an infant attempting to eat solid food or an adolescent who desires to grow up too soon.

In the act of sin, Irenaeus believed that humans lost the "likeness" though not the "image" of Christ. He was clear that salvation would be impossible apart from God's grace and apart from the cross. Irenaeus avoided even a hint of Pelagianism (to use an anachronistic label), and at certain points the contrast between his thought and that of Augustine has been overblown.[61] Humans are born, as Irenaeus puts it, into the "house of bondage" and shackled with the chains of Adam's sin.[62] Yet he was less explicit than Augustine in claiming that the damning guilt for Adam's act

---

57. At this point, Augustine's Platonic view of sexuality shows itself. See T. A. Noble, "Original Sin and the Fall: Definitions and the Proposal," in *Darwin, Creation and the Fall*, ed. R. J. Berry and T. A. Noble (Nottingham: Apollos, 2009), 109.

58. For a careful and concise treatment of Augustine's doctrine, see Paul Rigby, "Original Sin," in *Augustine Through the Ages: An Encyclopedia*, ed. Allan D. Fitzgerald (Grand Rapids: Eerdmans, 1999), 607–14.

59. *Haer.* 4.38.1. This translation is that of Behr, *Irenaeus*, 195. Irenaeus may have borrowed this childlike view of Adam and Eve from Theophilus of Antioch. See Jacobsen, "Genesis 1–3 in the Theology of Irenaeus," 301.

60. As Behr notes, "An infant may well be born with 'perfect' limbs, but will nevertheless be unable to walk." Behr, *Irenaeus*, 195.

61. See A. N. S. Lane, "Irenaeus on the Fall and Original Sin," in *Darwin, Creation and the Fall*, ed. R. J. Berry and T. A. Noble (Nottingham: Apollos, 2009), 141–42.

62. See *Haer.* 5.21.1 (*ANF* 1:548–49).

was passed down via lust and heredity. And he was clearly different from Augustine in his emphasis that the world of Adam (in Gen 1–2) was not yet perfect.[63] On both of these points, Irenaeus has something to teach us.

In modern times, an Irenaean emphasis upon the intended growth of God's creation has been seized upon to wrestle with the challenges of science and (in some cases) with the search for alternatives to Augustine's version of original sin and guilt.[64] For some, Irenaeus's emphasis on a God who "takes his time" perfecting creation provides helpful hints for how one might interpret the Genesis narratives in light of evolutionary theory. In the Bible, after all, the original creation is declared good, not perfect. The command is therefore to work and keep (or perhaps "guard") the garden, not merely to maintain it in a static state of perfection. I will revisit all these themes in the next chapter.

| RETRIEVING RECAPITULATION |

On the atonement specifically, the centuries since the Reformation have also witnessed a partial retrieval of Irenaeus's recapitulative logic. Along these lines, John Calvin (1509–64) wrote that "our lord came forth as true man and took the person and name of Adam . . . in order to take Adam's place in obeying the Father."[65] Christ therefore "abolished sin" not merely by penal substitution but "by the whole course of his obedience," for "from the time when he took on the form of a servant, he began to pay the price of liberation in order to redeem us."[66] John Owen (1616–83) spoke similarly when he claimed, "There is no contemplation of the glory of Christ that ought more to affect the hearts of them that do believe with delight and joy than this, of the *recapitulation* of all things in him."[67]

Some of the greatest theologians of the twentieth century—perhaps most notably Karl Barth and T. F. Torrance—also returned to Irenaeus to show how the redemptive repercussions of Christ's work may carry over

---

63. See Lane, "Irenaeus on the Fall," 142–43.

64. Because Irenaeus wrote much less than Augustine on these matters, and because his writings have been less familiar to the Western church, the danger is that modern scholars might simply use Irenaeus (or the mysterious and hypergeneralized "East") as a blank canvas on which to anachronistically project their own theories. See Lane, "Irenaeus on the Fall," 130. I will return to this problem in the subsequent chapter.

65. *Inst.* 2.12.3.

66. *Inst.* 2.16.5.

67. John Owen, "The Person of Christ: His Mediatorial Office in Heaven," in *Works of John Owen*, ed. William H. Goold (London: Banner of Truth Trust, 1965), 1:372, italics added.

to *all* humanity. If the Son is the archetype of "Adam" (and not merely his descendant), then, as T. F. Torrance wrote,

> the true secret of our humanity is lodged in the Word. In the incarnation of the Word, Christ became the "proper man" as Luther called him, the true man . . . [and] because all mankind consist in him, he is the only one who can really represent all men and women from the innermost centre and depth of human being. He came then, not only as the creator of our race, but as the head of our race, for in him the whole race consists (Col 1.15–20). It was thus that Christ, true God took upon himself our flesh and became true man, and as such made atonement.[68]

The twenty-first century too has brought renewed interest in recapitulation. In a celebrated work on the atonement, Hans Boersma points to Irenaeus as the one whose view of recapitulation "holds out rich promise in overcoming seemingly insuperable polarities between the various models of the atonement," and in showing "the way in which the various models might relate to one another."[69] Likewise, there is a parallel between the atonement argument of Irenaeus and that of New Testament scholar N. T. Wright. Specifically, Irenaeus's concept of recapitulation, which deals primarily with Christ and Adam, is quite similar to Wright's concept of reconstitution as it pertains to Christ and the vocation of Israel.[70] In Wright's view, Christ takes upon himself the vocation of both Israel and Adam in order to bring salvation. The Messiah comes to do and be what Israel and Adam failed to do and be.

This mission is highlighted by the way Jesus seems, intentionally, to be walking through the story of Israel, specifically the exodus. Where his precursors succumbed to Satan's temptation, Jesus responds faithfully. Like Israel, Jesus goes into Egypt under sentence of death (Matt 2:13), and like Israel he emerges to pass through the Jordan (in baptism). Christ surrounds himself with an advance guard of twelve disciples, a move that mirrors both the twelve tribes and the twelve spies that set out into

---

68. T. F. Torrance, *Atonement: The Person and Work of Christ*, ed. Robert Walker (Downers Grove, IL: IVP Academic, 2009), 126. See also *CD* IV/1, 512–13. This does not mean, of course, that either Barth or Torrance accepted an ancient understanding of the literal or "historical" Adam. I must delay this debate until the following chapter.

69. Hans Boersma, *Violence, Hospitality, and the Cross: Reappropriating the Atonement Tradition* (Grand Rapids: Baker Academic, 2004), 14.

70. See, for instance, N. T. Wright, *Jesus and the Victory of God*, Christian Origins and the Question of God, vol. 2 (Minneapolis: Fortress, 1996), 615. Boersma notes this connection in *Violence, Hospitality, and the Cross*, 126.

the promised land. In all of this, Christ is reliving and reconstituting the Israel story. And it sounds an awful lot like an Israel-focused notion of recapitulation. When the focus turns back to Adam, Wright is likewise clear that Jesus's resurrection in a garden, on the first day of a new week, is meant to echo the Adam story, just as Jesus is presented as a "new Adam" who is simultaneously the representative of a new humanity.[71] Here, too, Wright's view resonates with the Irenaean concept of recapitulation, even while he adds the Israel-emphasis alongside the Adam one.

Others have recently argued that recapitulation presents helpful possibilities for contemporary culture as we celebrate atonement as a remedy to human shame, not just human guilt.[72] The claim here is that feelings of guilt (I have done wrong) may be dealt with by punishment or making amends while abiding shame (I *am* wrong, awful, worthless) requires a more pervasive cure. For T. Mark McConnell,

> A global work of recreation is needed—the scope of atonement needs to be as wide as the scope of shame. Those struggling with shame would be helped to know that in Christ God has recreated every aspect of their life in the renewed image of God. If true humanity is lost in shame as the research shows, it is recreated in Christ through recapitulation.[73]

In this account of atonement, Jesus identifies with the human creature all the way down, even sharing in the shame of Adam's nakedness as he hangs naked on a Roman cross: "God's shame-bearing symbol for the world."[74] In this moment, he is not just *Christus Victor* but *Christus Nudus*,[75] the one who simultaneously scorns (Heb 12:2) and bears our shame. By penetrating to these dark recesses of the human story, Christ brings the love of God to bear on a shame-filled humanity and heals us by an act of recapitulation.

---

71. For more on Wright's treatment of Christ as the new Adam, see N. T. Wright, *The Climax of the Covenant: Christ and the Law in Pauline Theology* (Minneapolis: Fortress, 1991), 18–40; And more recently, *The Day the Revolution Began: Reconsidering the Meaning of Jesus's Crucifixion* (New York: HarperOne, 2016), 273–76.

72. See T. Mark McConnell, "From 'I Have Done Wrong' to 'I am Wrong': (Re)Constructing Atonement as a Response to Shame," in *Locating Atonement: Explorations in Constructive Dogmatics*, ed. Oliver D. Crisp and Fred Sanders (Grand Rapids: Zondervan, 2015), 168–88.

73. McConnell, "From 'I Have Done Wrong,'" 182.

74. Robert H. Albers, "The Shame Factor: Theological and Pastoral Reflections Relating to Forgiveness," *Word & World* 16, no. 3 (June 1, 1996): 352; cited in McConnell, "From 'I Have Done Wrong,'" 186.

75. On this phrase, see Dan Lé, *The Naked Christ: An Atonement Model for a Body-Obsessed Culture* (Eugene, OR: Pickwick, 2012).

| CONCLUSION |

These recent applications should motivate Christians to do precisely what I have tried to do in the present chapter—namely, to attempt to understand what Irenaeus meant when he viewed the work of Jesus through the lens of recapitulation.

For Irenaeus, Adam himself was fashioned in the image and likeness of the incarnate Christ. Thus Jesus was not merely a *son* of Adam but also Adam's *source* and archetype. At the deepest root of our expanding family tree there is one greater than Adam, one who reclaims headship from our fallen founder and relives the human story faithfully on our behalf. Since the Messiah is the mold for all humanity, and the true image after which all of us were patterned, Irenaeus's account of recapitulation lends explanatory power to the idea that Christ may act on behalf of others. In later chapters, this recapitulatory insight will prove foundational for other models of atonement, since it shows how the past can exert a mysterious but pervasive influence upon the present and the future. "For as in Adam all die, so in Christ all will be made alive" (1 Cor 15:22).

In this biblical and Irenaean understanding of Christ and Adam, one can recognize the meaning of recapitulation. But in merely outlining this view of the atonement, I have not yet shown whether its ancient argument still has credibility. In the following chapter, I will therefore turn to a contemporary issue that threatens to shatter the foundation of my mosaic Christ, like the smashing stone in Nebuchadnezzar's vision (Dan 2:34), crushing the *feet*, which turned out to be partly made of clay.

CHAPTER 2

WHERE ARE YOU, ADAM?

RECAPITULATION AND THE
HUMAN ORIGINS DEBATE

The Fall [is] the only encouraging view of Life.
It holds . . . that we have misused a good world,
and not merely been entrapped into a bad one.

G. K. Chesterton

"Where are you?" is the first question God asks in the Bible. The inquiry is addressed to the figure we call Adam and to his wife, Eve (Gen 3:9).[1] In the story, the couple responds to the shame of disobedience by hiding in hopes of disappearing. But in modern times, their "disappearing act" has seemed more successful. As it has with many doctrines, science has long questioned older views on human origins. Thus names like Darwin and Dawkins bring to mind the supposed "war" between science and faith.

In the wake of these modern controversies, many Christians have sought a kind of truce. This comes, for instance, by adopting a more contextualized reading of the Genesis creation narratives or other portions of the Bible.[2] Once this path is taken, one can see the earth as far older than the meagre tally of the biblical genealogies and can (perhaps) carve out more space for evolutionary processes. There is no tenet of orthodoxy,

---

1. In Hebrew,'*adam* is a generic term for human. The word is not used as a proper name until the genealogy in Gen 5.
2. See, for instance, John H. Walton, *The Lost World of Genesis One: Ancient Cosmology and the Origins Debate* (Downers Grove, IL: IVP Academic, 2009).

after all, that forbids belief in a God who might wisely endow certain creatures with the ability to adapt and evolve over time as part of his patient plan. Provided that God is still affirmed as the Creator, the move away from seeing the Bible as literalistic science textbook is meant to allow Christians to understand the claims of both "books," Scripture and nature, more faithfully.[3]

For evangelicals, the compromise has helped many to maintain belief in a historical Adam and Eve as the literal parents of the entire human race. In support of this conclusion, the suppositions often have run as follows: Perhaps the earth is billions of years old; perhaps evolution exists in some form or another; and perhaps this is not a problem for the Christian faith. After all, one might well be an "old-earth creationist" while still believing in a singular Adam, whose sin affected the future in profound ways.[4]

But with the recent rise of genetic mapping (as seen most notably in the Human Genome Project), the shaky truce is again being challenged. Over the last decade or so, a plethora of books and articles have emerged to deal with the science as it pertains to human origins.[5] And many now claim that any "wiggle room" for belief in Adam and Eve as the literal progenitors of the entire human race has been eliminated.[6] In the words of the geneticist (and Christian) Dennis Venema, "The sun is at the center of our solar system, humans evolved, and we evolved as a population. . . . To date, every genetic analysis estimating ancestral population sizes has agreed that we descend from a population of thousands, not a single ancestral couple."[7] But what does this have to do with the atonement?

Because this is not a book on "science and the Bible," many questions in the above debate may be passed over for sake of space and subject matter.

---

3. See Kathryn Applegate and J. B. Stump, eds., *How I Changed My Mind about Evolution: Evangelicals Reflect on Faith and Science* (Downers Grove, IL: IVP, 2016).

4. See, for instance, C. John Collins, "A Historical Adam: Old-Earth Creation View," in *Four Views on the Historical Adam*, ed. Ardel B. Caneday and Matthew Barrett (Grand Rapids: Zondervan, 2013).

5. For a small sampling, see Peter Enns, *The Evolution of Adam: What the Bible Does and Doesn't Say about Human Origins* (Grand Rapids: Brazos, 2012); C. John Collins, *Did Adam and Eve Really Exist? Who They Were and Why You Should Care* (Wheaton, IL: Crossway, 2011); Barrett and Caneday, eds., *Four Views on the Historical Adam*; John H. Walton, *The Lost World of Adam and Eve: Genesis 2–3 and the Human Origins Debate* (Downers Grove, IL: IVP Academic, 2015); Dennis Venema and Scot McKnight, *Adam and the Genome: Reading Scripture after Genetic Science* (Grand Rapids: Brazos, 2016); William T. Cavanaugh and James K. A. Smith, eds., *Evolution and the Fall* (Grand Rapids: Eerdmans, 2017).

6. See Karl W. Giberson and Francis S. Collins, *The Language of Science and Faith* (Downers Grove, IL: IVP, 2001), 209–10; see also Francis S. Collins, *The Language of God: A Scientist Presents Evidence for Belief* (New York: Free Press, 2006), ch. 5.

7. Venema and McKnight, *Adam and the Genome*, 55.

I do not, for instance, have any desire to venture into the increasingly unfruitful culture wars between so-called "young-earth creationists" (YECs) and their scientific foils. I am not a scientist. And I am most certainly not a part of the Christian cottage industry of nonscientists pretending to be scientists.[8] This is a book on the atonement; I am merely a theologian.

Yet the question of Adam is relevant to discussions of Christ's work. As seen in the prior chapter, both Paul and Irenaeus viewed Jesus as a kind of second Adam, who acted on behalf of the entire human race. Recapitulation therefore involves a "reheadshipping" of the human family in a way that reverses and exceeds Adamic failure. Salvation is possible in part because Christ, the head, may act on behalf of the whole.[9] Since the human was fashioned in the image of the incarnate Christ, Irenaeus saw Jesus as entering the story not just as Adam's *son* but also as his *source* and archetype. Christ is the root of the entire human tree, not merely an offshoot of the tribe of Judah. Just as many died by the trespass of the "one man" Adam (Rom 5:15), so "in Christ all will be made alive" (1 Cor 15:22). Put simply, the Bible brings together Christ and Adam at the nexus of atonement.

But what if there was no historical Adam who was the first and only hominin in the beginning?[10] What if scientific claims preclude this old notion of the "one man" who was the literal father of the human race just as they preclude credible belief in a flat earth and a sun that orbits us? Should orthodox Christians accept these scientific claims? And what might that mean for recapitulation?

While the prior chapter sought only to frame recapitulation as a view of the atonement, the present one deals with a contemporary "land mine" (science) that threatens to blow up this age-old understanding of Christ's work. I will begin with an overview of the scientific conversation as it currently stands. Next, I will touch upon some available Christian responses,

---

8. This industry indeed exists. Several years ago at a faculty workshop, I recall being lectured to for several hours by one of these itinerant "experts." The discourse ranged confidently from philosophy, to theology, to geology, to physics, and so on. Since the audience was filled with PhDs from these fields, and since our speaker had encouraged Christians to question the credentials of so-called authorities, someone eventually asked about his own training. He then admitted that he had only an undergraduate degree in English literature. So far as I remember, this was just about the only subject on which he had not claimed to be an authority.

9. See ch. 1.

10. Anthropologists now use *hominin* (rather than *hominid*) to speak of the grouping of humans with what are seen to be their prehuman relatives. Theologically speaking, when I say "human," I mean always to highlight those who bear the image of God in a way that distinguishes us from all other creatures. In this way, *human* (i.e., image bearer) and *hominin* are not necessarily synonymous.

along with their respective implications. Finally, I will offer a series of theological proposals on the subject of Adam and atonement.

In the end, I will argue that indeed *some belief in the historical "Adam" as the head of God's image bearers is necessary if one wishes to affirm a robust view of Scripture, sin, and the atonement.* For these reasons, neither Adam nor the fall can simply be discarded without serious consequences to the logic of redemption. Still, the precise wording of the italicized sentence is important. One need not feel compelled to advocate for such things as a "young earth," heavy-handed biblical literalism, or even the notion that Adam was the first and only hominin at the time of his creation. While geneticists and Bible scholars may continue to explore this topic, the logic of recapitulation does not require these specific commitments. My conclusion, therefore, is that there may be more common ground between science and orthodox theology than is sometimes thought. If this is true, then something like an Irenaean understanding of recapitulation may be maintained as a foundational piece in the mosaic of atonement.

| SNAPSHOTS OF SCIENCE |

I begin with a snapshot of the scientific argument. Long before the mapping of the human genome, evolutionary thinking had begun to challenge traditional views on Adam and Eve. While Darwin deftly avoided the question of human evolution in his *Origin of the Species* (1859), the seeds were clearly sown within the work. And it was but a short step to the prevailing wisdom that humans share a common ancestor with the great apes.[11] The emerging consensus was straightforward: Life evolved via a process of natural selection from simpler to more complex forms.[12]

The Fossil Record

Then came fossils. With the discovery of what appeared to be transitional species between anatomically modern humans and their evolutionary ancestors, many claimed to have a "smoking gun" against Adam's historicity.[13]

---

11. Charles Darwin, *On the Origin of Species by Means of Natural Selection* (London: Murray, 1859). Darwin would take up an account of human origins in *The Descent of Man, and Selection in Relation to Sex* (New York: D. Appleton, 1871).

12. Unless otherwise specified, when I use the term *evolution* in the remainder of this chapter, I am using it with this definition in mind.

13. See William Stone (a pseudonym), "Adam and Modern Science," in *Adam, the Fall, and Original Sin: Theological, Biblical, and Scientific Perspectives*, ed. Hans Madueme and Michael Reeves (Grand Rapids: Baker Academic, 2014), 54; likewise, Venema and McKnight, *Adam and the Genome*, ch. 3.

After all, if we have hard evidence (literally) that *Homo sapiens* evolved from prior primates, then the Sunday School image of a fig-draped Adam might seem imperiled. Indeed, when it came to the evolution of life in general, the fossil evidence appeared virtually incontrovertible to specialists in the field.[14]

For many Christians, however, the fossils alone did not rule out belief in the historical Adam. In a recent book on the subject, a Christian paleoanthropologist argued (albeit under a pseudonym to protect his professional reputation) that it is possible to accept many tenets of evolutionary theory while placing the biblical Adam at the origin of the genus *Homo*. This would purportedly locate such a figure as living about 1.8 million years ago. Still, the claim is hardly free from difficulties. The view would place Adam far earlier than the apparent setting in Genesis and long before the earliest cultural remains in the paleontological record.[15] In spite of these challenges, the pseudonymous scientist illustrates how some have sought to affirm the fossil record while still viewing Adam as the father of the entire human race. What the above argument entirely sidesteps, however, is that the debate no longer centers on the fossils.[16]

Genetics

Genetics is the new frontier. With the mapping of the human genome and those of other species in the early twenty-first century, scientists claimed a mountain of new evidence to corroborate Darwin's theory of evolution via natural selection.[17] While the details are complex, Francis Collins, the leader of the project and a professing evangelical Christian, claims that one result is clear: "The study of genomes leads inexorably to the conclusion that we humans share a common ancestor with other living things."[18]

This conclusion is said to be supported by multiple and independent lines of genomic data. Geneticist Dennis Venema identifies the basic evidence.

---

14. See, for instance, Darrel R. Falk, *Coming to Peace with Science: Bridging the Words Between Faith and Biology* (Downers Grove, IL: IVP Academic, 2004), ch. 4. Beyond such theological publications, see Donald Johanson and Blake Edgar, *From Lucy to Language* (New York: Simon & Schuster, 2006).

15. See Stone, "Adam and Modern Science," 81; and John Bloom, "On Human Origins: A Survey," *Christian Scholars Review* 27, no. 2 (1997): 199n72.

16. See Stone, "Adam and Modern Science," 61n32. On the one hand, one cannot blame a paleoanthropologist for avoiding questions of genetics. It is lamentable, however, that a book which seeks to touch upon the science of the debate would all but ignore the most important findings of recent decades.

17. See also Dennis R. Venema, "Genesis and the Genome: Genomics Evidence for Human-Ape Common Ancestry and Ancestry and Ancestral Hominid Population Sizes," *Perspectives on Science and the Christian Faith* 62, no. 3 (September 2010): 166–78.

18. Collins, *The Language of God*, 127–28.

First, there is the astonishing similarity of genes (called *homology*) between species thought to have a common ancestor (e.g., humans and chimpanzees). Second, there is the conservation of a precise gene order between related species (called gene *synteny*). And thirdly, there is the evidence from *pseudogenes*—the mutated remains of gene sequences that persist even after inactivation by way of prior evolutionary mutations.[19] Since these pseudogenes (sometimes called "junk DNA") serve no functional purpose, opponents of human evolution are forced to answer why "the designer" would implant something in us that has no function other than to give the strong impression that we share a common ancestor with other primates.[20] In other words, why would the Christian God place inactive remnants of nonfunctional DNA within us, at just the right places, simply to trick us into believing that our race evolved?

Finally, there is the issue of ancestral population size. The claim here is that one may now compose a "family tree" of sorts, based on a detailed map of the existing genetic diversity.[21] This science has even gone mainstream with the ability to check one's genetic and ancestral history by way of a simple mail-order test. Unlike the roots and branches of biblical genealogies, this tree leads allegedly not to a single human ancestor but to many (no fewer than a few thousand). This notion is referred to as *polygenism*.[22] Venema sums up the argument:

> Some ideas in science are so well supported that it is highly unlikely new evidence will substantially modify them. . . . Put most simply, DNA evidence indicates that humans descend from a large population because we, as a species, are so genetically diverse in the present day that a large ancestral population is needed to transmit that diversity to us.[23]

In the end, this argument challenges a literalistic reading of the "one man" (Rom 5:15) from whom God "made all the nations" (Acts 17:26).[24]

---

19. See Venema, "Genesis and the Genome," 166–67; cf. Venema and McKnight, *Adam and the Genome*, chs. 3–4. See also Collins, *The Language of God*, 138–39.

20. Venema, "Genesis and the Genome," 173.

21. See Venema, "Genesis and the Genome," 174.

22. Some crucial scientific studies are noted in Venema, "Genesis and the Genome," 178n40. For an early and influential work, see Francisco Ayala, "Molecular Genetics of Speciation and Human Origins," *Proceedings of the National Academy of the Sciences* 91, no. 5 (July 1994): 6787–94. See also David Wilcox, "Finding Adam: The Genetics of Human Origins," in *Perspectives on an Evolving Creation*, ed. Keith B. Miller (Grand Rapids: Eerdmans, 2003), 234–53.

23. Venema and McKnight, *Adam and the Genome*, 55.

24. A minority of biblical scholars take Acts 17:26 as referring to Noah, yet this exegetical possibility gives no help with the genetic evidence. See, for instance, Walton, *Lost World of Adam and Eve*, 106–7.

From Science to Theology

But if the question "Where are you, Adam?" no longer has a simple answer, Christians are also left with deeper questions about the origin of almost everything that we call evil. Regarding humans especially,[25] the atonement has always been taken to deal with things like sin and death as *problems*—and as unwelcome intruders into God's good world. To cite Cornelius Plantinga, Christianity holds that "sin is unoriginal, that it disrupts something good and harmonious, that (like a housebreaker) it is an intruder, and that those who sin deserve reproach." From this perspective, the present state of selfishness, violence, and deceit is "not the way it's supposed to be."[26]

Still, the science has led some Christians to question even *this* contention.[27] Bible scholar Daniel Harlow claims that we now have "a range of evidence [that] establishes that virtually all of the acts considered 'sinful' in humans are part of the natural repertoire of behavior among animals." These behaviors include thievery, bullying, infanticide, and rape. His claim is that instead of corrupting the animal kingdom with the contagion of sin and fallenness, "humans inherited these tendencies from our animal past."[28] These terrible realities came about, in the view of the Reformed theologian John Schneider, "by the creative-destructive will of God."[29] In a stark reversal of Plantinga's description of sin as unoriginal to the created order, this argument implies that the violence, selfishness, and death that sustain both animal and human "kingdoms" *is* precisely how it is supposed to be.[30]

From one perspective, this frightening conclusion may seem to fit the appearance of the world around us. Consider, for instance, the brutal "circle of life" (and death) depicted in popular nature documentaries.

---

25. The question of animal death and suffering is an important and complicated question that I cannot address here. See Michael Murray, *Nature Red in Tooth and Claw: Theism and the Problem of Animal Suffering* (Oxford: Oxford University Press, 2008); Ronald Osborn, *Death Before the Fall: Biblical Literalism and the Problem of Animal Suffering* (Downers Grove, IL: IVP Academic, 2014); Christopher Southgate, *The Groaning of Creation: God, Evolution, and the Problem of Evil* (Louisville: Westminster John Knox, 2008).

26. Cornelius Plantinga, *Not the Way It's Supposed to Be: A Breviary of Sin* (Grand Rapids: Eerdmans, 1995), 16.

27. See especially John R. Schneider, "Recent Genetic Science and Christian Theology on Human Origins: An 'Aesthetic Supralapsarianism,'" *Perspectives on Science and Christian Faith* 62, no. 3 (September 2010): 196–212; Daniel C. Harlow, "After Adam: Reading Genesis in an Age of Evolutionary Science," *Perspectives on Science and Christian Faith* 62, no. 3 (September 2010): 179–95.

28. Harlow, "After Adam," 180. See also Daryl Domning, *Original Selfishness: Original Sin and Evil in the Light of Evolution* (Aldershot: Ashgate, 2006).

29. Schneider, "Recent Genetic Science and Christian Theology," 207.

30. In critique of Schneider's claim, see the careful work of Thomas H. McCall, *An Invitation to Analytic Christian Theology* (Downers Grove, IL: IVP Academic, 2015), 128.

It can seem, says David Bentley Hart, "as if the entire cosmos were somehow predatory."[31] This bloody observation led Darwin to conclude that "the sufferings of millions of the lower animals throughout almost endless time" seem irreconcilable with a creator of "unbounded" goodness.[32] Thus some have been led to the unsettling assumption that if there is a Designer, he apparently designed it like this.[33] In the chilling words of Hannibal Lecter, "Typhoid and swans, it all comes from the same place."[34]

This jarring statement brings the Christian to an uncomfortable reality. This is not an abstract discussion. In dealing with the results of the fall, we are dealing with those parts of life that most haunt and grieve us. On a personal level, when I first sat down to write this chapter, my own brother-in-law lay not far away with tubes protruding from his body. At age thirty, he was in the final stages of a disease called ALS. In that painful season, the family gathered to say goodbye and to mourn what Christians say is the result of a "fallen" world. Surely, we say, this is "not the way it's supposed to be."[35]

Both here and elsewhere, the question is whether the suffering and perceived injustices within the present world are actually *contra Deum* ("against God").[36] Not only must we ask, What do scientists say? We must also ask how Christians should respond to the scientific treatment of Adam, the fall, and the atonement.

| POSSIBLE RESPONSES |

At least three major options are on the table. For those who wish to maintain their Christian faith and a high view of Scripture, one may, at each point,

1. *dispute* the scientific arguments,
2. *ignore* the scientific arguments, or
3. *harmonize* the scientific arguments with one's reading of the Scriptures and tradition.

---

31. David Bentley Hart, *The Doors of the Sea* (Grand Rapids: Eerdmans, 2005), 50.

32. See Darwin's letter to Hooker, July 13, 1856, in *More Letters of Charles Darwin*, ed. F. Darwin and A. Seward (London: Murray, 1903), 1:94.

33. According to Jill Carroll, "To reclaim violent models of God is simply to be honest about the universe we live in and the cosmic, natural powers that seem to 'brood and light' within it." Carroll, *The Savage Side: Reclaiming Violent Models of God* (Lanham, MD: Rowman and Littlefield, 2001), 116.

34. Thomas Harris, *The Silence of the Lambs* (New York: St. Martin's, 1988), 22.

35. Daniel Robert Berg went to be with Christ in 2015. He is greatly missed.

36. The gravity of this question is set forth by McCall, *Analytic Christian Theology*, 145.

These choices should not be viewed as hermetically sealed approaches (though they have been in some cases). One need not select one option at the outset and then apply it to every claim of science along the way.[37] *At each point* one may accept and harmonize certain scientific claims while bracketing or disputing others.

Disputing Science

I begin with the more contentious path. The response of many Christians, especially within the movement of young-earth creationism, has been to fight science with "science"—or at least with what passes for science in the eyes of the faithful.[38] From this perspective, the problem is not with the evidence, but with what is claimed to be the highly biased, dishonest, and anti-Christian motives that guide the guild of scientists at large. If only one is allowed to view the "real evidence" (that is, the data that most peer-reviewed academic journals do not want you to hear) then one may see the truth.[39]

Unfortunately, what passes as "creation science" has often been of dubious credibility.[40] Instead of merely lampooning the movement, however, Christian academics would do well to hear the words of Mark Noll, in his otherwise scathing critique of evangelical anti-intellectualism. In Noll's words:

> Creation scientists have performed an excellent service by denying that vast cosmological claims about the self-sustaining, closed character of the universe can ever arise from scientific research itself. They are just as insightful when claiming that such grand conclusions are as much

---

37. This is a significant problem with the options as set forth by both Enns and Harlow. In both cases, they give the impression that one must choose a single approach at the outset and then adopt it in regard to every claim of science and the Scriptures. See Harlow, "After Adam," 180; Enns, *Evolution of Adam*, xvii–xviii.

38. For the definitive history of this movement, see Ronald Numbers, *The Creationists: The Evolution of Scientific Creationism* (Berkeley, CA: University of California Press, 1992).

39. Among the first of such attempts came the 1961 publication of *The Genesis Flood* by John C. Whitcomb and Henry M. Morris.

40. An example of this tendency comes from one of the most well-known (and well-funded) creationists in recent years, who has argued that the presence of "dragon-stories" in various cultures provides evidence that dinosaurs indeed coexisted with humans. No word yet on the scientific implications of cultures that tell stories about the Cookie Monster. For a Christian refutation of young-earth creationism, see Davis Young and Ralph Stearley, *The Bible, Rocks and Time: Geological Evidence for the Age of the Earth* (Downers Grove, IL: IVP, 2008). For an essential historical treatment of the movement, see George M. Marsden, "Why Creation Science?," in *Understanding Fundamentalism and Evangelicalism* (Grand Rapids: Eerdmans, 1991).

an act of faith as any other large-scale religious claim. . . . In a word, fundamentalist and evangelical resentment at how capital-*s* Science is practiced, funded, preached, and prescribed in our culture could not be more appropriate. It is quite otherwise with the fundamentalist practice of science. Fundamentalist social resentment may be well grounded, but not fundamentalist science.[41]

While many insights of evolutionary theory may pose no threat to orthodox theology, there has been a widespread (though nonsensical) effort by some scientists to smuggle the quasi-religious claims of atheistic naturalism into a definition of evolution.[42] One example of the tendency can be found in the ridiculous claim of Stephen J. Gould, who states that "before Darwin, we thought that a benevolent God had created us," but now, after Darwin, we realize that "no intervening spirit watches lovingly over the affairs of nature."[43] Case closed.

What Gould's statement fails to mention, of course, is how the credible claim of evolving creatures could possibly disprove the existence of a Creator who may have patiently overseen this process. Indeed, although evolutionary development requires an incredible amount blood and death to move things forward, one might view the apparent wastefulness of the process as something more akin to "sacrifice." After all, Christians have long claimed that life emerges from a death of incalculable proportions.[44] We call this the doctrine of atonement.

Christ himself likened God's patient method of building to seeds falling on all types of soil. And since it is this same Son through whom God made the world (Heb 1:2), N. T. Wright suggests that the parable of the sower may help us understand God's involvement in the long and prodigal process of creaturely development. Whether in building his kingdom or in cultivating creation, a pattern emerges: "Some seeds go to waste; others bear remarkable fruit. Some projects start tiny and take forever but suddenly produce a great crop." *This* is simply God's long-established method of

---

41. Mark Noll, *The Scandal of the Evangelical Mind* (Grand Rapids: Eerdmans, 1994), 186.

42. For an explanation of why naturalism should be seen as a "quasi religion," see Alvin Plantinga, *Where the Conflict Really Lies: Science, Religion, and Naturalism* (Oxford: Oxford University Press, 2011), x.

43. Gould, "In Praise of Charles Darwin," in *Darwin's Legacy* (San Francisco: Harper & Row, 1983), 6–7.

44. Daniel Harrell proposes this possibility in his afterword to Venema and McKnight's *Adam and the Genome*, 195.

overcoming chaos, however slow or wasteful it may appear to both New Atheists and fundamentalists alike.[45]

Yet not all disputations of the scientific consensus come from the web-based wasteland of the fundamentalist fringe. In more recent years, some scientists have questioned, for instance, the nonfunctionality of the previously mentioned *pseudogenes* (sometimes called "junk DNA").[46] And on the question of polygenism specifically, it has recently been argued that scientists like Venema have confused genetic data with genealogical evidence when the two are not the same. In the argument of S. Joshua Swamidass, "It is likely that there have been many individuals, and potentially couples, across the globe who are each individually genealogical ancestors of all those alive when recorded history began."[47] As a nonspecialist, I cannot speak to this debate. Still, it is important to remember that science also evolves, especially when the evidence is relatively new, as with genetics. If this happens, then perhaps the years to come will create more room for thoughtful disputation.[48]

Ignoring Science

A second approach is simply to set aside or otherwise *ignore* the scientific arguments regarding human origins.[49] This may take place out of an embarrassment over the pseudoscience of fundamentalists; it may reflect an acknowledgment that one is not qualified to speak as a scientific authority; or it may represent a silence that seems required when little friendly evidence seems readily at hand.

45. N. T. Wright, "Christ and the Cosmos: Kingdom and Creation in Gospel Perspective," in *Christ and the Created Order: Perspectives from Theology, Philosophy, and Science*, ed. Andrew B. Torrance and Thomas H. McCall (Grand Rapids: Zondervan, 2018), 103. Wright's point is that both atheists and fundamentalists have often failed to grasp this point, even as both have tended to divorce Christ's kingdom-teachings from the doctrine of creation.

46. See Erika Check Hayden, "Life Is Complicated," *Nature* 464 (2010): 664–67 (published online, March 31, 2010), as cited in C. John Collins, *Did Adam and Eve*, 118.

47. S. Joshua Swamidass, "The Overlooked Science of Genealogical Ancestry," *Perspectives on Science and Christian Faith* 70, no. 1 (March 2018): 19–35. Swamidass is a physician, scientist, and Assistant Professor of Laboratory and Genomic Medicine at Washington University in Saint Louis. While dealing with complex scientific data, he provides an accessible argument that a person might be a genealogical ancestor of "all living" without necessarily passing on any genetic material to those alive today.

48. This possibility, along with a call for caution, is held out by Collins, *Did Adam and Eve*, 118–19.

49. Despite its strong points, this is the unfortunate impression left by the recent volume edited by Hans Madueme and Michael Reeves, *Adam, the Fall, and Original Sin*. While the subtitle claims to approach the issues from "Theological, Biblical, and Scientific Perspectives," the lone chapter dealing with the "science" simply brushes aside any treatment of genetics in a single furtive footnote. See again Stone, "Adam and Modern Science," 61n32.

For many Christians, a lack of engagement with science may be sustainable. After all, most people are not immersed in the fields of genetics, geology, or paleoanthropology. And the fields are so specialized that one may often avoid the theological ramifications of one's work. For example, Congregational minister Daniel Harrell tells of asking a geneticist in his church if she had ever thought about the connections between her research and what the Bible says of Adam. "No, she said, her funding only permitted her to focus on a single gene."[50] The fact that nearly fifty percent of Americans claim to believe in young-earth creationism may simply reflect a lack of interest or familiarity with science in general.[51]

Yet for those who do desire a deep understanding of *both* God's Word and God's world, ignoring science is not an option. And if the evidence continues to mount, this approach may prove deadly. It creates the perception that Christians should fear evidence, and it can cause students especially to abandon the faith when scientific data begins to contradict teachings that may not be requirements for orthodoxy in the first place. What then is the final option?

Attempted Harmonies

"Concordism" is often understood as the belief that harmony, or positive concord, should be sought between the claims of science and Scripture. In extreme forms, this involves a literalistic attempt to read the Bible as a "science text" that provides a play-by-play of how the physical universe functions and how it came to be. In the view of most scientists and Bible scholars, this approach is folly.[52]

The truth, however, is that virtually all Christians seek a "concord" between the Scriptures and the world around us. The reason should be clear: many doctrines involve historical events that either happened or not. Science claims that bodily organs do not suddenly revivify after death and decay have taken hold, but the Scriptures beg to differ when it comes to Jesus's resurrection (and our future one). So while the study of biology alone does not support the likelihood of Easter, Christians cling to

---

50. Daniel Harrell, afterword to *Adam and the Genome*, by Venema and McKnight, 193.
51. A 2012 Gallup poll registered that nearly half of Americans "believe in the creationist view that God created humans in their present form at one time within the last 10,000 years." Frank Newport, "In U.S., 46% Hold Creationist View of Human Origins," Gallup, June 1, 2012, http://www.gallup.com/poll/155003/hold-creationist-view-human-origins.aspx. Other studies reportedly show that around 90 percent of American evangelicals affirm young-earth creationism. See Denis Lamoureux, *I Love Jesus and I Accept Evolution* (Eugene, OR: Wipf and Stock, 2009), 15.
52. See the evenhanded treatment in Collins, *Did Adam and Eve*, 105–7.

resurrection as central to our faith—and rightly so. At this point, believers trust the "rule of faith" over mountains of so-called scientific evidence.[53]

For this reason, the simplistic claim that one may "assign the Bible and science to two separate spheres of authoritative discourse"[54] is not ultimately sustainable. At certain points the theological claims of Scripture and the claims of scientists may flatly contradict one another. And in these cases, the slogan "separate but authoritative"—like the segregation falsehood "separate but equal"—is simply nonsense.[55]

Likewise, if the apostle Paul loads *theological* freight into the notion of a historical Adam and a historical fall, then it would be problematic to say that Paul was wrong about the history but right about theology. At certain points, history and theology are bound together. We know God by what he has done within the divine economy. The question is therefore not about "concordism" versus "anticoncordism" but about what kind of concord one should seek between the claims of science and Scripture.[56] On Adam and atonement several options exist.

Adam as a Strictly Literary Figure

One approach is to view Adam as a purely literary figure within a story that is nonetheless inspired.[57] As the parables of Christ reveal, some biblical characters need not be historical in order to bear the weight of revelation. By this account, a literary Adam is paralleled with a historical Jesus in order to explain aspects of the human plight and the atonement. For Paul, the point of the parallel is said to be that all people (both Jews and gentiles) are enslaved to the powers of sin and death and that Christ has made redemption possible for all.

In this view, Paul's theology is seen as valid, even though Adam himself was not a historical person. For example, Peter Enns claims that the

53. This is not to say that there is no evidence for the resurrection. See N. T. Wright, *The Resurrection of the Son of God* (Minneapolis: Fortress, 2003).

54. Harlow, "After Adam," 180. Enns makes a similar claim to that of Harlow. See Enns, *Evolution of Adam*, xvii–xviii.

55. This segregation of science and faith is often dubbed "NOMA" for the supposedly "Non-Overlapping Magisteria" of the two fields. It was proposed by the same Stephen Jay Gould who elsewhere claimed that Darwin had disproven the possibility of a loving God. See Gould, "Non-Overlapping Magisteria," *Natural History* 106 (March 1997): 16–22.

56. In the view of James K. A. Smith and William T. Cavanaugh, the best approach will be to follow the example of Chalcedon in resisting an unimaginative either/or between "science" and "faith." This is precisely the simplistic false choice that was rejected by the council when it refused to buy into the ruling philosophy of the day that it was impossible for someone to be both human and divine. See Cavanaugh and Smith, introduction to *Evolution and the Fall*, xvii.

57. This is basically the approach of Harlow, Enns, Schneider, and Lamoureux.

biblical Adam is a symbol of the Israel story. By this symbol, Israel's special creation, sinful rebellion, exilic punishment, and gracious upholding are projected onto a primordial canvas. *Israel is Adam.* And while there is no literal first couple to be found within the evolutionary process, the literary Adam reveals spiritual truths, both for Israel and the wider world.[58]

While this view fits easily with recent scientific arguments, it would seem more difficult to harmonize with a high view of Scripture. Most versions of the literary Adam theory claim that Paul believed that Adam was an actual person and that Paul (as an ancient man) was simply wrong.[59] A deeper problem, however, involves what this perspective may imply of Jesus's fallibility. In the view of C. John Collins, the Gospels portray Jesus as believing that Adam and Eve "were actual people, and that their disobedience changed things for their descendants."[60] This claim rests partly upon Christ's reference to Abel as a real person (Matt 23:35; Luke 11:51) and partly upon Jesus's claim regarding divorce that "it was not this way from the beginning" (Matt 19:8), which he says immediately after citing two separate parts of the Adam story (Gen 1:27; 2:24). As Collins puts it, "The obvious candidate for making that change [regarding divorce]—indeed, the only one—is the sin of Adam and Eve, with its consequences for all human beings."[61]

Finally, if some primal fall did not happen, however symbolically portrayed in Scripture, then one is forced to come up with alternative explanations for the "wrongness" of the violence, selfishness, and sin that haunt the human experience. For while something like the fall of cosmic spiritual powers (or "the Satan") may be leveraged to account for the conflict and predation that afflict the animal kingdom prior to Adam,[62] Scripture still places a unique burden of culpability upon God's image bearers for the failure to expand the beachhead of *shalom* that was birthed in Eden.[63]

Without a historical fall, Christians are therefore left with two equally unacceptable options: either a

---

58. See especially Enns, *Evolution of Adam*, ch. 7.

59. This is the claim of Enns, *Evolution of Adam*, 119–22.

60. Collins, *Did Adam and Eve*, 78. See also Christopher J. H. Wright, *Old Testament Ethics for the People of God* (Downers Grove, IL: IVP, 2004), 349–51.

61. Collins, *Did Adam and Eve*, 77.

62. This subject of Satan and "the powers" must be delayed until ch. 9.

63. See Brian Brock, "Jesus Christ the Divine Animal? The Human Distinctive Reconsidered," in Torrance and McCall, *Christ and the Created Order*, 70. Brock's claim is that human sin is a moving backward into the already universal (pre-Eden) state of predation and selfishness—but now, for humans, in a way that carries culpability and spiritual "death." Such forces did not exist in the pre-Eden world because no animal had been ushered into an image-bearing relationship with God that entailed moral responsibility.

1. *dualism* whereby good and evil are simply coeternal principles, or a
2. *monism* whereby God is both good and evil.[64]

The views of Harlow and Schneider tend toward the latter, while Enns tries to carve out a third option by remaining silent on the origins of sin and death as "problems."[65] None of these approaches seem likely to satisfy.

Adam as an (Evolutionary) Ancestor

A second harmonizing option is more traditional than the literary Adam theory in that it accepts three central notions:

1. a primal fall,
2. a paternal Adam (the physical progenitor of all humans), and
3. portions of the scientific data.

The proposal here is that Adam was a real person, who was either created or specially modified by God somewhere within the evolutionary process.[66] In this way, the science for both an "old" earth and an evolutionary trajectory is respected, even while it is taken to be biblically and theologically important to maintain Adam as the literal progenitor of the entire human family.

The next move often involves varying levels of speculation regarding *when* such an ancient ancestor might have lived. If the apparent setting of Genesis is followed, Adam may be taken as a Neolithic farmer around 10,000 BC.[67] If factors of human culture and population expansion are taken into account, Adam may be located between 70,000 to 50,000

64. Hans Madueme helpfully presents the starkness of these two options. See "The Most Vulnerable Part of the Whole Christian Account: Original Sin and Modern Science," in *Adam, the Fall, and Original Sin*, 232. Some theologians may attempt to carve out a third possibility by claiming that God is simply (to cite Nietzsche) "beyond good and evil." Yet once again, this view seems impossible to square with the traditional Christian view of God as Holy Love. The latter point is helpfully made by T. A. Noble, "Original Sin and the Fall: Definitions and the Proposal," in *Darwin, Creation and the Fall*, ed. R. J. Berry and T. A. Noble (Nottingham: Apollos, 2009), 113–14.

65. Enns's argument seems sloppy at this point. On the one hand, he is clear that Paul presents the historical Adam as the source of such problems. Then he goes on to contradict this claim by stating that the origin of sin and death "does not seem to be a question that Scripture is prepared to answer" (126). While Enns may well be right about both Paul and Adam, the latter statement about Scripture clearly contradicts his prior argument.

66. Because this view has been touched upon already, my present treatment may be brief. Proponents of this view tend to accept some degree of evolutionary theory while differing amongst themselves regarding the question of human evolution. See Stone, "Adam and Modern Science"; and Madueme, "Most Vulnerable Part," 236–37.

67. See the suggestion of John Stott, *Romans* (Downers Grove, IL: IVP, 1995), 162–66.

years ago.[68] And if one wishes to locate Adam as the first member of the genus *Homo*, then the proposed date may stretch back nearly two million years.[69]

Among other objections,[70] the biggest challenge to these views seems to be the perceived requirement for monogenesis as it connects to new genetic data. (Although if Swamidass is right, then perhaps the genomic assumptions also stand in need of reconsideration as they relate to genealogy.)[71] Whatever the case, one thing seems clear: the flaming sword that barred reentry into Eden (Gen 3:24) also bars our attempts at such detailed historical reconstructions.[72] Despite these challenges, and despite the diversity of speculative dates within this second attempt at harmonization, all such views are willing to accept *some* recent scientific evidence, while either disputing or ignoring the argument for polygenism.

Adam as a Representative Head

In the third and final option, the biblical Adam is seen as pointing back to a real person (or persons[73]) either created or selected by God to serve as a *representative head* for humanity. Most importantly, this "Adam" need *not* be the literal father of all successive generations even though he is our representative forebear and the father of the fall. From this perspective, Adam may have been chosen from a preexisting mass of hominins who had not yet been endowed with a special relationship to God. The important point is that the historical Adam stands distinct by virtue of (1) election and (2) *imago Dei*. In this way, a historical reality lies beneath the literary (and symbolic) layers of the biblical accounts. Even though all Scripture is "God-breathed" (2 Tim 3:16), not all passages are designed to be read as a literalistic play-by-play of the events described. The Bible contains poetry, parables, and a variety of symbolic literature. With this in mind, the present perspective rejects a literalism that allegedly

---

68. This is the suggestion of Fazale Rana with Hugh Ross, *Who Was Adam? A Creation Model Approach to the Origin of Man* (Colorado Springs: NavPress, 2005), 248.

69. See Stone, "Adam and Modern Science," 81.

70. See, for instance, Richard Mortimer's critique of one such attempt to locate Adam as an ancient ancestor in "Blocher, Original Sin and Evolution," in *Darwin, Creation and the Fall*, 188. See also A. Day, "Adam, Anthropology and the Genesis Record," *Science and Christian Belief* 10, no. 2 (1998).

71. See Swamidass, "Overlooked Science of Genealogical Ancestry," 19–35; cf. Venema and McKnight, *Adam and the Genome*, 59.

72. Credit for this imagery goes to T. A. Noble, "Original Sin and the Fall," 119.

73. See Walton's ensuing point that when the definite article precedes '*adam*, it should be taken as a generic Hebrew word for humankind, rather than a personal name. Thus some have suggested the possibility of a representative group.

flies in the face of both the modern science and the ancient contexts of the biblical literature.[74]

Evidence for other people in proximity to Adam has been suggested in three different references from Genesis 4. Upon hearing of his exile from the family land, (1) Cain is openly fearful that "whoever finds me will kill me." (2) The Lord then gives Cain a "mark" to protect him from these others. (3) And Cain departs and finds a wife, who seemingly emerges out of nowhere (Gen 4:14, 15, 17).[75] While the passage gives rise to multiple and somewhat strained interpretations,[76] it certainly raises the possibility of other persons existing around the time of Adam who are not his biological offspring. If this is correct, then Adam would not be the literal father of all humans but more like humanity's chosen representative (or "federal head").

Evangelical Old Testament scholar John Walton sets forth a related argument. Walton points to things like the definite article that precedes the word *adam* in the vast majority of its occurrences in Genesis 1–5. In his view, we cannot think of this as a mere personal name, for *adam* is the Hebrew word for humankind. The preceding definite articles provides reason to believe that the image bearer represents all humanity as their archetype.[77] Walton also highlights the phrasing of Genesis 2:15, which shows Adam "taken" and "placed" in the garden, as pointing to the notion that the archetypal human is "removed from the everyday realm of human experience [and perhaps from the realm of other hominins] and placed in a specially prepared place" in order to function as a federal representative.[78] For Walton, these textual clues help make it possible to harmonize the biblical and scientific evidence for polygenism without denying the historical Adam or the truthfulness of Scripture.

Another version of this viewpoint came years ago from C. S. Lewis. In a famous passage from *The Problem of Pain*, he writes:

---

74. John Walton's work, for example, deals with the ancient contexts of the Adam story. See *The Lost World of Adam and Eve*.

75. See John H. Walton, "Origins in Genesis: Claims of an Ancient Text in a Modern Scientific World," in *Knowing Creation: Perspectives from Theology, Philosophy, and Science*, ed. Andrew B. Torrance and Thomas H. McCall (Grand Rapids: Zondervan Academic, 2018), 117.

76. Some have seen the feared "others" as animals, while the wife is claimed to be a relative. For more on this debate, see Collins, *Did Adam and Eve*, 111–13, 124.

77. Critics might respond to Walton's claim by noting that there is no reason why an "archetypal Adam" could not *also* be an "ancestral Adam"; that is, the literal father of all subsequent humans. See Walton, "A Historical Adam: Archetypal Creation View," in *Four Views on the Historical Adam*, 91; cf. Walton, *Lost World of Adam and Eve*, 58–62.

78. Walton, "A Historical Adam," 93–94.

For long centuries, God perfected the animal form which was to become the vehicle of humanity and the image of Himself. . . . Then, in the fullness of time, God caused to descend upon this organism . . . a new kind of consciousness which could say "I" and "me," which could look upon itself as an object, which knew God, which could make judgments of truth, beauty and goodness. . . . We do not know how many of these creatures God made, nor how long they continued in the Paradisal state. But sooner or later they fell. Someone or something whispered that they could become as gods. . . . They wanted some corner in the universe of which they could say to God, "This is our business, not yours." But there is no such corner. They wanted to be nouns, but they were, and eternally must be, mere adjectives. We have no idea in what particular act, or series of acts the self-contradictory, impossible wish found expression. For all I can see, it might have concerned the literal eating of a fruit, but the question is of no consequence.[79]

According to Lewis, the reality of a primal fall is crucial, even while the Adam story need not lead to a denial of either evolution or the existence of prior hominins. In his own poetic style, Lewis makes no attempt to explain how his suggestion fits with the biblical logic of sin and the atonement, yet other scholars have attempted to fill in this gap.[80]

For C. John Collins, if there were "more human beings than just Adam and Eve at the beginning," we should view them "as a single tribe . . . under the leadership of Adam and Eve."[81] This view of Adam as a sort of "king" is seen to be important to ensure a biblical understanding of how headship functions, and to explain how other humans may be held accountable for Adam's disobedience. In support, examples like David fighting Goliath are then used to show how the anointed leader ("head") may act on behalf of the "whole" without literally fathering the group. Indeed, Jesus himself is not the literal father of anyone, yet he is still spoken of as the "last Adam" (1 Cor 15) and the "head" of the church (Eph 5:23; Col 1:18).

Derek Kidner offers a somewhat different explanation. He proposes that after establishing Adam and Eve as vice regents, "God may . . . have conferred his image on Adam's collaterals, to bring them into the same realm of being." Thus "Adam's 'federal' headship of humanity extended

---

79. C.S. Lewis, *The Problem of Pain* (1940; repr., San Francisco: Harper Collins, 1996), 72.
80. Lewis recognizes this as a potential tension but does not seem overly worried. See the more extensive discussion in Collins, *Did Adam and Eve*, 128–29.
81. Collins, *Did Adam and Eve*, 121.

outwards to his contemporaries as well as onwards to his offspring." In this case, as with the previous suggestions, the unity of humanity "in Adam" need not involve *heredity* but rather *solidarity* by divine appointment.[82] New Testament scholar Scot McKnight[83] and theologian-philosopher James K. A. Smith assert something similar.[84] What should one make of such views?

Taking Stock

In response, some will argue that any denial of Adam as the father of all humans runs afoul of both the biblical narrative[85] and the perceived necessity that all must have been "in" Adam (physically) in order to inherit the effects of his sin.[86] Yet as I have shown, there are other arguments for how headship functions in the Bible, just as there are other arguments to address how the effects of sin spread. One of these is described as a "radiation" model (as opposed to a "biological" model) of original sin. By this account, the fall opens a door to a form of disorder and evil that then metaphorically irradiates the entire cosmos. It opens Pandora's box, so to speak.[87] In another suggestion, the introduction of human sin through Adam should be viewed as a moving *backward* into a state of violence and self-promotion that had long existed in the animal realm. Now, however, there was the added catastrophe that God's image bearers had become morally responsible for bringing spiritual death into the world.[88] As such, the fall is like slipping backward into chaos, but with the additional weight of moral culpability, idolatry, and human rebellion that did not exist previously in God's good creation.[89] Whether correct or not, these views provide

82. Derek Kidner, *Genesis*, Tyndale OT Commentary (Downers Grove, IL: IVP, 1967), 29–30.

83. Venema and McKnight, *Adam and the Genome*, ch. 8.

84. James K. A. Smith, "What Stands on the Fall?," in Cavanaugh and Smith, *Evolution and the Fall*, 61–62.

85. For Henri Blocher, "The tension with the 'natural sense' of Scripture is hard to bear." Blocher, "The Theology of the Fall and the Origins of Evil," in Berry and Noble, *Darwin, Creation and the Fall*, 171.

86. This, as we have seen, was the view of Augustine, who believed that both the guilt for Adam's sin and its debilitating punishment (*concupiscence*, "disordered desire") were inherited by way of propagation. For a succinct overview of Augustine's view, see Paul Rigby, "Original Sin," in *Augustine Through the Ages: An Encyclopedia*, ed. Allan D. Fitzgerald (Grand Rapids: Eerdmans, 1999), 607–14.

87. This description is taken from John Walton, "A Historical Adam," in *Four Views on the Historical Adam*, 106n37.

88. See Brock, "Jesus Christ the Divine Animal?," 70.

89. Walton sees this shift as a move from the "nonorder" that existed prior to the fall (see Gen 1:2; 2:15) to the "disorder" that was introduced by human sin. See Walton, "Origins in Genesis," 117.

alternatives to the necessity of original sin being passed on as a kind of genetic disorder from a primal parent.

The suggestions, however, are not without critics. Peter Enns dismisses the representative headship view with the claim that such "ad hoc" theories present a narrative that is "utterly foreign to the biblical portrait."[90] After all, the Bible does not explicitly describe the presence of other hominins around the time of Adam, just as it does not give clear evidence to suspect a "representative headship" view over the more common "ancestral" one. This may be true. Yet it is not clear why Enns sees such foreignness as a problem, since his own view is quite foreign to both the mind of Paul and the text of Genesis.

Others contend that the representative headship view falls victim to a kind of "Adam-of-the-gaps" fallacy. Representative headship allegedly grants the current scientific narrative a place of unquestioned preeminence and then attempts to plug an anemic-looking Adam into whatever space remains within the scientific storyline.[91] On the other hand, if the claims of Walton and others are correct, then perhaps there are actually good biblical reasons to question some of the old (Augustinian) assumptions about Adam and the fall. Where then should we go from here?

| CONSTRUCTIVE PROPOSALS |

The overarching question of this chapter is whether the Pauline and Irenaean claims regarding Christ and Adam can withstand the recent flood of scientific evidence. In response, I will now move to evaluate the prior arguments in order to set forth a series of proposals on how Christians *ought* to think of Adam and atonement.

On Keeping Certain Options Open

It seems wise for Christians to remain open to multiple interpretive possibilities with regard to science and the historical Adam. The letter of Titus warns readers to avoid unnecessary squabbles over "genealogies"

---

90. Enns, *Evolution of Adam*, 139 and xvii, respectively.

91. See Madueme, "Most Vulnerable Part," 237. Venema refers to something like this phenomenon as the latter stage of "ratcheting" concord in his article, "Genesis and the Genome," 176. In Venema's words, "Those who employ it, at first, resist the implications of new research that conflict with their concordist expectations, often deferring a decision on the claim of insufficient evidence. However, if contrary evidence continues to mount against their position, eventually such an individual may concede the point, discard the specific concordist expectation in question, and 'ratchet' over to the next available position that retains the balance of their expectations."

(3:9), and indeed there has often been a need to apply this wisdom to the heated discussions surrounding Genesis.

For conservatives, if prior skirmishes between science and faith have taught anything (whether the Scopes "Monkey Trial" or the oft-caricatured case of Galileo[92]), it is that a quick dismissal of scientific evidence can have profound consequences. One might even argue that an antagonistic stance toward science may betray an un-Christian view of God and the created order. The notions that the universe can be known and studied and that our well-gathered evidence can be trusted is partly the product of Judeo-Christian theology.[93] Good science requires belief in the universe's orderly arrangement, and it requires disbelief in the pagan notion of the gods as cosmic tricksters.[94] Simple dismissals of science can entail some rather pagan presuppositions. For if the collective mountain of evidence (of bones, stones, and genomes!) is really so misleading, then the "designer" seems quite different from the trustworthy God of the Christian tradition.[95] A better approach is to leave some options open.

The same goes for progressives. If both Paul and Jesus speak of the early figures in Genesis as real people, then surely Christians must take these figures' historicity seriously, however embedded within a stylized or typological narrative.[96] Likewise, it would be foolish for Christians to accept every emerging claim that wraps itself in the banner of science like a politician in the flag.[97] To go to this extreme is to watch science become a *power* in the biblical sense, a structure that was created good but has a tendency to usurp its bounds and make transcendent claims to

92. Galileo's case is complex because he was in fact challenging the "science" of his day (the Ptolemaic system) and not merely the claims of religious tradition. Thus, while elements of the church would come to oppose him, so too did defenders of the current "scientific consensus." This reality should be remembered before caricaturing "religion" as the primary opposition to emerging science.

93. In the words of Colin Gunton, "If the world as a whole is divine or the body of God, it is unlikely that anyone will think it proper to dissect it in a laboratory." For this and other insights on the relation between science and the doctrine of creation, see Gunton, *The Triune Creator: A Historical and Systematic Study* (Grand Rapids: Eerdmans, 1998), 111.

94. See R. Hooykaas, *Religion and the Rise of Modern Science* (Edinburgh: Scottish Academic Press, 1972); and Peter Harrison, *The Bible, Protestantism, and the Rise of Natural Science* (Cambridge: Cambridge University Press, 1998).

95. Ronald Osborn refers to this as the "Deceiver God Dilemma." This "deceiver god" emerges when some creationists account for seemingly insurmountable scientific data by claiming that God must have created the world with the appearance of a prior history. This notion not only sets aside the science but also the traditional understanding of God's character—a frightfully high cost. See *Death Before the Fall*, 131.

96. Jesus refers to Abel in Matt 23:35 (cf. Luke 11:51). Collins sees such references as implying the historicity of such a figure. *Did Adam and Eve*, 76–77.

97. This analogy comes from Alvin Plantinga, *Where the Conflict Really Lies: Science, Religion, and Naturalism* (Oxford: Oxford University Press, 2011), x–xi.

divine power.[98] Evidence of this unsettling tendency can be seen in the way words like *evolution* have sometimes been poorly defined.[99] There is, for example, a widespread misconception, propelled by certain atheistic scientists, that an acceptance of the adaptation of life-forms via genetic mutation and natural selection somehow entails a metaphysical naturalism (no god; no purpose). And in the words of Alvin Plantinga, this claim "is error, and whopping error at that."[100]

"Scientism" is itself a pseudoscience, not least because a great many truths lie beyond the reach of scientific inquiry. And Christians have always believed that the biblical narrative gives insights that explain the human situation more deeply than a mere study of the physical evidence. Across virtually all theological traditions these insights include:

1. a good God who creates a good world,
2. a human fall into sin and its consequences, and
3. a gracious solution through Israel's Messiah and the Holy Spirit.

It is possible, of course, to believe that all these claims are nonsense, but this suggestion is hardly provable by science. To claim otherwise is a category mistake akin to thinking that because one's thermostat can read temperatures, it can also read Shakespeare.

If the Christian story explains our situation more deeply than a mere study of the genome or the fossil record (as I believe it does), then progressive Christians should also leave certain harmonizing options open—especially when they are crucial in addressing the *problems* that the atonement is meant to solve.

God Is Not the Author of Sin

To trace the human behaviors that we call evil to none other than the "creative-destructive will of God" (given to us through our animal ancestors[101]) is a move that seems disastrous for Christian theology.[102]

---

98. See Brian Curry, "Christ, Science, and the Powers: Elements in a Christian Doctrine of Creation," in Torrance and McCall, *Christ and the Created Order*, 92–94.

99. See McCall's critique of Enns, Harlow, and Schneider for failing to distinguish what they mean by such terms. *Analytic Christian Theology*, 136–44.

100. Alvin Plantinga, *Where the Conflict Really Lies*, 308.

101. See Schneider, "Recent Genetic Science and Christian Theology," 207.

102. In a related conclusion, Hans Boersma, in his brilliant and self-consciously Reformed approach to the atonement, critiques Calvinist notions of supralapsarianism and double predestination for "drawing violence from history into the heart of God." The remark is relevant to the present discussion, since Harlow has dubbed his own view a kind of "aesthetic

To prove the point, a legion of texts could indeed be cited, but perhaps the most obvious is James 1:13–15: "When tempted, no one should say, 'God is tempting me.' For God cannot be tempted by evil, nor does he tempt anyone; but each person is tempted when they are dragged away by their own evil desire and enticed. Then, after desire has conceived, it gives birth to sin; and sin, when it is full-grown, gives birth to death."[103] Even though Christians have a variety of ideas to address *how* sin spread to humanity at large,[104] virtually the entire tradition has agreed that God cannot be blamed for sinful behavior.[105] God is not the author of evil. "God is light; in him there is no darkness at all" (1 John 1:5). While we may inherit any number of sinful propensities from our forebears, if we ascribe our present drives toward rape, murder, and wanton selfishness to God's design, then we are no longer dealing with the Christian God. Whatever doors one leaves open, this one must remain firmly shut.[106]

A Fall in Harmony with Science

If God is not the author of sin, then there are only so many options left within a Christian worldview. One might blame some other fallen creature (for instance, "the Satan"),[107] or one might blame humanity. The Scriptures do a bit of both. But if humanity is held responsible for sin, one is left invariably with some sort of historical fall. The question then is how this theological necessity may fit with scientific evidence.

One option would be to say that at some point God endowed the human creature with a kind of freedom and ethical responsibility that is simply nonexistent within the animal kingdom. It may be entirely appropriate for a lion to hunt the most vulnerable gazelle,[108] but it is both wrong and sinful for a loan shark—or a prosperity preacher—to prey upon vulnerable

---

supralapsarianism." See Boersma, *Violence, Hospitality, and the Cross: Reappropriating the Atonement Tradition* (Grand Rapids: Baker Academic, 2004), 56.

103. The passage becomes even more relevant if one grants that it is a theological reflection on Gen 1–3. See Joel B. Green, "'Adam, What Have You Done?' New Testament Voices on the Origins of Sin," in Cavanaugh and Smith, *Evolution and the Fall*, 112.

104. One need not agree with Augustine that all humans (save Jesus) sinned in Adam or that all humans inherit "original guilt" by virtue of this fall. See Oliver Crisp, "Original Sin," *IJST* 17, no. 2 (April 2015): 1–15.

105. See Christopher Hays and Stephen Herring, "Adam and the Fall," in *Evangelical Faith and the Challenge of Historical Criticism*, ed. Christopher M. Hays and Christopher Ansberry (Grand Rapids: Baker Academic, 2013), 45.

106. For support, see Smith's resistance to what he calls the "naturalizing" of sin in "What Stands on the Fall," 63.

107. I will return to a discussion of the demonic realm in ch. 9.

108. It is worth noting that the book of Job views the awe-inspiring wildness of the animal kingdom (including predation) as a sign of the Creator's remarkable design.

people. By God's will, humans have a special responsibility to behave in ways that subvert the evolutionary logic of "the strong eat the weak." And in this way, the question of whether this ethical responsibility was endowed *within* the evolutionary progression is less important than the fact that it did, at some point, happen.

If the prior suggestions are considered valid from a Christian standpoint, then the following chain of logic emerges:

1. Scientific evidence should be taken seriously but not uncritically.
2. Sin and evil exist as problems, but God is not their author.
3. Humans bear an ethical imperative to behave differently than animals.

On the basis of these conclusions, it seems inescapable that we are left with something quite like the Genesis and Pauline accounts of Adam and the fall. This likeness need not be woodenly literal, of course, but there must be an "intended historical referentiality."[109] The scriptural account should therefore be viewed as "a stylized account of a real historical event."[110] And if so, then G. K. Chesterton is right to state that "the Fall [is] the only encouraging view of Life," for "it holds . . . that we have misused a good world, and not merely been entrapped into a bad one."[111]

| CONCLUSION |

At long last it is possible to answer the question that began this chapter: What does the current science mean for atonement via recapitulation? As seen in chapter 1, a crucial factor in the Irenaean understanding of recapitulation was a unique view of the *imago Dei* as *imago Christi*. Because Adam was fashioned in the image of the incarnate Christ, the Messiah enters the human story as the rightful head of the entire human race. And in the logic of the Bible, the head may act on behalf of the whole.

If other hominins lived before Adam, then one must account for what makes Adam distinct. The divine image is an excellent candidate. Suppose, one might argue, that the Creator crafted (or refurbished) a particular

109. Collins, *Did Adam and Eve*, 109.

110. Brock, "Jesus Christ the Divine Animal?," 70.

111. G. K. Chesterton, *As I Was Saying*, ed. Robert Knille (Grand Rapids: Eerdmans, 1985), 160, cited in C. John Collins, "Adam and Eve as Historical People, and Why It Matters," in *Perspectives on Science and Christian Faith* 62 (September 2010): 158.

creature that would live in a new and special relationship to God and to the world. This creature would then be patterned after the one who *is* the true image of the invisible God: the incarnate Christ.[112] Part of this Christ-patterning would be a relationship that had never before existed on Planet Earth, a vocation of authentic moral responsibility that allowed Adam to transcend animal instinct in order to mirror (or fail to mirror) the image of Christ.

In this account, the *imago Christi* and the vocational responsibilities that come with it are what separated Adam from all animals. While primal urges may rightly drive other creatures with no concern for moral scruples,[113] the *Christic* image bearers stand distinct, not anatomically or even (merely) rationally but by a Spirit-birthed relation to the Son. Here again, the Messiah formed the mold for Adam's making, not just physically, but *morally* as well. For this reason, humans feel the tug of righteousness, the temptation of sin, and the terrible reality that things are not as they should be.[114] In all of this, the Son of God remains the deepest "root" of the entire human family. Thus, with a nod to Acts 17, one might say that "from one man [that is, *Christ*], God made all the nations."

If these image bearers were indeed selected from the mass of (nonhuman) hominins, then the parallels between Adam and Israel may be accepted, and even deepened. As N. T. Wright proposes, "Just as God chose Israel from the rest of humankind for a special, strange, demanding vocation, so perhaps what Genesis is telling us is that *God chose one pair from the rest of early hominins for a special, strange, demanding vocation. This pair . . . were to be the representatives of the whole human race.*"[115] In this way, the election of Adam bears a relation to the election of Israel, just as the bestowal of the image upon Adam's "collaterals" (to use Kidner's term) bears a resemblance to the New Testament inclusion of the nations within

---

112. For while Jesus of Nazareth was yet to be born in Adam's time, this does not stop him from claiming that "before Abraham was, I am" (John 8:58). See the similar argument in Oliver Crisp, *The Word Enfleshed: Exploring the Person and Work of Christ* (Grand Rapids: Baker Academic, 2016), 66–68.

113. As the poet states: "The killer whale's heart weighs one hundred kilos / but in other respects is light." Wislawa Szymborska, "In Praise of Self-Deprecation." I was alerted to this fantastic line by Osborn, *Death Before the Fall*, 125.

114. To cite Chesterton again (*As I Was Saying*, 160), there is "that sublime sense of loss that is in the very sound of all great poetry, and nowhere more than in the poetry of pagans and sceptics. . . . [It is the cry] that happiness is not only a hope, but also in some strange manner a memory; and that we are all kings in exile."

115. N. T. Wright, "Excursus on Paul's Use of Adam," in John Walton, *Lost World of Adam and Eve*, 177, italics in original.

God's great family. This is what happens when one begins to think about both creation and redemption through the lens of Christ.

Paul's theology clarifies that one need not be a genetic child of Abraham to be reckoned as his offspring. This is simply how election and salvation work within the Scriptures. *God elects the one from the many, for the good of creation, and glory of his Name.* If this also happened with regard to Adam (and I have no idea if it did), then perhaps the emerging science may help us read the story in a way that is even more harmonious with God's electing actions throughout the biblical economy.

CHAPTER 3

HOW BEAUTIFUL THE FEET

RECAPITULATION AND THE FOUNDATION OF ATONEMENT

The highest does not stand without the lowest.

Thomas à Kempis

The central claim of this book is that particular models of atonement may be understood like pieces in a grand mosaic. Even if such models are noticeably distinct from one another, their distinctness need not prevent them from being fitted together in particular ways, so as to achieve a more holistic picture of Christ's work. The purpose of this chapter is to address *how* the recapitulation model fits together with the models addressed in later chapters: penal substitution, *Christus Victor*, and moral influence.

In chapter 1, I sought merely to explain the concept of recapitulation by way of its most famous proponent: Irenaeus of Lyons. For Irenaeus, because the Messiah formed the pattern for Adam's making, Christ enters the human storyline as the archetype and head of the entire human family. And in the Bible, the head may act on behalf of the whole. In chapter 2, I addressed a contemporary challenge to this model in the claims of evolutionary science. I argued that while science must be taken seriously, and while certain options should be left open, even recent genetic evidence does not rule out a biblically rooted understanding of atonement as recapitulation. In the Scriptures, headship is about more than physical fathering, for as both Abraham and Jesus illustrate, God often chooses one from among the many to represent and redeem the group. With the explanatory (ch. 1) and apologetic (ch. 2) work done, the current chapter turns to the task of integration (ch. 3).

| THE THESIS |

I will argue that Christ's recapitulative identity as the true Adam (and true Israelite) should be seen as a foundation that lends stability to other models of atonement. In my mosaic of atonement, I identify recapitulation with the feet of the crucified and risen Jesus. While firmly planted in the dust of fallen creation, these feet bring good news, because the other models stand, both logically and biblically, upon ideas inherent within the view of Jesus as the true and faithful Adam and the true and faithful Israel.

This is not to say, however, that recapitulation is somehow "most important" among the "pieces" of Christ's work. A further claim of this book is that both (1) defensive hierarchy and (2) disconnected plurality may be avoided when one part of Christ's mosaic body refuses to say to the others, "I have no need of you!" (1 Cor 12:21). Each model to be surveyed is indeed essential, for each fulfills certain indispensable functions within the biblical mosaic of atonement. In this way, my unfolding claim is that certain problems within atonement theology may be dealt with if one begins to note the varied ways the pieces fit together.

| A PROBLEM FOR PENAL SUBSTITUTION |

Penal substitution, in its basic form, refers to the notion that in Christ God has graciously borne the judgment for human sin on our behalf. Jesus willingly experienced condemnation both "in our place" and "instead of us."[1] Because a detailed look at this model awaits part 2 of this book, the concern here is only to explore how a particular version of recapitulation provides some help with a question that is often raised against penal substitutionary logic.[2] The question is this: How is it just for an innocent person to "stand in" for the guilty when it comes to punishment? How does this not create a legal fiction, a farce of logic, and an offense against

---

1. For the distinction between these two descriptions, see Simon Gathercole, *Defending Substitution: An Essay on Atonement in Paul* (Grand Rapids: Baker Academic, 2015), 15–16.
2. The treatment of other critiques of penal substitution must await ch. 5.

God's justice?[3] In what follows, I will refer to this dilemma as the problem of penal nontransference.[4]

One need not be a legal expert to recognize the potential pitfalls. As Proverbs states, "Acquitting the guilty and condemning the innocent— the Lord detests them both" (17:15). No human judge would therefore be commended for handing down a prison sentence to, say, the victim of pedophilia instead of the perpetrator. Justice doesn't work like that. And it makes no difference whether all parties within this diabolical exchange are (oddly) willing to go through with it. Civil cases may permit a gracious friend to pay the fine of the offender—say, giving the money for a delinquent parking ticket—but criminal matters are something else entirely. Here things like punishment and vindication are not seen as justly transferable between the innocent and guilty parties.[5] If God is just, there appears to be a problem with the reality of penal nontransference.[6]

| ON THE LIMITS OF METAPHORS |

In response to such critiques, a common move in recent years has been to highlight the metaphorical quality of all atonement imagery. Simply put, no model or metaphor is identical to the thing it depicts. For example, as a young boy I enjoyed assembling tiny replicas of US fighter jets. From

---

3. The question is by no means an exclusively modern one. As Anselm has Boso ask in *Cur Deus Homo?*, "What justice is there in his suffering death for the sinner, who was the most just of all men? What man, if he condemned the innocent to free the guilty would not himself be judged worthy of condemnation?" (1.8). In recent years, it has become common to assume that Anselm never considered the offense of such an argument, yet that is clearly not the case. Anselm, *Cur Deus Homo?*, in *Proslogium; Monologium; an Appendix in Behalf of the Fool by Gaunilon; and Cur Deus Homo*, trans. Sidney Norton Deane (repr., Chicago: Open Court, 1926).

4. Along related lines, Mark C. Murphy argues that "penal substitution is unintelligible" because "punishment will be non-transferrable" by its very definition. See Murphy, "Not Penal Substitution but Vicarious Punishment," *Faith and Philosophy* 26, no. 3 (July 2009): 256–57. For a careful rebuttal to this logic, see Daniel J. Hill and Joseph Jedwab, "Atonement and the Concept of Punishment," in *Locating Atonement: Explorations in Constructive Dogmatics*, ed. Oliver Crisp and Fred Sanders (Grand Rapids: Zondervan, 2015), ch. 7. The problem of penal nontransference also bulks large for Eleonore Stump, *Atonement* (Oxford: Oxford University Press, 2018), 24.

5. As Steve Holmes notes, "We are not talking about a fine when we come to the atonement; we are talking about an execution." Holmes, "Can Punishment Bring Peace? Penal Substitution Revisited," *SJT* 58, no. 1 (2005): 120.

6. More precisely, one might say that it is *guilt* that is nontransferable, whether in criminal or civil cases. See Oliver Crisp, "Scholastic Theology, Augustinian Realism and Original Guilt," *EuroJTh* 13 (2004): 18. In Crisp's view, this constitutes "the central [logical] problem with penal substitution." See also Crisp, "The Logic of Penal Substitution Revisited," in *The Atonement Debate: Papers from the London Symposium on the Theology of Atonement*, ed. Derek Tidball, David Hilborn, and Justin Thacker (Grand Rapids: Zondervan, 2008), 223.

these models, I learned much about the actual aircraft; still it remains obvious that there are massive differences between my plastic version of an F-16, and the 165-million-dollar reality. I would be foolish, therefore, to think that because my glued-together replica was unflyable, so too was the jet itself.

The same goes for atonement models. As Christians agree, the saving work of Christ is an utterly singular reality. There is truly nothing else to match it.[7] Because of this, any metaphor that we import from other experiences—whether battlefield victory, courtroom acquittal, or reconciled relationships—necessarily falls short. In the words of Colin Gunton, all metaphors are "calculated category mistakes."[8] Thus we ought to hold them knowing that the thing depicted is larger and more complex than that which we can wrap words and fingers around, like my tiny model aircrafts.[9] Sallie McFague is therefore correct to note that metaphors "always contain the whisper, 'it is and it is not.'"[10]

This is a helpful reminder as we find potential problems with all the images of Christ's work. Models and metaphors have limits.[11] Yet the question is whether a retreat to metaphorical limits—or the playing of

---

7. Scripture therefore views the cross as a "once for all" occurrence. See Rom 6:10; Heb 9:28; 10:12; 1 Pet 3:18.

8. Colin Gunton, *Actuality of Atonement: A Study of Metaphor, Rationality and the Christian Tradition* (London: T&T Clark, 1988), 28. Gunton credits this insight to Nelson Goodman, *Languages of Art: An Approach to a Theory of Symbols* (Oxford: Oxford University Press, 1969), 73.

9. This obvious reality is not the same as using a recognition of metaphorical atonement imagery as an excuse "to unsettle or even to dismantle" classical doctrines. Indeed, metaphors point to realities and, in some cases, more effectively than so-called "literal" language. On this point, see Henri Blocher, "Biblical Metaphors and the Doctrine of the Atonement," *JETS* 47, no. 4 (December 2004), 629–45.

10. Sallie McFague, *Metaphorical Theology: Models of God in Religious Language* (Philadelphia: Fortress, 1982), 13.

11. For instance, while the Bible uses the language of "ransom" (Gk *lutron*) to describe Christ's death, one need not picture a backroom bargain between a dealing devil and a duplicitous deity. Likewise, when Isa 53:10 says that "it was the LORD's will to crush [the Servant]," this need not carry the maniacal laugh of a sadistic human father. In both cases, the metaphors of ransom and vicarious penalty-bearing must include the caveat that it is *not* like this.

At the same time, this hardly means that an embrace of "literal" language is either possible or desirable. While John Locke once claimed that metaphors only "insinuate wrong *ideas*, move the passions, and thereby mislead the judgment," contemporary philosophers and sociolinguists argue that all speech is irreducibly metaphorical and that well-chosen metaphors actually offer a "thicker" account of reality than what might be seen as a more "literal" account. See Erin Heim, "Paths Beyond Tracing Out: The Hermeneutics of Metaphor and Theological Method," in *The Voice of God in the Text of Scripture: Explorations in Constructive Dogmatics*, ed. Oliver Crisp and Fred Sanders (Grand Rapids: Zondervan, 2016), 114–15; the Locke quotations comes from *An Essay Concerning Human Understanding*, bk. III, ch. 10 (italics in original), as cited in Heim, "Paths Beyond Tracing Out," 114.

the "metaphor card" by theologians—sufficiently addresses all the pitfalls of, say, penal substitution. After all, it will not do to excuse an absurd or unbiblical model of atonement on the claim that "no metaphor is perfect." Some are clearly better than others. The early church ruled certain ways of speech heretical when used, for instance, to describe the Trinity. It does not help to preface the untriune analogy of water existing as (1) liquid, (2) solid, and (3) gas with the admission that the metaphor is "inexact." It is inexactly Trinitarian because it is *exactly* modalist.

So even though no model of Christ's work is exact, appealing to the limitations of metaphors does not exempt Christians from asking hard questions about particular construals of the cross. Now back to the preceding question: How does an Irenaean account of recapitulation help solve the problem of penal nontransference?

| RECASTING INDIVIDUALITY |

In dealing with the dilemma of penal nontransference, it becomes clear that the critique carries some assumptions about the separate identities of the characters within the judicial analogy.[12] These include (1) the innocent party who strangely now receives the punishment, (2) the guilty party who is inexplicably acquitted, and (3) the apparently unjust judge who oversees this farce of logic and judiciary practice. Sometimes, the judge is simultaneously caricatured as an angry father, and the punished plaintiff as an innocent son who takes the beating as a "whipping boy" on behalf of the guilty. In any case, this distorted account of penal substitution involves the notion that the three "characters" within this storyline are separate individuals.[13]

With regard to the Father and the Son, this assumption is plainly wrong, at least if one affirms an orthodox account of the Trinity, yet the assumption is also seriously flawed with respect to the Son's relation to

---

12. The Socinians (c. 1600s–1700s) were among the first to raise this objection. For them, the problem was insuperable, in part, because they denied both the Trinity and the deity of Christ. Hence Christ was just one individual human amongst others, and united neither with God the Father, nor with humanity at large. See Faustus Socinus (1539–1604), *De Jesu Christo Servatore* (1574).

13. See again Colin Gunton's definition of individualism as "the view of the human person which holds that there is so much space between people that they can in no sense participate in each other's being." Gunton, "Trinity, Ontology and Anthropology: Towards a Renewal of the Doctrine of the *Imago Dei*," in *Persons, Divine and Human: King's College Essays in Theological Anthropology*, ed. Christoph Schwöbel and Colin Gunton (Edinburgh: T&T Clark, 1991), 55.

other humans. As seen in Irenaeus (ch. 1), the presuppositions of reca-pitulation imply a rejection of modern assumptions regarding individual autonomy and disconnectedness. To return to the organic imagery of the Scriptures, recapitulation maintains that as the deepest root of God's expanding family tree, the Son is *not detached* from either the stump of Jesse (Isa 11:11) or the wild olive shoots that have now been grafted in to the existing branches (Rom 11:17). All are connected, for these metaphors point to a participation that demolishes assumptions of an atomistic individualism.

The words of Christ also undermine a completely disconnected view of human personhood. In Luke 9, Jesus proclaims, "Whoever welcomes this little [child] in my name welcomes me; and whoever welcomes me welcomes the one who sent me" (v. 48). While the statement may be variously interpreted, the claim appears to *draw together* the identities of Christ and the child, so that to welcome the little one is to welcome Jesus incognito.[14] Matthew 25 contains a similar statement about the final judgment. Here, the separation of sheep and goats hinges upon a response to Jesus. Yet the twist occurs when hearers learn that they have unknowingly encountered Christ in their interaction with the naked, the hungry, and the imprisoned: "Whatever you did for one of the least of these brothers and sisters of mine, you did for me" (v. 40). Here again, the lines between Jesus and other humans blur—individualism be damned.

In these and other cases, we encounter claims of a connectedness that exists between what we might think of as separate individuals. When it comes time to explain this mysterious connectedness, two possibilities have often been suggested.

Realism

First, in a so-called *realist* rendering, one might say that all humans truly are bound together in the sense that all were literally inside the body of Adam, albeit in some seminal form. In this way of thinking, Adam's actions are seen as my actions because I was in him in the beginning. The guilty verdict handed down to Adam is therefore also rightly handed down

---

14. In a startling turn, Christ then quickly parallels this unseen correspondence (between himself and the child) with a statement about the connection that exists between himself and God the Father. While this does not mean that the relations are identical (or even strictly analogical), Jesus clearly wants us to understand that, at least in certain instances, to welcome one person is to welcome another unseen person also. We are not as disconnected as we may be tempted to believe.

to me, or so the story goes. This idea is found most notably in the theology of Augustine and his heirs.[15]

Yet there are potential pitfalls. Augustine's realism requires belief in monogenesis (the notion that Adam was the physical progenitor of all humanity), and as the previous chapter has shown, many genetic scientists are highly skeptical of this. A further problem involves the dubious logic by which the unborn offspring of one sinner may be condemned for an act that occurred before the child's birth, even if the crime was perpetrated by a primal parent. It is one thing to claim that our genes (or heritage) affect us, but it is quite another to hold one criminally guilty for the actions of an ancestor. Hence Deuteronomy states, "Parents are not to be put to death for their children, nor children put to death for their parents; each will die for their own sin" (24:16).[16] Here again, there is the problem of penal nontransference.

In the end, my own argument regarding recapitulation rejects some aspects of this realist proposal (most notably, belief in original guilt). I will however affirm the realist's desire to take more seriously the genuine connectedness of humankind. In my view, Christians must hold together two realities: First, as Scripture teaches, we are truly bound together with all humanity in a way that counters the currents of modern individualism. Yet, second, it is equally true that each one is to be punished for their own sins, not the sins of another (Jer 31:30).

Federalism

A second way of understanding the "bound-together-ness" of humankind is known as *federalism*. While the word may evoke thoughts of modern politics, it derives from the Latin term for covenant (*foedus*). Thus we are speaking here of covenant theology. The most basic claim of federalism is that God has sovereignly ordained that all humanity be bound up with the moral actions of a single human (whether Adam or Christ). And this singular person therefore acts as a federal head, on behalf of others.

In most federalist theology, Adam is also seen as the forefather of

---

15. See ch. 1.

16. See also 2 Kings 14:6. On this topic, Garry Williams argues that even Old Testament texts that speak of the Lord punishing children for the iniquity of parents (e.g., Deut 5:9) do not involve the innocent being punished for the guilty. Rather, such texts may be seen to point to the guilty being punished for and with the guilty, since both the children and the parents are seen as having rejected God. See Garry Williams, "The Cross and the Punishment of Sin," in *Where Wrath and Mercy Meet: Papers from the Fourth Oak Hill College Annual School of Theology*, ed. David Peterson (London: Paternoster, 2001), 76.

the entire the human race,[17] but this monogenetic reality is not logically necessary for how the schema functions. The crucial idea is that God has sovereignly *covenanted* that human destiny would hinge upon the faithfulness of just one man acting on behalf of the many. The operative principle is therefore not a parental connection but the will of God, the covenant maker.[18] This chapter will argue that a modified version of this federalist approach can help one grasp the foundational link between the (1) recapitulation and (2) penal substitution pieces of our mosaic.

FROM RECAPITULATION TO PENAL SUBSTITUTION

As with federalism, an Irenaeus-inspired view of recapitulation affirms that the actions of Christ and Adam redound to others because each functions as the representative of a larger community. Yet with the realist tradition, recapitulation affirms that Christ's headship involves more than mere appointment.[19] For Irenaeus, Christ acts as the true head of all humanity *because* he is both the creator and the archetype after which the human creature was formed in the beginning. The *imago Dei* is the *imago Christi* because Adam was crafted after the image of the (yet-to-be) incarnate Son. Christ's life and our lives share a mysterious but real connection.

In this recapitulative framework, it is not merely Christ's perfection, his divine-humanity, or his divine appointment that allows him to stand in for others. Rather, it is the fact that all humanity possesses a unique connection to him as the one who has stamped us as images (literally, "icons") of himself. All exist "in him" who is "the firstborn over all creation" (Col 1:15–20). Not only is this the language of headship ("firstborn") but also of incorporation ("in him"). In fact, to even speak of headship implies incorporative imagery, for a head is united to a body.[20] The result, as T. F. Torrance wrote, is that our existence in the Son means that Christ "is the

---

17. See, for instance, the claims of the *Westminster Confession*, 6.1; 19.1.

18. To cite N. T. Wright, it is as if God always intended to have "a human being [Christ] at the helm of the universe." Wright, *Paul and the Faithfulness of God* (Minneapolis: Fortress, 2013), 534.

19. It is not merely that Christ, as a fully human and divine person, was sovereignly "chosen" to stand in for others. The logic involves more than a mere appeal to an all-powerful divine choice.

20. With this bodily metaphor in mind, Thomas Aquinas argued that grace—like anointing oil, when poured onto the "head" (Christ) in abundance—runs down onto the members of the "body." *Commentary on the Epistle to the Hebrews* (South Bend, IN: St. Augustine's, 2006), nn63–65. See also Brandon Peterson, "Paving the Way? Penalty and Atonement in Thomas Aquinas's Soteriology," *IJST* 15, no. 3 (July 2013): 273.

only one who can really represent all men and women from the innermost centre and depth of human being."[21]

A similar incorporative existence can be glimpsed in Acts 17. Here, when referencing the relationship between the Creator and those *outside* the covenant community, the Paul of Acts draws upon a pagan poet to claim that it is "in him" (God) that "we live and move and have our being" (Acts 17:28). On the one hand, such imagery seems strange. As a good Jew, Paul believed in a distinction between the Creator and the creation. Thus both pantheism and idolatry are excluded. Still, the passage claims that *all humans* (whether Jewish or pagan) somehow exist "in" the One who made us. What should we make of this?

While the exact meaning of this imagery may not be obvious, one way of corroborating the reference would be to connect the "him" of Acts 17 to the "him" of Colossians 1: "In him [that is, the Son] all things were created," and "in him all things hold together" (1:16, 17).[22] In saying this, the implication is that *all humanity* is somehow bound up *in* the Messiah after whose image humanity was fashioned. Israel's Christ is also the root and ruler of the entire human race, and this corporate person somehow contains our lives within his life. This allows Jesus to recapitulate the human story successfully on our behalf.

This recapitulative insight also helps as we return to the problem of penal nontransference. If all humanity is somehow bound up *in* and *with* the Son, then the cross presents us not with one innocent and disconnected individual bearing the punishment for other guilty ones. Instead, the cross involves the judgment of the sin of the entire human race in the body of the one person who really does (somehow) contain us all. For that reason, Irenaeus could state that Christ "also summed up [humanity's] death," which God had ordained as the punishment for Adam's sin.[23] Christ did this "so that neither should justice be infringed upon, nor should the hand-iwork of God go to destruction."[24] I will return to these ideas momentarily as they relate to the themes of vicarious judgment and penal substitution.

One finds similar themes of recapitulation, headship, and penalty-bearing

---

21. T. F. Torrance, *Atonement: The Person and Work of Christ*, ed. Robert Walker (Downers Grove, IL: IVP Academic, 2009), 126.

22. In Colossians 1, it is not merely all humanity but also all creation that is bound up with the Son. Thus the atonement may be seen to have redemptive implications for the entire created order. For a recent treatment of this, see Adam Johnson, *Atonement: A Guide for the Perplexed* (London: T&T Clark, 2015), ch. 6.

23. *Haer.* 5.23.2.

24. *Haer.* 5.1.1.

in the writings of Gregory of Nazianzus (ca. 330–90).[25] In his fourth *Theological Oration*, Gregory drew upon Paul's language of Christ being made "sin" and "a curse for us" (2 Cor 5:21; Gal 3:13).

As for my sake He was called a curse, Who destroyed my curse; and sin, who taketh away the sin of the world; and became a new Adam to take the place of the old, just so He makes my disobedience His own as Head of the whole body. As long then as I am disobedient and rebellious, both by denial of God and by my passions, so long Christ also is called disobedient on my account.[26]

The incorporative logic of Christ as the new Adam and "Head of the whole body" helped Nazianzen explain how Christ may bear our disobedience and our curse.

A related claim is found in the writings of John Calvin (1509–64): "Our Lord came forth as true man and took the person and the name of Adam in order to take Adam's place in obeying the Father, to present our flesh as the price of satisfaction to God's righteous judgment and, in the same flesh, to pay the penalty that we had deserved."[27] In this quotation, recapitulative obedience ("to take Adam's place") is married to the notion that Christ may offer "our flesh" to "pay the penalty" because he is the new Adam. In short, Christ may bear the judgment for our sin because he does, in some sense, *bear us*.[28]

| AN ANALOGY FROM SCIENCE FICTION |

Obviously, the above claim does nothing to dispel the mystery of the atonement. The mystery actually deepens when Scripture speaks of all humanity existing in the Son. Modern thought affords few analogies for this kind of

---

25. For an argument in favor of finding penal substitution in Gregory, see Steve Jeffery, Michael Ovey, and Andrew Sach, *Pierced for Our Transgressions: Rediscovering the Glory of Penal Substitution* (Wheaton, IL: Crossway, 2007), 173–74.
26. Gregory of Nazianzus, *Fourth Theological Oration*, in NPNF² 7:311.
27. *Inst.* 2.12.3. This linkage is similarly noted by Ben Pugh, *Atonement Theories: A Way through the Maze* (Eugene, OR: Cascade, 2014), 77.
28. A classic articulation of this argument from a federalist perspective can be seen in the work of John Owen (1616–83). For Owen: "the federal head and those represented by him are not considered as distinct, but as one; for although they are not one in respect of personal unity, they are, however, one;—that is, one body in mystical union, yea, *one mystical Christ* . . . and when the head is punished, the members are also punished." *A Dissertation on Divine Justice*, 2.5, in *Works of John Owen*, ed. William H. Goold (London: Banner of Truth Trust, 1965), 10:598, italics in original.

incorporation. Perhaps it is fitting then that the following example comes from the realm of science fiction.

In Orson Scott Card's popular novel *Ender's Game*, a gifted boy named Ender Wiggin is tasked with directing a fleet of starships against a race of alien invaders.[29] He must control his fleet remotely, as if the entire war is a kind of high-stakes video game—and in this "game" the odds seem hopeless. The aliens are more numerous, better equipped, and more intelligent than their human adversaries. Yet, eventually, Ender learns a pivotal reality. While the alien fleet consists of thousands of ships, they operate somewhat like a hive of bees. Each ship is mysteriously connected to a single "queen." If the queen is destroyed, the thousands of underlings lose their potency. The operative principle is clear: As with the queen, so with the hive. In the story, there is an unseen connection between the life of the leader and the lives of the followers. In her the others live and move and have their being.

An Irenaean view of recapitulation posits something similar (albeit resulting in victory) between Jesus and his people. Upon this incorporative foundation, the critique of penal nontransference begins to lose its force. If humans exist in the Son, who is the archetype and head of the entire image-bearing family (as recapitulation claims), then what happens to the Son, even with respect to judgment, may be said to have happened to us.[30]

The apostle Paul also appears to be operating with something like this incorporative framework when he claims that "one has died for all; therefore all have died" (2 Cor 5:14). Elsewhere, Paul claims to have been "crucified with Christ" (Gal 2:20), despite the fact that Saul of Tarsus was far from placing faith in Jesus at the time of Jesus's execution. In some mysterious sense, what happened to Christ on the cross is seen as having happened to others also. Because of this "bound-up-ness" (for lack of a better word), contemporary New Testament scholar Scot McKnight argues, "If union with Christ is given a fair hearing, imputation follows."[31] "Incorporation is the foundation for justification."[32]

In sum, if the incorporative presuppositions of recapitulation are true, then the sentence of divine judgment has been passed upon the one human *in whom* all humanity has a mysterious but genuine connectedness.

---

29. Orson Scott Card, *Ender's Game* (New York: Tor, 1991).

30. See again the claim of Irenaeus that Christ recapitulated the death of humanity at Calvary in *Haer.* 5.23.2.

31. Scot McKnight, *A Community Called Atonement* (Nashville: Abingdon, 2007), 94.

32. McKnight, *A Community Called Atonement*, 97.

To modify a quote from C. S. Lewis, the Son is the "host" who "creates [and bears] his own parasites."[33] And because our very existence is in him, what is true of him may also be true of us, even with regard to judgment and vindication.[34] In this way, the sting of penal nontransference is removed because all humanity subsists in the Son, our archetype and head. Thus, as 1 John puts it, Christ "is the atoning sacrifice . . . not only for [our sins] but also for the sins of the whole world" (2:2).[35]

| WHY NOT UNIVERSALISM? |

Yet if one believes all this, a further question presents itself: Why not believe in universalism? If all humans are mysteriously bound up with Christ, then why do certain Scriptures,[36] and the vast majority of the Christian tradition, seem to reject the idea that all will ultimately be saved? In asking this, one is forced to grapple with the tension between texts that stress the universal implications of Christ's work and those (sometimes in close proximity!) that speak in more particular ways.[37] Theologies of recapitulation tend to see Christ as the head of the human race, yet Scripture also speaks of him more exclusively as the head of his body, the church.[38] While all are said to be "in him" in some general sense (e.g., Col 1), other passages reserve a special kind of bodily incorporation for those who believe.

What should one make of this? Taken as a whole, the Scriptures appear to maintain two points that must continually be held together: While "all

---

33. C. S. Lewis, *The Four Loves* (1960; repr., New York: Harcourt Brace, 1988), 127.

34. Wolfhart Pannenberg speaks, in a somewhat different vein, of an "inclusive substitution." In chapters 4 and 6, I will examine more carefully how the ideas of substitution and incorporation can coexist. Pannenberg, *Jesus: God and Man*, 2nd ed., trans. Lewis Wilkins and Duane Priebe (Philadelphia: Westminster, 1977), 263.

35. While this chapter intentionally avoids the debate regarding the scope of the atonement (universal versus limited/definite), it is now clear where my allegiance resides. My reading of Scripture demands that Christ be seen as having died "for all" without exception. For the alternative perspective, see David Gibson and Jonathan Gibson, eds., *From Heaven He Came and Sought Her: Definite Atonement in Historical, Biblical, Theological, and Pastoral Perspective* (Wheaton, IL: Crossway, 2013).

36. See, for instance, I. Howard Marshall, "Does the New Testament Teach Universal Salvation?" in *Christ in Our Place*, ed. T. A. Hart (Exeter: Paternoster, 1989).

37. For instance, while 2 Cor 5:19 speaks of God "reconciling the world to himself," the very next verse features an appeal for hearers to "be reconciled to God." Likewise, while Col 1:20 speaks of God reconciling "all things" through the Son, the writer then includes the following condition: "if you continue in your faith" (v. 23). In a similar way, John 3:16 famously holds together God's love for the "world" with the notion that "whoever believes" will be spared from perishing.

38. See especially Eph 5:23; cf. 1 Cor 12:27; Col 1:18.

things" have been reconciled to God through Christ's "blood" (Col 1:19), some powers and people may not ultimately experience this reconciliation, departing instead to what Jesus calls "eternal punishment" (Matt 25:46). This is an unsettling reality. Yet while the vast majority of questions surrounding the "afterlife" and "final states" cannot be tackled here, one issue that must be addressed is whether my account of recapitulation leads logically (or implicitly) to a form of universalism.

Irenaeus, for his part, did not think so. His view of Christ acting on behalf of all humans as a kind of last Adam coincided with his insistence on the necessity for faith and true repentance.[39] Apart from faith, "the righteous judgement of God [will fall] upon all who . . . have seen, but have not believed."[40] Irenaeus clearly disavowed universalism. Yet it is possible to disavow a particular conclusion even while the logic of one's thought appears to contradict that statement. Thus the question remains: How might the above argument concerning the universal and recapitulatory implications of Christ's work avoid universalism?

John Wesley's Answer

One possible answer can be seen in the theology of John Wesley (1703–91). In Wesley's view, Christ's work on behalf of *all humans* removed the original guilt that would otherwise condemn us. This Adamic guilt—which was quite real in Wesley's eyes—has been wiped away by the atoning work of Christ, the true Adam. Therefore, no one, and especially not unbaptized infants, will be sent to hell for Adam's sin.[41] This part of our predicament (original guilt) has been dealt with universally because of Christ.

Yet, in Wesley's view, original guilt is hardly the only thing that renders humans liable for condemnation; we also incur guilt when we willfully transgress the moral laws of God. For this reason, Wesley saw repentance and faith as essential for salvation if and when we become mature enough to understand right from wrong, to transgress these boundaries, and to incur just condemnation. While Christ's atonement universally removes the original guilt of Adam's sin, and while it universally brings about the salvation of those too young or infirm to understand the gospel, this does not change the fact that faith is required of those who do not fall into these categories.

---

39. See *Haer.* 2.32.5 (*ANF* 1:409); 3.6.2 (*ANF* 1:419); 4.28.3 (*ANF* 1:501–2).

40. *Haer.* 4.6.5 (*ANF* 1:468); see also 4.28.2–3 (*ANF* 1:501–2).

41. *The Letters of John Wesley*, ed. John Telford, vol. 6 (London: Epworth, 1931), 239. See also T. A. Noble, "Original Sin and the Fall: Definitions and the Proposal," in *Darwin, Creation and the Fall*, ed. R. J. Berry and T. A. Noble (Nottingham: Apollos, 2009), 126–27.

Beyond the removal of original guilt, Wesley also saw another universal benefit of Christ's atoning work. Like Calvin, he claimed to believe whole-heartedly in the debilitating effects of original sin. And if left to ourselves, this condition of total depravity would render us incapable of accepting God's grace. But unlike Calvin, Wesley went on to claim that Christ's action on behalf of all humans has led to a supernatural restoration of "a measure of free-will" so that all people may either accept or reject God's free offer of salvation.[42] This degree of freedom, however, does not come from innate human power, goodness, or potential. Instead, it is solely the product of God's prevenient grace—the grace that comes before salvation to all people, irrespective of their later decision to trust God.[43] In the end, Wesley steered clear of universalism while simultaneously affirming that the atoning work of Christ accomplished real benefits for all humans.[44] These benefits were to be seen in (1) the removal of original guilt and (2) the gracious restoration of a measure of free will by God's prevenient grace.[45]

T. F. Torrance's Answer

A second, and somewhat different, way of avoiding the universalist implications of "universal atonement" can be seen in the theology of T. F. Torrance (1913–2007).[46] For Torrance, because all things are created and sustained in the Word (John 1), or Son (Col 1), all humans are invariably bound up with the incarnate Christ "in [whom] our humanity is lodged."[47] Given this incorporative framework, Torrance saw Christ as reconciled not merely to an elect portion of humanity but to *all* humanity. "[The Son] took upon himself our twisted, lost and damned existence," said Torrance, "with all its wickedness, violence and abject misery, and substituted himself for us in the deepest and darkest depths of our perdition and godlessness, all in

---

42. John Wesley, "Predestination Calmly Considered," in *The Works of John Wesley* (Grand Rapids: Zondervan, 1958), 10:229–30.

43. See Thomas C. Oden, *John Wesley's Teachings* (Grand Rapids: Zondervan, 2014), 2:139–45.

44. This point has sometimes been misunderstood or misconstrued by later Wesleyan theologians. See, for instance, the assertions of Ray Dunning that Wesley's penal view of the atonement somehow must lead either to universalism, limited atonement, or a rejection of prevenient grace. H. Ray Dunning, *Grace, Faith, and Holiness: A Wesleyan Systematic Theology* (Kansas City, MO: Beacon Hill Press, 1988), 363–65.

45. In chapter 13, I will seek to modify Wesley's account of prevenient grace by speaking instead of the prevenient work of the Holy Spirit. Just as in all areas of atonement doctrine, the Spirit must not be left out of the discussion.

46. While Torrance was, of course, heavily influenced by Karl Barth on such matters, his own doctrine of atonement avoids some of Barth's apparent ambiguity on the subject of universalism.

47. Torrance, *Atonement*, 126.

order to save and redeem us through the atoning sacrifice of himself."[48] In this event, Torrance saw Christ as uniting all humanity to God: "As the creator and head of the race in whom all mankind consist, Christ died for all men and women, and the justification involved is total, for all."[49]

In spite of these universal overtones, Torrance likewise rejected what he calls the "heresy" of universalism.[50] This is made possible, in his view, because humanity retains a terrible freedom to refuse the reconciliation that has *already* taken place in Christ. To understand this possible rejection rationally would be futile, for the nature of evil itself is irrational, incomprehensible, and mysterious. Nevertheless, as Torrance saw it, the Scriptures attest that some will absurdly choose this course.[51] The overriding point for Torrance was that the ultimate condemnation of such persons emerges only from a stubborn and hard-won refusal of the reconciliation that has *already* been established for all people in the atoning work of Christ.[52]

Taking Stock of Torrance and Wesley

Torrance and Wesley reveal two ways to avoid universalism while simultaneously affirming that the atonement achieves real benefits for all humans, regardless of whether they consciously believe in Christ.[53] For Wesley, the logic is more straightforwardly that of *federalism* (or covenant theology) without much appeal to something like the ontic union that exists between Christ and all humanity.[54] This sets Wesley's view apart from that

---

48. Thomas F. Torrance, "The Atonement: The Singularity of Christ and the Finality of the Cross: The Atonement and the Moral Order," in *Universalism and the Doctrine of Hell: Papers Presented at the Fourth Edinburgh Conference in Christian Dogmatics, 1991*, ed. Nigel M. de S. Cameron (Grand Rapids: Baker, 1993), 236–37.

49. Torrance, *Atonement*, 128.

50. See Torrance's descriptions of limited atonement and universalism as "twin heresies" (*Atonement*, 248).

51. For Torrance: "If anyone goes to hell they go to hell, only because, inconceivably, they refuse the positive act of the divine acceptance of them, and refuse to acknowledge that God has taken their rejection of him upon himself, so acknowledging that they deserved to be rejected" (*Atonement*, 157).

52. See further Andrew Purves, *Exploring Christology and Atonement: Conversations with John McLeod Campbell, H. R. Mackintosh and T. F. Torrance* (Downers Grove, IL: IVP Academic, 2015), 229.

53. In the broad sense, this claim is not unusual, especially not if we consider something like the *Christus Victor* model. Here, Christ defeats Satan and the forces of evil (thus achieving a "real benefit") regardless of whether anyone believes in it or not. Likewise, the resurrection occurs prior to and apart from the disciples' faith. Yet in the context of the above discussion, I am speaking more exclusively of the believer's salvific standing before God.

54. See Stanley Rodes, "'From Faith to Faith': An Examination of the Servant-Son Metaphor in John Wesley's Theological Thought," PhD thesis, University of Manchester, 2011, as cited in T. A. Noble, *Holy Trinity: Holy People; The Historic Doctrine of Christian Perfecting* (Eugene, OR: Cascade, 2013), 99.

of Irenaeus, Torrance, and all those who would draw more overtly upon the logic of recapitulation.

In Torrance's thought, however, one finds something similar to a recapitulative account of Christ's incorporative identity, in which all humanity mysteriously subsists. The question, however, is whether he adequately accounted for the high value that the New Testament places upon the *believer's faith* as an apparent requirement for justification.[55] While Torrance frequently affirmed the importance of such faith, some allege that his highly objective account of the atonement has left the precise role of one's belief in Christ ambiguous, or at least underdeveloped.[56]

Still, it might be possible to combine certain aspects of these two approaches. Suppose, for instance, that one sides with Torrance (and Irenaeus) in affirming the genuine (albeit mysterious) ontological connection between the Son and all humanity. In this view, all humans are truly bound up *in* and *with* the Son because—as Irenaeus claimed—Christ is the archetype of the entire human family and the true *imago Dei*. In this way, the Son's headship is rooted in something more than simply the divine decree that he should represent us as our federal head. He is also the *Logos* in whom all are formed; thus all humans somehow cohere *in him*.

The benefit of this more realist rendering of the relation between Christ and humanity can be seen in the way that it deals more adequately with the critique of penal nontransference.[57] The judgment for human sin may be borne by Christ because all humanity has always subsisted in the Son. In this way, the cross is not the arbitrary punishing of an innocent victim but the just condemnation of sinful humanity bound up in the Son.

---

55. See the critique of Torrance at this point by Kevin J. Vanhoozer, "The Origin of Paul's Soteriology: Election, Incarnation, and Union with Christ in Ephesians 1:4 (with Special Reference to Evangelical Calvinism)," in *Reconsidering the Relationship between Biblical and Systematic Theology in the New Testament: Essays by Theologians and New Testament Scholars*, ed. Benjamin E. Reynolds, Brian Lugioyo, and Kevin J. Vanhoozer, (Tubingen: Mohr Siebeck, 2014), 192–211.

56. Robert Letham goes further, claiming that Torrance "would appear to render faith superfluous" to justification. See Letham, "The Triune God, Incarnation, and Definite Atonement," in *From Heaven He Came and Sought Her: Definite Atonement in Historical, Biblical, Theological, and Pastoral Perspective*, ed. D. Gibson and J. Gibson (Wheaton, IL: Crossway, 2013), 457. In denial of critiques like these, Torrance appeals to mystery, claiming that the precise place "of our human response" in the "equation" of redemption cannot "be understood logically." See Torrance, foreword to the new edition of *The Mediation of Christ* (Colorado Springs: Helmers & Howard, 1992), xii.

57. Crisp hints at a similar "realism" wherein "God makes the elect and Christ one metaphysical entity for the purposes of atonement." See Crisp, "The Logic of Penal Substitution," 227n26.

Yet suppose also that one were to side with Wesley (and others) in placing more of a developed emphasis upon the believer's faith as it relates to justification. One option here would be to say that while humanity's ontic union with Christ (by virtue of his recapitulative identity) allows the atonement itself to deal with aspects of our plight—say, atoning for sins committed in ignorance, saving those who are unable to hear and comprehend the gospel, or even securing some prevenient benefit for all people—the fact remains that Scripture consistently identifies faith in Christ as essential.[58] Thus, while we may have many unanswered questions about the possible exceptions to this trend,[59] those questions should not diminish the normative relation between belief in Christ and the believer's justification.[60]

This brief engagement with Wesley and Torrance has highlighted how both were able to emphasize the universal implications of Christ's work (that is, the way in which Jesus secures genuine benefits for all humanity) and deny universalism. Thus a commitment to recapitulation as I have described it does not lead to a belief in universal salvation. Despite their differences, both Wesley and Torrance saw Christ as acting successfully on behalf of all humanity as the true Adam, in whom all humans are somehow bound together. Likewise, both saw Jesus as bearing upon the cross the divine judgment for all human sin.

Because all humans are genuinely bound up *in* the Son, the true head of the entire human family (as recapitulation argues), Christ's subsequent bearing of divine judgment is *not* identical to the hideous transfer of punishment between isolated and disconnected individuals. So while Christ remains our substitute in that we did not physically experience the torture of the cross, our existence *in him* helps address the dilemma of penal non-transference.[61] In this way, my Irenaeus-inspired account of recapitulation provides a foundational presupposition upon which an understanding of penal substitution can stand more sturdily.[62]

---

58. See, for instance, John 3:17–18; Rom 10:9–10; and Heb 11:6.

59. See my treatment of Matt 25 and the separation of the "sheep" and the "goats" earlier in this chapter. Beyond this, another option has been to consider the possibility of a postmortem repentance. In this case, one's faith is clearly required for salvation, even while the opportunities for belief are not limited to this life. This discussion lies beyond the scope of my present inquiry.

60. See Oliver Crisp's treatment of "The Nature and Scope of Union with Christ," for a slightly different solution to what he calls "Vanhoozer's Worry" regarding Torrance's soteriology. Crisp, *The Word Enfleshed: Exploring the Person and Work of Christ* (Grand Rapids: Baker Academic, 2016), ch. 9.

61. In ch. 5, I will further explore how the ideas of "incorporation" and "substitution" may coexist in atonement doctrine.

62. I must suspend judgment on the other critiques of penal substitution until part 2 of this book.

What though of the relation between recapitulation and the other models in this mosaic of atonement? While the following connections will take less time to demonstrate, they are by no means less important. I will turn first to the foundational relation between recapitulation and the larger theme of divine triumph.

| FROM RECAPITULATION TO *CHRISTUS VICTOR* |

The connection between recapitulation and the *Christus Victor* motif is in some ways too obvious. After all, some see recapitulation as but one version of the triumph theme. Gustaf Aulén certainly thought so. In his view, "The Divine victory accomplished in Christ stands in the centre of Irenaeus' thought, and forms the central element in the *recapitulatio*."[63] But if recapitulation is simply a version of the *Christus Victor* paradigm, then why distinguish it? Why speak of recapitulation as the foundational *feet* of this mosaic Christ, while referring to the resultant victory as the crowned *head*?

First, although recapitulation is rightly associated with the larger family of *Christus Victor* explanations, one basis for its distinction involves the fact that according to the Scriptures Christ's ultimate victory involves more than just a successful reliving of the human story in Adam's place. As Milton rightly saw, the Son's resistance to temptation was indeed a victory.[64] Yet Milton overstepped in claiming that Christ "regain'd lost Paradise" simply by rebuffing Satan's wilderness enticements.[65] In contrast to this claim, I will argue later (ch. 7) that the full victory comes only by a more robust account of Jesus's bloody, sacrificial death—the beating heart of our mosaic Christ—the model known as penal substitution.

While the presuppositions of recapitulation bring coherence to penal substitution by dealing with the issue of penal nontransference, the recapitulative framework *alone* does not adequately account for the violent and sacrificial nature of Christ's death, nor for the centrality of the cross within the gospel proclamation. For Fleming Rutledge, "Compelling as

---

63. Gustaf Aulén, *Christus Victor: An Historical Study of the Three Main Types of the Idea of the Atonement*, trans. A. G. Hebert (New York: MacMillan, 1960), 21.

64. "'Tempt not the Lord thy God,' he said and stood. / But Satan smitten with amazement fell." John Milton, *Paradise Regained*, book 4, lines 561–62.

65. Milton, *Paradise Regained*, book 4, line 608. Despite this poetic overstatement, Milton is not so dull as to believe that the wilderness temptation alone accomplished full redemption. Thus his masterpiece famously ends, with these words, the first of which are spoken over Jesus: "Now enter, and begin to save mankind. / Thus they the Son of God our Saviour meek / Sung Victor, and from Heavenly Feast refresh / Brought on his way with joy; he unobserv'd / Home to his Mother's house private return'd" (book 4, lines 635–39).

Irenaeus's account is, it does not incorporate and make sense [sufficiently] of Christ's gruesome death. This is the lacuna—the blank space begging to be filled."[66] In fairness to Irenaeus, I have noted already how he spoke of Christ "summing up" the death of humanity, just as he also recognized the need for divine justice to be maintained concerning sin's punishment.[67] Irenaeus did not ignore the cross. Still, resolving to know "nothing but Christ and him crucified" (1 Cor 2:2) elevates the crucifixion in a way that is not explained sufficiently by Jesus reliving the Adamic (or Israelite) vocation.

Just as penal substitution stands upon the incorporative logic of recapitulation, so too (as I will argue later) does the biblical logic of divine triumph rest upon Christ's penal substitution.[68] Yet if this is so (and herein lies the crucial point for now), then recapitulation is also foundational to a full account of *Christus Victor* in the same way that a home's foundation supports not only walls but also (though less directly) the roof as well. "The highest does not stand without the lowest."[69] In this way, the progression of atonement logic remains important:

1. from Christ's recapitulative identity,
2. to his sacrificial and substitutionary death,
3. on to his victorious resurrection and ascension.

While the feet and the head of my mosaic Christ are indeed related, they must also be distinguished, in part because of the connective role of penal substitution.

There is a second sense in which recapitulation grounds the understanding of divine triumph. While other versions of the conquest motif have sometimes veered toward either docetism (as with the Gnostics)[70] or

---

66. Fleming Rutledge, *The Crucifixion: Understanding the Death of Jesus Christ* (Grand Rapids: Eerdmans, 2015), 549.

67. See Joshua Schendel, "'That Justice Might Not Be Infringed Upon': The Judgement of God in the Passion of Christ in Irenaeus of Lyons," *SJT* 71, no. 2 (2018): 212–25.

68. For a similar argument, see Jeremy R. Treat, *The Crucified King: Atonement and Kingdom in Biblical and Systematic Theology* (Grand Rapids: Zondervan, 2014), ch. 8. Henri Blocher makes a related point in "*Agnus Victor*: The Atonement as Victory and Vicarious Punishment," in *What Does It Mean to Be Saved? Broadening Evangelical Horizons of Salvation*, ed. John G. Stackhouse (Grand Rapids: Baker, 2002), 67–91.

69. Thomas à Kempis, *The Imitation of Christ*, trans. William Benham (Overland Park, KS: Digireads, 2016), 2.11.

70. Eugene Fairweather claims that "the specter of Docetism" hovers even over Aulén's account of *Christus Victor*, and on this point Boersma concurs. See Hans Boersma, *Violence, Hospitality, and the Cross: Reappropriating the Atonement Tradition* (Grand Rapids: Baker Academic, 2004), 185; Fairweather, "Incarnation and Atonement: An Anselmian Response to Aulén's Christus Victor," *Canadian Journal of Theology* 7 (1961): 167.

divine duplicity (as with some accounts of God deceiving the devil), Irenaeus shows that triumph actually comes through a peaceable and incarnational obedience. Even though Christ "robs" the strongman, "destroys" death, and "crushes" the devil,[71] he does not do so through "violent means."[72] He does not become a monster to defeat one. Likewise, Irenaeus claimed that God uses persuasion rather than force to call humans to himself, thereby protecting both freedom and justice. This becomes even more crucial to note if, as some allege, the *Christus Victor* motif is vulnerable not only to docetic or duplicitous articulations but also to triumphalist and violent misunderstanding. The classic case in point would be Constantine's construal of the cross, displaced from Calvary to the Milvian Bridge.

| FROM RECAPITULATION TO MORAL INFLUENCE |

What then of the relation between recapitulation and moral influence? As I will argue in part 4, Scripture teaches that the final victory is only consummated as the Spirit conforms and transforms particular Christians into the image of the Christ. Thus the victory is both already (in terms of Christ's incarnational triumph) and not yet (in terms of the final mopping up of evil). While the *already* portion involves Christ's recapitulative identity and his substitutionary death, the unfolding divine victory comes about, in part, by Spirit-driven moral influence.

Evidence for this reality can be seen in Paul's encouragement to the Christians in Rome: "The God of peace will soon crush Satan underneath your feet" (Rom 16:20). Here one finds a triumph text with a clear echo of the story of Adam and Eve through the so-called protoevangelium (Gen 3:15). Yet in Romans 16, the victory Paul speaks of has not yet happened. God will soon crush Satan. What's more, this future stomping out of evil involves the soles—not merely the pardoned *souls*—of ordinary Roman Christians. The believers' transformed lives are connected to the continued unfolding of the divine victory. This theme brings one to the atonement model known as moral influence.

How does recapitulation relate to moral influence? Once again, a sense

---

71. *Haer.* 3.23.7 (*ANF* 1:57); 5.21.1 (*ANF* 1:548–49).

72. *Haer.* 5.1.1 (*ANF* 1:527). This does not mean, however, that Irenaeus can be claimed as an advocate for a so-called "nonviolent atonement." He is a believer in the necessity of retributive justice, and he sees death (including the death of Christ) as the divinely ordained penalty for human sin. His point, then, is that God does not violate either the creature's freedom or the demands of justice when accomplishing atonement. See Schendel, "That Justice Might Not Be Infringed," 212–25.

of order is important. Before human hearts can be enflamed to follow Christ's example, Jesus must first *provide* this paradigm of faithfulness. He must relive the human story successfully. As Irenaeus put it, "Not despising or evading any condition of humanity."[73] In this way, Jesus's recapitulative obedience is foundational (as a precursor) to our Spirit-enabled moral influence. Apart from Christ reliving the human drama faithfully, we would have no perfect exemplar to follow. Christ's recapitulative identity as true Adam and true Israel reveals what it means to be fully and victoriously human, even in suffering and temptation. The recapitulative foundation must come first as an objective ground for moral influence.

While history provides many impressive exemplars of love and sacrifice, Christ's resurrection and ascension make him utterly unique. These realities reveal that, despite appearances, the way of the cross does not ultimately end in pointless tragedy. On the other side of "*Eloi, Eloi*" is resurrection, both for Jesus and for those bound up with him. Irenaeus's account of headship via the *imago Christi* provides a basic rationale, however mysterious, that reveals how Christ may represent us in a way that transcends all other "good examples." Other exemplars cannot claim this sort of headship, shared existence, or incorporative identity. Because it is *in him* that we live and move and have our being, the call to trust and obey is neither moralistic drudgery, nor idealistic gas. Here, too, the notion of Christ as true Adam (and true Israel) is foundational to what I will later expound as a Spirit-driven account of moral influence.

| CORROBORATION |

My thesis has been that a particular recapitulative account of Christ's person and work serves to ground the models to be surveyed in later chapters. Recapitulation grounds them by providing foundational presuppositions upon which they stand more sturdily. Hence recapitulation is represented by the mosaic's feet. If my claims are valid, one might expect to find corroboration in the broader scholarly community. Happily, this is the case.

---

73. *Haer.* 2.22.2 (*ANF* 1:390). Despite what Irenaeus says about Jesus becoming "an old man for old men," it is not necessary for Christ to encounter every *possible* human experience in order to fully identify with our humanity. He was not, so far as we know, "a cancer patient for cancer patients." Nor was he "a victim of sexual abuse for those who have been so molested." The point, instead, is that Christ is *fully human* and in this way fully open to human emotions, trials, and temptations. As with all humans, Christ's experiences were specific to his gender, personality, place of origin, and many other contextual factors. Still, we find in his navigation of these particular waters, a profoundly relevant example of obedience, courage, and grace.

Hans Boersma notes a similar way in which Christ's recapitulative identity provides a basis for other models of atonement. For him, the other models serve to build out and up, in more particular ways, from Christ's recapitulation of the human story. Therefore, "Christ's work of recapitulation has a prophetic element (moral influence), a priestly element (representative punishment), and a royal element (*Christus Victor*)."[74] Boersma's conclusion, then, is that an Irenaean view of recapitulation holds promise in "overcoming seemingly insuperable polarities between the various models of atonement."[75] Yet while recapitulation easily flows into other models, the *specificity* of these other "mosaic pieces" is crucial as well. For Boersma:

> When we say that Christ recapitulated Israel and Adam, we haven't yet said *in which way* Christ recapitulated them. This is where the three atonement models come in. As the representative of Israel and Adam, Christ instructs us and models for us the love of God (moral influence). As the representative of Israel and Adam, Christ suffers God's judgment on evil and bears the suffering of the curse of the Law (penal representation). As the representative of Israel and Adam, Christ fights the powers of evil, expels demons, withstands satanic temptation to the point of death, and rises victorious from the grave (*Christus Victor*).[76]

Boersma helps corroborate my claim that Christ's recapitulative vocation is foundational not merely to penal substitution but also to these other models of atonement.

| CONCLUSION |

So ends part 1. In the above pages, I have sought to frame the classic account of recapitulation in Christian history (ch. 1), to deal with a contemporary challenge to its viability (ch. 2), and to show how it forms the presuppositional "footing" upon which the later pieces may stand in order to display the beauty of God's Spirit-driven work in Christ. In the words of Irenaeus, "The glory of God is a living human."[77] Yet as this mosaic Christ must now go on to illustrate, the human figure is more than just feet.

---

74. Boersma, *Violence, Hospitality, and the Cross*, 122.
75. Boersma, *Violence, Hospitality, and the Cross*, 14.
76. Boersma, *Violence, Hospitality, and the Cross*, 113.
77. *Haer.* 4.34.5. My translation.

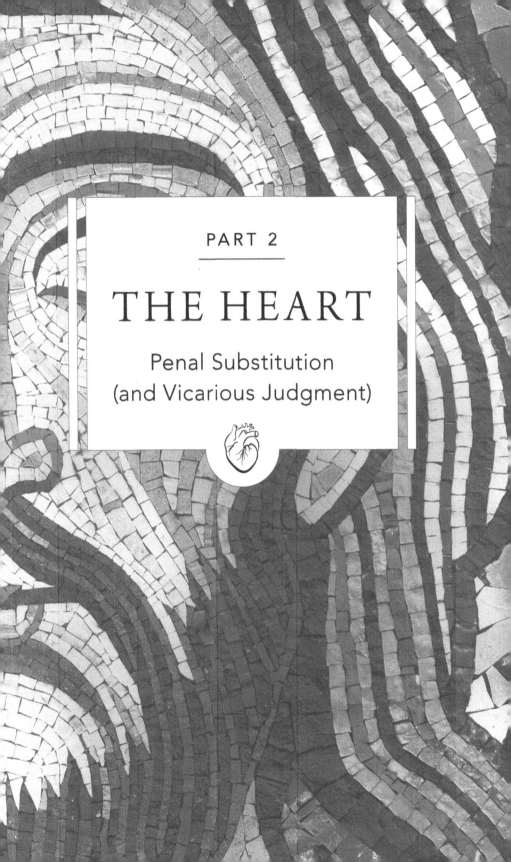

PART 2

THE HEART

Penal Substitution
(and Vicarious Judgment)

CHAPTER 4

OLDER THAN THE PEWS

PENAL SUBSTITUTION IN EARLY CHRISTIAN HISTORY

The age of one's church pews is not normally seen as relevant information in discussions of atonement doctrine. Yet, surprisingly, the subject has come up. In a much-publicized critique of penal substitution, a prominent British pastor claimed that Christians should abandon a view of the cross that is "not even as old as the pews in many of our church buildings."[1] Admittedly, in America, where both the age of buildings and the style of seating are (often) somewhat different, the statement makes less sense. Still, the implication is clear: If the logic of penal substitution is a relatively late development in the history of Christian doctrine—traced often to John Calvin in the sixteenth century[2]—then this ought to raise some questions.

Protestants have always been more interested in biblical support than appeals to church tradition, but it certainly seems that someone should have noticed this doctrine in their Bibles prior to the Reformation.[3]

---

1. Steve Chalke, "Cross Purposes," *Christianity* (September 2004): 45.
2. For a recent example of this conventional wisdom, see James Beilby and Paul R. Eddy, introduction to *The Nature of Atonement: Four Views*, ed. Beilby and Eddy (Downers Grove, IL: IVP Academic, 2006), 17. See also Paul Fiddes, *Past Event and Present Salvation: The Christian Idea of Atonement* (Louisville: Westminster John Knox, 1989), 89. Calvin, of course, would never have used the language of "penal substitution" (or its French equivalents). This phrase is often traced to Charles Hodge. See Ben Pugh, *Atonement Theories: A Way through the Maze* (Eugene, OR: Cascade, 2014), 46n5.
3. Despite the fact that no early creed is even suggested as advocating penal substitution, a recent defense of the model casually groups it alongside "the Trinity, the deity of Christ, and the bodily resurrection" as "foundational truths of the Christian faith." Steve Jeffery, Michael Ovey, and Andrew Sach, *Pierced for Our Transgressions: Rediscovering the Glory*

Both the church fathers and their medieval inheritors were thoughtful readers of Scripture, even if their interpretive frameworks may differ from our own.[4] So what should we make of this claim that the logic of penal substitution was virtually unheard of for the first fifteen hundred years of Christian history?

The present chapter focuses on the (1) nature and (2) origins of penal substitution, since it exists alongside vicarious judgment as the *heart* of my mosaic of atonement. In other words:

1. What are the essential elements of penal substitutionary atonement?
2. How did the logic of penal substitution emerge in Christian history?

Unlike recapitulation, which was introduced by attending primarily to one voice from the tradition (Irenaeus), the supposedly shallow roots of penal substitution demand a different approach. Rather than select a single representative, I will engage with several supposed exemplars. And because the early affirmation of the model has been doubted, I will focus upon figures from (roughly) the first five hundred years of postbiblical Christian history.

Before doing so, however, it is important to clarify the essential logic of penal substitution. This matters because, despite what some may think, there have been many versions of the model throughout history. Therefore, any discussion of the topic should start by establishing some minimum requirements for a view to be identified as penal substitution. Having done so, my next task will be to demonstrate that, contrary to common claims, the basic elements of penal substitution have been broadly present in church history, even from the earliest centuries.

In saying this, however, I will also move to chasten some of penal substitution's overzealous defenders, as they wrongly locate it in some parts of the tradition where it is not present—or when they make it the be-all and end-all of atonement. The chapter seeks to provide much-needed moderation to the "flame wars" that reignited a decade or so ago over the nature and origin of the model. With these caveats in place, my overarching claim is

---

of Penal Substitution (Wheaton, IL: Crossway, 2007), 24. In my judgment, this claim goes too far; for whether intended or not, it serves to bolster a "reductionism" that sets up one atonement model as most important.

4. See, for instance, the compilation of ancient scriptural wisdom in the multivolume *Ancient Christian Commentary on Scripture*, Thomas C. Oden, gen. ed. (Downers Grove, IL: IVP Academic, 1998–2010).

that while the age of church pews may differ, it is no longer possible to say that penal substitutionary atonement is a "latecomer" to Christian worship.

| MERE PENAL SUBSTITUTION |

In his famous introduction to orthodox belief, C. S. Lewis began with a disclaimer: "You will not learn from me whether you ought to become an Anglican, a Methodist, a Presbyterian, or a Roman Catholic." The goal instead was to introduce *Mere Christianity*—the essential common doctrines of the diverse Christian movement. These shared beliefs were then pictured as "the broad hall out of which doors open into several rooms" representing more particular groups. Despite their differences, these smaller groups were seen as sharing much in common, just as several rooms might share a common hall.[5]

My first task echoes Lewis. The goal here is to identify what might be termed "mere penal substitution"—the broad hall to which countless smaller rooms connect. As is well known, John Calvin (1509–64) has a room off this hall, as do Martin Luther (1483–1546) and Charles Hodge (1797–1878). Yet there are connecting chambers that were built far earlier. Even though all these rooms have interesting furnishings, my first goal is merely to describe the *shared space* between these doorways, while avoiding the false assumption that penal substitution is only a one-bedroom apartment. With this in mind, I will explore three essential elements of mere penal substitution under the headings of (1) substitution, (2) penalty, and (3) divine sanction.

Substitution

When it comes to substitution, it can be helpful to define the concept through a single, simple catchphrase. For Simon Gathercole, that phrase is "in our place, instead of us."[6] The idea is that Christ stands in for us so that something happens to him that does not happen (at least in the same way) to us. Substitution is hereby distinguished from a strictly incorporative or representative view of the atonement.[7] With incorporation, Christ acts "in our place, with us," because we are somehow bound up

---

5. C. S. Lewis, preface to *Mere Christianity* (New York: MacMillan, 1952).
6. Simon Gathercole, *Defending Substitution: An Essay on Atonement in Paul* (Grand Rapids: Baker Academic, 2015), 15.
7. See my prior treatment of humanity's incorporative existence in the Son (ch. 3). Incorporative views of atonement are sometimes referenced by way of "participation," or "inclusive place-taking."

in and with him. From this perspective, Paul claims that he was crucified "with" Christ (Gal 2:20) and that "all died" (2 Cor 5:15) with Jesus on the cross. In representation, Christ acts "in our place, for us"—but without a specification of exactly how this place-taking works. As such, substitution (in our place, instead of us) and incorporation (in our place, with us) are two different ways of expressing *how* Christ represents us.

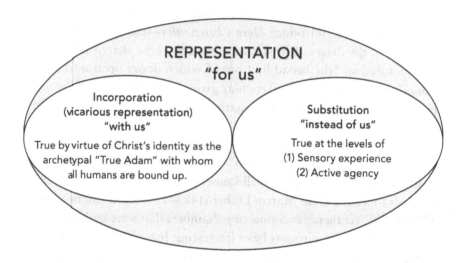

Some illustrations further show the difference. In the sport of soccer, Jones may enter the game as a substitute for Smith. Yet to do so, Smith must simultaneously exit. In this way, Jones plays instead of and in place of his teammate. On the other hand, if Sue runs a marathon while five months pregnant (perhaps to shame us for our laziness . . .) one might argue that the unborn child did complete the race with her, despite the fact that Sue did all the running, and despite the fact that the child was unaware of Mom's accomplishment.[8] Similarly, if Sue were to shame us further by hoisting up and carrying an injured runner (James) across the final meters, then James too would complete the course with her, but only in that he was borne upon her body.

All three of these concepts (representation, incorporation, and substitution) are necessary when it comes to the atonement.[9] On incorporative

8. The analogy to the atonement should be clear: in an incorporative viewpoint, I am bound up with Christ, despite the fact that I have no memory or sensory experience of the cross; indeed it happened before my birth.

9. See Adam Johnson, *Atonement: A Guide for the Perplexed* (London: T&T Clark, 2015), 44–46.

representation, Scripture clearly argues that we were bound up *with* Christ on the cross (e.g., Gal 2:20), so that what is true of him is (or can be) true of us. Likewise, chapter 3 showed how this bound-togetherness is useful in answering the critique of penal nontransference. Because Christ is the true Adam in whose image all humanity was patterned and in whom all things subsist (Col 1:16), Jesus may act on behalf of the human race as our representative head. In this way, all are bound up with Christ as our vicarious representative. Yet the imagery of substitution is also necessary, especially as it pertains to the levels of (1) sensory experience and (2) the active agency by which atonement happens.

With regard to sensory experience, it is clear that Jesus suffered some things that I did not. I did not feel the weight of divine forsakenness upon a Roman cross, nor did nails pierce my hands and feet.[10] Likewise, regarding agency, I contributed nothing (except my sin) to the strange triumph at Golgotha. While I was mysteriously bound up with Christ, I was not the agent of redemptive action. For these reasons, it seems that incorporation (or participation) describes things as they *really are* at some deep level,[11] and substitution describes the previously mentioned levels of agency and sensory experience.[12]

Finally, it bears noting that a substitutionary atonement need not necessarily be penal.[13] For example, Scottish theologian John McLeod Campbell (1800–1872) claimed that the Son offered substitutionary penitence on our behalf.[14] In this view, Christ offered vicarious repentance for us (in our place, instead of us) even while he did not suffer the punishment of divine wrath upon the cross. Substitution need not be penal, but the idea of Christ experiencing something in our place, instead of us, does comprise the first component of mere penal substitution.

---

10. While there are certainly those who *have* experienced both the pain of crucifixion and the perception of divine forsakenness, the point here is merely that being mystically bound up with Christ on the cross (e.g., Gal 2:20) does not itself include these sensory experiences.

11. Hence, "all died" with Christ (2 Cor 5:14), just as "in him all things were created . . . and in him all things hold together" (Col 1:16, 17).

12. Beyond the English language, the concepts may merge even further. This may be witnessed, for instance, by Barth's use of *Stellvertretung*. According to the editors of the English translation of his *Church Dogmatics*, this German term "enshrines the notions both of representation and substitution, and never the one without the other." See G. W. Bromiley and T. F. Torrance, editors' preface to *CD* IV/1, vii.

13. See Oliver Crisp, "Non-Penal Substitution," *IJST* 9, no. 4 (October 2007): 415–33.

14. John McLeod Campbell, *The Nature of Atonement*, 6th ed. (London: Macmillan, 1895 [1856]); See also, R. C. Moberly, *Atonement and Personality* (London: Murray, 1901).

Penalty

The second concept of penal substitution is that of penalty or punishment.[15] While philosophical definitions of these words have become complex,[16] a common understanding of *penalty* refers to the suffering in person, rights, or property brought about by a judicial decision on the grounds of a crime or public offense.[17] Within this definition, we might draw out three elements: punishment itself (e.g., thirty lashes with a wet noodle), the alleged infraction (e.g., wearing white after Labor Day), and the judicial authority by which the punishment is handed down (e.g., Judge Judy). Despite the ridiculous examples, a nuanced understanding of penal substitution requires careful attention to all three components.

Take, for instance, the supposed punishment itself. At this point, specific versions of penal substitution might claim that the divinely sanctioned penalty (or penalties) experienced by Christ included any or all of the following:

- death on a cross[18]
- bearing the divine or covenantal curses (including exile from the land of the living)
- experiencing divine wrath or judgment
- experiencing the divine abandonment (or withdrawal) that we deserved
- being forsaken unto death
- being God-forsaken
- descending into hell
- being pierced for our transgressions
- giving his life as a propitiating sacrifice for human sin

Any of these occurrences might be seen as penal, though some might dispute whether all of them are valid interpretations of the cross. The crucial

---

15. I take penalty and punishment to be more-or-less synonymous in today's culture. This approach, while not universal, is taken by such common legal sources as *Black's Law Dictionary*, 7th ed., ed. Bryan Garner (New York: West Group, 1999), s.v. "penalty." For one attempt to distinguish the two terms, see P. T. Forsyth, *The Work of Christ* (London: Hodder and Stoughton, 1910), 147.

16. See Mark C. Murphy, *Philosophy of Law* (Oxford: Blackwell, 2007), 113–16.

17. Adapted from the Merriam-Webster Dictionary. A similar legal definition for *penalty* may be found in *Black's Law Dictionary*.

18. For I. Howard Marshall, it is important that "the death of Jesus on the cross was not merely a physical death, but also the eternal death due to sinners." Marshall, *Aspects of the Atonement: Cross and Resurrection in the Reconciling of God and Humanity* (London: Paternoster, 2007), 3.

point is that one may employ penal substitutionary *logic* even without the explicit use of words like penalty or punishment.[19]

On the infraction that occasioned penalty, there is wide agreement: while Christ did not sin, the sin of humanity remains the offense for which the penalty is paid. However, in turning to the third element—the judicial authority behind the penalty experienced by Christ—we encounter the most controversial aspect of penal substitution.

Divine Sanction

Accounts of penal substitution see the penalty endured by Christ as having been sanctioned in some way by God himself. For this reason, God is viewed as the ultimate judicial authority behind atonement. In mentioning the Father's part in willing the cross, one can see the origin of the contemporary smear that the model is like "divine child abuse."[20] Though a fuller response to this charge awaits (ch. 6), all proponents of penal substitution acknowledge some level of divine sanction over the penal and judicial aspects of atonement. As Peter proclaims in Acts 4, "Indeed Herod and Pontius Pilate met together with the Gentiles and the people of Israel in this city to conspire against your holy servant Jesus, whom you anointed. *They did what your power and will had decided beforehand should happen*" (vv. 27–28, italics added).

When it comes to divine sanction, several "rooms" open from the broad hall of mere penal substitution. A strong view of divine punishment—and one more vulnerable to the charge of "divine child abuse"—might lead one to claim, following Martin Luther (1483–1546), that "God himself struck and punished Christ."[21] Here, the object of the action is Christ, and the subject is simply God. John Owen claimed something similar: "The person punishing is Jehovah, the person punished . . . [is] the Messiah, the Christ."[22] So while it has been asserted that evangelical accounts of

---

19. Failure to recognize this possibility is an example of the so-called "word-thing fallacy"—that is, the erroneous belief that unless a specific word is used, the author cannot be evoking the underlying idea.

20. See Steve Chalke and Alan Mann, *The Lost Message of Jesus* (Grand Rapids: Zondervan, 2003), 182. The allegation emerged first from certain feminist theologians. See Joanne Carlson Brown, "Divine Child Abuse," *Daughters of Sarah* 18, no. 3 (1992): 28.

21. Martin Luther, *Werke: Kritische Gesamtausgabe*, vol. 40, pt. 3, *Weimar Ausgabe*, ed. J. K. F. Knaake (Weimar: Böhlaus, 1930), 715, cited in Daniel J. Hill and Joseph Jedwab, "Atonement and the Concept of Punishment," in *Locating Atonement: Explorations in Constructive Dogmatics*, ed. Oliver Crisp and Fred Sanders (Grand Rapids: Zondervan, 2015), 151n29. The Latin reads as follows: *Ipse Deus percussit et punivit Christum.*

22. John Owen, *Works*, vol. 9, ed. Thomas Russell (London: Baynes, 1826), 443.

penal substitution have never claimed that God punished Christ,[23] the fact remains that several influential voices have said exactly this.[24]

But more nuanced views of divine sanction are possible. Allow me to list four possibilities briefly. First, instead of claiming that the Father actively tortured the Son to vent his retributive wrath, one might claim with Richard Mouw that the penalty endured was that of separation from God. While this judgment upon sin clearly involves a divine sanction, it is not the same as God "directly inflicting pain on the Son."[25] Similarly, Gregory Boyd suggests that divine wrath and judgment are not an active torturing of sinners or of Christ upon the cross, but rather a "withdrawal" of God's protective presence, which allows sin to be punished by other violent agents.[26] Both approaches could fit under the umbrella of mere penal substitution since both involve a divine sanction for the judgment of human sin at the cross.[27]

Second, one might place any number of intermediaries between God the Father and the meting out of the divinely ordained penalty for sin. Here, Jesus may be seen as bearing the covenantal curses in place of others.[28] Because God established the covenant, there is surely a divine sanction,[29] yet this is not the same as crassly claiming that "God killed Jesus."[30] In another example, some theologians have even claimed that God allowed the devil, as an unwitting intermediary, to mete out the divinely ordained penalty for human sin, through the hands of evil men.[31]

---

23. In the heat of renewed debates over penal substitution, I. Howard Marshall claimed that "Indeed at some point the challenge needs to be issued: where are these evangelicals who say that God punished Christ? Name them!" Marshall, "The Theology of the Atonement," in *The Atonement Debate: Papers from the London Symposium on the Theology of Atonement,* ed. Derek Tidball, David Hilborn, and Justin Thacker (Grand Rapids: Zondervan, 2008), 63.

24. For further examples, see Hill and Jedwab, "Atonement and the Concept of Punishment," 150–53.

25. Richard J. Mouw, "Violence and the Atonement," in *Must Christianity Be Violent: Reflections on History, Practice, and Theology* (Grand Rapids: Brazos, 2003), 167.

26. Gregory A. Boyd, *Crucifixion of the Warrior God: Interpreting the Old Testament's Violent Portraits of God in Light of the Cross,* vol. 2, *The Cruciform Thesis* (Minneapolis: Fortress, 2017), 768, 781.

27. Though Boyd muddies the waters by assuming that penal substitution must *always* claim that the Father actively "poured out" or "vented" his wrath upon Jesus, like a torturer personally pouring scalding water on an innocent victim. In this way, Boyd is operating with a definition of penal substitution that is too narrow and too caricatured. See Boyd, *Crucifixion of the Warrior God,* 2:781n44; cf. 2:1061.

28. See Jeremy Treat, "Atonement and Covenant: Binding Together Aspects of Christ's Work," in *Locating Atonement: Explorations in Constructive Dogmatics,* ed. Oliver Crisp and Fred Sanders (Grand Rapids: Zondervan, 2015), 110–11.

29. "The law, we remember, is God's law and therefore it is God who imposes the curse." Marshall, *Aspects of the Atonement,* 46.

30. E.g., Tony Jones, *Did God Kill Jesus? Searching for Love in History's Most Famous Execution* (New York: Harper Collins, 2015).

31. I will return to this idea when I survey Augustine's treatment of atonement. Boyd

Third, one might emphasize Christ's initiative. The result would be to say that Jesus freely took upon himself the divinely sanctioned penalty for human sin.[32] P. T. Forsyth (1848–1921) is an exemplar of this move: "There is a penalty and curse for sin; and Christ consented to enter that region. . . . It is impossible for us to say that God was angry with Christ; but still Christ entered the wrath of God. . . . He bore God's penalty upon sin."[33] While this imagery may not necessarily contradict the abrasive claim that God punished Christ, it does place the accent on a very different and more nuanced point.

Fourth and finally, one might follow Karl Barth in emphasizing that the Son himself is both God and Judge. The result of this move is that "God [himself] goes down into the dock,"[34] as Christ becomes "the Judge judged in our place."[35] Not all of these options may be agreeable, yet each one shows how different theologians have accounted for a level of divine sanction for the penalty endured by Christ. And in this way, each one may connect to the broad hall of mere penal substitution.

To sum up, every version of "mere" penal substitution agrees that Christ acted and experienced certain things both in our place and *instead of us*. Likewise, all agree that Christ takes on the penalty for human sin even while this penalty can be described in diverse ways. Finally, all accounts maintain varying levels of divine sanction behind the penalty despite the fact that "wicked men" (Acts 2:23) were to blame for the injustice of the crucifixion. All three components—substitution, penalty, divine sanction—allow room for diversity as one moves from the broad hall into the particular rooms of specific theologians.

| EARLY CHRISTIAN VOICES |

Having briefly defined the parameters of mere penal substitution, I will now examine when these ideas emerged in Christian history and whether they are, so to speak, "older than the pews."[36]

---

appears to endorse this claim as well, albeit without supporting penal substitution. Boyd, *Crucifixion of the Warrior God*, 2:782.

32. This is the route taken by Marshall, "The Theology of the Atonement," 63.

33. Forsyth, *The Work of Christ*, 147. Forsyth preferred to speak of judgment rather than penalty and of representation rather than substitution. Nonetheless, all these ideas were present in his thought to varying degrees, and one could argue that his view of the cross qualifies under my definition of mere penal substitution. See also Theng-Huat Leow, "'The Cruciality of the Cross': P. T. Forsyth's Understanding of the Atonement," *IJST* 11, no. 2 (April 2009): 190–207.

34. CD IV/1, 220.

35. CD IV/1, 236, 254.

36. In recent years, several voices have sought to rebut the old claim that penal substitution emerged first with the Protestant Reformers. I will therefore draw occasionally upon these

Justin Martyr: Christ Took the Curses of All

Even prior to Irenaeus and his theology of recapitulation, Justin Martyr (ca. AD 100–165) set forth claims about atonement that have been likened to penal substitution. The crucial material appears in his *Dialogue with Trypho* (ca. 130). In the relevant passage, Justin responded to a Jewish man named Trypho, who questioned whether Jesus could possibly be the Christ, given that he was crucified and therefore hung upon a tree. The objection concerns the claim of Deuteronomy, that "anyone who is hung on a tree is under God's curse" (21:23). Surely, Trypho reasoned, the Messiah could not be accursed by God.

Justin responded that Christ was not cursed for his own sins. Rather, "the whole human race" is under a curse, for we have failed to do those things "written in the book of the law" (Deut 27:26; Gal 3:10).[37] In a crucial passage, Justin built upon Paul's argument in Galatians 3:13, that the Father "wished His Christ for the whole human family to take upon Him the curses of all." Thus Christ "submitted to suffer these things according to the Father's will, as if he were accursed."[38] Some claim to find the doctrine of penal substitution here, for, as one assessment puts it, Jesus is presented as taking "upon himself the curse of God that had rested upon [humanity]."[39]

Yet this is almost certainly wrong. Justin emphatically denied that Christ was accursed by either God or the law. For him, "Though a curse lies in the law against persons who are crucified, yet no curse lies on the Christ of God."[40] As he stated in the next chapter, it was "not [that] He who has been crucified is cursed by God." Rather, Justin claimed that Jesus "submitted to the suffer . . . according to the Father's will *as if* He were accursed"—and the *as if* is crucial.[41] But if Christ was not accursed by either God or the law, then what did Justin mean when he said that Jesus took "upon Himself the curses of all"?

---

scholars even while differing from the overzealous attempts to find the model in every nook and cranny of the tradition or to elevate it as the most important model. For the attempted location of penal substitution in the early Christian tradition, see Jeffery, Ovey, and Sach, *Pierced for Our Transgressions*, ch. 5; Henri Blocher, "Biblical Metaphors and the Doctrine of the Atonement," *JETS* 47 (2004): 629–45; Blocher, "*Agnus Victor*: The Atonement as Victory and Vicarious Punishment," in *What Does It Mean to Be Saved? Broadening Evangelical Horizons of Salvation*, ed. John G. Stackhouse Jr. (Grand Rapids: Baker Academic, 2002), 74–77.

37. Justin Martyr, *Dialogue with Trypho, a Jew* 95 (ANF 1:247).
38. Justin, *Dialogue with Trypho* 95 (ANF 1:247).
39. Jeffery, Ovey, and Sach, *Pierced for Our Transgressions*, 166.
40. Justin, *Dialogue with Trypho* 95 (ANF 1:247).
41. Justin, *Dialogue with Trypho* 95 (ANF 1:247), italics added.

The best possibility is to read the "all" as speaking of those *humans* who cursed Christ. This reading is strengthened by the fact that Justin immediately and repeatedly returned to the idea that unbelievers (including Trypho) continue to "curse" Christ today and so bring judgment on themselves.[42] Whatever the case, it is flatly wrong to claim that Justin presented Christ as bearing God's curse on our behalf. He explicitly rejected this notion. Justin saw a divine sanction for Christ's suffering (it was the Father's "will" and "wish"), but in his work the notion that Christ bears God's curse (or penalty) instead of us is far from obvious. Thus Justin should not be claimed as an early exemplar of penal substitution.[43]

Irenaeus of Lyons—Nonpenal Propitiation

The next patristic possibility is a familiar one: Irenaeus of Lyons (ca. AD 130–202). While recapitulation provides the primary lens for Irenaean atonement,[44] a few have suggested that he hinted at something close to penal substitution.[45] The suggestion hinges upon the fact that Irenaeus occasionally spoke of Christ as "propitiating" (*propitians*) the Father on our behalf. Irenaeus wrote,

> By transgressing [God's] commandment we became his enemies. And therefore in the last times the Lord has restored us into friendship through his incarnation, having become "the Mediator between God and men"; propitiating for us the Father against whom we had sinned, and cancelling our disobedience by his own obedience; conferring also upon us the gift of communion with, and subjection to, our Maker.[46]

A similar claim appears in book 4 of *Against Heresies*. Here, he wrote that Jesus performed "the offices of the high priest, propitiating God for men . . . Himself suffering death, that exiled man might go forth from condemnation."[47]

---

42. Justin, *Dialogue with Trypho* 95–96 (*ANF* 1:247).
43. Contra Jeffery, Ovey, and Sach, *Pierced for Our Transgressions*, 166.
44. See ch. 1.
45. Andrew J. Bandstra, "Paul and an Ancient Interpreter: A Comparison of the Teaching of Redemption in Paul and Irenaeus," *Calvin Theological Journal* 5 (1970): 43–63; Hans Boersma, *Violence, Hospitality, and the Cross: Reappropriating the Atonement Tradition* (Grand Rapids: Baker Academic, 2004), 161–63.
46. *Haer.* 5.17.1 (*ANF* 1:544). The crucial words in Latin are as follows: "*propitians quidem pro nobis Patrem, in quem peccaveramus, et nostrum inobedientiam per suam obedientiam consolatus.*"
47. *Haer.* 4.8.2 (*ANF* 1:471): "*propitians pro hominibus Deum . . . uti exiliatus homo exiret de condemnatione.*"

Both passages clearly speak of propitiation, and as the twentieth century demonstrated, that concept would become a flash point. The English word and its Latin precursor (*propitiatio*) refer to the placation, assuaging, removal, or turning aside of divine wrath, often through a sacrifice or gift.[48] Hence the notion is important for those who claim that Jesus bore the weight of divine wrath in our place. Yet while the meaning of the Latin word is clear enough, scholars are divided over whether *propitiatio* is a proper rendering of the Hebrew and Greek words (most notably, *kipper* and *hilastērion*) often used to describe atonement.

Two camps formed within the modern era. First, following C. H. Dodd (1884–1973), some claim that the Bible speaks only of an "expiatory sacrifice" by which sin is cancelled, purged, or forgiven. By this account, neither Paul nor the New Testament depict Jesus as assuaging God's active wrath toward sin and sinners. This view would allegedly be too pagan in its connotations, setting forth an angry God who must vent wrath in order to be pacified. For Dodd, God's wrath is not a personal attitude of anger but an "inevitable process of cause and effect in a moral universe."[49] By analogy, if one drinks a keg of beer on Tuesday night, one will experience the "wrath" of a headache (or worse) by Wednesday morning. Yet this is not the product of a vengeful God who sends "anger rays" toward one's cranium. Rather, there is simply an inevitable relation between the action and consequence. According to Dodd's account, propitiation is not a Christian way to speak about Christ's work.

For others, led most notably by Leon Morris (1914–2006), the *hilaskomai* word group, along with certain uses of *kipper* in the Old Testament, does (sometimes) include the notion of propitiation,[50] despite the massive differences between the God of the Bible and capricious pagan deities.[51] God's wrath is simply the just outflow of his settled opposition to evil, and an outworking of God's essential love and holiness.[52] In such accounts, divine wrath may be retributive, restorative, or both. Yet the key idea is that

---

48. See Leon Morris, "Propitiate, Propitiation," in *The International Standard Bible Encyclopedia*, vol. 3, ed. Geoffrey W. Bromiley (Grand Rapids: Eerdmans, 1986), 1004.

49. C. H. Dodd, *The Epistle of Paul to the Romans* (London: Hodder & Stoughton, 1932), 21.

50. The argument here is that propitiation and expiation need not be mutually exclusive. See Leon Morris, *The Apostolic Preaching of the Cross* (Leicester: Inter-Varsity Press, 1965).

51. For a classic and accessible discussion of how God's wrath and propitiation are radically different than those of pagan deities, see J. I. Packer, *Knowing God* (Downers Grove, IL: InterVarsity Press, 1973), chs. 15, 18.

52. See the excellent treatment by Tony Lane, "The Wrath of God as an Aspect of the Love of God," in *Nothing Greater, Nothing Better: Theological Essays on the Love of God*, ed. Kevin Vanhoozer (Grand Rapids: Eerdmans, 2001), 138–67.

if God were not both grieved and angered over evil, he would be neither holy nor loving, like an apathetic parent who remains indifferent to a child's destructive behaviors. Beyond this, Morris and others have argued that the Bible does speak of wrath being actively poured out in response to evil,[53] just as it sometimes speaks of wrath being propitiated by virtue of a particular action.[54] The result of this position is the claim that *both* expiation and propitiation deserve a place within atonement doctrine.[55]

But what of Irenaeus? On the surface, his use of *propitiatio* appears to affirm a central contention of Morris and his interpretive kin. When one speaks of expiation, the object is usually sin, while the object of propitiation is God or divine wrath. In the above quotations, Irenaeus clearly views God the Father as the object of the action. Thus Jesus's high priestly work is viewed as "propitiating for us the Father against whom we had sinned." Likewise, the thing requiring propitiation is the transgression by which we "became [God's] enemies."[56] The point, therefore, is not merely that Irenaeus spoke of propitiation but that he made God the object because of our prior status as his enemies.

Yet there is an added wrinkle. While Irenaeus wrote originally in Greek, the above passages exist today (as with most of his work) in a later Latin translation.[57] Hence one might claim that the propitiation language reflects the mind of Irenaeus's translator more than his own.[58] Perhaps partly

---

53. To cite just two examples, neither the great flood (Gen 6), nor the striking down of Ananias and Saphira (Acts 5) seem anything like an impersonal process of cause and effect. The land is not spontaneously immersed in water every time the sin of humanity reaches critical mass, nor do those who are dishonest about their monetary donations normally drop dead in church (thankfully). For other biblical examples, see Thomas R. Schreiner, "Penal Substitution View," in *The Nature of the Atonement: Four Views*, ed. James Beilby and Paul R. Eddy (Downers Grove, IL: IVP Academic, 2006), 79–82. Likewise, Lane, "The Wrath of God," 149–51.

54. See, for instance, the priestly work of Aaron in Num 16:41–50 and the zealous actions of Phinehas (who "turned away [God's] anger from the Israelites) in Num 25:6–12. For a classic and accessible defense of these points, see John R. W. Stott, *The Cross of Christ*, 20th anniv. ed. (Downers Grove, IL: IVP, 2006), esp. 104–11; 166–79.

55. For one account of the coexistence of expiation and propitiation, see N. T. Wright, *The Letter to the Romans*, in *The New Interpreter's Bible*, vol. 10 (Nashville: Abingdon, 2002), 476.

56. *Haer.* 5.17.1 (*ANF* 1:544–45).

57. An Armenian translation of books four and five of *Against Heresies* was discovered in 1904. Only a single paragraph from the work comes down to us in Greek. See Behr, *Irenaeus*, 13.

58. The twentieth-century French translation of *Against Heresies* by Adelin Rousseau attempts a reconstruction the original Greek, based partly upon existing fragments and the complete Greek text of Irenaeus's *Demonstration of Apostolic Preaching*. In the reference to Christ "propitiating" God, it is notable that the Greek suggestion is indeed a participle form of *hilaskomai* (*hilasamenos*). See Irénée de Lyon, *Contre Les Hérésies*, livre 5, tome 2 (Paris: Les Éditions du Cerf, 1969), 223 (5.17.1).

because of this, John Lawson acknowledges that the use of *propitians* in the above passages only appears to teach "Divine Appeasement." The reasons given stem from the fact that (1) Irenaeus did not normally speak of propitiation and (2) the original Greek word may be given a biblical sense in which appeasement is not present. On the latter point, Dodd's shadow lingers in the background.[59]

In response to Lawson, two points should be made. First, it is certainly accurate to say that Irenaeus did not usually speak of atonement as propitiation. Still, the fact that someone *usually* doesn't do something is no grounds for claiming that they never do it. Jesus usually walked on land, but this is no proof that he never walked on water. Second, it is also true that the meaning of *hilastērion* is sometimes more akin to expiation than propitiation.[60] But if this is so for Irenaeus, then it seems singularly odd that both passages from *Against Heresies* identify the Father as the one who is propitiated. If Lawson were correct, then Irenaeus should have spoken of sin as the object of this action—but Irenaeus did not.[61] In the end, both objections to the concept of propitiation in Irenaeus (as the turning away of divine wrath) seem unconvincing.

Of course, none of this means that Irenaeus espoused a view of penal substitution in his references to divine propitiation. Key parts of the doctrine are either missing or muted in these texts.[62] Most notably, the theme of punishment is entirely absent. And while cultic imagery is present, Irenaeus pictured Jesus not as the sacrificial *victim* that absorbs divine wrath but as "the high priest," who propitiates God by "cleansing lepers" and "healing the sick."[63] When Christ's death is mentioned, it is not viewed as a propitiatory sacrifice but as the death of the high priest, which according to the law was the event that signaled to certain exiled persons that they might return from their cities of refuge without fear of punishment (Num 35:25).[64] A crucial distinction should therefore be noted: the presence of sacrificial themes (including propitiation) in an author do

---

59. John Lawson, *The Biblical Theology of Saint Irenaeus* (London: Epworth, 1948), 193.

60. See D. A. Carson, "Atonement in Romans 3:21–26," in *The Glory of the Atonement*, ed. Charles E. Hill and Frank A. James III (Downers Grove, IL: IVP, 2004), 130–31.

61. In light of this, one wonders if Lawson's conclusion stems more from a prior assumption that any talk of propitiation (or as he tellingly calls it "Divine Appeasement") is inherently problematic in its overtones, and thus must be ruled out from the start.

62. *Haer.* 4.8.2 (*ANF* 1:477); 5.17.1 (*ANF* 1:544–45).

63. *Haer.* 4.8.2 (*ANF* 1:477).

64. With this (nonpenal) high priestly background in mind, Irenaeus says that Christ suffered death "that exiled man might go forth from condemnation, and might return without fear to his own inheritance." *Haer.* 4.8.2 (*ANF* 1:477). Thanks to Jerome Van Kuiken for alerting me to the Old Testament background here.

not necessarily reflect belief in penal substitution, and interpreters should avoid the folly of finding penal substitution in *every* reference to priests and sacrifices.

Elsewhere, however, Irenaeus did speak of Christ redeeming us "by his blood,"[65] just as he wrote that Jesus "gave himself as a redemption for those who had been led into captivity."[66] Alongside these claims, my treatment of recapitulation (ch. 1) showed that Irenaeus even viewed Christ as summing up the human death which was the divinely sanctioned penalty for sin "so that neither should justice be infringed upon, nor should the handiwork of God go to destruction."[67] These statements come much closer to penal substitutionary themes, even while the emphasis is more representative than explicitly substitutionary.[68] On Irenaeus, the verdict is therefore a "yes" on propitiation and vicarious judgment but a "no" on an explicit account of penal substitution. This trend will change, however, with the next figure.

Eusebius of Caesarea: He Transferred to Himself Our Penalty

While Eusebius of Caesarea (ca. 260–339) is often dubbed the father of church history, he has also been seen as an early exemplar of penal substitution. Aside from chronicling the rise of Christianity in his *Ecclesiastical History*, and controversially praising the Emperor Constantine in his *Life of Constantine*, Eusebius also crafted theological and exegetical treatises.

In his *Proof of the Gospel*, Eusebius mounted a defense of Christianity that is aimed at those from pagan backgrounds. Here, he claimed the following with regard to Christ's death:

And the Lamb of God . . . was chastised on our behalf, and suffered a penalty He did not owe, but which we owed because of the multitude of our sins; and so He became the cause of the forgiveness of our sins, because He received death for us, and transferred to Himself the scourging, the insults, and the dishonor, which were due to us, and drew down upon Himself the appointed curse, being made a curse for us.[69]

---

65. Irenaeus, *Demonstration of Apostolic Preaching*, trans. A. Robinson (New York: MacMillan, 1920), 72, 78, 88.

66. *Haer.* 5.1.1 (*ANF* 1:527).

67. *Haer.* 5.23.2 (*ANF* 1:551).

68. See Joshua Schendel, "'That Justice Might Not Be Infringed Upon': The Judgement of God in the Passion of Christ in Irenaeus of Lyons," *SJT* 71, no. 2 (2018): 219–23.

69. Eusebius of Caesarea, *Proof of the Gospel*, trans. and ed. W. J. Ferrar, vol. 2 (New York: Macmillan, 1920), 195.

Recent studies have called this an "explicit"[70] and "unequivocal statement of penal substitution," and indeed it does seem quite straightforward.[71] The passage combines sacrificial and Passover imagery of the "Lamb of God" with echoes from Isaiah 53 and a Pauline emphasis on Jesus becoming a curse for us (Gal 3:13).

Yet the text is also notable for what it does not claim. Specifically, it does not argue that the Father transferred our "penalty" to the Son. Although Jesus is spoken of as having "suffered a penalty . . . which we owed," the initiative for this exchange remains his own. As Eusebius wrote, Christ *"transferred to Himself* the scourging, the insults, and the dishonor, which were due us, and drew down upon Himself the appointed curse." In this statement, the three elements of mere penal substitution are all apparent (substitution, penalty, and divine sanction), yet there is not a hint of "divine child abuse." Instead, it is the Lamb who willingly and sovereignly takes our punishment and curse upon himself.

Athanasius: A Substitute for the Life of All

If Eusebius was the greatest historian of the fourth century, Athanasius (ca. 295–373) was the greatest theologian.[72] At barely thirty years old, he was present at the Council of Nicaea, and just three years later he succeeded his bishop, Alexander, in a long and tumultuous episcopacy, marked by five exiles at the hands of four different emperors. Most famously, however, Athanasius engaged in polemical combat with the movement he successfully dubbed "Arianism" and with its belief that the Son was not *homoousios* with God the Father.[73]

Not surprisingly, Athanasius's insistence upon the Son's full divinity dovetailed with his view of the atonement. The human predicament, as he portrayed it, is that rebellion against God has corrupted humanity and placed us under the dominion of death. So we came from nothing in the beginning (*ex nihilo*), and our sin and subsequent corruption meant that

---

70. Henri Blocher, "Biblical Metaphors and the Doctrine of the Atonement," *JETS* 47, no. 4 (December 2004): 630. See also Blocher, *"Agnus Victor,"* 75.

71. Jeffery, Ovey, and Sach, *Pierced for Our Transgressions,* 167.

72. Because Augustine's mature theology is written mostly after 400 AD, I rank him as the greatest theologian of the fifth century, and as the most influential theologian of all postbiblical history.

73. For recent treatments of the complex history, see Lewis Ayres, *Nicaea and Its Legacy: An Approach to Fourth-Century Trinitarian Theology* (Oxford: Oxford University Press, 2004); Khaled Anatolios, *Retrieving Nicaea: The Development and Meaning of Trinitarian Doctrine* (Grand Rapids: Baker Academic, 2001).

we were "on the way to returning . . . to non-existence."[74] This reality poses a dilemma for God.

> It was unworthy of the goodness of God that creatures made by Him should be brought to nothing through the deceit wrought upon man by the devil. . . . Yet it was unthinkable that God, the Father of Truth, should go back upon his word regarding death in order to ensure our continued existence. He could not falsify Himself; what, then, was God to do?[75]

The solution for Athanasius was the incarnation. Yet in describing how the Christ-event solved our problem, various images converged. Participation was the most common one. Here Athanasius saw human nature itself as being taken up and healed by the incarnation. Behind his view was the metaphysical assumption that human beings all participate in a universal human nature. And with the perfect union of the human and divine natures in Jesus, communion was restored between God and humanity. The result of this participatory logic was "deification" (or *theopoiesis*). For as Athanasius wrote, God "assumed humanity that we might become god."[76]

Alongside his participatory emphasis came sacrificial imagery. For Athanasius, Christ presented his body as an "offering" and "sacrifice" to the Father.[77] The result of this sacrifice was an unlikely triumph, by which Christ's apparent "poverty and weakness on the cross . . . overturns the pomp and parade of idols, and quietly . . . wins over the mockers and unbelievers to recognize him as God."[78] At the intersection of these (1) participatory and (2) sacrificial themes, we find passages that have been taken as exemplars of penal substitution.[79] In *Against the Arians*, Athanasius wrote:

---

74. Athanasius, *On the Incarnation* (New York: St. Vladimir's Seminary Press, 1993), sect. 1.

75. Athanasius, *On the Incarnation*, sects. 6–7, pp. 32–33. Athanasius is also clear that repentance alone would not be sufficient, for (1) it would not deal with the subsequent corruption to our nature, brought about by sin, and (2) it would still mean that God had gone back on his word regarding death.

76. Athanasius, *On the Incarnation*, sect. 54.3. While the notion is prone to misconstrual, Athanasius insists that we will be deified only in the Son, "without losing our own proper substance." Athanasius, *De Decretis*, 3.14; cited in Michael Horton, "Atonement and Ascension," in Crisp and Sanders, *Locating Atonement*, 240.

77. See Anatolios, *Retrieving Nicaea*, 107.

78. Athanasius, *On the Incarnation*, sect. 1.

79. The following are also noted by Jeffery, Ovey, and Sach, *Pierced for Our Transgressions*, 169–73. Blocher likewise finds penal substitution in these passages, "Biblical Metaphors," 630.

Formerly the world, as guilty, was under judgment from the Law; but now the Word has taken on Himself the judgment, and having suffered in the body for all, has bestowed salvation to all.[80]

Similarly, in *On the Incarnation*, he stated:

He surrendered His body to death in place of all, and offered it to the Father. This He did out of sheer love for us, so that in His death all might die, and the law of death thereby be abolished because, having fulfilled in His body that for which it was appointed, it was thereafter voided of its power for men. . . . Thus He would make death to disappear from them as utterly as straw from fire.[81]

And once more, in a justly famous passage from the same work:

The Word perceived that corruption could not be got rid of otherwise than through death; yet He Himself, as the Word, being immortal . . . could not die. For this reason, therefore, He assumed a body capable of death, in order that it . . . might become in dying a sufficient exchange for all, and, itself remaining incorruptible through His indwelling, might thereafter put an end to corruption for all others as well, by the grace of the resurrection. It was by surrendering to death the body which He had taken, as an offering and sacrifice free from every stain, that He forthwith abolished death for His human brethren by the offering of the equivalent. For naturally, since the Word of God was above all, when He offered His own temple and bodily instrument as a substitute for the life of all, He fulfilled in death all that was required.[82]

In response to these passages, some have claimed that "Athanasius not only affirmed the doctrine of penal substitution, but also placed it squarely at the centre of his theology."[83]

To say that not everyone agrees with this assessment, however, would be a massive understatement. In response, Benjamin Myers alleges that modern proponents of penal substitution wrongly "project" their "Calvinist

---

80. Athanasius, *Against the Arians*, sect. 60.
81. Athanasius, *On the Incarnation*, sect. 8.
82. Athanasius, *On the Incarnation*, sect. 9.
83. Jeffery, Ovey, and Sach, *Pierced for Our Transgressions*, 173.

assumptions" onto Athanasius, as well as other early Christian sources.[84] According to Myers, penal substitution is not only absent from the center of Athanasius's theology, it is absent altogether. Myers's charge focuses on the way that death and sacrifice are spoken of in the above passages.

I will begin with death. For Athanasius, the threat of eternal death—that is, of God's good creation forever collapsing into nonexistence—is perhaps the greatest problem to be solved in incarnation and atonement. If this happens, then God's goodness is impugned and his project of creation fails. Yet if God reneges on the requirement of death, then he is shown to be a liar. Furthermore, as Myers argues, divine impassibility also poses problems. For Athanasius and others, the way to extinguish death is to bring it into contact with the eternal life of the divine nature. Yet herein lies a problem: since the divine nature is impassible and immortal, it is seen to be incapable of undergoing change from life to death.

The solution, once again, is the union of humanity and divinity in the incarnation. Since "the Word was not able to die . . . [he] takes to himself a body capable of death."[85] This death is a privation of being, just as darkness is a privation of light. When Christ offers himself to death, the privation encounters life itself, and eternal death is immediately cancelled like a shadow removed by light.[86]

But what of sacrifice? For Myers, Athanasius's sacrificial imagery simply emphasized the universality of Christ's work: "In sacrifice, one particular thing is offered on behalf of the many." Thus "the oneness of the community is symbolized and enacted in the sacrifice."[87] The contention here is that there was no connection between the sacrifice and the notion of a divinely sanctioned penalty borne in our place. For Myers, this can be seen in the fact that Athanasius depicted "Christ as a sacrifice offered to *death*" rather than to God.[88] Myers concludes then that there was no penal substitution. Rather, there was a metaphorical mixing of sacrificial and participatory images whereby the divine life extinguishes death by coming into contact with it.

Is Myers right? While there are many insightful aspects in his survey of

---

84. Benjamin Myers, "The Patristic Atonement Model," in Crisp and Sanders, *Locating Atonement*, 86.

85. Athanasius, *On the Incarnation*, sect. 9.

86. See Myers, "Patristic Atonement Model," 80. Thus, while Christians still die, this death is not eternal, but instead a pathway to resurrection and life eternal.

87. Myers, "Patristic Atonement Model," 84.

88. Myers, "Patristic Atonement Model," 85, italics in Myers; citing Athanasius, *On the Incarnation*, sect. 9.

patristic atonement doctrine, his argument on Athanasius appears flawed in two key respects. First, the above quotation from *On the Incarnation* shows Athanasius speaking of Christ's death as a sacrifice "offered to the Father," not merely as a sacrifice offered to death.[89] Both ideas are clearly asserted, and one need not oppose the other. Second, and more importantly, Myers never asks the most significant question: Did Athanasius view death itself as penal? The idea of death as a privation does not exclude the possibility that it is also a divinely sanctioned penalty for sin. Athanasius seemed to view death in both ways.

In *Against the Arians*, Athanasius saw Christ as suffering "in his body for all." And the thing that he suffered was "the judgment of the Law."[90] Yet whose law was it? Who instituted it? And what was this judgment if not a penalty for sin? The Athanasian treatment of the divine dilemma in fact illustrates that it was God who pronounced the death sentence as the consequence of sin. Hence God would be a liar if the sentence were not carried out. One wonders how Athanasius, who was a careful reader of Scripture, could view death as anything but the required penalty for sin. Thus, when he stated that Christ "offered His own temple and bodily instrument as a substitute for the life of all," the death experienced by Christ should be seen as simply that—the divinely pronounced penalty. This is why Athanasius stated in the next sentence that Christ "fulfilled in death all that was required."[91] The requirement, as he has already argued, was that man must die as a penalty for sin. Given this, the view of death as a privation should in no way exclude the notion of death as penal; both notions coexist in Athanasius's thought.

In sum, all three elements of mere penal substitution are indeed present in Athanasius. First, he spoke of Christ as a "substitute." Second, he spoke of Christ as undergoing, on our behalf, the judgment of the law, which is death. And third, he followed Eusebius and others by emphasizing the Son's freely willed initiative ("he takes a body capable of death"), so that even though there was divine sanction for this act, no reader could confuse such passages with divine child abuse. While the Son offers himself as a sacrifice to the Father, the judgment spoken of is that of the law.

Of course, it is wrong to claim that penal substitution represents "the centre of [Athanasius's] theology."[92] As I have noted, this place is rightly

89. Athanasius, *On the Incarnation*, sect. 8.
90. Athanasius, *Against the Arians*, sect. 60.
91. Athanasius, *On the Incarnation*, sect. 9.
92. Jeffery, Ovey, and Sach, *Pierced for Our Transgressions*, 173.

reserved for the participationist notion of the Word taking up and redeeming human nature from death, through the incarnation. While this logic is not antithetical to penal substitution, the emphasis is more often incorporative than substitutionary. Substitution is mentioned less frequently.[93] My own look at Athanasius seeks to modify both the wrongful denials and the exaggerated affirmations of penal substitution in his thought.

John Chrysostom: The King's Son, Punished in Our Stead

In recent years, some have alleged that the real problems with penal substitution come in the pulpit. Although an academic version of the model may be defended, it soon becomes nonsensical, unbiblical, and even dangerous when simplified in sermon illustrations (more on this in ch. 5).[94] With this critique in mind, it is fitting that the next representative is heralded as the greatest preacher of the early church: John Chrysostom (ca. 350–407).[95]

John's most famous use of penal substitutionary logic emerged from a sermon analogy. The illustration involved a ruler who gives his only son to be killed in the place of a convicted criminal.

> If one that was himself a king, beholding a robber and malefactor under punishment, gave his well-beloved son, his only-begotten and true, to be slain; and transferred the death and guilt as well, from him to his son (who was himself of no such character), that he might save the condemned man and clear him from his evil reputation . . .[96]

Suppose further, said Chrysostom, that this pardoned criminal was then "promoted to great dignity" and "glory unspeakable." How terrible then, and how nonsensical, if this man were to display a lack of gratitude toward his king and benefactor.

There is no doubt that the above imagery could be labeled penal substitution.[97] Likewise, there is no doubt that the analogy could create massive

---

93. See again the rare but overt mention of substitution in Athanasius, *On the Incarnation*, sect. 9.

94. See Mark Baker and Joel Green, *Recovering the Scandal of the Cross: Atonement in New Testament*, 2nd ed. (Downers Grove, IL: IVP Academic, 2011), esp. 183–91. Here, Baker and Green praise accounts of penal substitution set forth by Hans Boersma, Stephen Holmes, and (especially) Kevin Vanhoozer. At the same time, they attempt to focus their criticism on the popular construals.

95. Even what sounds today like a name is a comment on his oratory (Chrysostom means "Golden-mouthed").

96. John Chrysostom, *Homilies on Second Corinthians* 11.6 (*NPNF*[1] 12:335).

97. Elsewhere, Chrysostom makes a similar, though less developed, and less parabolic, statement: "God was about to punish them, but He forbore to do it. They were about to perish,

problems if taken too far. Here, the appearance of parental abuse and the problem of penal nontransference both show forth. Chrysostom pictured the king as transferring not only the death sentence but also the guilt to his innocent and beloved son, which runs counter to the common assumption that guilt is not transferable. In addition, note that the sermon was not primarily about the cross. The sermon focused on how we should not be ungrateful to God. Instead, we should be "full of remorse" for "the provocations we have offered our Benefactor."[98]

According to a recent treatment of the passage, "The fact that [Chrysostom] can allude to [penal substitution] in this incidental way shows that it must have been widely accepted and understood by his hearers, for he would hardly have chosen to illustrate his point with an analogy that was unfamiliar or controversial."[99] In my own view, this assumption seems far from obvious.

A more likely conclusion is that Chrysostom's illustration was not meant to be a precise and familiar description of how atonement happens but a compelling (though inexact) story by which to induce "remorse"—the very theme he landed on—in the hearts of his hearers. In this way, Chrysostom's sermon would not be far removed from some emotionally charged modern analogies of penal substitution, which have brought forth repentance from some and indignation from others.[100] In any case, the illustration does show that the most famous preacher of the early church employed the imagery of penal substitution (however imperfectly) before his congregants—and whatever seats these fourth-century parishioners sat on (if any), they most certainly were older than our pews.

Augustine of Hippo: Christ Took Our Punishment

In the words of Jaroslav Pelikan, much of Western doctrine could indeed be written "as series of footnotes" to Augustine of Hippo (350–430).[101] As Stephen Holmes writes, Augustine "towers like a colossus over Western theology."[102] In terms of the atonement, Augustine's thought is often associated with the so-called ransom mechanism by which divine victory

---

but in their stead He gave His own Son." Chrysostom, *Homilies on 1 Timothy* 7.7 (*NPNF*[1] 12:431).
98. John Chrysostom, *Homilies on Second Corinthians* 11.6 (*NPNF*[1] 12:334).
99. Jeffery, Ovey, and Sach, *Pierced for Our Transgressions*, 176.
100. For a popular-level critique of such preaching, see Jones, *Did God Kill Jesus*, ch. 1.
101. Jaroslav Pelikan, *The Christian Tradition: A History of the Development of Doctrine*, 5 vols. (Chicago: University of Chicago Press, 1971–85), 1:330.
102. Stephen Holmes, *The Quest for the Trinity: The Doctrine of God in Scripture, History, and Modernity* (Downers Grove, IL: IVP Academic, 2012), 129.

was achieved through trickery. Along these lines, Augustine claimed on more than one occasion that the cross should be viewed as a "trap" or "mousetrap," baited with the blood of Christ to ensnare the devil.[103] Thankfully, this was not Augustine's only way of viewing the atonement.[104] It has been argued that in *Against Faustus the Manichean* he gave "a straightforward statement of penal substitution."[105] In a crucial passage, Augustine wrote, "Christ, though guiltless, took our punishment, that He might cancel our guilt, and do away with our punishment."[106] The statement is indeed explicit. Like Athanasius, Augustine clearly viewed death as penal, for it comes upon us "as the punishment of sin."[107] Yet to understand Augustine properly, more context is needed.

The discussion in this portion of *Against Faustus* pertains to what it means for Christ to bear a "curse" as one who is hung upon a tree (Deut 21:23; cf. Gal 3:13). For Faustus, who rejected the Old Testament, this meant that Moses must have erred, for surely Christ was not accursed by God.[108] Answering this objection, Augustine argued that the sinless Christ died for our offenses just as he bore *our* curse:

As He died in the flesh, which He took in bearing our punishment, so also, while ever blessed in His own righteousness, He was cursed for our offences, in the death which He suffered in bearing our punishment. . . . The believer in the true doctrine of the gospel will understand that Christ is not reproached by Moses when he speaks of Him as cursed, not in His divine majesty, but as hanging on the tree as our substitute, bearing our punishment.[109]

---

103. A helpful overview of Augustine's sermons with this theme can be found in David Scott-Macnab, "Augustine's Trope of the Crucifixion as a Trap for the Devil and Its Survival in the English Middle Ages," *Vigiliae Christianae* 68, no. 4 (September 2014): 409–15.

104. In truth, Augustine employs a variety of atonement motifs. By J. N. D. Kelly's estimation, these include a certain "physical doctrine," ransom theory, a moral exemplar theme, and (centrally, in his view) the notion of redemption by way of an expiatory sacrifice. See Kelly, *Early Christian Doctrines*, rev. ed. (San Francisco: HarperSanFrancisco, 1978), 393. Somewhat differently, Gerald Bonner has demonstrated the importance of participation and deification in Augustine's thought. See Gerald Bonner, "Augustine's Concept of Deification," *Journal of Theological Studies* 37 (1986): 369–86; Bonner, "The Doctrine of Sacrifice: Augustine and the Latin Patristic Tradition," in *Sacrifice and Redemption: Durham Essays in Theology*, ed. S. W. Sykes (Cambridge: Cambridge University Press, 1991).

105. Jeffery, Ovey, and Sach, *Pierced for Our Transgressions*, 179.

106. Augustine, *Against Faustus*, 14.4 (NPNF[1] 4:208).

107. Augustine, *Against Faustus*, 14.3 (NPNF[1] 4:208).

108. For an accessible overview of the work, see Matthew Levering, *The Theology of Augustine: An Introductory Guide to His Most Important Works* (Grand Rapids: Baker Academic, 2013), ch. 2.

109. Augustine, *Against Faustus*, 14.6–7 (NPNF[1] 4:209).

It takes some fairly impressive interpretive maneuvers to read this as anything other than penal substitution. And the case becomes even stronger when one turns to Augustine's use of propitiation language. In the *Enchiridion*, he wrote:

> Since men are in this state of wrath through original sin—a condition made still graver and more pernicious as they compounded more and worse sins with it—a Mediator was required; that is to say, a Reconciler who by offering a unique sacrifice, of which all the sacrifices of the law and the prophets were shadows, should allay that wrath.[110]

In the judgment of Adonis Vidu, "This is clearly penal substitutionary language."[111] Yet the pagan imagery of an angry god who suddenly transforms to love after the giving of a sacrifice is completely absent. Also absent is the notion of the Son as a passive victim. Augustine rejected both of these false notions in *De Trinitate* when he wrote, "The Father loved us . . . not only before the Son died for us, but before he created the world. . . . Nor was the Son delivered up for us as it were unwillingly."[112]

A remaining question is how to square Augustine's penal substitutionary logic with his previously mentioned ransom imagery. Once again, it bears noting that the mousetrap imagery emerges in Augustine's sermons, and as such, the image may be partly the product of a preacher grasping for an evocative illustration to allow the listener to conceptualize the cross.[113] Certainly those of us who preach regularly would not want every one of our illustrations held up to the probing light of academic analysis. Perhaps, then, the attempt to reconcile these two perspectives on the cross is ill-advised.

Or perhaps not. There is a way in which Augustine's ransom imagery may be harmonized with his emphasis on Christ propitiating divine wrath

---

110. Augustine, *Enchiridion*, trans. Albert C. Outler, 10.33, https://www.ccel.org/ccel/augustine/enchiridion.chapter10.html.

111. Adonis Vidu, *Atonement, Law, and Justice: The Cross in Historical and Cultural Contexts* (Grand Rapids: Baker Academic, 2014), 35–36. Vidu's claim is that while it is "problematic" to find a "theory" of penal substitution in Augustine, he does employ penal substitutionary logic (34). Presumably, in speaking of the absence of the "theory," Vidu means to reference a more comprehensive and fully worked out explanation of the mechanism by which atonement occurs.

112. Augustine, *De Trinitate*, 13.11.15 (*NPNF*[1] 3:175).

113. For a focused treatment of atonement doctrine in Augustine's sermons, see Stanley P. Rosenberg, "Interpreting Atonement in Augustine's Preaching," in *The Glory of the Atonement: Biblical, Historical and Practical Perspectives*, Charles Hill and Frank A. James, eds. (Downers Grove, IL: IVP, 2004), ch. 11.

by bearing our punishment. In these passages, Augustine always stopped short of claiming that God punished Christ.[114] And in this way, he differs from the likes of Martin Luther, John Owen, Francis Turretin, and even Charles Wesley.[115] Yet as I have defined mere penal substitution, this strong view of divine punishment is not the only way to speak of divine sanction. One of the previously mentioned options involves the use of "intermediaries" by which the divinely ordained penalty for sin is meted out. These intermediaries might include things like the law, the covenantal curses, or those evil men who nonetheless "did what [God's] power and will had decided beforehand should happen" (Acts 4:28). But might the devil be such an intermediary? Might Satan be the unwitting means by which the propitiating sacrifice for human sin was rendered and through whom the penalty was meted out? Augustine seemed to think so.

The role of Satan bulks large in Augustine's treatment of the cross, and not just in the infamous mousetrap analogy. In book 4 of *De Trinitate*, readers learn that it was Satan who "stripped himself" of authority over us when he laid hold of the sinless Christ.[116] Elsewhere, Augustine clarified that the devil was allowed to bring death to humanity as a penalty for sin.[117] Thus, while Augustine saw death as a divinely sanctioned punishment, he also distanced God from death itself by picturing the devil as its intermediary (literally, "the mediator of death") and enforcer.[118] In a passage from *De Trinitate*, he stated,

"God made not death" (Wis. 1.13), since He was not Himself the cause of death; but yet death was inflicted on the sinner, through His [i.e., God's] most just retribution. Just as the judge inflicts punishment on the guilty; yet it is not the justice of the judge, but the desert of the crime, which is the cause of the punishment. Whither, then, the mediator of

---

114. See Vidu, *Atonement, Law, and Justice*, 38.

115. While Luther and Owen are cited previously in this chapter, Turretin claimed that "Christ is justly punished by God the judge both in body and soul in order to make expiation for sinners." Francis Turretin, *De Satisfactione Christi Disputationes* (Geneva: De Tournes, 1666), *Disputatio VI, Quae Quarta est de Veritate Satisfactionis*, pt. 4, ch. 20, sect. 51. Similarly, Charles Wesley, in a hymnbook that was edited by his brother John, wrote, "For what you have done, his blood must atone; The Father hath punished for you his dear Son." Charles Wesley, "All Ye That Pass By" (Hymn 707), in *A Collection of Hymns*, ed. John Wesley (London: Edward Dalton, 1889), 71. These references are drawn from Hill and Jedwab, "Atonement and the Concept of Punishment," 151.

116. Augustine, *De Trinitate*, 4.13.17 (NPNF[1] 3:78).

117. See Augustine, *On the Merits and Forgiveness of Sins and on Infant Baptism*, 2.21.51.

118. See Vidu, *Atonement, Law, and Justice*, 38; see also Frederick Van Fleteren, "Devil," in *Augustine Through the Ages: An Encyclopedia*, ed. Allan D. Fitzgerald (Grand Rapids: Eerdmans, 1999), 268–69.

death [i.e., Satan] caused us to pass . . . to the death of the flesh, there our Lord God introduced for us the medicine of correction, which He deserved not, by a hidden and exceeding mysterious decree of divine and profound justice. In order, therefore, that as by one man came death, so by one man might come also the resurrection of the dead. . . . For we, indeed, came to death through sin; He through righteousness: and, therefore, as our death is the punishment of sin, so His death was made a sacrifice for sin.[119]

Herein lies the relation between Augustine's penal substitutionary emphases and his treatment of the devil seizing upon Christ like bait in a mousetrap.

For Augustine, Christ died as our substitute, was punished on our behalf, and became a sacrifice that propitiates divine wrath. Each of these claims was clearly asserted in the catena of earlier citations. Yet at the same time, Augustine saw this divinely sanctioned punishment as being *meted out* (unwittingly) by Satan. Thus the devil "was permitted to effect [death] upon that mortal element which the living Mediator had received from us," and "there in every respect [the devil] was conquered."[120] In the end, Augustine affirmed the logic of penal substitution yet in a way that fits his patristic emphasis on a divine victory that comes through trickery.

After Augustine: Cyril, Gelasius, and Gregory the Great

If space permitted, one might embark upon a fuller survey of penal substitutionary imagery from other sources in the early years of Christian history. For example, around the same time as Augustine, Cyril of Alexandria (ca. 376–444) wrote that "we have paid in Christ himself the penalties for the charges of sin against us: 'For he bore our sins, and was wounded because of us,' according to the voice of the prophet. Or are we not healed by his wounds?"[121] By citing Isaiah 53, Cyril made use of the *locus classicus* of penal substitution in the Old Testament. And as with others, he viewed the death that Christ endured as penal. After all, it had been "hanging over us" like the Damoclean sword "as the result of our sin." Still, the above passage is more aptly understood as setting forth an incorporative view of the atonement, for as Cyril said, it is *we* who "have paid in Christ . . .

---

119. Augustine, *De Trinitate*, 4.12.15 (NPNF[1] 3:77).
120. Augustine, *De Trinitate*, 4.13.17 (NPNF[1] 3:78).
121. Cyril of Alexandria, *De adoratione et cultu in spiritu et veritate*, in PG 68:293, 296; English translation from Garry Williams, "Penal Substitution: A Response to Recent Criticisms," in Tidball, Hilborn, and Thacker, *The Atonement Debate*, 190n29.

the penalties" for sin.[122] For this reason, Cyril's view might be seen more accurately as penal incorporation or, perhaps, penal participation.

Shortly after Cyril's time, a lesser-known historian who was once given the name Gelasius of Cyzicus (c. 400s AD) made assertions that support the logic of penal substitution.[123] This author (whatever his real name) wrote a history of the Council of Nicaea that included an account of Christ's life and work. Here he claimed that Christ "came and received the punishments which were due to us into his sinless flesh, which was of us, in place of us, and on our behalf." What makes this straightforward account of penal substitution even more interesting is the claim that follows it: "This is the apostolic and approved faith of the church . . . transmitted from the beginning from the Lord himself through the apostles."[124] If Gelasius was correct, then such penal substitutionary logic was hardly uncommon in the early days of Christianity.

Finally, at the end of the first five centuries AD, there was Gregory the Great (ca. 540–604). As "the last of the church fathers and first of the popes," Gregory provides a fitting conclusion to this survey of patristic voices.[125] In *Morals on the Book of Job*, Gregory found in Job's suffering a prefiguring of Christ's own anguish. "For 'he [Christ] was destroyed without cause,' . . . and yet being without offense took upon Himself the punishment of the carnal."[126] In response to Gregory, Stephen Holmes— who is hardly known to identify numerous exemplars of penal substitution prior to the Protestant Reformers—claims that Gregory's words offer a clear and unambiguous example of penal substitution.[127] For Gregory, Christ himself took our punishment, so while he suffers a penalty instead of us, none could claim that we see a vengeful father victimizing an unwitting son. Penal substitution is present, but it is nothing close to divine child abuse. Indeed, this has been true of almost all the voices surveyed in this chapter.

---

122. Pace Jeffery, Ovey, and Sach, *Pierced for Our Transgressions*, 181. While Jeffery, Ovey, and Sach see both participation and substitution in the passage, it would certainly seem that that the incorporative or participatory emphasis is primary.

123. The name itself may be inaccurate; the use dates to Photius I of Constantinople and may be erroneously attached to an anonymous historian who wrote *The Acts of the First Council of Nicaea*.

124. Gelasius of Cyzicus, *Church History* 2.24, in *Die Griechischen Christlichen Schriftsteller der ersten drei Jahrhunderte*, vol. 28 (Leipzig: Preussische Akademie der Wissenschaften, 1918), 100; English translation from Williams, "Critical Exposition." Cited in Jeffery, Ovey, and Sach, *Pierced for Our Transgressions*, 181–82.

125. Pelikan, *Christian Tradition*, 1:349.

126. Gregory the Great, *Morals on the Book of Job*, vol. 1 (Oxford: John Henry Parker, 1844), 3.14.

127. Stephen Holmes, *The Wondrous Cross: Atonement and Penal Substitution in the Bible and History* (London: Paternoster, 2007). For Holmes, Gregory is the only early writer who teaches penal substitution "clearly and unambiguously" (51).

| CONCLUSION |

I have sought to describe the broad hall that is "mere penal substitution," by way of three basic components—(1) substitution, (2) penalty, and (3) divine sanction. Having done so, I then surveyed roughly the first five hundred years of postbiblical Christian history in order to counter the allegation that penal substitution is primarily a modern innovation.

The logic of penal substitution has been broadly present from almost the very beginning of church history. If there *is* a modern myth to be retired, it is the false notion that penal substitution first emerges with the Protestant Reformers.[128] At the same time, I have also sought to temper claims by some overzealous archaeologists of penal substitution, who either have wrongly located the view where it does not exist or have wrongly elevated it to the pinnacle of atonement doctrine in the patristic period.[129] In this way, the goal has been to bring some needed balance to the discussion of this model in early Christian history.

Finally, I should conclude by noting what this survey does not mean. It does not mean that readers must accept penal substitution in any form as helpful, true, or biblical, for to do so merely on the basis of these patristic sources would be, in the words of Mary Wollstonecraft, "to reverence the rust of antiquity" without sufficient reason.[130] I have not yet shown that penal substitution is either biblically faithful or culturally coherent. These arguments await in the next two chapters. Still, by defining the "mere" meaning of the model and by locating its presence in the work of several early theologians, I have demonstrated that the pedigree of penal substitution is far older—and far more well-worn—than even the oldest of church pews.

---

128. It was encouraging to see this point affirmed from the mainline (Episcopal) perspective of Fleming Rutledge, *The Crucifixion: Understanding the Death of Jesus Christ* (Grand Rapids: Eerdmans, 2015), 480.

129. See especially the prior discussion of Athanasius.

130. Mary Wollstonecraft, *A Vindication of the Rights of Men* (1790; repr., Oxford: Oxford University Press, 1999), 8.

CHAPTER 5

ACCORDING TO THE SCRIPTURES

THE BIBLE AND PENAL SUBSTITUTION

The prior chapter sought to define the essential logic of penal substitution and then to locate it within the early church tradition. The next two chapters will address some further critiques of this model of atonement. These criticisms will be organized under the headings of (1) canon, (2) character, and (3) culture. For sake of space, only the first of these will be discussed in the present chapter. Still, it may be helpful to spell out the meaning of each term from the outset.

In terms of canon, I am asking whether the Bible supports penal substitution, for indeed it hardly matters if Athanasius and Augustine endorsed the model if the Scriptures do not. Regarding character, I will address the claim that penal substitution misrepresents the character of God, perhaps by allowing wrath to trump mercy or by limiting God's sovereignty so that sin cannot be forgiven without retribution. Finally, responding to specific cultural critiques, I will tackle some practical and pastoral concerns regarding the model. In truth, these three categories are often inextricably related, and I cannot hope to address every conceivable objection to penal substitution. Especially in recent years, much ink has been spilled in the debates surrounding this understanding of the cross, and the disagreements have sometimes generated more heat than light. I have no interest in furthering this fight or the false assumption that those who object to this model have somehow betrayed the faith. Nonetheless, the questions are important. Thus I hope to address some of the most pressing claims against this model of atonement, and I begin with the biblical objection.

"The fathers, the fathers, the fathers!" was the exasperated response of

Martin Luther when he was confronted not with biblical reasons for why his views were wrong but with quotations from later church tradition. The exclamation was not meant to disparage the fathers—of whom Luther had his favorites—but to highlight that the true test of doctrine is the canon of Scripture. With that, one meets the most pressing question regarding penal substitution: Does the Bible teach it? Many fine scholars have claimed it does not.[1] In what follows, my goal will be to counter this conclusion, not by answering each individual argument but by looking at some of the central biblical themes and passages involved. The first is sacrifice.

| CHRIST AND SACRIFICE |

In the Old Testament, God clearly commands blood sacrifice as a means of atonement, but how exactly this atonement works has been a subject of debate. One clue, according to Leviticus, is that the life of the creature is seen as being "in the blood." Therefore, it is the blood that "makes atonement for one's life" (Lev 17:11).[2] In response to this idea, a later biblical author even claims that without the shedding of blood there can be no forgiveness (Heb 9:22).

In the New Testament, Christ's death is seen as sacrificial. He is "our Passover lamb . . . sacrificed for us" (1 Cor 5:2), and our great high priest, who "sacrificed" not an animal but "himself" (Heb 7:27; cf. 9:26). He is "the Lamb of God who takes away the sin of the world!" (John 1:29) and the "atoning sacrifice [hilasmon] for our sins" (1 John 4:10; cf. Rom 3:25). Elsewhere, Christ is spoken of as "a fragrant offering and sacrifice to God" (Eph 5:2), and his "blood" is that of "the covenant . . . poured out for many for the forgiveness of sins" (Matt 26:28). Over all such passages there is a crucial takeaway: Unlike the sacrifices of the Old Testament, Christ's work is actually *sufficient* to deal with sin in a full and final sense (Heb 10:4).

However else the Messiah's death is interpreted, the theme of sacrifice

---

1. For just a few examples, see Paul Fiddes, *Past Event and Present Salvation: The Christian Idea of Atonement* (Louisville: Westminster John Knox, 1989), 89, 98; Stephen Travis, "Christ as Bearer of Divine Judgment in Paul's Thought about the Atonement," in *Atonement Today: A Symposium at St John's College, Nottingham,* ed. John Goldingay (London: SPCK, 1995), 21–38; Joel B. Green, "Must We Imagine the Atonement in Penal Substitutionary Terms? Questions, Caveats and a Plea," in *The Atonement Debate: Papers from the London Symposium on the Theology of Atonement,* ed. Derek Tidball, David Hilborn, and Justin Thacker (Grand Rapids: Zondervan, 2008), 167; Tom Smail, "Can One Man Die for the People?" in *Atonement Today,* 73–92. John Goldingay, "Old Testament Sacrifice and the Death of Christ," in *Atonement Today,* 3–20.

2. While the statement in Leviticus follows discussion of the fellowship offering, the clear implication is that this principle is relevant to all blood sacrifices.

is central for the New Testament writers.[3] It was perhaps the first image by which the early Christians came to understand the atonement.[4] Yet as I have noted previously (ch. 4), sacrificial imagery does not lead automatically to a view of penal substitution.

Goldingay's Grievance

In the view of evangelical Old Testament scholar John Goldingay (b. 1942), "Sacrifice [for Israel] does not involve penal substitution in the sense that one entity bears another's punishment. By laying hands on the offering, the offerers identify with it and pass on to it not their guilt but their stain. The offering is then not vicariously punished but vicariously cleansed."[5] A further point for Goldingay's argument is that "the idea of punishment belongs to the framework of law rather than the framework of worship, and we get into difficulties when we mix ideas from the different frameworks such as these."[6]

In response to these contentions, no careful reader of the Old Testament would go so far as to claim that all of Israel's sacrifices should be seen as penal substitutions. Some were more akin to the thankful giving of a gift, or the symbolic depiction of feasting and fellowship. Sacrifice had many purposes. Not all offerings involved atonement, not all were bloody, and not all evoked ideas of punishment.[7] Still, the fact that *some* sacrifices carried no penal or substitutionary connotations hardly proves that none did. A more careful analysis is needed.

A Response to Goldingay

Along these lines, I. Howard Marshall points out that sacrifices invariably cost the worshiper something valuable. They were *costly*, and in certain instances the idea of a penalty or judgment depicted in the animal's death is difficult to ignore. For instance, in the sealing of a suzerain-vassal covenant (as depicted in Gen 15), the curses of punishment for breaking the agreement were acted out in a sacrificial killing.

---

3. See Robert Sherman, *King, Priest, and Prophet: A Trinitarian Theology of Atonement* (London: T&T Clark, 2004), 169–71.
4. See Fiddes, *Past Event*, 61.
5. Goldingay, "Old Testament Sacrifice," 10.
6. Goldingay, "Old Testament Sacrifice," 10.
7. On this point, I. Howard Marshall argues that sacrifices variously included and combined ideas of (1) gift, (2) communion, and (3) atonement. Marshall, *Aspects of the Atonement: Cross and Resurrection in the Reconciling of God and Humanity* (London: Paternoster, 2007), 124.

Hence, to make a covenant was to "cut" (*karat*) one.[8] Ancient covenants included stipulations, and the acted-out curses for breaking them were clearly penal in their nature.[9] By passing through the divided pieces of the sacrificial victim, the implication was clear: "May this happen to me and more if I break the words of the covenant."[10] Yet in Genesis 15, the stunning fact is that God, not Abraham, passed between pieces. In the words of Markus Barth, "God alone . . . walks the bloody road between the carcasses."[11] According to this logic, it is God who places himself on the line if the agreement is broken.[12]

Some sacrifices were explicitly substitutionary. Further on in the Genesis story, we read that Abraham "took the ram and sacrificed it as a burnt offering *instead of* his son" (Gen 22:13, italics added). The substitution here cannot be doubted. In Jewish tradition, this event was referred to as the *Akedah*, or the binding of Isaac. According to Peter Leithart, this event becomes part of "the foundation of Israelite sacrifice."[13] The New Testament therefore echoes it in referring to Christ's own death. In John's Gospel, Jesus carries the beam of his own cross as he approaches Golgotha (19:17), evoking images of Isaac climbing Moriah beneath the weight of sacrificial wood.[14] Likewise, Paul writes in Romans that God "did not spare his own Son, but gave him up for us all" (8:32). This claim may also be intended as an echo of the Akedah since the Septuagint uses the same verb to state that Abraham "did not spare (*ephisato*) his own Son."[15] In the end, similar reflections on a number of texts lead Gordon Wenham to conclude that, in certain instances, "in giving the animal

8. This is a fairly standard interpretation of the ritual. See, for instance, David M. Carr, *An Introduction to the Old Testament: Sacred Texts and Imperial Contexts of the Hebrew Bible* (Malden, MA: Wiley-Blackwell, 2010), ch. 5.

9. See Scott J. Hafemann, "The Covenant Relationship," in *Central Themes in Biblical Theology: Mapping Unity in Diversity*, ed. Scott J. Hafemann and Paul R. House (Grand Rapids: Baker Academic, 2007), ch. 1.

10. See also Jer 34:18: "Those who have violated my covenant . . . I will treat like the calf they cut in two and then walked between its pieces."

11. Markus Barth, "Was Christ's Death a Sacrifice," *SJT Occasional Papers 9* (Edinburgh: Oliver and Boyd, 1961), 17.

12. See Jeremy Treat, "Atonement and Covenant: Binding Together Aspects of Christ's Work," in *Locating Atonement: Explorations in Constructive Dogmatics*, ed. Oliver Crisp and Fred Sanders (Grand Rapids: Zondervan, 2015), 104.

13. Peter J. Leithart, *Delivered from the Elements of the World: Atonement, Justification, Mission* (Downers Grove, IL: IVP Academic, 2016), 89n30.

14. The rabbinical author of *Genesis Rabbah* (56:3) claimed that Isaac bore the wood "like one carries his stake [read: cross] on his shoulder." See D. A. Carson, *The Gospel according to John*, The Pillar New Testament Commentary (Grand Rapids: Eerdmans, 1991), 609.

15. See Douglas J. Moo, *The Epistle to the Romans*, NICNT (Grand Rapids: Eerdmans, 1996), 541n18.

to God, the worshiper is reminded that he should die for his sins had the animal not taken his place."[16]

Another weakness in Goldingay's argument involves his segregation of the frameworks of law and worship. While many modern cultures place firm boundaries between the sacred and the legal, ancient Israel did not. For the Hebrews, law and worship were intimately intertwined. A major purpose of the Law (that is, the Torah) was to structure worship, and as many first-time readers of Leviticus can attest, it is sometimes startling to see how the legal and the liturgical (to use anachronistic terms) are bound up together. To say that Israel operated with separate silos labeled "law" and "worship"—each with its own stock of mutually exclusive metaphors—is simply wrong.[17] And while this hardly proves that certain sacrifices should be viewed through the lens of penal substitution, it does mean that we should not exclude the possibility based on an imagined separation.[18] This too calls for closer analysis of particular sacrificial rituals.

| THE DAY OF ATONEMENT |

Near the center of the debate regarding penal substitution in the Old Testament stands the Day of Atonement (*Yom Kippur*; Lev 16). On this day, the high priest entered the holy of holies to make atonement for sins not covered by the other sacrifices. The ritual had several parts, but the most important part for my purposes is that involving two goats:

> [Aaron] is to cast lots for the two goats—one lot for the LORD and the other for the scapegoat. Aaron shall bring the goat whose lot falls to the LORD and sacrifice it for a sin offering. But the goat chosen by lot as the scapegoat shall be presented alive before the LORD to be used for making atonement by sending it into the wilderness as a scapegoat. (Lev 16:8–10)[19]

Then, after the first goat was slaughtered,

---

16. Gordon J. Wenham, *Numbers* (Downers Grove, IL: IVP Academic, 1981), 228.

17. The dichotomy is further undermined by the penalties that accompany improper worship, as in the case of Nadab and Abihu (Lev 10), and in the punishments prescribed for wrongful presentation of fellowship offerings (Lev 7:20–1). See Steve Jeffery, Michael Ovey, and Andrew Sach, *Pierced for Our Transgressions: Rediscovering the Glory of Penal Substitution* (Wheaton, IL: Crossway, 2007), 48n26.

18. N. T. Wright has continually pointed this out in particular regarding the apostle Paul.

19. I will not delve into the debate concerning the translation "for the scapegoat" (16:8 NIV) versus the goat "for *Azazel*" (16:8 NRSV).

> [Aaron] is to lay both hands on the head of the live goat and confess over it all the wickedness and rebellion of the Israelites—all their sins—and put them on the goat's head. He shall send the goat away into the wilderness in the care of someone appointed for the task. The goat will carry on itself all their sins to a remote place; and the man shall release it in the wilderness. (Lev 16:21–22)

Though there is much that remains mysterious about the ritual, for some advocates of penal substitution the meaning is clear. In the words of Thomas Schreiner, "The live goat functions as the substitute that bears the penalty (eviction to the desert) for Israel's sins."[20] Although it may seem odd that the animal's death is not mentioned, it bears mentioning that, for Israel, the paradigmatic punishment for sin is *exile*, of which death is but a species.[21] In Leviticus, to be banished from the camp is to experience God's penalty for sin.[22]

Not only was one goat sent away; another was sacrificed. Even though the interpretation of blood sacrifice is disputed, one can make the case that *both goats* offer differing angles on the same reality. Hebrews likens Christ's blood to that of the sacrificial goat. And in the Scriptures, doubling images or storylines (like the two goats) often provides a way to tell the same narrative from slightly different angles. This is certainly true of Joseph's two dreams in Genesis 37 (sheaves bowing; heavenly bodies bowing), the two dreams of pharaoh in Genesis 41 (seven cows; seven heads of grain), or even the doubling of the creation stories in Genesis 1–2.[23] If all this is taken into account with regard to the scapegoat and the sacrificial victim, then a compelling case can be made that Yom Kippur involves an element of penal substitution. But there is a notable objection.

---

20. Thomas Schreiner, "Penal Substitution," in *The Nature of the Atonement: Four Views*, ed. James Beilby and Paul R. Eddy (Downers Grove, IL: IVP Academic, 2006), 84. For Schreiner, "It may also be the case that the goat was sent into the wilderness to die."

21. N. T. Wright refers to exile as the "curse of all curses," and in his own work, Hans Boersma builds on this theme to make what is perhaps the most notable recent defense of penal substitution. Here, Christ's death is linked to the covenantal penalty of exile. See N. T. Wright, *The Climax of the Covenant: Christ and the Law in Pauline Theology* (Minneapolis: Fortress, 1942), 140; Hans Boersma, *Violence, Hospitality, and the Cross: Reappropriating the Atonement Tradition* (Grand Rapids: Baker Academic, 2004), 176.

22. Lev 7:20–27; 17:4, 9–14; 18:29; 19:8; 20:3, 5–6, 17–18; 22:3; 23:29. See Jeffery, Ovey, and Sach, *Pierced for Our Transgressions*, 49.

23. Credit for this insight into the Torah's use of doubling goes to my colleague, Jerome Van Kuiken.

The Tübingen Alternative

In German scholarship, a movement out of Tübingen has focused on Yom Kippur as the key to understanding both the Old Testament and the Pauline treatments of atonement. Emerging from the work of Hartmut Gese (b. 1929) and Otfried Hofius (b. 1937), the argument is that atonement occurs not by substitution but by "inclusive place-taking."[24] With regard to the scapegoat, the claim is that by laying hands on the animal and confessing the sins of Israel, the act does not transfer transgressions but *conjoins* the priest (and people) to the animal. In other words, "What happens on this line of interpretation is that the laying on of hands establishes a connection between the human being and the animal, and so when the animal goes through death, it symbolically takes the person to death with it. . . . The people cannot simply escape death; they must pass through it."[25] In this explanation, one can see the meaning of "inclusive [or incorporative] place-taking." Likewise, when turning to the New Testament, the inclusive paradigm has obvious links to Paul's claims that humanity has died "with" Christ (e.g., 2 Cor 5:14; Gal 2:20).

A Response to Tübingen

There is much to appreciate about the Tübingen perspective. But while the argument rules out what some call "simple substitution" (whereby the sacrifice and the people are not in *any way* bound together),[26] the logic in no way contradicts the overlapping and complementary nature of Christ's incorporative and substitutionary work. To revisit a statement from the last chapter: incorporative participation with Christ describes things as they *really are* at some deep and unseen level while substitution describes the levels of agency and sensory experience.

If all humanity is somehow bound up *with* Christ, then he may justly bear the penalty for human sin (hence the claims of penal nontransference

---

24. The German phrase here is *inkludierende* as opposed to *exkludierende Stellvertretung* ("exclusive place-taking"). For insight into the German scholarship on the topic, see Simon Gathercole, *Defending Substitution: An Essay on Atonement in Paul* (Grand Rapids: Baker Academic, 2015), 30–38; Richard H. Bell, "Sacrifice and Christology in Paul," *Journal of Theological Studies* 53 (2002): 1–27; and Daniel Bailey, "Concepts of *Stellvertretung* in the Interpretation of Isaiah 53," in *Jesus and the Suffering Servant: Isaiah 53 and Christian Origins*, ed. William Bellinger Jr. and William Farmer (Harrisburg, PA: Trinity Press International, 1998), ch. 13. As noted previously with regard to Karl Barth, the German *Stellvertretung* can be ambiguous as to whether we are speaking of representation or substitution. In Gese and Hofius, however, the meaning appears to be more akin to representative or inclusive place-taking.

25. Gathercole, *Defending Substitution*, 32.

26. Bell, "Sacrifice and Christology in Paul," 3.

lose their force).[27] Given the recapitulative presuppositions surveyed earlier (part 1), this aspect of the Tübingen perspective fits perfectly with my argument about the incorporative foundation of atonement. Exactly why this "inclusive place-taking" must rule out *all* substitutionary elements, however, seems far from obvious.[28]

Clearly some level of substitution is present with regard to the scapegoat. While the people may be pictured as spiritually bound up with the animal (as claimed by the Tübingen perspective), they do not physically *experience* the subsequent exile and presumed death. Nor do they actively and personally embark upon that lonely walk of banishment and condemnation. After the sins of the people are placed on the head of the scapegoat, the animal alone is physically banished, while the people still stand physically in the midst of the camp.[29]

In the Day of Atonement, as with Calvary, the language of "in our place, instead of us," still seems best when speaking of the elements of (1) sensory experience and (2) active agency. Beyond this, I have noted already that a strong case can be made that the banishment and presumed death of the sin-bearer has the penal connotations that exile has elsewhere within the Torah. For these reasons, Yom Kippur appears to present us with an image of penal substitution joined with vicarious judgment. One need not accept a false choice between these two options.

The Suffering Servant

Even more than the Day of Atonement, Isaiah's Suffering Servant is often held up as the clearest Old Testament example of penal substitutionary logic.[30] While the entire text is justly famous, the following verses have been especially emphasized:

---

27. See ch. 3.
28. This is similar to Peter Leithart's claim regarding the substitutionary *and* inclusive nature of sacrifices in general. Leithart, *Delivered from the Elements*, 106–7n35: "The sacrificial system assumes exile from Eden; the worshiper approaches a God who is enthroned behind a screen of cherubic guardians with swords of fire. The worshiper cannot draw near without dying; so he sends an animal ahead on his behalf. The animal is sent to bring the worshiper into God's presence; the animal dies and is turned to smoke, and the worshiper remains quite alive and nonsmoky. The only word that fits what happens is 'substitute.' It is important to recognize the inclusive character of the substitution. . . . But that has to be balanced with the recognition that the animal's ministry takes place *outside* the worshiper."
29. See also Scot McKnight, *A Community Called Atonement* (Nashville: Abingdon, 2007), 111.
30. For sake of consistency, and in keeping with much Christian tradition, I have chosen to capitalize the references to "the Servant" throughout this section.

But he was pierced for our transgressions,
   he was crushed for our iniquities;
the punishment that brought us peace was on him,
   and by his wounds we are healed. (Isa 53:5)

For many, the meaning seems clear: "Isaiah 53 teaches that God's Servant willingly took the place of his people, bearing the penalty for their sins in order that they might escape punishment."[31] Thus "those who deny the theme of penal substitution in this chapter appear to be guilty of special pleading."[32]

The passage brims with sacrificial imagery, despite the jarring reality that the offering appears to be a human being. The Suffering Servant will "sprinkle"[33] many nations (52:15); he is "led like a lamb to the slaughter" (53:7); "the LORD has laid on him the iniquity of us all" (53:6), and "the LORD makes his life an offering for sin" (53:10). What's more, this sacrificial death is then simultaneously and explicitly described as a "punishment" that brings "peace" to others (53:5). Given all this, those who would deny all penal connotations to Hebrew sacrifice are left to explain the convergence of these themes.[34] It is clear that Isaiah brings together sacrificial and penal language as applied to the redemptive work of the human Servant.

THE SUFFERING SERVANT IN THE NEW TESTAMENT

In the New Testament, Isaiah's Suffering Servant passage is applied to Christ. Luke has Jesus quoting from Isaiah 52:12 and then applying it to himself: "It is written: 'And he was numbered with the transgressors'; and I tell you that this must be fulfilled in me" (22:37). In Acts 8, the Ethiopian eunuch reads how the Servant "was led like a sheep to the slaughter," and in response "Philip began with that very passage of Scripture and told

---

31. Jeffery, Ovey, and Sach, *Pierced for Our Transgressions*, 61.
32. David Peterson, "Atonement in the Old Testament," in *Where Wrath and Mercy Meet: Proclaiming the Atonement Today* (Carlisle: Paternoster, 2001), 21.
33. "Startle" is an alternative possibility, as illustrated by the LXX. See John N. Oswalt, *The Book of Isaiah: Chapters 40–66*, The New International Commentary on the Old Testament (Grand Rapids: Eerdmans, 1998), 374n56.
34. On the sacrificial imagery of the passage, see Sue Groom, "Why Did Christ Die? An Exegesis of Isaiah 52.13–53.12," in Tidball, Hilborn, and Thacker, *The Atonement Debate*, 101–2; J. Alan Groves, "Atonement in Isaiah 53: 'For He Bore the Sins of Many,'" in Tidball, Hilborn, and Thacker, *The Glory of Atonement*, 61–89.

him the good news about Jesus" (vv. 32–34). Beyond these texts, there are many likely allusions to Isaiah's Servant. One is found in Christ's statement that "the Son of Man did not come to be served, but to serve, and to give his life as a ransom for many" (Mark 10:45). In response to the dual images of a (1) Servant who gives his life as a ransom for (2) "the many" (cf. Isa 53:11–12 LXX), Sue Groom argues that the only possible Hebrew background that unites these themes is Isaiah 53.[35]

Perhaps the most important New Testament reference to the Servant occurs in 1 Peter 2:22–25. The passage intends to provoke believers to imitate Christ's actions. In doing so, the author quotes directly from the portion of Isaiah that speaks of the Servant sacrificially bearing the sins of the people, and thereby bringing healing:

> "He committed no sin,
>   and no deceit was found in his mouth." [Isa 53:9] . . .

> "He himself bore our sins" in his body on the cross, so that we might die to sins and live for righteousness; "by his wounds you have been healed." For "you were like sheep going astray," [Isa 53:4–6 (see LXX)] but now you have returned to the Shepherd and Overseer of your souls.

In response to the New Testament data, N. T. Wright argues that this entire section of Isaiah became thematic for Christ's ministry.[36] Along these lines, one may even note a kind of three-step progression, whereby the reestablishment of the covenant (Isa 54) follows the work of the Servant (Isa 53) and results in the fruit of new creation (Isa 55).[37]

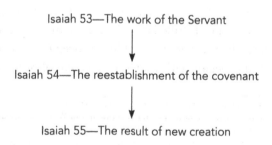

Isaiah 53—The work of the Servant

Isaiah 54—The reestablishment of the covenant

Isaiah 55—The result of new creation

35. Sue Groom, "Why Did Christ Die," 104.

36. N. T. Wright, *Jesus and the Victory of God* (Minneapolis: Fortress, 1996), 602–4; also Wright, "The Servant and Jesus: The Relevance of the Colloquy for the Current Quest for Jesus," in *Jesus and the Suffering Servant*, 294.

37. N. T. Wright, *Justification: God's Plan and Paul's Vision* (Downers Grove, IL: IVP Academic, 2009), 226.

The New Testament seems to portray the Messiah as embodying the Servant's actions. And in Isaiah, these actions entail the sacrificial bearing of sin (53:12) and punishment (53:5), so that the many are justified (53:11), and the people find healing and peace (53:5). In sum, the case for penal substitution seems almost unavoidable.

Morna Hooker's Objection

The most notable objection to this conclusion exists in the work of Morna Hooker (b. 1931).[38] Although Hooker's argument is detailed, it may be summarized in three basic points. First, there is "no convincing evidence" that the Suffering Servant played "any significant role in Jesus's own understanding of his ministry."[39] Second, there is little evidence that the other New Testament writers used the text to interpret the meaning of Christ's death.[40] And third, there is no case for penal substitution in either Isaiah 53 or the Bible at large.

In place of these traditional claims, Hooker sees the Servant as embodying an "'inclusive' rather than 'exclusive place-taking.'"[41] Her argument is therefore similar to the claims seen previously from the Tübingen school.[42] For Hooker, the Servant suffers as a result of and alongside others, yet the Servant is not a substitute because "*both* the culprits and the innocent bear the consequences of sins."[43] The Servant shares the people's experience of suffering—he does not suffer instead of the people.

A Response to Hooker

On a positive note, Hooker is certainly correct to claim that several New Testament quotations of Isaiah 53 make no attempt to interpret the

---

38. Hooker's early work may be found in *Jesus and the Servant* (London: SPCK, 1959), and her mostly "unrepentant" reflections of forty years later are detailed in "Did the Use of Isaiah 53 to Interpret His Mission Begin with Jesus," in *Jesus and the Suffering Servant*, William Bellinger Jr. and William Farmer, eds. (Harrisburg, PA: Trinity Press International, 1998), 88–103.

39. Hooker, "Did the Use of Isaiah 53," 88.

40. For Hooker, the primary exception is 1 Peter 2:22–25, but she still seems unimpressed by the passage because of concerns over (1) date, (2) authorship, and (3) an implied discomfort over the apparently oppressive ends toward which the text is used (i.e., "the author [of 1 Pet] is appealing to slaves to be submissive to their masters and to put up with undeserved punishment"), 92–93. In contrast to her earlier work, Hooker now sees Paul, in Rom 3:25, as using Isa 53 to interpret Christ's mission. See Hooker, "Did the Use of Isaiah 53," 102–3.

41. Hooker, "Did the Use of Isaiah 53," 102.

42. It is noteworthy, however, that Hofius disagrees with Hooker on Isaiah's Suffering Servant. In his view, the passage *does* speak of substitution (or "exclusive place-taking") between the Servant and the people. Still, he (somewhat oddly) rules it out as a valid description of Christ's death because of Hebrew prohibitions against human sacrifice, and because of the supposed preference for "inclusive place-taking" in the New Testament. See Bailey, "Concepts of *Stellvertretung*," 237.

43. This explanation is that of Daniel Bailey, "Concepts of *Stellvertretung*," 234–45.

text in terms of either penal substitution or atonement in general. This much is undisputed. It would be unwise to apply an entire Old Testament passage unequivocally to Christ if indeed the New Testament does not endorse this approach.[44] In this sense, Hooker provides a helpful caution to conventional assumptions.

However, Hooker's argument has several problems. I will briefly note three. The first weakness involves her propensity to ignore the New Testament's many *likely allusions* to Christ as the Servant. Hooker only deals with a handful of proof texts, but many biblical scholars find several more references to the Suffering Servant in the New Testament. Stephen Dempster, for one, argues that the New Testament "contains forty-eight references" to Isaiah's fourth Servant song, making it second only to the Danielic Son of Man in New Testament attestation.[45] And some of these allusions are linked directly to Christ's atoning work. For instance, if Christ's statement about coming "to serve" and give his life as "a ransom for many" (Mark 10:45) is, as many think, an allusion to the Servant, then Hooker's case regarding Christ's self-understanding falls apart.[46] The idea of the Suffering Servant may be present in a text apart from a lengthy word-for-word quotation.

Second, Hooker's complete sidestepping of 1 Peter 2 ("'He himself bore our sins' in his body on the cross . . . [and] 'by his wounds you have been healed'") simply because of date and authorship concerns is also telling.[47] If one is dealing, as I am, with a canonical approach to doctrine, then one cannot simply sideline disagreeable texts on the grounds that they lack authority. While this should not be taken as a blanket denunciation of all critical concerns, the danger is readily apparent. Too often, texts that do not fit the interpreter's fancy are simply sidelined from the outset.

Third, the most significant problem with Hooker's theological argument has to do with the *achievement* of the Servant's suffering. In the words of

---

44. For instance, while parts of 2 Sam 7 seem to point to Christ, we do not assume that the verse about the "son" actually committing "iniquity" (v. 14) applies literally to him. Whether he is *counted* as having committed iniquity, however, is, of course, a different shade of meaning.

45. Stephen G. Dempster, "The Servant of the LORD," in *Central Themes in Biblical Theology: Mapping Unity in Diversity*, ed. Scott J. Hafemann and Paul R. House (Grand Rapids: Baker Academic, 2007), 165.

46. To bolster the prior claim of Groom, "Why Did Christ Die," 104, Dempster notes that the triadic combination of themes: (1) servanthood, (2) ransom, and (3) "the many" (which chimes like a bell throughout the Servant song), make Hooker's claim regarding Christ's self-understanding unlikely. See Dempster, "The Servant of the LORD," 157, 169.

47. Her contempt for the passage is palpable: "Perhaps we ought not to include it among the quotations at all." Hooker, "Did the Use of Isaiah 53," 92.

Isaiah, "The punishment that brought us peace was on him, and by his wounds we are healed" (Isa 53:5). Though Hooker briefly acknowledges this verse (and the quotation of it in 1 Peter), she quickly dismisses the idea of penal substitution. She states, "There are many ways in which the sufferings of one person can save a whole community."[48] In turning to Paul and the New Testament, Hooker then claims that atonement occurs through a process of "interchange." Here, Christ—much like the Servant—shares the *experience* of the people's suffering and death, so that the people might share his resurrection.[49] Salvation therefore comes by identification and interchange "in Christ," not because Christ has borne a penalty instead of us.[50]

What seems to be lacking in Hooker's argument is an explanation as to *why* the Servant's sharing in the people's suffering should bring peace and healing for the people (53:5). How does the Servant "justify many" (53:11) merely by suffering with them? By way of analogy: Why should a cancer patient be cured simply because her doctor tests positive for the same condition? It may be comforting to know, as one novelist writes, that "God came into the world and screamed alongside us,"[51] but the idea of shared pain by itself is not a satisfying explanation of atonement. The idea that "God saves" does not flow logically or automatically from the claim that "Christ suffers."

Turning to Hooker's treatment of Christ and the New Testament, Gathercole echoes this critique with the charge that she does "not sufficiently account for what is achieved by the *death* of Christ." By this, he means that her treatment of atonement displays a stunning "lack of place for a *positive* role for the cross."[52] Instead, Hooker often appeals to vague formulas[53] and retreats to mystery: "In some *unfathomable* way Christ is identified with what is opposed to God, in order that man should be reconciled to him."[54] Although this statement could be taken as an endorsement of penal substitution, Hooker explicitly rejects the notion on the grounds that such an answer peers too deeply into the divine darkness.

---

48. Hooker, "Did the Use of Isaiah 53," 98.

49. Morna Hooker, *From Adam to Christ: Essays on Paul* (Cambridge: Cambridge University Press, 1990), ch. 1.

50. See the judicious yet critical treatment of this argument in Gathercole, *Defending Substitution*, 38–46.

51. From Susan Howatch's novel, *Absolute Truths* (New York: Fawcett Crest, 1994), 307.

52. Gathercole, *Defending Substitution*, 41, italics in original.

53. See especially Hooker's repeated citation of the Irenaean dictum, as if it were an explanation for how atonement works: "He became what we are so we might become what he is." See Hooker, *From Adam to Christ*, 22; citing *Haer.* 5, preface (*ANF* 1:526).

54. Hooker, *From Adam to Christ*, 17, italics added.

On Mystery and Mechanism: A Caveat

In response to Hooker's last argument, a brief word should be said about two concepts that affect every model of atonement: (1) mystery and (2) mechanism. With regard to mystery, there are bound to be aspects of Christ's work that remain opaque to us. As Paul exults, God's judgments are "unsearchable" and his ways "unfathomable" (Rom 11:33). Thus, none should presume to understand Christ's work exhaustively. As Conrad's character in the novel *Heart of Darkness* notes, the "map" of our theology contains "blank spaces." This should not surprise us. We are, after all, dealing with a holy, transcendent, and invisible God. Yet at the same time, a premature or unnecessary appeal to mystery often betrays a weakness in one's argument. Though the cross mocks worldly wisdom (1 Cor 1), this does not mean that it has no underlying logic.[55]

This brings me to mechanism. By this apparently unspiritual word, I mean the basic rationale by which the events of the incarnation are thought to bring about redemption. In other words, how Christ's work *works*. For some, however, even to be preoccupied with this question is evidence of error. For Joel Green, proponents of penal substitution especially have been "far more concerned with identifying the 'how' of our salvation than either the Bible or the tradition has been."[56] While no examples are named and no evidence given, Green blames the mechanistic preoccupation on a favorite whipping boy of contemporary theologians: René Descartes. It was Descartes who saw the universe as a big machine, so (by Green's judgment) he must be to blame for those who are focused on the "how" of the atonement.[57] Green's charge is so sweeping that it provides a more extreme example, but others have made similar claims.[58]

Rather than simply dismiss the unsubstantiated allegation, we should first recognize the important grain of truth within it. It is possible for accounts of the atonement to be overly mechanical. And some proponents of penal substitution have likely overemphasized the "how" of Christ's work. In resistance to this error, T. F. Torrance warns against foisting "logico-causal" categories upon a personal God.[59] If this happens, one may

---

55. For Donald MacLeod: "The apostles clearly saw it as their duty not only to proclaim the cross, but to explain it"—at least *somewhat*. MacLeod, *Christ Crucified: Understanding the Atonement* (Downers Grove, IL: IVP Academic, 2014), 15.

56. Joel B. Green, "Must We Imagine the Atonement in Penal Substitutionary Terms: Questions, Caveats and a Plea," in Tidball, Hilborn, and Thacker, *The Atonement Debate*, 166.

57. Green, "Must We Imagine," 164.

58. See Fiddes, *Past Event*, 83.

59. See T. F. Torrance, *Scottish Theology: From John Knox to John McLeod Campbell*

end up with what Edward Irving called a "stock-exchange divinity" for whom redemption occurs by a grotesque balancing of debts and credits on the cross.[60] This is not the gospel. As Kevin Vanhoozer points out, the love of God on the cross is no mere balancing of accounts. Divine love is excessive: "God did not merely compensate for human sin; he did more. He did not simply make up sin's deficit; he destroyed it. The New Testament, of course, knows this 'excess' by its proper covenantal name: *grace*."[61] Yes and amen!

In the face of these helpful warnings against an overly mechanistic view of the atonement, it would be equally absurd to accuse any attempt at clarifying the logic of redemption of being unduly indebted to Descartes's view of the world as a giant machine.[62] Fideism is not the gospel either. And appeals to mystery can function as a cloak for incoherence or the simple lack of an argument.[63] While one may choose to reject any or all of the traditional atonement models, each is an attempt to offer a rationale regarding how atonement happens. To blame this on the influence of a seventeenth-century French philosopher is nonsense.[64] Mystery and mechanism must "kiss" within atonement doctrine, as they do within the New Testament.

| THE GOSPELS |

With this claim in mind, I turn now to the Gospels themselves. Understandably, in these books, less time is spent interpreting Christ's passion than in describing it. Still, the writers of the Gospels are also theologians, not mere court reporters. And there are statements from the life of Jesus that are important for the archaeology of penal substitution. In what

---

(Edinburgh: T&T Clark, 1996), xi. Likewise, Torrance, *Atonement: The Person and Work of Christ*, ed. Robert T. Walker (Downers Grove, IL: IVP, 2009), 437–47.

60. Edward Irving, *The Last Days: A Discourse on the Evil Character of These Our Times: Proving Them to Be the "Perilous Times" of the "Last Days"* (London: Seeley and Burnside, 1828), 506. Cited in Colin Gunton, *Actuality of Atonement: A Study of Metaphor, Rationality and the Christian Tradition* (London: T&T Clark, 1988), 129. Although, in truth, Irving's own view was hardly better.

61. Kevin J. Vanhoozer, "The Atonement in Postmodernity: Guilt, Goats, and Gifts," in *The Glory of the Atonement*, ed. Charles Hill and Frank James (Downers Grove, IL: IVP, 2004), 403–4.

62. While Torrance and Vanhoozer are hardly guilty of this, the claims of Green, Fiddes, and Hooker are more suspect.

63. See the helpful discussion of this in Thomas H. McCall, *An Invitation to Analytic Christian Theology* (Downers Grove, IL: IVP Academic, 2015), 19.

64. It bears noting that Anselm was acutely concerned with the logical "how" of atonement doctrine, centuries before Descartes.

follows, I will look briefly at two themes: (1) Christ's treatment of the cup that he must drink, and (2) the unintentional prophecy of Caiaphas that one should die on behalf of the nation.

The Cup of Divine Judgment

One of the most gut-wrenching moments in Christ's passion plays out amidst the gnarled branches of Gethsemane. Here, the Lord cries out through blood-like tears: "My Father, if it is possible, may this cup be taken from me" (Matt 26:39). It is this drink that Christ must drain. And in the Hebrew Scriptures, the cup is associated with God's wrath and judgment. Psalm 75:8 is just one example:

> In the hand of the Lord is a cup
> full of foaming wine mixed with spices;
> he pours it out, and all the wicked of the earth
> drink it down to its very dregs.

Similar imagery is found throughout the Scriptures,[65] most famously in the book of Revelation with the bowls of wrath poured out on human sin (Rev 16).[66] In terms of penal substitution, the image fits with the idea that Christ willingly endured the divinely sanctioned penalty (wrath or judgment) for human sin upon the cross. The penal overtones are clear. But does he drink this cup *instead* of us? This idea is sometimes less obvious. At one point, Christ even promises that his disciples "will drink the cup I drink" (Mark 10:39; cf. Matt 20:23), which might seem to contradict the notion of a simple substitution.[67]

Yet this last statement can be understood in several ways. Perhaps it refers merely to the fact that his disciples will suffer similar punishments at the hands of earthly authorities. Or perhaps, as Matthew's Gospel hints, we are to hear a eucharistic echo: "You will indeed drink from *my* cup" (Matt 20:23). As with many of Christ's statements, several meanings intermingle. Whatever the verdict with regard to straightforward substitution, however, the view of the cross as entailing Christ's draining of the cup of divine wrath fits perfectly with the penal aspects of atonement.

---

65. See especially Isa 51:17 and Jer 25:15ff.
66. See G. K. Beale, *The Book of Revelation: A Commentary on the Greek Text* (Grand Rapids: Eerdmans, 1999), 812ff.
67. See, for instance, the claim of Donald MacLeod that "He drinks the cup so that we should not." MacLeod, *Christ Crucified*, 85.

The Prophecy of Caiaphas

My second case study from the Gospels involves the unintentionally prophetic words of Caiaphas: "It is better . . . that one man die for the people than that the whole nation perish" (John 11:50). While said with the calculated chill of political pragmatism, the writer of John views this as an inadvertent preaching of atonement doctrine. "He did not say this on his own, but as high priest that year he prophesied that Jesus would die for the Jewish nation, and not only for that nation but also for the scattered children of God, to bring them together and make them one" (vv. 51–52).

In response, two points stand out. First, the statement draws on sacrificial themes. Caiaphas is the high priest, and in the Hebrew cultus and culture, a redeeming death "for the people" can hardly be seen as anything but sacrificial. It is a metaphor, of course—since Caiaphas is not proposing the literal burning of Christ upon the altar—but the metaphor is one of sacrifice. Second, the sacrificial death is both "in place of" and "instead of" the nation. It is substitutionary. This is the point of both the prophecy and the pragmatism: Christ perishes so that others do not—at least not in the same way.[68] In the end, there is sacrifice *and* substitution.[69]

On the heels of prior discussions in this chapter, the importance of these dual emphases should not be missed. While some (e.g., the Tübingen perspective) argue that sacrificial imagery does not include the idea of substitution, the prophecy of Caiaphas begs to differ. And presumably, as high priest of Israel, he knew something of these matters—indeed, a good bit more than modern scholars.

While more Gospel passages could indeed be cited,[70] when taken together, these two case studies, the cup and the Caiaphas prophecy, come together to form an image of Christ's cross as a penalty endured under divine sanction and a substitutionary sacrifice by which Jesus perishes so that others do not. In sum, these emphases fulfill the basic requirements of what was previously identified as "mere penal substitution."[71]

---

68. In both the cup metaphor and the Caiaphas statement, one must remember that the New Testament does not see God's wrath as so utterly absorbed by the Son that none is left for those who reject him (for instance, in the Synoptics, the fall of Jerusalem in AD 70 is clearly viewed as a divine judgment on Israel for rejecting the Messiah's way of peace). Thanks for this helpful reminder goes to my colleague, Jerome Van Kuiken.

69. Ch. 12 will address an alternative reading of this text by René Girard.

70. Ch. 6 will turn to an objection to penal substitution that is based, in part, upon the Gospel parable of the prodigal son.

71. Paul Fiddes argues, somewhat oddly, that while the New Testament presents Christ's death in both penal and substitutionary terms, it does not warrant the conclusion of "penal substitution." Despite many praiseworthy aspects of Fiddes's study of atonement doctrine,

| PAUL |

"Jesus have I loved, but Paul . . . ?" Some have accused the Apostle to the Gentiles of adding both controversy and conundrum to the Christian faith.[72] The Pauline corpus has provocative statements on election, sexuality, the roles of women, and the rights of ruling authorities, just to name a few. Unsurprisingly, Paul is also central to the controversy over penal substitution. Because of the immensity of the topic, the following exploration must again be limited to a few central passages.

1 Corinthians 15:3–4

If one desired a straightforward summary of Paul's gospel, one could hardly do better than the opening verses of 1 Corinthians 15: "For what I received I passed on to you as of first importance: that Christ died for our sins according to the Scriptures, that he was buried, that he was raised on the third day according to the Scriptures" (vv. 3–4). While there is much to talk about within this text, I must begin with a few core insights.

First, Paul clarifies that his understanding of Christ's work was "received" and then "passed on" as "of first importance." If this is so, then whatever is contained within this brief credo has the combined authority of an even earlier and broader tradition. Second, Paul claims that Christ dying "for [huper] our sins" was foretold by the Old Testament. It was "according to the Scriptures." As Simon Gathercole notes, this claim is fascinating since there are few passages in the Hebrew Bible that foretell of one *human being* dying redemptively for the sins of others. While death is frequently a consequence for sin(s) in the Old Testament, the normal pattern is that one dies for their own transgressions.[73]

What is the most likely Old Testament background for Paul's statement? At the front of the pack, by some distance, is Isaiah 53. In fact, if one wants evidence for how widespread this consensus is, one need look no further than the scholar who once famously denied the apostolic use of Isaiah 53

---

this sounds rather like admitting that one side of the equation is "two plus two" (2+2=) while insisting that the answer is not four. See Fiddes, *Past Event*, 98.

72. See J. R. Daniel Kirk, *Jesus Have I Loved, but Paul? A Narrative Approach to Pauline Christianity* (Grand Rapids: Baker Academic, 2011).

73. See Gathercole, *Defending Substitution*, 60. For instance, in 1 Kgs 16:18–19: "[Zimri] died for [huper, LXX] the sins he had committed." As Gathercole notes, the Greek here in the Septuagint is almost identical to that of Paul (both passages contain the phrase: *apethanen huper tōn hamartiōn*), except for the obvious difference that Zimri dies for his own sins. See Gathercole, *Defending Substitution*, 71.

in interpreting Christ's death: Morna Hooker.[74] Hooker now concedes that the Suffering Servant is indeed the most likely Old Testament background for Paul's statement.[75] If this is so, and the widely held opinion is correct that Isaiah 53 presents a version of substitutionary redemption, then it would seem likely that 1 Corinthians 15:3–4 views things similarly.[76] In the end, a good case can be made that the most natural way to interpret the gospel statement in 1 Corinthians 15 is through the lens of substitution.

Romans 8:1–4

Additional Pauline passages affirm the penal nature of Christ's death and the divine sanction behind it. In Romans 8, one of the great mountain vistas of Christian Scripture, Paul tells with exuberance that

> there is now no condemnation for those who are in Christ Jesus, because through Christ Jesus the law of the Spirit who gives life has set you free from the law of sin and death. For what the law was powerless to do because it was weakened by the flesh, God did by sending his own Son in the likeness of sinful flesh to be a sin offering. And so he condemned sin in the flesh, in order that the righteous requirement of the law might be fully met in us, who do not live according to the flesh but according to the Spirit. (vv. 1–4)

Condemnation (*katakrima*) is clearly penal language. And the text tells us that Christians face none of it because "God condemned sin in the flesh" of Christ.

At this point Paul's atonement doctrine features both clarity and nuance. He does not say flatly that God punished Jesus (contra Luther and Owen; see ch. 4). Nor does he say that the Father was angry personally with the Son. John Calvin was therefore correct to say:

> We do not . . . insinuate that God was ever hostile to him or angry with [Christ]. How could he be angry with his beloved Son, with whom his soul was well pleased? Or how could he have appeased his Father by his intercession for others if he were hostile to himself? But this we say,

---

74. Remember that while Hooker acknowledges 1 Pet 2, she does not place it on the same level as the other New Testament allusions to Isa 53.

75. Hooker, "Did the Use of Isaiah 53," 103.

76. This is precisely Simon Gathercole's conclusion. See Gathercole, *Defending Substitution*, 78–79.

that he bore the weight of the divine anger, that, being smitten and afflicted, he *experienced* all the *signs* of an angry and avenging God.[77]

In many ways, this statement may be viewed as a careful outworking and expansion of Paul's thought.

According to Romans 8, sin (not the Son!) is the ultimate target of God's cross-directed condemnation. Yet it so happens that this sin is borne "in the flesh" of him who knew none (2 Cor 5:21). This is possible, as I have previously suggested,[78] because all humanity is somehow bound up "with Christ," the true Adam. Because our sin is borne by Christ, Jesus experiences God's condemnation of sin as if it were a divine judgment on his very person—despite the fact that it is not.[79] The poetic words of P. T. Forsyth are apt: the crucified Christ proclaims that the Father's judgment is holy when it "strikes the sinful spot if even I stand on it."[80]

In the view of Romans 8, God condemned human sin in the flesh of Christ so that the redeemed experience both righteousness in him and "no condemnation." Here, too, the ground for justification and imputation rest upon the incorporative union between Christ and humanity.[81] With regard to condemnation, the language is clearly (1) *penal*, (2) the act occurs under *divine sanction*, and (3) there is *substitution* in the sense that Christ experiences the weight of divine judgment while we do not. Although humanity is bound up with Christ, the realms of active agency and sensory experience are his alone. This is a crucial part of the larger gospel message. And it is also penal substitution.[82]

Romans 3:25–26

The same notion accords with a certain interpretation of Romans 3:25–26:

God presented Christ as a [*hilasterion*], through the shedding of his blood—to be received by faith. He did this to demonstrate his

---

77. *Inst.* 2.16.11.
78. See ch. 3.
79. This also accords well with a reading of the cry of dereliction, in which Christ is really forsaken unto death, but not utterly forsaken in the sense that the Father ceases to love him, or the Trinity ceases to exist in its essential three-in-oneness. See Thomas H. McCall, *Forsaken: The Trinity and the Cross, and Why It Matters* (Downers Grove, IL: IVP Academic, 2012).
80. P. T. Forsyth, *The Work of Christ*, 2nd ed. (London: Independent Press, 1938), 150.
81. See again, McKnight, *Community Called Atonement*, 94, 97; see also my prior treatment of recapitulation as a foundation for penal substitution (ch. 3).
82. See also Michael F. Bird, *Romans*, The Story of God Bible Commentary (Grand Rapids: Zondervan, 2016), 261.

righteousness, because in his forbearance he had left the sins committed beforehand unpunished—he did it to demonstrate his righteousness at the present time, so as to be just and the one who justifies those who have faith in Jesus.

While I have no time to descend the rabbit hole of arguments that threaten to engulf this passage (propitiation, expiation, mercy seat, passive or active wrath, etc.), a few points must be noted since they accord well with my conclusions on the other passages.

First, by juxtaposing the "unpunished," or "passed over" (*paresin*), sins of the past with the shedding of Christ's blood on the cross, it is natural to adopt a reading of Christ's sacrifice that includes the idea of divine judgment poured out on human sin. If what was previously "passed over" was punishment,[83] then it would stand to reason that this penal judgment was not bypassed but "poured out" at the cross. For this reason, God is both just and the one who justifies the ungodly (Rom 4:5). This idea fits perfectly with Paul's later point that God condemned sin in the flesh of Christ (Rom 8:3). Likewise, in Romans 3, penal imagery coexists alongside sacrificial imagery, just as it does in Isaiah 53 and in covenant-ratifying ceremonies like Genesis 15. Not all sacrifices carried penal connotations, but some did. And a case can be made that Romans 3 fits in the latter category.[84]

Second, in light of similar passages from the Maccabean martyr literature, there is precedent for good Jews to connect the death of a righteous human to the propitiation of divine wrath and the cessation of divine judgment upon the nation. In 4 Maccabees 6:28–29, a Jewish martyr prays for God to "be merciful to your people and let our punishment suffice for [*huper*] them. Make my blood their purification, and take my life in exchange for theirs" (RSV). Here, too, the punishment of the righteous (at the hands of pagan soldiers) is seen through a sacrificial lens as the hoped-for means by which the nation may go free.

Likewise, in 2 Maccabees 6–7, a book likely written not long before the time of Jesus, one finds an Israelite praying not only for a future resurrection, but that the suffering of he and his fellow martyrs might have the result of dealing with Israel's sins in the present so that God's people might receive mercy in the future (6:12–17). In the following chapter, the prayer

83. See James D. G. Dunn, *Romans 1—8*, WBC (Waco, TX: Word, 1988), 173.

84. See also Ben Witherington, "The Death of Sin in the Death of Jesus: NT Atonement Theology," *Wesleyan Theological Journal* 50, no. 1 (Spring, 2015): 12–14; see also Bird, *Romans*, 117–19.

is that the martyrs' horrific deaths might "bring to an end the wrath of the Almighty that has justly fallen on our whole nation" (7:38). Of course, the great difference between these texts and those of Paul (e.g., Rom 3) is Paul's shocking claim that God presented Christ as this sort of a saving sacrifice, despite the fact that Christ had never sinned (2 Cor 5:21). There is not only divine sanction but divine initiative. God is not "made loving" by the cross; instead, he is Love, for if he were not, the incarnation would never have happened. This holy love therefore stands behind the biblical logic of penal substitution and vicarious judgment.

| CONCLUSION |

While more biblical passages could indeed be cited, these case studies have been sufficient to demonstrate that the logic of "mere penal substitution" is present within the canon of Scripture. This is not to say, however, that every version of penal substitution is "biblical." I have attempted to demonstrate that a blanket dismissal of the model on the grounds of biblical evidence has been weighed and found wanting. Thus, with a treatment of the canon now concluded, I must turn next to address some other critiques of penal substitution under the headings of divine *character* and contemporary *culture*.

CHAPTER 6

RIGHT BUT REPULSIVE?

FURTHER CRITIQUES OF PENAL SUBSTITUTION

The Bible is the ultimate proving ground for Christian doctrine, but it is not the only one. Scripture may be misread. One way of testing an interpretation is to ask what it entails for the character of God. If the exegesis provides a deity whose nature is something other than holy love, then there is reason to examine it more closely. Likewise, if a construal of the cross is not "good news," then one may also ask some questions about that telling of the story. For Stephen Holmes, the designation "right but repulsive!" has been a constant danger for evangelical theology.[1] And if a doctrine is repulsive enough, perhaps it is not right. At least that is what many seem to think of penal substitution. In the view of Fleming Rutledge, "It is not an exaggeration to say that in some circles there has been something resembling a campaign of intimidation, so that those who cherish the idea that Jesus offered himself in our place have been made to feel that they are neo-Crusaders, prone to violence, oppressors of women and enablers of child abuse."[2]

In the present chapter, I will move beyond the (1) biblical critiques of penal substitution (ch. 5) to several criticisms regarding (2) divine character and (3) contemporary culture. As before, I will claim that even though the

---

1. Stephen Holmes, *The Wondrous Cross: Atonement and Penal Substitution in the Bible and History* (London: Paternoster, 2007), 10. As Holmes notes, the phrase was first used by W. C. Sellar and R. J. Yeatman to describe the followers of Oliver Cromwell.
2. Fleming Rutledge, *The Crucifixion: Understanding the Death of Jesus Christ* (Grand Rapids: Eerdmans, 2015), 464.

charges against penal substitution are serious, they do not invalidate the model when it is properly understood. Hence the treatments of divine character and contemporary culture will bolster my prior case from Scripture. The aim, however, is not to provide a comprehensive defense of penal substitution but to answer some of the most prominent charges before integrating the model into a larger mosaic of atonement.

| CRITIQUES OF CHARACTER |

"What is God like?" is perhaps the most basic question in all theology. In the New Testament, one answer is clear: God is Christlike. To cite the book of Hebrews, "The Son is the radiance of God's glory and the exact representation of his being" (1:3). Christ is "the image of the invisible God" (Col 1:15; cf. 2 Cor 4:4). In light of these biblical statements, some reject penal substitution because it purportedly distorts the divine character as witnessed in Christ.

According to these critics, penal substitution distorts the divine character by allowing the perceived necessity of wrathful retribution to trump God's freedom to show mercy. To quote Paul Fiddes, "A law [of necessary punishment] is set above the character of God" so that penal substitution "requires God to act in a way which is confined by legal restraints." In this way, "It does not allow God the freedom to exercise a justice of another kind, a justice which certainly requires a penalty to fall upon rebellious creatures while they are in the state of rebellion, but which is satisfied when they repent and return to him."[3] Ultimately, "Penal substitution fails to unify the love of God with his wrath."[4]

Does the Prodigal Son Discredit Penal Substitution?

Each of the above contentions must be addressed in turn, I will begin by looking at a biblical story that both Fiddes and others cite as evidence: the parable of the prodigal son (Luke 15:11–32).[5] In this tale, the father is fully satisfied by the mere return of his child "and refuses to accept that there is any debt outstanding against him." The parable then portrays the elder brother as the one who insists on a rigid rule of retribution,[6] and

---

3. Paul Fiddes, *Past Event and Present Salvation: The Christian Idea of Atonement* (Louisville: Westminster John Knox, 1989), 101.
4. Fiddes, *Past Event*, 103.
5. In addition to Fiddes, see Mark Baker and Joel Green, *Recovering the Scandal of the Cross: Atonement in New Testament*, 2nd ed. (Downers Grove, IL: IVP Academic, 2011), 174.
6. Fiddes, *Past Event*, 101.

the father, in his extravagant love, dismisses the idea.[7] All this is seen as countering the notion that a penalty for sin must be given in order for humanity to be reconciled to God.

What then might the parable look like through the lens of penal substitution? Robin Collins offers a creative (and satirical) retelling. In his account, the father cannot merely forgive the returning son, for "it would be against the moral order of the entire universe." "Such is the severity of my justice that reconciliation will not be made unless the penalty is utterly paid. My wrath—my avenging justice—must be placated." The elder brother then speaks up with an unexpected offer to endure the required punishment: "Let me work extra in the field on his behalf and thereby placate your wrath." Finally, "when the elder brother died of exhaustion, the father's wrath was placated against his younger son and they lived happily for the remainder of their days."[8]

The retelling is clever, but is it really damning to penal substitution? One problem with the argument of Fiddes and Collins is the attempt to make the parable address something that it was never intended to explain—namely, how (specifically) atonement happens. In Luke's account, the story is the third in a series of parables (the lost sheep, the lost coin, the lost son), all of which illustrate that God delights in restoring lost people to himself. This is why Jesus "welcomes sinners and eats with them" (Luke 15:2). His heart is a perfect reflection of the Father, who "so loved the world that he gave his one and only son" (John 3:16).

No thoughtful account of penal substitution would deny this notion. But rejecting the necessity of Christ's vicarious sacrifice just because it isn't mentioned in the parable is both an argument from silence and a rather obvious example of decontextualization. The tendency to overread the parables has always been there,[9] yet the error becomes more apparent as we look to other examples. Take, for instance, the parable of the rich man and Lazarus (Luke 16). Just as the purpose of this story is not to provide a detailed geography of hell—complete with a broad chasm and the ability to send unfilled drink orders (v. 24)—so too the tale of the prodigal son is not meant to give a detailed map of atonement doctrine. The latter story is

---

7. For a winsome retrieval of the original meaning of *prodigal* (recklessly extravagant), see Timothy Keller, *The Prodigal God: Recovering the Heart of the Christian Faith* (New York: Riverhead, 2008).

8. Robin Collins, "Understanding Atonement: A New and Orthodox Theory," 1995, http://home.messiah.edu/~rcollins/Philosophical%20Theology/Atonement/AT7.HTM.

9. E.g., the patristic slant toward hyper allegory.

about a more basic reality: God delights in welcoming repentant sinners, and he calls "elder brothers" to join the celebration.

Still, as some may object, forgiveness does come in the parable apart from any obvious penalty. Thus if one must account for the absence—a move that I have already acknowledged as highly suspect—the question still remains: How might penal substitution answer? One option would be to acknowledge that a penalty of sorts appears in the story. As would be obvious to early hearers, the father *himself* absorbs a massive loss of property and honor in forgiving the son. Indeed, this kind of forgiveness is always costly.[10] As H. R. Mackintosh notes, it is a "shattering experience" in which the forgiver must "set out on voyages of anguish."[11] For example, consider grieving parents who choose (incredibly) to visit the prison and forgive their child's murderer. Acts of love like this set aside the desire for outward retribution, wage peaceful war against vengeance, and absorb what must feel like a kind of penalty.[12] So too in Christ's parable of the prodigal son. In both the parable and in penal substitution in general, God absorbs the blow.[13]

Is Necessary Punishment Placed Above Divine Freedom?

Now for Fiddes's next contention. The claim here is that penal substitution places a law of necessary punishment *above* God so that God cannot forgive apart from retribution. This allegedly violates both divine power and divine freedom. Many discussions turn at this point to some version of the Euthyphro dilemma.[14] Yet another route to answering the charge

---

10. For I. Howard Marshall, forgiveness "involves some kind of cost borne by the forgiver." Marshall, *Aspects of the Atonement: Cross and Resurrection in the Reconciling of God and Humanity* (London: Paternoster, 2007), 50.

11. H. R. Mackintosh, *The Christian Experience of Forgiveness* (Welwyn: Nisbet, 1927), 191, 211. Cited in Fiddes, *Past Event*, 173, 175.

12. I say, "a *kind* of penalty," because it should be obvious that these examples differ from a judicially imposed penalty from without (see ch. 5). Still, in speaking of atonement in general one must also admit that even the judicial metaphors are used analogically to those of human courtrooms.

13. Christina Baxter explains this idea: "Penal ideas can be understood either actively or passively. If I have been offended, I can either be an actor who initiates revenge or I can choose to bear the penalty myself so that it becomes my passion. The penal substitutionary theory of the atonement is not saying that God the Father is an actor who initiates revenge against Jesus his Son, because he does not want to initiate revenge against the true perpetrators. It is saying that God has chosen to carry the penalty himself so that it becomes his passion." Christina Baxter, "The Cursed Beloved: A Reconsideration of Penal Substitution," in *Atonement Today: A Symposium at St John's College, Nottingham*, ed. John Goldingay (London: SPCK, 1995), 72.

14. In Plato's *Euthyphro*, Socrates asks: "Is the pious loved by the gods because it is pious, or is it pious because it is loved by the gods?" In Christian theology, the question often turns on whether God commands and does things *because they are right* (which would seem to

has already been touched upon; it involves the nature of the covenant relationship.[15]

In the covenant, God links himself to a people in "a binding relationship based on obligations and sealed with an oath that makes two parties as close as family."[16] Here the legal and the familial-relational components of atonement (so often set at odds) are unified into a seamless garment called covenant. One need not choose between them. And as the above definition makes clear, the covenant involves obligations, with ensuing curses if the terms are broken.[17] With this in mind, one can now answer Fiddes's critique.

When the divine Son takes the curses (or penalties) of the covenant upon himself, it is not that a law is placed above the free character of God. Rather, it is the holy character of God that established the law in the first place. No external necessity forced God to enter into such a union. And no exterior force arranged this "marriage" against his will. In total freedom and in continuity with his character, Yahweh made a covenant in which these curses—like exile, and that final exile, death—would be binding. And because Yahweh is righteous, he keeps his covenant, even at great cost. In the words of 2 Timothy: "If we are faithless, he remains faithful, for he cannot disown himself" (2:13).

In light of this covenantal reality, it is simply false to claim that penal substitution does away with God's ontological freedom by making him subservient to a law of necessary punishment. As Barth noted, God is "the one who loves in freedom,"[18] and he is not constrained by anything apart from his nature and decision.[19] If there are limits to God's freedom, they are self-imposed within the covenant, on the basis of his sovereign choice and holy love.

---

place a law above God), or whether "the right" is simply right because God does it (which would seem to make morality arbitrary).

15. See Jeremy Treat, "Atonement and Covenant: Binding Together Aspects of Christ's Work," in *Locating Atonement: Explorations in Constructive Dogmatics*, ed. Oliver Crisp and Fred Sanders (Grand Rapids: Zondervan, 2015). I have dealt with this theme already in chs. 3 and 4.

16. Treat, "Atonement and Covenant," 103.

17. See, again, Scott J. Hafemann, "The Covenant Relationship," in *Central Themes in Biblical Theology: Mapping Unity in Diversity*, ed. Scott J. Hafemann and Paul R. House (Grand Rapids: Baker Academic, 2007), 35.

18. *CD* II/1, 306.

19. Ironically, a full-throated affirmation of this very point comes in a later portion of Fiddes, *Past Event*, 158–60. Here, Fiddes is critiquing views of divine impassibility, yet he seems not to have recognized that the same logic could be used against his prior critique of penal substitution (101).

Does Penal Substitution Fail to Unify God's Wrath and Mercy?

This brings me back at last to the overarching question regarding wrath and mercy. Does penal substitution fail to unify these attributes? As seen previously, divine wrath has long been controversial.[20] For some classical thinkers, the notion rubbed against divine impassibility,[21] while for some moderns it seems too close to hatred for comfort. In either case, divine anger must be explained away either as an unbridled anthropomorphism or as an impersonal process of cause and effect.[22] Regardless of the motivation, the result is much the same: God's active wrath is relativized, and in both cases the argument founders like a ship on the rocky crags of the biblical narrative.

In the Bible, one meets a personal God who acts powerfully to judge and save. And while passages from both Testaments could be multiplied to illustrate the point, the exercise is largely unnecessary. No side denies that Scripture *portrays* God as actively bringing wrathful judgment.[23] The question is what to do with these texts. The most profitable path begins with the notion that divine wrath is merely the outflow of God's holy love and a consequence of his opposition to the evil that afflicts his beloved creation.[24] In this way, divine wrath is simply what happens when holy love goes toe-to-toe with evil and refuses to slink backward into apathy.[25] The biblical God slinks nowhere.

At the same time, divine wrath is clearly not synonymous with human anger. The two are only analogically related. Because humans fall short of God's perfection, when we respond to evil, we do so with imperfect understanding and with a love that is tainted by less holy motives. Hence the concerns of anthropomorphism are not entirely ill-placed. Still, human abuse does not disprove the divine archetype. A nonwrathful God would be indifferent to the plight of the oppressed and to the sheer destructiveness of sin. In the words of the Catholic theologian Hans Urs von Balthasar (1905–88),

---

20. See my prior treatment of C. H. Dodd's position in ch. 4.

21. Lactantius (ca. 250–ca. 325) records this as an objection of certain Stoic and Epicurean thinkers. See *A Treatise on the Anger of God* in ANF 7:259.

22. In both cases, Dodd's voice bulks large. See Yang and Davis, "Atonement and the Wrath of God," in Crisp and Sanders, *Locating Atonement*, 156–57.

23. Hans Urs von Balthasar does a good job of surveying the biblical support for this reality. See *Theo-Drama: Theological Dramatic Theory*, vol. 4, *The Action*, trans. Graham Harrison (San Francisco: Ignatius, 1994), 338–51.

24. See the admirable argument by Tony Lane, "The Wrath of God as an Aspect of the Love of God," in *Nothing Greater, Nothing Better: Theological Essays on the Love of God*, ed. Kevin Vanhoozer (Cambridge: Eerdmans, 2001).

25. This should not be taken as implying that wrath is at odds with forgiveness. It is perfectly possible for a being to be angry over sin and forgiving toward it. More on this momentarily.

A God who only loved and did not hate evil . . . would contradict himself. . . . In such a case, we would not owe him reverence. . . . Furthermore, it is impossible for God to announce to the world a law or reward for the good and punishment for evil and then let this law operate so to speak without his own active participation. Having established the world order, he cannot renounce his freedom nor retire from his obligation to punish and forgive.[26]

To be faithful to the covenant, evil must be dealt with. And because God is just and loving, evil arouses divine anger, not as an uncontrolled emotional explosion but as a consistent outflow of God's holy love.[27] For such reasons, wrath and mercy are not contradictory in a proper account of penal substitution, or anywhere else for that matter.

Does Punishment Preclude Forgiveness?

Others contend, however, that there is a logical problem with the simultaneous existence of Christ's penalty-bearing and divine forgiveness. If the price for sin is *paid* at the cross, can we really say that God *forgave* it? Theologian Gregory Boyd (b. 1957), for example, raises this objection.[28] For Boyd, "If God must always get what is coming to him in order to forgive (namely, 'a kill'), does God ever really forgive?"[29] After all, "If you owe me a hundred dollars and I hold you to it unless someone or other pays me the owed sum, did I really forgive your debt? Yes, you got off the hook. But forgiveness is about releasing a debt—not collecting it from someone else."[30] What should be said in response?

For starters, the Scriptures are crystal clear that God is a forgiver.[31]

---

26. Balthasar, *Theo-Drama*, 4:339.

27. See also the conclusion of N. T. Wright, "Romans," in *New Interpreter's Bible*, ed. L. E. Keck et al. (Nashville: Abingdon, 2002): "The creator is neither a tyrannical despot nor an indulgent, *laissez-faire* absentee landlord. . . . This God has a passionate concern for the creation and humans in particular, that will tolerate nothing less than the best for them. The result is 'wrath'—not just a settled attitude of hostility toward idolatry and immorality, but actions that follow from such an attitude when the one to whom it belongs is the sovereign creator" (431).

28. Alongside Boyd, see Eleonore Stump, "Atonement According to Aquinas," in *Philosophy and the Christian Faith*, ed. Thomas V. Morris (Notre Dame, IN: University of Notre Dame Press, 1988), 62.

29. Gregory Boyd, "Christus Victor Response," in *The Nature of the Atonement: Four Views*, ed. James Beilby and Paul R. Eddy (Downers Grove, IL: IVP Academic, 2006), 104.

30. Gregory Boyd, "The Danger of the Penal Substitution View of Atonement," ReKnew, November 20, 2014, http://reknew.org/2014/11/the-danger-of-the-penal-substitution-view-of -atonement/.

31. A few examples: In the Old Testament, Daniel proclaims: "To the Lord our God belong mercy and forgiveness . . ." (9:9). Likewise, Psalm 130 exults in the fact that "If you, Lord,

Boyd's critique therefore involves the meaning of divine forgiveness rather than its presence. The issue is as follows: Does the forgiveness of an offender necessitate that no punishment may be handed down for the offense? Clearly, it does not. Because Boyd's case proceeds by analogy, so too will my response. Consider again the example of the grieving parents who chose to forgive their child's murderer.[32] Their stunning act of forgiveness by no means implies that all penalties must be waived. Indeed, no thoughtful person would respond to the parents' gracious action by proclaiming: "Well, that's very nice, but it's *not* forgiveness because the criminal is still in jail." Forgiveness is not antithetical to legal consequences.[33]

In the biblical examples, Israel's forgiveness often comes after or alongside the enactment of certain penalties, such as exile or the deaths of certain perpetrators. Here, too, forgiveness need not imply a total lack of punishment. Often, as with Christ, forgiveness comes through the shedding of blood (Matt 26:28; Eph 1:7), for this has been woven into the covenant relationship. Boyd's claim misunderstands both the meaning of forgiveness in our contemporary setting (e.g., the example of the parents) and the meaning of forgiveness within the biblical and covenantal narrative.

Forgiveness Prior to the New Covenant

If one accepts my argument, a further question emerges with regard to atonement: How did God forgive before the cross? A careful account of penal substitution should acknowledge that Christ's work is retroactive in its scope. The redemptive shadow of the cross spreads backward over human history, as well as forward. Since this is true, any full and final reconciliation with God is possible only by the atoning work of Jesus.

Something like this logic shows forth in the way Paul deals with the forgiven sins of the past centuries. How, for instance, was David forgiven for his horrific crimes (e.g., Ps 51)? Paul's answer centers on the blood of Jesus. Speaking of the sins that were forgiven before the time of Christ,

---

kept a record of sins . . . who could stand? But with you there is forgiveness" (vv. 3–4a). The New Testament is equally clear. As 1 John states: "If we confess our sins, he is faithful and just to forgive us our sins and to cleanse us from all unrighteousness" (1:9). And as Christ says at the Last Supper: "This is my blood of the covenant, which is poured out for many for the *forgiveness* of sins" (Matt 26:28, italics added).

32. The repetition of this example from the prior discussion of the prodigal son is fitting in that Boyd too cites the parable as proof in his argument. See Boyd, "Christus Victor Response," 104.

33. Of course, the conclusion rests largely on the type of analogy that is chosen. By choosing the metaphor of a parking ticket (a civil offense), forgiveness and payment seem antithetical. But other cases are quite different. In dealing with an execution, one is clearly dealing with a criminal matter, not something as frivolous as a parking ticket.

Paul writes that "in his forbearance [God] had left the sins committed beforehand unpunished"; now, God's righteousness, which presumably includes the bearing of the covenantal curses, has been demonstrated in the sacrificial shedding of Christ's blood (Rom 3:25).

One reason that the Father can freely and justly welcome repentant sinners in any era is because the covenantal curse for sin has been borne. Indeed, according to several translations of Revelation 13:8, it was borne "from the creation of the world."[34] A cross-shaped shadow touches every moment of human history. For this reason, King David is forgiven freely, as we all may be, by the blood of Christ. In the end, it is not that the Father must vent sadistic wrath in order to forgive. Instead, in order for the covenant to be upheld, the curse must be borne. The claim of penal substitution is therefore that God—the one God—in his unfathomable mercy chose to take the penalty upon himself.

The Trinity as Hinge-Point

With reference to the one God, I must now address a further set of criticisms: the Trinitarian ones. I do so now because the Trinity also involves the character (or nature) of God. Yet, in a twist, the Trinity also forms a kind of "hinge-point" as I move next to address some critiques from contemporary culture. Why is this? Some might argue that few things seem less relevant to modern society than words like *ousia*, *hypostasis*, and *perichoresis*. Still the fact remains that many of the cultural critiques of penal substitution arise from issues in Trinitarian theology.

First, take the rather tired meme that penal substitution is "divine child abuse." The analogy is meant to resonate with the concerns of a culture that (rightly) finds abuse abhorrent. This point is made more pressing as we have recently been confronted with numerous horrific examples in which abusive behavior has been swept under the rug, even by religious leaders. Yet the image of divine child abuse in atonement doctrine only makes sense if one operates under a view of God that is both subordinationist and tritheistic. These are Trinitarian errors. In the penal substitutionary caricature, the Father becomes the "big god" who tortures a helpless son in a scene akin to Greek mythology. The doctrine of the Trinity forbids this portrait, not merely on the grounds of divine love but because, as Augustine taught,

---

34. The NIV's translation is somewhat disputed because the phrase "from the creation of the world" can modify either "the Lamb who was slain" or those "whose names have been written in the book of life" (Rev 13:8). Thankfully, as Paul demonstrates in Rom 3:25, the retroactive power of the cross does not hang on this verse alone.

the outward acts of the Trinity are undivided.[35] The Father, Son, and Spirit *always* act together and in harmony.

Second, on the other side of triune error is the tilt toward modalism. In close proximity to this imbalance, some have critiqued penal substitution for (allegedly) claiming that one member of the Godhead *could* act upon another as a subject to an object. Along these lines, Joel Green and Mark Baker claim that "any atonement theology that assumes . . . that in the cross God did something 'to' Jesus is . . . an affront to the Christian doctrine of the triune God."[36] Similarly, Tom Smail asks what it could even mean to say that God propitiated himself: "Can the verb really have the same person for its subject and object and still retain its meaning?"[37] In fairness, both claims are attempting to deny that the cross presents us with one member of the Trinity actively torturing another. Quite right.

The problem with such claims, however, is the modalist-leaning assumption that one member of the Trinity cannot act upon (or toward) another as a subject to an object. This is clearly false. Scripture gives many examples to the contrary (e.g., the Father "loves the Son [John 3:35]; the Father "sent the Son" [John 3:17]).[38] Regarding the cross in particular, consider Isaiah 53:6: "The LORD has laid on him the iniquity of us all." If one reads the passage christologically, then the LORD is clearly doing something "to" the Son. While one should accept a certain degree of metaphorical distance in this statement (the Father is not literally heaving a parcel labeled "human sin" upon the Son's back), it is by no means obvious that the laying of iniquity upon Christ violates the doctrine of the Trinity any more than the Father loving the Son.

In response to Smail's point, if the Father, Son, and Spirit are distinct *hypostases*, then there is nothing un-Trinitarian in the idea that Christ's action on the cross might deal with the divine wrath toward sinners. In speaking of God, we are not dealing with a solitary monad any more than we are dealing with three atomistic *individuals* who may be set at odds. In the words of Garry Williams, "The logical implication of the denial that one person of the Trinity can act on another is the denial of

---

35. See Augustine, *De Trinitate*, 1.7. See also Adonis Vidu, "The Place of the Cross Among the Inseparable Operations of the Trinity," in Crisp and Sanders, *Locating Atonement*, ch. 1.

36. Green and Baker, *Recovering the Scandal*, 83.

37. Tom Smail, *Once and for All: A Confession of the Cross* (London: Darton, Longman & Todd, 1998), 87.

38. See Garry Williams, "Penal Substitution: A Response to Recent Criticisms," in *The Atonement Debate: Papers from the London Symposium on the Theology of Atonement*, ed. Derek Tidball, David Hilborn, and Justin Thacker (Grand Rapids: Zondervan, 2008), 179.

the distinction between them—namely, modalism."[39] Here again, at the hinge-point between the critiques of divine character and contemporary culture, is the Trinity.

| CULTURAL CRITIQUES |

With Trinitarian theology now in place as a hinge-point between the two halves of this chapter, I turn next to some critiques from the contemporary culture.[40] The first batch of cultural allegations involves the claim that penal substitution is actually dangerous to society at large. The charge is that it causes not just logical or theological inconsistences but actual pain, injustice, and violence in our world.

Although it emerged from the ranks of feminist theology,[41] this allegation soon spread to other quarters. Its basic claims are threefold: First, penal substitution serves to justify violence (or "the myth of redemptive violence"[42]) since God apparently orchestrated this sadomasochistic means of redemption. Second, the model tacitly encourages the victims of violence to continue suffering in silence, just as Jesus was oppressed and "opened not his mouth" (Isa 53:7 KJV; cf. Acts 8:52). And third, penal substitution sounds dangerously close to a form of "divine child abuse" by which a father vents wrath upon an innocent son.[43]

The Myth of Redemptive Violence

I begin with the desire for a "nonviolent atonement."[44] On the surface, this hope sounds rather odd. After all, it seems unavoidable that a crucifixion

---

39. Williams, "Penal Substitution: A Response to Recent Criticisms," 181. This is not to say that folks like Green, Baker, and Smail are de facto modalists; indeed, they are not. The problem is rather a failure to recognize consistently what Trinitarian dogma does and does not preclude when it comes to atonement theology.

40. To be clear, this shift in emphasis should not be taken as leaving behind my prior concerns, whether with the canon (ch. 5), the divine character, or the Trinitarian doctrines. All of these issues remain inextricably intertwined.

41. See Rita Nakashima Brock, "And a Little Child Will Lead Us: Christology and Child Abuse," in *Christianity, Patriarchy, and Abuse: A Feminist Critique*, ed. Joanne Carlson Brown and Carole R. Bohn (New York: Pilgrim, 1989); Beverly W. Harrison and Carter Heyward, "Pain and Pleasure: Avoiding the Confusions of Christian Tradition in Feminist Theory," in *Christianity, Patriarchy, and Abuse*; and Joanne Carlson Brown and Rebecca Parker, "For God So Loved the World?," in *Christianity, Patriarchy, and Abuse*. For a related, though slightly more nuanced approach from a feminist perspective, see Darby Kathleen Ray, *Deceiving the Devil: Atonement, Abuse, and Ransom* (Cleveland: Pilgrim, 1998).

42. A phrase coined by Walter Wink, with inspiration from René Girard.

43. See also Holmes, *The Wondrous Cross*, 107–8.

44. See, for instance, the use of this phrase in J. Denny Weaver, *The Nonviolent Atonement* (Grand Rapids: Eerdmans, 2001).

is an act of violence. All accounts of the atonement involve an execution, a tortured savior, and a healing that comes by wounds (1 Pet 2:24; cf. Isa 53:5). What proponents of a nonviolent atonement object to is the idea that God would sanction or demand the punishment of the cross as a way of dealing with the penalty for sin. Their charge is that violence *never* remedies violence and that retribution "begets the very thing it seeks to destroy."[45] The result is merely an endless feedback loop of bloodshed.[46]

In later chapters, I will examine the seminal works of René Girard and Walter Wink, which often stand behind this conversation. For both, the violence of the cross (and of other religious systems) comes entirely from the human side of the equation. God does not endorse it. He works to end it. What the cross reveals, therefore, is God unmasking the myth of redemptive bloodshed for what it truly is: demonic.[47] In due time, I will argue that there are some helpful insights in the arguments of both Girard and Wink, alongside serious problems. For now, I will deal only with "the myth of redemptive violence" as it pertains to penal substitution.

In response to this charge, a first observation is that other models of atonement are hardly left untouched by the claim that violence cannot be enacted to achieve redemptive outcomes. For example, if one accepts the Abelardian idea that the cross is ordained by God as a powerful demonstration of divine love, violence is again being used to bring about a good result—namely, the enflaming of our hearts to love God in return. Similar things could be said about many traditional *Christus Victor* viewpoints. Here, too, God conquers death by arranging and suffering a violent death.[48] So the supposed problem with the myth of redemptive violence is not unique to penal substitution.

Second, the presuppositions behind the myth of redemptive violence often proceed under some previously discounted assumptions regarding the passive nature of divine wrath, punishment, and covenantal justice. Here, God is never seen as actively or violently punishing sin, which, as I have shown, runs counter to the biblical narrative at many points. Indeed, in the famous argument of Miroslav Volf, the very practice of Christian

---

45. Steve Chalke and Alan Mann, *The Lost Message of Jesus* (Grand Rapids: Zondervan, 2003), 129.

46. See Walter Wink, *Engaging the Powers: Discernment and Resistance in a World of Domination* (Minneapolis: Fortress, 1992).

47. See René Girard, *Things Hidden since the Foundation of the World*, trans. Stephen Bann and Michael Metteer (Stanford: Stanford University Press, 1987); and Girard, *Violence and the Sacred* (Baltimore: Johns Hopkins University Press, 1986).

48. See again Myers, "The Patristic Atonement Model," in Crisp and Sanders, *Locating Atonement*, ch. 3.

nonviolence in the present may require a belief in divine vengeance in the future. For Volf, "It takes the quiet of a suburban home for the birth of the thesis that human nonviolence corresponds to God's refusal to judge. In a scorched land, soaked in the blood of the innocent, it will invariably die. And as one watches it die, one will do well to reflect about many other pleasant captivities of the liberal mind."[49]

Of course, none of this discounts the obvious truth that *human* violence often spirals in compounding ways. In this regard, the myth of redemptive violence stands on solid—blood-soaked—ground. Still, this human reality cannot be used as proof against the divine decision to punish sin (whether on the cross or elsewhere).[50] Finally, in what may be the most heralded recent study on violence and atonement doctrine, Hans Boersma argues that "all acts of hospitality in history" require "some degree of violence."[51] This is so, says Boersma, because "hospitality is an art that is impossible to practice when we refuse to challenge evil."[52] In the same way, "God's hospitality on the cross implies . . . redemptive violence," even while the true scandal resides in the fact that God takes such violence upon himself. For all these reasons, the myth of redemptive violence is exactly that—a myth—when it comes to the cross. It is not a persuasive refutation of penal substitution.

A Catalyst for Abuse?

What of the charge that penal substitution catalyzes further abusive relations by idealizing the passive victim who opens not her mouth (cf. Isa 53:7 KJV)? Emerging from feminist and liberation theologies, these claims have often been couched in inflammatory terms. For Beverly Harrison and Carter Heyward, penal substitution presents a kind of "sadomasochism" in which the Father willfully inflicts punishment and the Son masochistically accepts it.[53] Likewise, for Darby Kathleen Ray, penal substitution and several other models have "deadly consequences" in that they "feed the

49. Miroslav Volf, *Exclusion and Embrace: A Theological Exploration of Identity, Otherness, and Reconciliation* (Nashville: Abingdon, 1996), 304.

50. On "the inadequate idea of sin" that lies behind many such critiques, see Holmes, *The Wondrous Cross*, 108.

51. Hans Boersma, *Violence, Hospitality, and the Cross: Reappropriating the Atonement Tradition* (Grand Rapids: Baker Academic, 2004), 257. Unfortunately, Boersma's definition of "violence" includes far more than acts causing physical injury to another (44–45). Personally speaking, I find this ever-expanding definition of the term unhelpful, not least because of how "violence" can then be used to describe any words or actions with which one disagrees.

52. Boersma, *Violence, Hospitality, and the Cross*, 35.

53. Harrison and Heyward, "Pain and Pleasure," 153.

violence of the few and the passivity of the many."[54] By this, she means that "romantic visions of a martyred Savior function . . . to keep victims of abuse in their death-dealing situations."[55] Finally, Paul Fiddes joins the chorus by claiming that "if the Father is envisaged as requiring the death of Christ as a reparation for his offended justice, the cross will only legitimize other patterns of oppression in our world."[56]

Once again, it is important to note that these claims do not strike merely at penal substitution. In particular, Ray singles out versions of the moral influence and *Christus Victor* motifs as providing justification for the silent suffering of victims (moral influence) and the triumphal conquest of powerful (*Christus Victor*). And for Joanne Carlson Brown, "Christianity" itself "is an abusive theology that glorifies suffering." Thus "we must do away with the atonement."[57] Given the sweeping nature of such charges, Stephen Holmes seems right to note that if these arguments work, "this particular bomb is powerful enough to destroy the whole building, not just the one room we don't like."[58] What then is the best response?

A first observation involves the tendency of these critics to deal in inflated language and in caricatures devoid of source citation. Indeed, in many cases, it seems to be assumed that extreme rhetoric can take the place of careful research. And often, the charges cite no examples whatsoever of theologians claiming things that sound like sadomasochism, divine child abuse, or even the barest insinuation that victims should silently accept abuse. In place of footnotes and examples is talk about "what this kind of thinking leads to" and what is "really" going on beneath the surface of orthodox Christianity.[59] Despite the fact that abuse must *always* be brought into the light and confronted with genuine justice, my claim will now be that this blanket critique against a biblical account of penal substitution is unconvincing.[60]

---

54. Ray, *Deceiving the Devil*, 18, 88.
55. Ray, *Deceiving the Devil*, 57.
56. Fiddes, *Past Event*, 192.
57. Joanne Carlson Brown, "Divine Child Abuse," *Daughters of Sarah* 18, no. 3 (Summer 1992): 28, as cited in Richard J. Mouw, "Violence and the Atonement," *Must Christianity Be Violent: Reflections on History, Practice, and Theology*, ed. Kenneth R. Chase and Alan Jacobs (Grand Rapids: Brazos, 2003), 162.
58. Holmes, *The Wondrous Cross*, 108.
59. See Mouw's point about the "subtext" theme in such critiques, "Violence and the Atonement," 159.
60. I am indebted at this point to sentiments expressed by Rachael and Jacob Denhollander, "Justice: The Foundation of a Christian Approach to Abuse," paper presentation, Evangelical Theological Society, Denver, Colorado, November 13, 2018. In a testimony that received worldwide attention, Rachael Denhollander, JD, was the first woman to publicly accuse Michigan State gymnastics coach Larry Nassar of sexual abuse. In the previously cited paper,

An Evasive Move: "We Are Not Talking to Academics"

In response to pushback against a lack of source citation to illustrate the abusive versions of penal substitution, Mark Baker and Joel Green have been quick to clarify that they are not primarily responding to the published accounts by academic theologians. Instead, they are concerned with "the way atonement is conceived and articulated at the popular level by Sunday school teachers, Christian camp counselors, . . . and in small group Bible studies."[61] Fair enough. Indeed, as one who preaches regularly, I must admit to having sometimes expressed particular doctrines in a less-than-fully-nuanced way from the pulpit. And when it comes to "pop versions" of penal substitution, I once heard a well-educated pastor tell his congregation that the way we can know that God is not angry with us is that "he already got fully angry with Jesus on the cross." The intent was praiseworthy; the articulation was not.

Still, the problem with the evasive move by Baker and Green is that they *are* claiming that penal substitution is inherently problematic, not just prone to misconstrual.[62] Thus the attempt to avoid critique by claiming that they are only talking about "pop versions" of the doctrine does not ring true. If the test of a doctrine's truth and usefulness is that it cannot possibly be misinterpreted or misapplied from the pulpit, then no Christian truth-claim would be left standing. The doctrine of the Trinity has, for instance, often been articulated (especially by nonacademics) with analogies that imply tritheism, modalism, or plain incoherence. Yet these dangers are hardly grounds for sidelining the doctrine. Despite the attempted clarification by Green and Baker, the problems of caricature and a lack of evidence cannot be sidestepped by this particular evasive move. Now back to my prior argument on atonement and abuse.

Further Thoughts on Atonement and Abuse

A second problem in the above critiques is a tacit assumption that each Christian doctrine must do the ethical work of all the others. This is clearly nonsense. Yes, Christ willingly endured violence by his oppressors on the cross. And yes, the Bible teaches that his suffering (alongside his entire life

---

she and her husband argue that a proper account of penal substitution upholds a view of justice that is foundational for the treatment of both the victims and perpetrators of abuse.

61. Baker and Green, *Recovering the Scandal*, 46n42. This response, in the book's second edition, is given to those who leveled the above charge against the first edition.

62. See, for instance, Joel Green, "Must We Imagine the Atonement in Penal Substitutionary Terms? Questions, Caveats, and a Plea," in Tidball, Hilborn, and Thacker, *The Atonement Debate*, 153–70.

and ministry) was redemptive. Yet the Bible also repeatedly condemns the mistreatment of any creature (especially poor and vulnerable ones), even as it calls rich and powerful oppressors to account. The examples are too numerous to mention.

Likewise, whatever "submission to the ruling authorities" means for Paul (Rom 13), it clearly does not forbid Christian dissent. Nor does it undermine the wisdom of seeking safety from dangerous or abusive persons. The same Paul who wrote of God condemning sin in the flesh of Christ (Rom 8:3)—one of the clearest penal references in the canon—also fled Damascus by way of a basket to escape the harm of violent men (Acts 9:25). Later on, he employed his Roman citizenship to end a violent beating (Acts 22). So while Paul was willing to suffer violence if it were an unavoidable result of his gospel witness, he clearly did not see it as a good in itself.

Christians should gain insights from the entire narrative of Scripture rather than expecting a model of atonement to tell us everything about how to navigate a violent world. In the end, the same canon that supports a version of penal substitution, also provides numerous resources for condemning abuse, protecting victims, and bringing wrongdoers to justice.

Culturally Incomprehensible?

Not only is penal substitution said to be dangerous; it is also said to be incomprehensible in certain contexts. For Baker and Green, "penal substitution is simply unintelligible" in cultures that do not share a Western view of justice, guilt, and punishment.[63] In particular, they contend that it is meaningless in shame-based (as opposed to guilt-based) cultures. In shame-based cultures, the focus is said to be less upon the wrongful act and its required punishment, and more upon the disgrace and alienation that hang over the perpetrator. In these cultures, there is said to be a communal mindset, whereas penal substitution is "structured around individualism."[64] Given this reality, Baker and Green propose that Christians should embrace alternative depictions of the cross, since "for a huge percentage of the world's population . . . penal substitution . . . is a stumbling block to people's experiencing salvation in Jesus Christ."[65]

---

63. Baker and Green, *Recovering the Scandal*, 175.

64. Green, "Must We Imagine the Atonement in Penal Substitutionary Terms?," 164.

65. Baker and Green, *Recovering the Scandal*, 206. Eleonore Stump also critiques all "Anselmian" models of atonement (including penal substitution) for failing to deal with the problem of human shame. In Stump's view, "having an innocent person suffer the penalty or pay the debt incurred by one's own sin does not take away the shame. If anything, it seems

Paul Fiddes makes similar claims about the model's unintelligibility. In his view, Calvin could simply assume that if a law was broken, punishment must follow. Yet in many contexts, this may no longer be the case. In an increasingly "sinless" society, many people do not even think they need forgiveness. As an extreme example, a recent US presidential nominee managed to claim in one breath that he was an evangelical Christian and that he had never asked God for forgiveness. In response to similar examples of doctrinal illiteracy, Fiddes concludes that "every preacher ought to ask . . . whether a theory of penal substitution can even be understood in a society where it is no longer possible to use such words as 'Christ suffered the death penalty for us.'"[66]

Four points should be noted in response. First, as my prior survey of both Scripture and church history illustrates, the core elements of "mere penal substitution" are hardly confined to modern Western theologians sharing modern Western views of justice. They can be found not only in the ancient context of the Bible but also in a variety of patristic sources, writing from diverse locations, and long prior to modernity. Hence the idea that penal substitution requires modern Western lenses has already been disproven.[67]

Second, in light of recent research, it bears noting that a rigid and exclusive split between guilt- and shame-based cultures has also been challenged. Anthropologists today have come to reject the simplistic idea that guilt- and shame-based cultures are easily defined as exclusive and polar opposites. Stephen Holmes notes that "every culture, has shaming mechanisms and concepts of guilt, although the balance might be somewhat different in different cultures."[68] Beyond this, the old thesis that shame cultures are communal and non-Western whereas guilt cultures are the product of Western individualism has also been adjusted.[69] A more

---

to add to it." Eleonore Stump, *Atonement* (Oxford: Oxford University Press, 2018), 25. One irony in the claims of Baker, Green, and Stump is that Anselm's medieval, feudal culture was far *more* attuned to issues of honor and shame than are the cultures of the modern West. If anyone should have noticed the "shame problem" in penal satisfaction it was Anselm!

66. Fiddes, *Past Event*, 102–3. No doubt, Fiddes's point is meant specifically for cultures (like his own) in which the death penalty has been abolished. Fair enough. Yet surely twenty-first-century British citizens are quite capable of "understanding" what the death penalty *is*, even if their country no longer practices it. By this account, the cross itself (and the idea of "Christ crucified") would be completely incomprehensible in cultures that no longer practice crucifixion. With all respect to Fiddes's brilliant work, this claim fails to give the "understanding" of his compatriots enough credit.

67. See chs. 4–5.

68. Holmes, *The Wondrous Cross*, 111–12.

69. See especially McConnell, "From 'I Have Done Wrong' to 'I am Wrong,'" in Crisp and Sanders, *Locating Atonement*, 170–71. For McConnell, this simplistic typology gained traction

credible distinction now focuses on guilt as a response to "what I have done" whereas shame is a perception about "what I am" at some deep level. Of course, none of this invalidates the fact that the atonement must speak to human shame, yet it does challenge the neat assumption that penal substitution is not comprehensible in non-Western, communal, and shame-focused societies.

Third, it seems strangest of all to accuse penal substitution of only functioning within the confines of individualism. As I have shown already, individualism presents the biggest challenge to penal substitution through the idea of penal nontransference.[70] By my account, penal substitution is coherent only when one reimagines the human race as somehow mysteriously bound together as a whole. This communal state of being can then picture "the many" as being bound up *with* and *in* the one Christ, the true Adam (e.g., Col 1). In fact, this communal reimagining was part of the reason for picturing penal substitution as resting upon the incorporative presuppositions of recapitulative headship. Rigid individualism is not a prerequisite for penal substitution but its death knell.[71]

Fourth, it seems odd, and even somewhat unchristian, to sideline a particular doctrine because it presents a "stumbling block" to a given group.[72] Does not the cross itself do this (1 Cor 2:14)? Indeed, for Justin Martyr, the cross was so nonsensical and offensive in his own day that to believe it was a sign of "madness."[73] While Christians must contextualize the gospel message for every culture, the ultimate task, as Donald MacLeod states, "is not to ask what moderns are willing to believe, but what God has commanded us to say."[74] If we tailor our message to whatever a culture *already* believes, then we no longer have good news.

---

from a work by Ruth Benedict, *The Chrysanthemum and the Sword: Patterns of Japanese Culture* (1946), which, tellingly, was published despite the fact that the author had done no actual fieldwork in Japan. Since then, non-Western writers like Takeo Doi have criticized the binary typology and the rigid split between guilt and shame-based cultures as overly simplistic. See Takeo Doi, *The Anatomy of Dependence* (Tokyo: Kodansha International, 1973).

70. See ch. 3.

71. As Garry Williams notes: "the more individualistic penal substitution becomes, the less tenable it is, since it holds precisely that the guilty individual is not punished for his or her sins as an individual. Rather, corporate categories are powerfully at work in the historic doctrine of penal substitution." Williams, "Penal Substitution: A Response to Recent Criticisms," 181.

72. Indeed this reason seems almost farcical in a book entitled *Recovering the Scandal of the Cross*. Green and Baker, 206.

73. See Justin Martyr, *First Apology* 13 (ANF 1:166–67).

74. Donald MacLeod, *Christ Crucified: Understanding the Atonement* (Downers Grove, IL: IVP Academic, 2014), 109.

| CONCLUSION: HOW THEN SHALL WE PREACH? |

Having addressed several critiques regarding (1) canon, (2) divine character, and (3) contemporary culture, I now arrive at a final question to be answered as a way of gathering together all the points made thus far: How should one preach this model of atonement? It may be helpful to conclude by clarifying what version of penal substitution should be proclaimed. The critics seem correct in saying that the doctrine may be misunderstood. For this reason, I conclude the survey of critiques by setting forth some brief (and by no means comprehensive) thoughts for those who do believe that this model can speak accurately of the Bible and winsomely to the culture at large.

Preach the Cross, Not Crass Analogies

As with the doctrine of the Trinity, the atonement is sometimes afflicted by the hunt for appropriate analogies. One problem here is that the thing being gestured toward is in both cases *sui generis*, and therefore any analogy from other spheres of life is bound to fail. Given this challenge, Christians should preach the cross itself rather than any of the crass analogies on offer.[75] When this is done well, the picture is that of a God who has freely chosen to take upon himself the penalty for human sin.

In eschewing crass analogies, the preacher acknowledges that some words and images are better than others. Words connote as well as denote, and teachers must be aware of the dangers. While words like *punishment*, *penalty*, and *judgment* may amount to the same thing in certain instances, they each carry connotations that may make one more helpful than another in a given context.[76] Personally, I prefer not to speak of Christ being punished in our place as it may be misunderstood along the lines of torturing an innocent victim for the sins of the guilty. Instead, it seems better to speak of God (in Christ) choosing to bear the penalty for human sin. When coupled with the incorporative imagery of humanity being bound up in and with Christ, this way of preaching the cross is far preferable to crass analogies.

---

75. One of the worst of these analogies pictures God as a railroad switchman who chooses to divert a train from crushing a crowd of people and toward a track that will result in it crushing his own son. See Baker and Green, *Recovering the Scandal*, 141. There are myriad others as well.

76. Hence, P. T. Forsyth preferred to speak of judgment rather than penalty or punishment. See Forsyth, *The Work of Christ*, 2nd ed. (London: Independent Press, 1938).

Do Not Pit the Father Against the Son

Second, several critiques of penal substitution pertain to a version of the model, either real or imagined, that appears to pit the Father (angrily) against the Son. Indeed, some well-known preachers have unfortunately used emotive language of the Father punishing the Son, which could be taken to imply as much. To take just two examples, R. C. Sproul depicts the Father as shouting "God damn you, Jesus!" over the crucifixion,[77] while Wayne Grudem writes that "Jesus became the object of [God's] intense hatred" on the cross.[78] This language may be meant to impress upon its hearers the weight of sin and the greatness of Christ's sacrifice, but it is also deeply problematic. It is supported neither by Scripture[79] nor by the deepest roots of the Calvinist tradition from whence it claims to spring.[80] It is unnecessary and prone to misconstrual. Preachers should stick closer to the Bible and to the vast majority of the Christian tradition.

To pit the Father against the Son runs afoul not only of God's loving character but also of the doctrine of the Trinity.[81] So while the Son may be seen as bearing the covenantal penalty for sin, it is important to emphasize that the Son is fully God, and the members of the Godhead always act in harmony. One way of emphasizing this reality in preaching would be to say that, in the cross, *God* graciously takes upon himself the penalty for human sin. Here, the oneness of the triune God can be a great help. For as Katherine Sonderegger notes, "Monotheism is not a shame word."[82] The Father is not punishing the Son. Rather, the Father, Son, and Spirit are working in perfect harmony to bring forth salvation.[83]

---

77. See the use of such imagery in R. C. Sproul, "The Curse Motif of the Atonement," in *Proclaiming a Cross-Centered Theology*, ed. Mark Dever, Ligon Duncan, Albert Mohler, and C. J. Mahaney (Wheaton, IL: Crossway, 2009), ch. 5.

78. Wayne Grudem, *Systematic Theology* (Grand Rapids: Zondervan, 1994), 575.

79. Alongside my treatment of the Scriptures, see Tony Lane's related critique of the exaggerated and emotion-laden language used by Jonathan Edwards in his famous sermon, "Sinners in the Hands of an Angry God." While Lane defends the concept of active divine wrath, he also chastens the exaggerated tone of Edwards (and others) on the basis of Scripture. See Lane, "The Wrath of God," 146.

80. See again Calvin's clear rejection of the idea that the Father could ever be angry with the Son in *Inst.* 16.11.

81. See again Thomas H. McCall, *Forsaken: The Trinity and the Cross, and Why It Matters* (Downers Grove, IL: IVP Academic, 2012).

82. Katherine Sonderegger, *Systematic Theology*, vol. 1, *The Doctrine of God* (Minneapolis: Fortress, 2015), xiv.

83. At this point, John Stott's classic words are still instructive: "We must not, then, speak of God punishing Jesus or of Jesus persuading God, for to do so is to set them over against each other as if they acted independently of each other or were even in conflict with each other. We must never make Christ the object of God's punishment or God the object of Christ persuasion, for both God and Christ were subjects not objects, taking the initiative together

Sin (Not the Son) Is the Focus of God's Judgment

Thirdly, it is important to see the true focus of divine punishment as being *sin* and not the Son. This point is expressed succinctly by the apostle Paul: "God condemned sin in the flesh" of the Messiah (Rom 8:3). Clearly, because Christ's flesh was one with him, Jesus experienced this act as if it was directed against his person. Yet the distinction is important to avoid the caricature of a cruel and sadistic God.[84]

I have noted previously how P. T. Forsyth made this point commendably. In his view, it was not that God merely needed a "kill," a whipping boy, or a chance to vent his wrath. Rather, human sin demanded justice—on the basis of the covenant. For this reason, Forsyth placed these creative and compelling words on the lips of Christ: "Thou art holy in all Thy judgements, even in this judgement which turns not aside even from Me, but strikes the sinful spot if even I stand on it."[85] It was not that the Father needed to punish the Son but, as Paul asserts (albeit mysteriously), that Christ was made to "be sin" (2 Cor 5:21), and sin must be dealt with according to the covenant. Sin (and not the Son) is the focus of divine wrath on the cross.

Reclaim the Covenant as Context

Other potential problems with penal substitution pertain to presuppositions regarding which legal context to assume when speaking of things like justice, law, and punishment. For some early theologians the assumptions were tied to Roman law, while for later thinkers they were (perhaps) influenced by medieval feudalism or modern Western penal codes. In light of these competing contexts, preachers would do well to reclaim the biblical context of the covenant as the crucial backdrop for understanding atonement in general and penal substitution in particular.[86]

Indeed, this covenantal context helps with a variety of questions, three of which I will briefly address here.

Question one: Why must sin be punished? Why couldn't God simply forgive it apart from any penal justice? While much could be said here, the fact

to save sinners." John R. W. Stott, *The Cross of Christ*, 20th anniv. ed. (Downers Grove, IL: IVP, 2006), 151.

84. See also N. T. Wright, *The Day the Revolution Began: Reconsidering the Meaning of Jesus's Crucifixion* (New York: HarperOne, 2016), 287.

85. Forsyth, *The Work of Christ*, 150, cited in Theng-Huat Leow, "'The Cruciality of the Cross': P. T. Forsyth's Understanding of the Atonement," *IJST* 11, no. 2 (April 2009): 196.

86. See again Treat, "Atonement and Covenant." Also Michael J. Gorman, *The Death of the Messiah and the Birth of the New Covenant: A (Not So) New Model of the Atonement* (Eugene, OR: Cascade, 2014).

is that the covenant—like virtually all covenants in the ancient world—had blessings and curses that were connected to the keeping or breaking of the vows.[87] With respect to the curses, these penalties included things like exile or that final exile, death. So even though God may be able (ontologically) to forgive apart from any punishment, the nature of the covenant clearly required penalties and blessings. And God is faithful to his covenant.[88]

Question two: How is it *just* for God to take our penalty upon himself? Here again, there may be multiple answers.[89] Yet by virtue of the self-maledictory oath of Genesis 15 (in which Yahweh passes between the sacrificial pieces), God's bearing of our curse was part of the original agreement. In passing through the pieces, God was calling down upon himself the covenantal curses if his partners should prove unfaithful.[90] This may seem strange, and indeed it is radical, but it is not "unlawful" for the simple reason that the covenant had always stipulated that God himself would bear the blow for the unfaithfulness of his people. The arrangement therefore proclaims sin's frightful seriousness without nullifying either divine love or divine justice.

Question three: How can we hold together the legal and relational aspects of atonement? After all, the Bible uses both forensic and familial language for redemption. In the history of the doctrine, these two spheres have often been pitted against each other, with some theologians favoring metaphors of relational union and others opting for courtroom categories. But ancient covenants never separated these two spheres. Covenants were legally binding while simultaneously establishing a family relationship, like a marriage, between the parties. At this point, the legal and relational metaphors converge and "kiss" (Ps 85:10) within the covenant. In the end, the claim here is that certain difficulties with penal substitution, as well as with other models, may be dealt with more effectively if preachers can recover the neglected context of the covenant.[91]

---

87. See also Hafemann, "The Covenant Relationship," 32–40.

88. At this point, one might ask: But why did God institute this covenant (and these curses) in the first place? Here again, many answers could be given. The curses help to educate us by teaching the seriousness of sin and the holy nature of God's character. They also serve to protect and restrain humanity, by giving further reason to avoid destructive actions. Indeed, as Marshall notes, a sign proclaiming that "trespassers will be forgiven" is less likely to be effective either as a deterrent or as a tool to train up moral citizens. Marshall, *Aspects of the Atonement*, 25.

89. In my own argument, the problem of penal nontransference must also be dealt with by recognizing the mystical union and incorporative headship between Christ (the true Adam) and humanity at large.

90. See Robert Letham, *The Work of Christ* (Downers Grove, IL: InterVarsity, 1993), 48.

91. Indeed, reclaiming the ancient Near Eastern covenantal context may also make penal

Integrate Penal Substitution with Other Models

My final exhortation serves as a bridge to the next chapter. A further way to preach penal substitution more effectively is to integrate it thoroughly with other models of atonement: the Christ-Adam imagery of recapitulation, the triumph tones of *Christus Victor*, and the compelling love language of the moral influence paradigm, among others. In so doing, one takes the load-bearing stress off a single beam that (while crucial) was never meant to support the whole weight of atonement doctrine. There are other pieces in the grand mosaic of redemption.

Proponents of penal substitution have sometimes failed at this point, giving unnecessary arguments about how penal substitution is the "primary" or most important model of atonement. Such reductionism is hardly obvious from a biblical perspective, nor is it an adequate response to the relativism that simply affirms a multiplicity of models with no logical relationship between the "pieces." This brings us to a final question: How exactly should we integrate the logic of penal substitution with the other pieces in this Christ-shaped mosaic? This is the subject of the next chapter. So with the critiques now finally addressed, I turn now to integrate the beating "heart" of penal substitution with the other pieces of this mosaic doctrine of atonement.

---

substitution more intelligible to the non-Western world, as well as grounding our atonement doctrine in the story of Israel. For Peter Leithart, what we need in careful accounts of penal substitution, are not just "appropriate cautions and qualifications," but "*context*." And as I have argued, the most important context is that of covenant. Peter Leithart, *Delivered from the Elements of the World: Atonement, Justification, Mission* (Downers Grove, IL: IVP Academic, 2016), 17, italics in original.

CHAPTER 7

THE BEATING
HEART

PENAL SUBSTITUTION AS THE HUB
(NOT THE WHOLE) OF THE ATONEMENT

Neither defensive hierarchy nor disconnected plurality but a mosaic of atonement models—this was the goal when I first introduced this account of interconnected "pieces" of atonement doctrine. With defensive hierarchy, one model is prioritized over the rest;[1] while with disconnected plurality, a variety of models are simply spread out on the table, like isolated puzzle pieces. Each one is then rightly upheld as saying something important.[2] Yet the risk in this "kaleidoscopic" view (as it is sometimes called) is that one may fail to note the specific ways in which particular models of atonement are meant to fit together, not as a puzzle in which the primary goal is to "figure it out" but as pieces in a grand mosaic, an image of the Image, for which the goal is worship.[3]

How does penal substitution (and vicarious judgment) fit within this picture?[4] I will argue that the theme of Christ's judgment in our place

---

1. A classic example of the hierarchal tendency may be found in Anselm (*Cur Deus Homo*), who, while affirming exemplarist (2.18–19) and *Christus Victor* (2.21) emphases, clearly favors the account by which the God-man satisfies the offended divine honor. Ironically, a recent counterpart to this reductionism exists in one of Anselm's strongest critics. See Eleonore Stump, *Atonement* (Oxford: Oxford University Press, 2018). Despite brilliant insights and pastoral sensitivity, Stump gives the unfortunate impression that all "theories" other than her own Thomistic one are not just incomplete but flatly wrong.
2. See Joel Green, "Kaleidoscopic View," in *The Nature of Atonement: Four Views*, ed. Beilby and Eddy (Downers Grove, IL: IVP Academic, 2006), ch. 4.
3. See Adam Johnson's claim that "properly developed theories of the atonement . . . are non-competitive and mutually reinforcing explanations" of Christ's work. Johnson, *Atonement: A Guide for the Perplexed* (London: T&T Clark, 2015), 27.
4. I say vicarious judgment *and* penal substitution because one must continually remember

forms the hub—or beating *heart*—of this mosaic Christ. Penal substitution rests upon the incorporative presuppositions of recapitulation (the Adamic *feet*), while supplying lifeblood to the outstretched *arms* (moral influence). Furthermore, as I hinted in chapter 3, Christ's sin-bearing death also supports the crowned *head* of *Christus Victor* by revealing the crucial means by which Jesus conquers. In so doing, it answers an important question that often hangs over affirmations of divine triumph—namely, how does God defeat death and Satan by way of the cross? All this will be argued below. Yet I begin with a more basic question: Why the heart?

Whatever else is involved in penal substitution, blood is central. For some, this is part of the problem. Blood is sticky and repulsive, and its flow is often accompanied by pain. Hence, the idea that God would ask for it as a means of atonement provokes unflattering adjectives. "Bloodthirsty" is one. Still, the Scriptures remain clear that the vast field of atonement doctrine is itself an *Akeldama*, a "field of blood" (to borrow a phrase from Acts 1:19). Because the creature's life is seen as being in this substance, it has been given to make atonement (Lev 17:11). And without its shedding, "there is no forgiveness" (Heb 9:22). For these reasons, the heart is a fitting image for penal substitution; it is the body's blood-sending organ, and perhaps more than any other model, the life of penal substitution is in the blood.

As seen in chapter five, the New Testament explicitly views Christ's blood as sacrificial. And I argued that there are good reasons for viewing certain sacrifices through the lens of penal substitution. Yes, the worshiper may be mystically bound up *with* the victim, but the sacrifice alone bleeds. Or in the case of the scapegoat, the victim alone embarks on the lonely path of sin-bearing exile. So too with Jesus. Given this reality, the response to the question of the old African American spiritual "Were you there when they crucified my Lord?" is both yes and no. Indeed, humans are bound up "with" and "in" Christ in a mystical union (Gal 2:20; Col 1:17). Yet to annotate Isaiah, "the punishment that brought us peace was on him," not us. And "by his wounds [not ours] we are healed" (Isa 53:5). As in the

---

that being mystically and vicariously bound up with Christ is the ground for his just action on our behalf (see ch. 3's treatment of penal nontransference). As I have argued, Christ is our substitute in terms of (1) active agency and (2) sensory experience, even while we are bound up "in" and "with" him in a spiritual sense, as the true Adam and true Israel. For ease of reference, I will not mention both of these concepts at each point along the way; but that fact should not lead the reader to believe that one is being affirmed at the expense of the other. Since part 1 of the book focused upon incorporative elements of atonement, part 2 has honed in more explicitly on substitution.

Akedah, so also on the cross. In both cases, the victim's blood stains the sacrificial wood because he is offered "instead of" (Gen 22:13) Abraham's offspring.

Yet there is another reason for choosing the heart as a mosaic metaphor. The Latin word for *heart* is *cor,* and as I will argue, the logic of penal substitution and vicarious judgment stands, in many ways, closest to the core or crux of this mosaic. It is in the middle of my Christic icon (hence "core"), and it is unrelentingly cross-focused (hence *crux*). However, do not take this as a claim that penal substitution is somehow superior. Middle does not mean "most important." Penal substitutionary logic stands only on the feet of Christ's recapitulative identity (as the true Adam),[5] and it is ultimately aimed toward the triumph of the Lamb, an event that is fully realized as the Spirit births a transformative moral influence in God's people.[6] It is the hub, but not the whole. Thus again, one must resist the urge to rank the indispensable.[7]

With these introductory points in mind, I now move to show how penal substitution is, in some ways, the missing link between the foundation of recapitulation and the result of *Christus Victor.*

| *CHRISTUS VICTOR* BY PENAL SUBSTITUTION |

In chapter 3, I gave reasons for distinguishing recapitulation—the "feet" of our mosaic Christ—from the larger family of *Christus Victor* themes (the "head"). One basis for distinction is that God's ultimate victory involves more than just a successful rerun of the Adam story. If this were not so, then it is hardly clear why the cross would be required.

---

5. See ch. 3.

6. See again Rom 16:20. Boersma hints at this relationship by saying that "salvation in Christ only overcomes the bondage of sin and violence if our lives begin to reflect the life of Jesus Christ." Hans Boersma, *Violence, Hospitality, and the Cross: Reappropriating the Atonement Tradition* (Grand Rapids: Baker Academic, 2004), 116. The precise relation between moral influence and the final victory of God will be detailed in part 4 of this book.

7. In my view, this tendency to rank the models is a lingering deficiency in the otherwise excellent studies of both Henri Blocher and Hans Boersma. While both see penal substitution as the mechanism of Christ's victory, they use this point to make opposing claims. For Blocher, penal substitution is primary because Christ's triumph depends on it, while for Boersma, *Christus Victor* deserves pride of place because it is the "end" toward which the substitution is aimed. In contrast, Jeremy Treat seems right to claim that "the recognition of instrumentality should not lead to the conclusion that either penal substitution or *Christus Victor* is subordinate." Rather, "they play different roles." Jeremy R. Treat, *The Crucified King: Atonement and Kingdom in Biblical and Systematic Theology* (Grand Rapids: Zondervan, 2014). See Boersma, *Violence, Hospitality, and the Cross,* 182; Blocher, "The Sacrifice of Jesus Christ: The Current Theological Situation," *EuroJTh* 8 (1999): 31.

In the Scriptures, victory comes only because the true Adam (and true Israel undergoes the vicarious judgment mandated as the covenantal penalty for sin.[8] Like penal substitution, which stands more sturdily upon the incorporative and representative logic of recapitulation, a full account of divine triumph rest upon Christ's vicarious judgment on our behalf. The mosaic icon thus proceeds upward: from "feet" (recapitulation) to "heart" (penal substitution) to "head" (*Christus Victor*).[9]

Related Problems and Solutions

To make this case, I must begin with a pair of problems. On the one hand, from the perspective of penal substitution, the key problem to be solved by atonement is the rupture within the divine-human relationship brought about by sin. Here the human failure to worship and obey represents a break in covenant fidelity,[10] which in turn makes the people liable to covenantal curses, expressed as wrath and punishment. On the other hand, in the triumph motif, the key trouble to be overcome is the creaturely bondage to death and "to him who holds the power of death, that is, the devil" (Heb 2:14). In the New Testament, Satan is called the "ruler of this world" (John 12:31); thus "the Son of God appeared . . . to destroy the devil's work" (1 John 3:8).[11]

According to the Scriptures, both problems (sin and Satan) are quite real and inextricably related. Yet scholars differ on how exactly to connect them. For Gregory Boyd, the satanic snag must take precedence, for in a traditional reading of the biblical narrative, it emerged (so to speak) *before* the sin of humanity and helped give rise to it. It was, after all, the serpent's deceit that led God's image bearers astray. Likewise, as Boyd

---

8. See my treatment of the covenant structure in chs. 5–6.

9. This point has been set forth recently by scholars such as Jeremy Treat (*Crucified King*, ch. 8), and Henri Blocher, "*Agnus Victor*: The Atonement as Victory and Vicarious Punishment," in *What Does It Mean to Be Saved? Broadening Evangelical Horizons of Salvation*, ed. John G. Stackhouse (Grand Rapids: Baker, 2002), 67–91. To say that it comes "by way of penal substitution" is not to say that it comes "exclusively" by penal substitution. This too would be reductionistic. As I will describe in part 4 of this book (with a Spirit-driven account of moral influence), the victory has layers, stages, and more than one battle on the way to new creation. Thus, while the cross and resurrection bring triumph, there remains a victory to come in which the God of peace will crush Satan under the feet of the saints (Rom 16:20).

10. Even prior to Abraham and Moses, one may argue that the theme of covenant is present in the biblical narrative. Indeed, many scholars have traced it even to Adam. See Scott J. Hafemann, "The Covenant Relationship," in *Central Themes in Biblical Theology: Mapping Unity in Diversity*, ed. Scott J. Hafemann and Paul R. House (Grand Rapids: Baker Academic, 2007), 40–42.

11. Part 3 of this book will address more detailed questions for the *Christus Victor* model; these will include the ontological status of Satan and the demonic.

sees it, the satanic problem has a greater scope than that of human sin and punishment because all of creation is enveloped by this bondage to the Evil One.[12]

Despite some partial truths in Boyd's argument the biblical emphases run somewhat differently. As Jeremy Treat points out, "The responsibility in Scripture is always placed first and foremost on humanity, regardless of whether they are tempted (as was Adam) or in bondage (as are all under Adam)." This is evidenced in passages like Romans 5:12, which states that "Sin came into the world through one man . . . and so death spread to all men because all sinned." Satan's rule on earth is therefore dependent upon the reign of sin brought forth by human disobedience. "Only because Adam rejected God as king did Satan become his ruler."[13] Much more on Satan's overthrow awaits part 3 of this book. Yet for now, Treat's point is well made: "Bondage to Satan is derivative of the God-human problem."[14] It seems reasonable therefore that resolving the rift between the Creator and his image bearers would have implications for the Satan problem also.[15]

In this way, Treat's argument confirms my conclusion: "Christ defeats Satan (*Christus Victor*) by removing the ground of Satan's accusation, which Jesus does by paying the penalty for sin (penal substitution)."[16] Or, to use my language, the *head* of divine triumph must receive the lifeblood of the *heart*. It is not merely that both models are important; both are connected by particular logic—neither defensive hierarchy nor disconnected plurality but a mosaic of mutually supporting models of atonement.

---

12. See Gregory Boyd, *God at War: The Bible and Spiritual Conflict* (Downers Grove, IL: IVP, 1997), 242.

13. Treat, *Crucified King*, 197.

14. Treat, *Crucified King*, 199.

15. Despite many insightful aspects in his treatment of atonement (to which I shall return in ch. 9), Boyd seems to suppose wrongly that *Christus Victor* and penal substitutionary logic must *always* be pitted against each other. This error apparently stems from the notion that penal substitution must always and only be defined in a rather narrow and caricatured fashion whereby God "vents" his anger on the Son, and "transfers" our guilt onto an innocent victim. Because of this overly narrow definition of what penal substitution *must* entail, Body seems unaware that the following sentence from his most recent work simply *is* a straightforward version of what I have dubbed "mere penal substitution." In Boyd's view, "Jesus rather bore our punishment in the sense that he voluntarily suffered the divine abandonment that we deserved and suffered the destructive consequences inherent in sin." Boyd, Gregory A. Boyd, *Crucifixion of the Warrior God: Interpreting the Old Testament's Violent Portraits of God in Light of the Cross*, vol. 2, *The Cruciform Thesis* (Minneapolis: Fortress, 2017), 1061–62.

16. Treat, *Crucified King*, 204. For further support for this claim, see Sinclair Ferguson, "*Christus Victor et Propitiator*: The Death of Christ, Substitute and Conqueror," in *For the Fame of God's Name*, ed. Sam Storms and Justin Taylor (Wheaton, IL: Crossway, 2010), 171–89.

Corroborating Voices

In recent years, others have concurred with this judgment about the relation between penal substitution and *Christus Victor*.[17] For John Stott, "The payment of our debts [is] the way in which Christ has overthrown the powers."[18] And for Sinclair Ferguson, "The atonement, which terminates on God (in propitiation) and on man (in forgiveness), also terminates on Satan (in the destruction of his sway over believers). And it does this last precisely because it does the first two."[19] Similarly, the New Testament scholar Michael Bird writes that "Jesus's substitutionary death constitutes the basis and center of the divine victory"; hence, "penal substitution and Christus Victor do not compete against each other, for the former is clearly the grounds for the latter."[20] In the words of Garry Williams, "Deny penal substitution and *Christus Victor* is hamstrung."[21] Or as Graham Cole puts it, "*Christus Victor* needs the explanatory power of substitutionary atonement."[22]

The argument is not new. Describing Martin Luther's position, Paul Althaus wrote that "the Powers [being] spoiled of all right and power" depends on "the satisfaction of God's justice."[23] And Calvin claimed that the hostile powers "are disarmed" precisely because "the certificate of our guilt was itself cancelled," an act which in Calvin's thought may be described as penal substitution.[24] John Owen was even more explicit:

> When the sinner ceaseth to be obnoxious unto death, the power of Satan ceaseth also . . . for "there is no condemnation unto them that are in Christ Jesus" [Rom 8:1]; and this because he died. He died for their sins, took that death upon himself which was due unto them; which

---

17. In saying this, one need not endorse every argument of the following theologians with regard to penal substitution.

18. John R. W. Stott, *The Cross of Christ*, 20th anniv. ed. (Downers Grove, IL: IVP, 2006), 234–35, cited in Treat, *Crucified King*, 204n34.

19. Ferguson, "*Christus Victor et Propitiator*," 185.

20. Michael Bird, *Evangelical Theology: A Biblical and Systematic Introduction* (Grand Rapids: Zondervan, 2013), 418.

21. Garry Williams, "Penal Substitution: A Response to Recent Criticisms," in *The Atonement Debate: Papers from the London Symposium on the Theology of Atonement*, ed. Derek Tidball, David Hilborn, and Justin Thacker (Grand Rapids: Zondervan, 2008), 187.

22. Graham Cole, *God the Peacemaker: How Atonement Brings Shalom* (Downers Grove, IL: IVP, 2009), 184.

23. Althaus, *Die Theologie Martin Luther* (Gütersloh: Gütersloher Verlagshaus, 1963), 193; cited in Blocher, "*Agnus Victor*," 89.

24. See Calvin, *Calvin's Commentaries*, trans. Calvin Translation Society (Grand Rapids: Baker, 1999), on Col 2:15. See also *Inst.* 2.16.6.

being conquered thereby, and their obligation thereunto ceasing, the power of Satan is therewith dissolved.[25]

Likewise, George Smeaton (1814–89), the Edinburgh theologian, claimed that "when the guilt of sin was abolished [via penal substitution], Satan's dominion over God's people was ended." Thus "all the mistakes [regarding the means of victory] have arisen from not perceiving with sufficient clearness how the triumph could be celebrated on His cross."[26]

In sum, this chorus of corroborating voices indicates that the idea of divine triumph by way of penal substitution is present within the Christian tradition, even though it may deserve a greater emphasis. With this in mind, I will now note how this integrated approach addresses a pressing question for certain versions of the *Christus Victor* theme.

The "How" of Triumph

The idea of victory by crucifixion stands in need of a more specific rationale to show how triumph comes through such an ignominious means. Indeed, although the resurrection and ascension remain essential if one is to view the cross as a victory, the New Testament can nonetheless speak of Christ's crucifixion specifically as his exalted enthronement and as his means of triumph.[27] Thus a key question still hangs over many *Christus Victor* proclamations. For Blocher, "The main query is basic indeed: *How* is the battle fought and the victory gained? If the metaphor [of conquest] is to bear doctrinal fruit, it should yield at least some intelligence of the mode and process."[28] Likewise, Kathryn Tanner goes so far as to claim that "*Christus Victor* is not a model at all in that it fails per se, to address the question of the mechanism of the atonement. Christ is battling the forces of evil and sin on the cross but how is the battle won?"[29]

Already in this book (ch. 4), I noted that some patristic sources had answers to this question, even if they are not ones that many moderns

25. John Owen, "The Epistle to the Hebrews," in *The Works of John Owen*, ed. William H. Goold, 24 vols. (Edinburgh: Johnstone & Hunter, 1850–55; repr., Carlisle, PA: Banner of Truth, 1991), 20:450.
26. George Smeaton, *The Apostles' Doctrine of the Atonement* (Edinburgh: T&T Clark, 1870), 307–8; cited in Ferguson, "*Christus Victor et Propitiator*," 184.
27. John's Gospel is most explicit in picturing the cross as Christ's enthronement in glory (John 12:23–32; cf. 3:14; 8:28). Still, the theme is also present elsewhere (e.g., Col 2:14–15). See especially Jeremy Treat, "Exaltation in and through Humiliation: Rethinking the States of Christ," in *Christology: Ancient and Modern*, ed. Oliver Crisp and Fred Sanders (Grand Rapids: Zondervan, 2013), ch. 5.
28. Blocher, "*Agnus Victor*," 78.
29. Kathryn Tanner, *Christ the Key* (Cambridge: Cambridge University Press, 2010), 253.

have accepted. In particular, thinkers like Athanasius, Gregory of Nyssa, Gregory of Nazianzus, and Cyril of Alexandria believed that when Christ's humanity succumbed to mortality, the divine nature was brought into contact with death, so that death itself was cancelled out by way of divine life—in the same way that darkness is expelled by turning on a light. For this reason, Benjamin Myers argues that many patristic sources did possess a mechanism to explain how divine triumph might come about through the horrific death of Jesus.[30]

Despite the fact that similar logic can be found in several early Christian sources,[31] there are also significant roadblocks to accepting what Myers calls *the* patristic model of atonement. First, the argument relies primarily on classical (and largely Platonic) assumptions about the "universals" in which all particulars participate. And for moderns, the idea that there is such a thing as a universal human nature that the Son may assume for the purpose of contacting "the privative state of death" may sound as outmoded as the idea of a flat earth resting atop a giant stack of turtles.

Second, the proposed mechanism lacks biblical support, largely because it proceeds in detachment from the Jewish narrative and categories of Scripture.[32] The Bible certainly sees persons as being bound up as one in the Messiah, but the destruction of the "privative state of death" via contact with the divine nature through the hypostatic union is not an idea that is easily discernable from Scripture. The rationale is thin biblically.

Third, while the argument does address how Christ's death (in general) might bring about atonement, it fails to address why God willed this *particular* death. Why, for instance, could Jesus not die peacefully at a ripe old age in a villa for retired rabbis? Since the only requirement is for the divine nature to contact "death" (via Christ's humanity and the hypostatic union), there is no explanation for why such a horrific and humiliating death was chosen "by the predetermined plan and foreknowledge of God" (Acts 2:23).

Fourth, as I argued in chapter 4, the patristic tradition had other ways

---

30. Myers, "The Patristic Atonement Model," in *Locating Atonement: Explorations in Constructive Dogmatics*, ed. Oliver Crisp and Fred Sanders (Grand Rapids: Zondervan, 2015), 73. It is quite possible (though not necessary, as illustrated by Nazianzen) for this notion to coincide with a ransom viewpoint in which the devil is deceived into taking the bait of Christ's flesh.

31. See my prior acknowledgment of this in ch. 4.

32. Heb 2:14–15 offers perhaps the closest analogue to Myers's model. Still, this passage (which I will examine momentarily) is notably devoid of specific philosophical assumptions about universals, particulars, and death as a privation that is undone by contact with an eternal divine essence.

of dealing with the "how" of the atonement. In some passages, thinkers like Eusebius of Caesarea, Athanasius, John Chrysostom, Augustine of Hippo, and Gregory the Great employed logic that may rightly be described as "mere penal substitution," despite expressing it in different ways than some modern preachers and theologians. The covenantal logic of penal substitution offers a more compelling biblical basis for Christ's cruciform triumph over death and the devil than does Myers's so-called "patristic model of atonement."[33] To prove this point, however, I must go back to the Bible and to three passages that lend support to the hypothesis: Colossians 2; Hebrews 2; and Revelation 12.

Colossians 2:14–5

Because Colossians pictures all things as being bound up *in* the Son (Col 1:17), it becomes easier to conceptualize (albeit mystically) how the Son is able to act on behalf of those who are *in* him and, most specifically, on behalf of his body, the church. Right on cue, the incorporative logic of this passage then flows into the imagery of (1) debt cancellation and (2) divine triumph:

> When you were dead in your sins and in the uncircumcision of your flesh, God made you alive with Christ. He forgave us all our sins, having canceled the charge of our legal indebtedness, which stood against us and condemned us; he has taken it away, nailing it to the cross. And having disarmed the powers and authorities, he made a public spectacle of them, triumphing over them by the cross. (Col 2:13–15)

The final emphasis is that of victory over evil powers, and the text gives two answers as to how the triumph comes. First, it is by the unlikely instrument of the cross.[34] And second, it is by the legal cancellation of debt, which brings both forgiveness (v. 13) and the disarming of evil rulers and authorities. Christ's victory over the evil powers comes precisely through his forgiveness-granting act of legal debt cancellation. But what does that mean?

---

33. In fairness to Myers, it is not obvious to me that he is advocating for a full acceptance of this patristic model today. He may simply be arguing that some early sources viewed the atonement through this lens. And on that point, he is surely correct.

34. While the Greek is more ambiguous than the English (*en auto*, meaning "by it" or "by him"), it remains clear, as MacLeod states, that "Christ crucified was God's agent in disarming Satan." Donald MacLeod, *Christ Crucified: Understanding the Atonement* (Downers Grove, IL: IVP Academic, 2014), 246.

In the passage, what has been cancelled and nailed to the cross is the *cheirographon*, or note of legal indebtedness. In modern terms, this is something like an IOU.[35] According to the Torah, what was legally owed by covenant-breakers was to undergo the curse of the law.[36] Thus Dunn states rightly that "the decrees of the law [give] the *cheirographon* its condemnatory force."[37] While this is clear enough, a crucial question remains: What is the relationship between the decrees of the law and the evil powers? Biblically speaking, Satan is "the Accuser" (literally, *ha satan* in Hebrew) of God's people. He functions somewhat like a gifted though unscrupulous prosecuting attorney, bringing charges before the divine Judge.[38] Never mind that the Accuser himself has enticed humanity to high treason, the fact remains that humans *are* guilty on the basis of the covenant.[39] Humanity chose to follow the lead of the serpent, so the Accuser also became "the ruler of this world" (John 12:31).[40]

This is the relation between the evil powers and the *cheirographon*. In MacLeod's colorful imagery, "Our guilt, our broken bond, was Satan's title to enslave us and drag us down to hell with himself."[41] Unless the covenantal penalty is paid, the devil's accusation, and the condemnation flowing from it, stands.[42] Yet if the curse of the law is borne by one in whom we all subsist (Col 1:17–18), then the devil's accusations lose their force (Col 2). If this happens, as it arguably does in a careful account of penal substitution and vicarious judgment, then God is shown to be both just and the one who justifies the ungodly (Rom 4:5). Sin is punished, sinners are saved, and by God's Spirit they are also transformed into saints. This is why there is now no condemnation for those who are in Christ Jesus (Rom 8:1). The same Christ who was stripped and nailed upon a tree has "stripped" (*apekdusamenos*) the evil forces (Col 2:15), nailed up their accusation (2:14), and pronounced the *cheirographon* "paid in full."

---

35. Treat, *Crucified King*, 166.
36. See, specifically, Lev 26 and Deut 28–31.
37. James Dunn, *The Epistles to the Colossians and to Philemon: A Commentary on the Greek Text*, NIGTC (Grand Rapids: Eerdmans, 1996), 165.
38. See, for instance, Job 1; Zech 3; Rev 12:9–11. In Hebrew, *ha satan* can actually refer either to an "accuser" in a legal setting, or an "adversary" on the field of battle. In its own way, this too may argue for an integration of forensic and "fighting" themes with regard to Satan and atonement.
39. See Blocher's excellent treatment of this theme, *"Agnus Victor,"* 82–83.
40. Full demonstration of this reality must await part 3 of this book.
41. MacLeod, *Christ Crucified*, 246. See also F. F. Bruce, *The Epistles to the Colossians, to Philemon, and to the Ephesians*, NICNT (1884; repr., Grand Rapids: Eerdmans, 1993). As Bruce argues of Col 2:14–15: Christ subjugated the powers through the cancellation "of the damning indictment [the *cheirographon*] [that] was a means of controlling [humanity]" (110).
42. See Blocher, *"Agnus Victor,"* 86–87.

Tetelestai. In short, Colossians 2 proclaims a victory that comes by way of vicarious judgment and penal substitution.

Hebrews 2:14–18

This theme continues with more overtly priestly emphases in Hebrews 2:14–18:

> Since the children have flesh and blood, he too shared in their humanity so that by his death he might break the power of him who holds the power of death—that is, the devil—and free those who all their lives were held in slavery by their fear of death. . . . For this reason he had to be made like them, fully human in every way, in order that he might become a merciful and faithful high priest in service to God, and that he might make atonement for the sins of the people. Because he himself suffered when he was tempted, he is able to help those who are being tempted.

Here too, it is specifically Christ's death that renders the devil powerless. In this sacrifice, Jesus makes priestly "propitiation" by his blood (cf. Heb 9:14).[43]

Yet the passage also emphasizes the sinless *life* of Christ as grounds for his atoning victory. He identified fully with our frail humanity, taking human flesh, mortality, and temptation, and giving support to Calvin's claim that "from the time he took on the form of a servant, he began to pay the price of liberation in order to redeem us."[44] This insight is important because penal substitution has been accused of focusing only on Christ's grisly death, to the exclusion of his life, resurrection, and ascension. Here in Hebrews, however, the emphasis upon a death-and-devil-crushing sacrifice coincides with an accent upon Christ's whole life as one of priestly vocation.[45] One might even trace a trajectory from recapitulation (by the possible new-Adam parallels in Heb 2:5–10),[46] to penal substitution (propitiation by blood sacrifice in 2:17; 9:14), and on to triumph over "him who had the power of death, that is, the devil" (2:14–15).[47]

---

43. See again the treatment of sacrificial expiation and propitiation in ch. 5.
44. *Inst.* 2.16.5.
45. As Alan Torrance has winsomely argued, Christ's priesthood even now continues. See Torrance, "Reclaiming the Continuing Priesthood of Christ: Implications and Challenges," in *Christology: Ancient and Modern*, ed. Oliver Crisp and Fred Sanders (Grand Rapids: Zondervan, 2013), ch. 10.
46. See Treat, *Crucified King*, 205.
47. Because of this work, death ceases to be penal for the Christian, becoming instead the "sleep" that is the prerequisite for resurrection.

Revelation 12:7–11

My third and final snapshot of victory via penal substitution comes in the book of Revelation. Here, in chapter 12, it states that "the accuser of our brethren" (v. 10), who is "that ancient serpent . . . the devil" (v. 9), has been "triumphed over . . . by the blood of the Lamb (v. 11)." In this case, to speak of the sacrificial Lamb's blood as the means of military triumph is again a hint toward my thesis. In reference to this passage, G. K. Beale notes that Satan's "accusations appear to be directed against the illegitimacy of the saints' participation in salvation. The devil's accusation is based on the correct presupposition that the penalty of sin necessitates a judgment of spiritual death and not salvific reward."[48] Thankfully, however, "the devil no longer had any basis for his accusations against the saints, since the penalty that they deserved . . . had at last been exacted in Christ's death."[49] Here again, it is victory via Christ's sacrificial, penalty-bearing death.

In this brief passage from Revelation, three key contexts of atonement come together: the legal acquittal, the military triumph, and the sacrificial offering.[50] Yet again it is not merely that the metaphors are spread out upon the table in no particular relation. It is rather that the substitutionary offering of a life removes Satan's legal case against the saints, thereby stripping Satan of his deceptive dominion. This is why John sees the slain Lamb atop the throne; it is because Christ has "purchased" with his "blood [persons] from every tribe and tongue and people and nation" (5:9). Once more, it is not just victory and penal substitution but victory *by way of* penal substitution.

The combined weight of these (and other[51]) scriptural passages comes together with tradition and covenantal logic to lend credence to the idea that the divine triumph over Satan comes by way of Christ's vicarious judgment and penal substitution on our behalf. In the words of Sinclair Ferguson, he is *Christus Victor et Propitiator*. Or as Henri Blocher puts it, he is *Agnus Victor*. The result of divine triumph flows forth from a central cause, like lifeblood from a beating heart.

---

48. Beale, *The Book of Revelation: A Commentary on the Greek Text*, NIGTC (Grand Rapids: Eerdmans, 1999), 659.

49. Beale, *Revelation*, 659.

50. Treat, *Crucified King*, 207.

51. I will note momentarily how 1 John also furthers this hypothesis. Likewise, one might note Rom 8, in which God's condemnation of sin in the flesh of Christ (v. 3) forms the logical ground for our being "more than conquerors through him who loved us" (v. 37). On the merits of this argument, and a similar case on 1 Cor 15, see Bird, *Evangelical Theology*, 417.

THE MORAL INFLUENCE OF PENAL SUBSTITUTION

Yet the heart pumps lifeblood also to the outstretched hands. In my mosaic metaphor, I linked these hands to a twofold approach to the so-called moral influence model. Here, I will eventually picture Christ as both beckoning us to thankful obedience and waiving us away from certain violent tendencies through the power of the Spirit.[52] While the detailed arguments await in part 4, my goal now is merely to address the relationship between penal substitution and the broader moral influence and exemplarist implications of atonement.

In turning to the Scriptures, none can deny Christ's work has a transformative moral influence. In the view of Peter Abelard (1079–1142), the incarnation exerts a redemptive sway on our attitudes and actions, the result of which is "that our hearts [are] enkindled by such a gift of divine grace," so that we "should not now shrink from enduring anything for [God]."[53] Likewise, for Thomas Aquinas (1225–74), the first two answers given for Christ's death strike similar themes: "In the first place, man knows thereby how much God loves him, and is thereby stirred to love him in return." Second, "he set us an example of obedience, humility, constancy, justice, and the other virtues displayed in the Passion, which are requisite for man's salvation."[54] In short, the merits of the moral influence model are indisputable.

Objective and Subjective Emphases

The most common critique of this so-called "subjective" model pertains to those instances when it excludes other pieces of atonement doctrine.[55] When this happens, the claim is that moral influence is not "objective" enough to deal with the deep effects of sin and satanic domination.[56] Before addressing this charge, however, some definition must be given to the terms

52. For the "beckoning" influence of divine love, I will turn to the oft-misunderstood work of Peter Abelard (ch. 11); while the revelation and "waiving off" of violent tendencies will be highlighted through attention to René Girard (ch. 12).

53. Peter Abelard, *Commentary on the Epistle to the Romans*, II, on 2:26, in *A Scholastic Miscellany: Anselm to Ockham*, ed. and trans. E. R. Fairweather, vol. 10, LCC (London: 1956), 283.

54. *Summa Theologica*, 3.46.3.

55. As I will note (ch. 11), the idea that Abelard was an exclusive "exemplarist" must now be firmly rejected.

56. For the preeminent contemporary defense of the objective value of the moral influence model, see Paul Fiddes, *Past Event and Present Salvation: The Christian Idea of Atonement* (Louisville: Westminster John Knox, 1989), ch. 7 especially.

"objective" and "subjective." In common usage, the objective features of Christ's work deal with problems outside of us, most commonly with regard to divine justice or satanic might. On the other side, the subjective implications of atonement deal with problems that are in some way internal to us, as evidenced by our fearful mistrust of God and our bent toward disobedience.

In truth, any account of the atonement must have both objective and subjective aspects.[57] To present a false choice between the two is folly. For those arguing for a strictly exemplarist (or moral influence) view of the atonement, a common rebuttal comes from the work of Anselm: "You have not yet considered the exceeding gravity of sin."[58] Based on my previous survey of the Scriptures, this point has merit (ch. 5).[59] The Bible reveals that an objective penalty (the covenantal curse) was borne by Christ in order for sinful persons to be brought justly into communion with a holy God. Likewise, it will now be argued that the central act of love that compels our grateful response is that of Christ's penal substitution and vicarious judgment on our behalf. The *hands* of moral influence work best when receiving the lifeblood of the *heart* (penal substitution). This is evidenced by the First Epistle of John.

1 John: This Is the Love, the *Hilasmon*

In truth, 1 John could have easily been included to support the claim that divine victory comes by penal substitution and vicarious judgment.[60] As the letter states, "The Son of God appeared for this purpose: to destroy the works of the devil" (1 John 3:8). Yet this claim emerges within a larger discussion of his vocation as "the *hilasmos* for the sins of the whole world" (1 John 2:2).

In support of translating *hilasmos* as "propitiation" (which in no way excludes the simultaneous possibility of expiation[61]) is the fact that the pre-

---

57. As evidence, it may be argued that it is because of a subjective reason (our sinful hearts) that divine justice finds us guilty, and Satan finds his prey. Thanks to my colleague Jerome Van Kuiken for this insight.

58. Anselm, *Cur Deus Homo*, 1.21.

59. Though one may also raise the question of whether Anselm too has failed to consider the full gravity of sin by reducing it largely to a matter of offending the divine honor.

60. Treat does so in *The Crucified King*, 207.

61. For support, see J. Ramsey Michaels, "Atonement in John's Gospel and Epistles," in *The Glory of Atonement: Biblical, Historical, and Practical Perspectives*, ed. Charles E. Hill and Frank A. James (Downers Grove, IL: IVP Academic, 2004), 114; likewise, Robert W. Yarbrough uses the phrase "expiatory propitiation," *1–3 John*, BECNT (Grand Rapids: Baker Academic, 2008), 77; similarly, Stephen Smalley, *1 ,2, 3 John*, WBC 51 (Waco, TX: Word, 1984), 40.

ceding verse presents "Jesus Christ, the Righteous One," as our "Advocate [*parakleton*] with the Father" (1 John 2:1). By this logic, God is presented as the object in the sacrificial drama, not merely the subject. To this extent, the context supports "propitiation" as the meaning of *hilasmos*.[62] Furthermore, if God is pictured as the Judge[63] and Christ as our Advocate, then 1 John's imagery also fits with the image of Satan as the prosecuting attorney who now has no case for condemning the saints. The reason for this overturned conviction is Christ's propitiating death. Again, the text fits well with the theme of *Christus Victor* by way of penal substitution.[64]

Yet 1 John also grounds the moral influence motif within the *hilasmon*. And in this way, the beckoning *hands* of Christ also receive the lifeblood of the *heart*. "This is love," proclaims 1 John 4:10–12, "not that we loved God, but that he loved us and sent his Son as an atoning sacrifice [*hilasmon*] for our sins. Dear friends, since God so loved us, we also ought to love one another. No one has ever seen God; but if we love one another, God lives in us and his love is made complete in us." Here again we find two key components of the moral influence motif: first, the revelation of God's love in Christ and, second, the imitation of God's love in us.[65] But in 1 John, the first point is seen specifically when one comes to view Christ's death as the objective sacrifice on our behalf (the *hilasmon*) that deals with sin.

In the Septuagint, this is the precise word that is used of the Day of Atonement (Lev 25:9), which I have previously come to view through the lens of penal substitution and vicarious judgment.[66] One may argue that

---

62. Michaels, "Atonement in John's Gospel and Epistles," 114. As Michaels points out here (in n32), even C. H. Dodd had to acknowledge the force of this point, while still denying the idea of propitiation. See Dodd, *The Bible and the Greeks*, 94–95. In further support of "propitiation" here, see I. Howard Marshall, *The Epistles of John*. NICNT (Grand Rapids: Eerdmans, 1978), 118.

63. Michaels unjustifiably describes God here as the "Prosecutor" who "himself sends and appoints the Defense Attorney to plead with the Prosecutor to show mercy!" This odd (and apparently schizophrenic) action on God's part is avoided if we picture a divine Judge and a satanic accuser. Indeed, this is more in line with the scriptural imagery elsewhere. See "Atonement in John's Gospel and Epistles," 116.

64. Given the progression of the argument in 1 John, Matthew Jensen concludes that "the destruction of the devil's work should be understood in terms of taking away sins." Jensen, "'You Have Overcome the Evil One': Victory Over Evil in 1 John," in *Christ's Victory Over Evil: Biblical Theology and Pastoral Ministry*, ed. Peter Bolt (Nottingham, UK: Apollos, 2009), 114.

65. The fact that God is said to have "sent" the Son (v. 10) for our redemption shows that the Father has *always* been lovingly disposed toward us and was not suddenly "made so" upon the death of Jesus.

66. See again Theilman, "The Atonement," in *Central Themes in Biblical Theology: Mapping Unity in Diversity*, ed. Scott J. Hafemann and Paul R. House (Grand Rapids: Baker Academic, 2007), 119.

Christ's death is only a genuine display of divine love if he truly is, as another Johannine text states, "the Lamb of God, who takes away the sin of the world" (John 1:29).

An Illustration from T. F. Torrance

This point was made vividly in a story told by T. F. Torrance. In his early days of teaching, a student came to see Torrance about an essay written for class. As Torrance recalls, "[The student] had spoken of the death of Christ simply as a demonstration of the love of God . . . expounding something like what was known as a 'moral influence theory' of the atonement." Rather than discuss the perceived inadequacies of such an exclusive approach, Torrance showed the boy a detailed copy of Grünewald's famous painting of the crucifixion. In particular, "I also showed him some of the enlargements of the painting . . . which focused on the fearfully lacerated flesh of Jesus." Then Torrance said,

Harold, you have written about that as a picture of the love of God. It is certainly a picture of the fearful sin and hatred of mankind, but if you can tell me WHY Jesus was crucified, WHY he endured such unbelievable pain and anguish, then you will be able to say something of the real meaning of the atonement, and about why the crucifixion of Jesus was and is indeed a revelation of the love of God—Christ was crucified like that FOR our sakes, to save us from sin and judgment. It is only in the light of that FOR that the death of Jesus is a picture of the love of God. . . . What I had been unable to say in words alone, could be conveyed with the help of that famous painting: "Behold the Lamb of God who takes away the sin of the world!"[67]

Something similar happens in 1 John. Here, the wrath-averting nature of Christ's devil-defeating death gives rise to the moral influence motif. The *hands*, much like the *head*, receive the lifeblood of the *heart*.

Beyond this, one might also argue that the objective necessity of Christ's death keeps the ghastly nature of the crucifixion from appearing unwarranted. If the terrible penalty for sin did not need to be dealt with in order to reconcile humanity with God, then the horror of the cross begins to look like the unnecessary act of a demented lover. Here, God may appear

---

67. T. F. Torrance, "Memories of Auburn 1938–39," unpublished typescript, as cited in Alister E. McGrath, *Thomas F. Torrance: An Intellectual Biography* (Edinburgh: T&T Clark, 1999), 54–55.

188 | The Mosaic of Atonement

like a cosmic Van Gogh, who self-mutilates to prove his love ("Here is my ear; now you know how much I care for you"). Yet as many lovers can attest, such unbidden and unnecessary acts of (self-)harm are more likely to appear manipulative than loving. While the person who *must* give up life to save others is esteemed, the one who simply chooses death "to make them love me" is unbalanced, controlling, or both. The First Epistle of John does not take this path; it grounds the loving influence of atonement in the objective reality of the *hilasmon*.

1 Peter 2: Imitate the Suffering Servant

A second text that is relevant for the relation between penal substitution and moral influence appears in 1 Peter 2. This passage, as I have noted already (ch. 5), repeatedly links Jesus to the substitutionary work of Isaiah's Suffering Servant while encouraging readers to imitate this sacrificial love. Controversially, slaves are then told to "[bear] up under the pain of unjust suffering" (v. 19),

> because Christ suffered for you, leaving you an example, that you should follow in his steps.

> "He committed no sin,
>   and no deceit was found in his mouth." [Isa 53:9]

> When they hurled their insults at him, he did not retaliate; when he suffered, he made no threats. Instead, he entrusted himself to him who judges justly. "He himself bore our sins" in his body on the cross, so that we might die to sins and live for righteousness; "by his wounds you have been healed." For "you were like sheep going astray," [Isa 53:4–6, see LXX] but now you have returned to the Shepherd and Overseer of your souls. (vv.21–25)

In regard to my mosaic metaphor, it is important to note that the text attaches our imitation of Christ to his prior work as the Servant who "bore our sins in his body on the cross" (1 Pet 2:24; cf. Isa 53:4). Just as in 1 John, Christ's sin-bearing death serves as the objective ground for our subjective response. Here again, the *imitatio Christi* is rooted in Jesus's role as *Christus propitiator*. Likewise, the most natural way to understand the Servant's work, both here and in Isaiah, is through the lens of penal substitution. In the view of the New Testament scholar Ben Witherington,

"The implied idea [for the readers] is that Christ bore the punishment for human sins *in their stead.* Thus, we have here a substitutionary atonement by the Suffering Servant."[68] Once more, the beckoning hands receive the lifeblood of the heart.

There is, however, a perceived danger with 1 Peter 2, and it once again pertains to the acceptance of abuse. For many, what is worrying in the passage is the clarity of relation between Christ's silent acceptance of violence and the so-called exemplarist approach. Here, the Messiah's own tolerance of unjust treatment leaves us "an example" that we "should follow in his steps." And to make matters worse, the instructions are given specifically to some of the most vulnerable members of society, slaves and wives (3:1).[69]

In response, some answers have already been given. I have noted previously that Scripture gives ample evidence for avoiding harm if possible, just as it gives ample critique of the oppressors. Likewise, as Witherington notes, "Nothing is said here about seeking martyrdom or suffering."[70] The passage is therefore neither a masochistic endorsement of pain, nor a call to overlook injustice. Indeed, in the next chapter, the same charge to "repay evil with blessing" is given not just to slaves but to "all of you" (3:9, 8), indicating that it is for all believers.[71] The charge in question pertains to instances in which suffering cannot be avoided; thus the letter entreats believers to make the best of a difficult situation. Still, it should never be used as a manipulative or guilt-laden ploy to encourage victims to stay in abusive environments when there is a way out. In these instances, the threatened should imitate Paul in his use of legal recourse (Acts 16:37–38), and in his flight over the wall and out of immediate danger (Acts 9:25; 2 Cor 11:33).

Another crucial caveat is also needed: while Christians are called to imitate the Servant's gracious response to unjust suffering, we are *not* called to imitate his penal substitution. Indeed, we cannot. Here, it is important to recall the phrase "instead of us" within the shorthand description of substitution as "in our place, instead of us."

---

68. Ben Witherington, *Letters and Homilies for Hellenized Christians,* vol. 2, *A Socio-Rhetorical Commentary on 1–2 Peter* (Downers Grove, IL: IVP Academic, 2007), 157, italics in original.
69. For critiques of the abusive implications of even moral influence paradigms, see Rita Nakashima Brock and Rebecca Ann Parker, *Proverbs of Ashes: Violence, Redemptive Suffering, and the Search for What Saves Us* (Boston: Beacon, 2001).
70. Witherington, *1–2 Peter,* 155.
71. See again, Witherington, *1–2 Peter,* 155–56.

In 1 Peter, readers are told that Christ's sin-bearing death was a one-time occurrence (e.g., 3:18) that cannot be replicated by his followers. Thus the claim of penal substitution is not that the suffering of the marginalized is somehow inherently redemptive. At this point, Richard Mouw distinguishes his generally Reformed account of atonement from the theology espoused by John Howard Yoder (1927–97). "To be sure," Mouw says, "Christians may be called to suffer in Christ's name." Yet he admits to being "troubled a bit by Yoder's insistence that the New Testament calls us to imitate the work of the cross 'consistently and universally.'"[72] For Mouw,

We do not have to—we *ought* not to—imitate Jesus' approach to dying [at least in every respect]. His suffering is in significant ways inimitable, because he bore the wrath of our cursed existence precisely in order that we do not have to suffer under that wrath. And this is important to emphasize with reference to the kinds of examples raised by those who worry that the Bible's depiction of the atoning work of Christ might encourage, say, women to think that they must patiently endure spouse abuse. In such cases, the most basic consideration for a woman in that kind of situation is to know that Christ has suffered the abandonment and abuse on her behalf, and that she does not need to endure those experiences in order to please God.[73]

For this reason, to speak of Christ's penalty-bearing death *before* speaking of our imitation of Christ (as both 1 John and 1 Peter do) may actually provide a safeguard to abusive applications of atonement doctrine. It does so not only by emphasizing God's justice in punishing evil but also by clarifying that the price of redemption has been fully paid by Christ alone. No further suffering by victims is necessary as a means of penance. Christ has unmasked this false view of sacrifice and suffering, as I will further note when I explore the "restraining" elements of the moral influence model (ch. 12).

---

72. Richard Mouw, "Violence and the Atonement," in *Must Christianity Be Violent? Reflections on History, Practice, and Theology*, ed. Kenneth R. Chase and Alan Jacobs (Grand Rapids: Brazos, 2003), 169; cf. John Howard Yoder, *The Politics of Jesus* (Grand Rapids: Eerdmans, 1972), 97.
73. Mouw, "Violence and the Atonement," 170.

| CONCLUSION |

The goal of this chapter has been to highlight the way in which penal substitution connects with two other models of atonement: *Christus Victor* and moral influence. In relation to the triumph motif, Christ's curse-bearing death reveals the crucial means by which the Messiah conquers sin, death, and the devil. In short, there is victory via penal substitution and vicarious judgment. Likewise, both 1 John and 1 Peter also ground the moral influence aspects of atonement in the objective status of Christ's work as a propitiating sacrifice (*hilasmos*). In this way, the beckoning and restraining *hands* of Christ also function because they receive the lifeblood of the beating *heart*.

In these respects, both objective and subjective aspects of atonement come together, and neither *head* nor *hands* can say to the *heart*, "I have no need of you." All are joined, for "God has put the body together, giving greater honor to the parts that lacked it, so that there should be no division" (1 Cor 12:24–5). May we take note and worship.

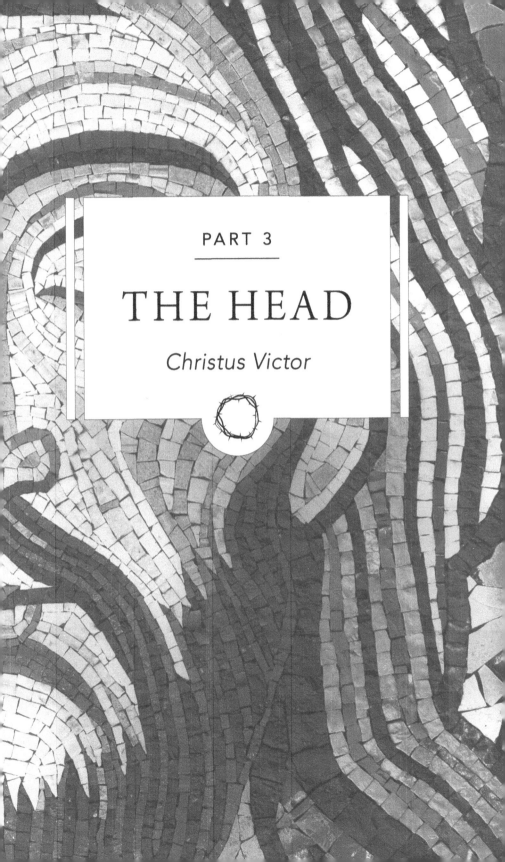

PART 3

THE HEAD

Christus Victor

CHAPTER 8

TRIUMPH THROUGH TRICKERY

REEXAMINING THE ROLE OF DECEPTION IN CHRIST'S VICTORY

None of the rulers of this age understood it, for if they had, they would not have crucified the Lord of glory.

1 Corinthians 2:8

For Augustine, the devil was "overcome, not by the power of God, but by his justice [*iustitia*]." In his view, while God is clearly sovereign, he does not redeem by sheer force. Instead, Christ conquers by the "justice game" rather than the "power game." Likewise, as Augustine argued, this calls forth imitation: we too should "conquer . . . by justice, not by power."[1] This idea fits with my prior claim that Christ's triumph comes through the demonstration of divine righteousness in Jesus's judgment-bearing, devil-defeating, and deliverance-giving work. But in my own construction, the divine triumph emerges because of Jesus's recapitulative obedience and his vicarious judgment on our behalf.

However, Augustine pointed to another element that deserved attention: the role of *trickery* in Satan's downfall. This may seem ironic given the apparent tension between righteousness and subterfuge. Nonetheless, this chapter reexamines a long-discarded element of atonement doctrine, the place of deception in the devil's defeat. I will begin, as I have done before, by exploring the historical roots of the idea. Next, I will note why the theme

---

1. Augustine, *De Trinitate*, 13.13; this translation is my own.

all but disappeared before an attempted retrieval in recent years. Finally, I will conclude by outlining what a more credible account of the devil's deception might look like, once it is shorn of its more questionable qualities.

| A HISTORY OF DECEPTION |

Inspiration for the divine deception motif may have come from Gnosticism.[2] In this diverse movement, humanity was seen as being under the oppressive power of the Demiurge and imprisoned in the paltry world of matter, time, and flesh.[3] The solution came through cunning. Here, the Logos took on the mere *appearance* of human flesh in order to defeat the Demiurge and bring freedom to a special few. For the Gnostic teacher Basilides, Christ's tricky triumph came by changing Simon of Cyrene's appearance so that Simon was crucified in Jesus's place. Meanwhile, the true Christ stood by laughing. In all of this, salvation came by a divine deception.[4]

The claim is that later Christians both *adopted* and *adapted* this logic, swapping out the Demiurge for the devil. While this is possible, explicit proof is hard to find. One recent study views Irenaeus as the "missing link" between the Gnostics and the Christian view of ransom by deception.[5] But Irenaeus himself did not endorse this logic. Though Irenaeus recorded the Gnostic views for posterity—believing that merely recounting such convolutions was nearly enough to overthrow them—he never openly claimed that God deceived the devil.[6]

The first Christian claim of this sort came from Origen of Alexandria (ca. 185–254). In reflecting on the biblical notion that Jesus offered his life as a ransom for humanity,[7] the brilliant Alexandrian began to speculate—as he was wont—about to *whom* the ransom was paid. "Could it not be the evil one?" he asked. "For he had us in his power, until the ransom for us should be given." Origen then moved to the theme of deception: "Since he (the evil one) had been deceived, and led to suppose that he was

2. This claim was made by R. S. Franks, *A History of the Work of Christ in Ecclesiastical Development*, vol. 1 (Nashville: Thomas Nelson, 1962), 16, and by L. W. Grensted, *A Short History of the Doctrine of the Atonement* (Manchester: University of Manchester Press, 1920). See also Ben Pugh, *Atonement Theories: A Way through the Maze* (Eugene, OR: Cascade, 2014), 3–5.

3. For a fuller treatment of Gnosticism, see ch. 1.

4. This account of Basilides comes by way of *Haer.* 1.24.4.

5. See Pugh, *Atonement Theories*, 4. This may be true to the extent that Irenaeus chronicled many Gnostic teachings.

6. See again ch. 1.

7. See Origen, *On Romans*, trans. Thomas P. Scheck (Washington, DC: Catholic University Press, 2001), II/13.

capable of mastering that soul, . . . he did not see that to hold Him [Christ] involved a trial of strength greater than he was equal to."[8]

Around this same time, Cyprian of Carthage (ca. 200–258) likened the Son's divine power to "a kind of fishhook hidden by the covering of human flesh" by which Satan was caught.[9] The motivation for the lurid imagery was twofold: First, by an allegorical reading of Job ("Can you pull in the Leviathan with a fishhook?" [41:1]), he concluded that the sea-beast was symbolic for Satan; thus the age-old passage actually spoke of Jesus's work. Second, the fishing analogy also claimed roots in Christ's words when he likened his time in the grave to that of Jonah in the "sea monster" (Matt 12:40). With respect to this text, Stephen Holmes suggests that perhaps Christ deliberately says "monster" (*ketous*) instead of "fish" (*ikthus*), in order to bring Leviathan to mind.[10] If so, then the church fathers may have been correct to link Job and Jesus in some way. For in going to the grave, Christ claimed to have entered the belly of the beast.

With these "early adopters" in place, the stage was now set for the famous words of Gregory of Nyssa (ca. 335–95):

> [Christ's] Deity was hidden under the veil of our [human] nature, so that, as with ravenous fish, the hook of the Deity might be gulped down along with the bait of flesh, and thus, life being introduced into the house of death, and light shining in darkness, that which is diametrically opposed to light and life might vanish; for it is not in the nature of darkness to remain when light is present, or of death to exist when life is active.[11]

Aside from the shocking imagery, it bears noting that there is a connection between Gregory's ransom logic and the so-called "Patristic Atonement Model" detailed previously (ch. 7).[12]

As Benjamin Myers argued, Nyssen employed the metaphysical assumption that death itself would be destroyed if it were to contact the immortality of the divine nature. The problem, of course, is that this contact

---

8. Origen, *Commentary on Matthew* in ANF 10:489.

9. Cyprian, *Expositio Symboli*, cited in Oden, *Systematic Theology*, vol. 2, *Word of Life* (Peabody, MA: Hendrickson, 2006), 400.

10. Stephen Holmes, *The Wondrous Cross: Atonement and Penal Substitution in the Bible and History* (London: Paternoster, 2007), 26.

11. Gregory of Nyssa, *Greater Catechism* in NPNF[2] 5:493.

12. Benjamin Myers, "The Patristic Atonement Model," in *Locating Atonement: Explorations in Constructive Dogmatics*, ed. Oliver Crisp and Fred Sanders (Grand Rapids: Zondervan, 2015), ch. 3.

seems impossible, for the immortal, by definition, cannot die. Only the incarnation makes this possible. In this way, said Gregory, "life [was] introduced into the house of death" and "darkness" was expelled by the "light" of Christ's divinity. But while this assumption explains the mechanism of victory, the reason for Satan's unwitting welcome of Jesus into "death's house" is the deceptive hiding of divinity beneath the veil of human flesh. Once again, salvation comes by cunning.

In the years that followed, many others embraced this "trickery" form of Christus Victor logic. Ambrose of Milan (337–97) spoke of a "pious fraud,"[13] by which the devil was deceived, while Cyril of Jerusalem (313–86) wrote of Christ's body as being made a "bait to death," which when gulped down by "the dragon," caused Satan to "disgorge" those whom he had "devoured."[14] I have noted already how Augustine grotesquely likened the cross to a "mousetrap" baited with Christ's blood.[15] Yet when such blood was offered to the devil "as a price for us," Satan "was not enriched but bound."[16]

Still, the specifics of this ransom logic were not unanimously accepted. John of Damascus (676–749) bristled at the notion that "the blood of the Lord should have been offered to the tyrant,"[17] preferring instead to picture "death" as that which swallowed "the bait" of Christ's humanity. Aside from this point, however, John's account of trickery was much the same: "Since the enemy had caught man with the bait of the hope of divinity, he himself was taken with the bait of the barrier of the flesh."[18]

Centuries later, even Martin Luther (1483–1546) expressed delight in the patristic "fishhook" imagery, noting that the Psalm quoted by Christ on the cross, had likened the speaker to a "worm, and not a man" (Ps 22:6).[19] In this way,

13. Ambrose, Expositio Evangelii secundum Lucam, 4.16; cited in Hans Boersma, Violence, Hospitality, and the Cross: Reappropriating the Atonement Tradition (Grand Rapids: Baker Academic, 2004), 191.

14. Cyril of Jerusalem, Catechetical Lectures, lecture 12 (NPNF² 7:72–81).

15. Augustine, Sermon 130, as cited in see Stanley P. Rosenberg, "Interpreting Atonement in Augustine's Preaching," in The Glory of the Atonement: Biblical, Historical and Practical Perspectives, Charles Hill and Frank A. James, eds. (Downers Grove, IL: IVP, 2004), ch. 11.

16. Augustine, De Trinitate, 13.15. My claim (ch. 4) was that, in Augustine, the ransom/ victory imagery coexists with a novel form of what might be called "mere penal substitution," in part because Augustine sees Satan as the one who unwittingly metes out the divinely sanctioned penalty (death) for human sin.

17. In this way, John partly followed the logic of Gregory of Nazianzus (329–90), to whom I shall return momentarily.

18. John of Damascus, On the Orthodox Faith in NPNF² 10:72.

19. For Luther's frequent imagery of Christ as a "worm" on the cross, see Kenneth Hagen,

God has cast into the world his only Son . . . and upon the hook has put Christ's humanity, as the worm; then comes the devil and snaps at the (man) Christ, and devours him, and therewith he bites the iron hook, that is, the godhead of Christ, which chokes him, and all his power thereby is thrown to the ground. This is called *sapientia divine*, divine wisdom.[20]

The account of triumph through the devil's deception has deep roots in the history of atonement doctrine.[21]

| DECEPTION DISAPPEARS |

Why then did it vanish? For several reasons. First, in terms of biblical support, many note that the Bible hardly shows anything like the lurid imagery of Satan snatching at Christ's flesh because he was deceived about his hidden divinity. Indeed, it is often the demons that seem clearest on Jesus's true identity (e.g., Mark 1:24). Likewise, Hans Boersma argues that in Matthew's telling of the story, the devil's desire appears to be to keep Christ *off* the cross rather than crucify him.[22] For these reasons, the biblical case for ransom by divine deception may seem lacking.

Second, the model's lurid literalism has done little to prolong its life span. The imagery of a blood-baiting deity, a salivating Satan, and a cosmic sting operation has led more than one reader to refer to it as "grotesque" and "mythic."[23] And while the Scriptures surely contain many vivid (even bloody) metaphors, one must remember that to take any one of these too literally is to create a myth and in this case a rather garish one.[24]

Third, regarding divine character, many Christians find it difficult to square a God of truth with a picture of atonement through divine deceit. In response to this concern, Gregory of Nyssa attempted to justify the "fraud" and "deception" in at least two ways.[25] On the one hand, he appealed to

"Luther on Atonement—Reconfigured," *Concordia Theological Quarterly* 61, no. 4 (October 1997): 267–71.

20. Martin Luther, *Table Talk*, trans. William Hazlitt (Philadelphia: Lutheran Publication Society), 197.

21. Herein lies the value of Gustaf Aulén's retrieval of the model, despite the flaws within his study. See Aulén, *Christus Victor: An Historical Study of the Three Main Types of the Idea of Atonement*, trans. A. G. Hebert (London: SPCK, 1931).

22. See Boersma, *Violence, Hospitality, and the Cross*, 191.

23. See Aulén's chronicle of these charges in *Christus Victor*, 17.

24. Colin Gunton, *Actuality of Atonement: A Study of Metaphor, Rationality and the Christian Tradition* (London: T&T Clark, 1988), 64.

25. Gregory of Nyssa, *An Address on Religious Instruction* 26, in *Christology of the*

justice as that which is "fitting." He pointed out the appropriate symmetry that "he who deceived man by the bait of sensual pleasure is himself deceived by the presentment of [Christ's] human form." Next, Nyssen also defended the justness of divine trickery by a claim of the salvific ends justifying the deceptive means. Divine trickery was thus compared to that of a doctor who hides medicine in food in order to bring healing. God's ruse was acceptable because it was done for the salvation of humanity and even for the "benefit" of him "who had wrought our ruin" (that is, the devil)![26] This final point highlights Nyssen's controversial suggestion, picked up from Origen, that even Satan might one day be redeemed because of Christ's atoning work. But few have followed Gregory.

A fourth reason for the argument's decline involved questions over Satan's "rights." Even in Nyssen's own lifetime, his fellow Cappadocian, Gregory of Nazianzus (329–90), argued that it was an "outrage" to suggest that "the robber should receive the ransom" from God.[27] Likewise, in the medieval era, Anselm of Canterbury (1033–1109) claimed that when one slave deceives another, what is deserved is punishment, not payment.[28] And in more modern times, Hastings Rashdall (1858–1924) argued that to speak of the devil's "just rights" over humanity was not just "immoral" but "childish."[29]

Fifth, the disappearance of this patristic paradigm coincided with the rise of juridical categories to speak of the atonement.[30] In the aftermath of the Reformation, legal language began to dominate the landscape as salvation was sometimes individualized as an exchange by which the believer received imputed righteousness while Christ took sin and guilt upon himself. While I have elsewhere attempted to defend the validity of legal language under the ancient context of the covenant, few would dispute that an exclusive focus on judicial categories sometimes squeezed out the biblical theme of *Christus Victor*.

Sixth, the Enlightenment's rational rejection of the unseen world also played a part in the model's waning influence. When the world of witches, fairies, and gibbering ghosts was progressively "disenchanted," so too was

Later Fathers, ed. Edward Hardy (Louisville: Westminster John Knox, 1954), 302.

26. Gregory of Nyssa, *Great Catechism*, in NPNF² 5:495.

27. Likewise, Nazianzen also found it unacceptable that such a ransom would be offered to the Father, "For it was not the Father who held us captive." Gregory of Nazianzus, *Oratio*, 45.22 (*NPNF²* 7:427).

28. See *Cur Deus Homo*, 1.7.

29. Hastings Rashdall, *The Idea of Atonement in Christian Theology* (London: MacMillan & Co., 1919), 364.

30. So claimed Aulén, *Christus Victor*, 88.

the atonement.[31] Thus the idea of a bloodthirsty Satan who "snaps at" and "devours" Christ,[32] was seen by many to have gone the way of other ignorant superstitions. In the infamous claim of Rudolf Bultmann: "We cannot use electric lights and radios . . . and at the same time believe in the spirit . . . world of the New Testament."[33]

Seventh and finally, some have claimed that more deterministic accounts of divine sovereignty have diminished many forms of the logic of *Christus Victor*. "Where providence extends to every minute detail of human life," writes Hans Boersma, "it may not be easy to see how real 'warfare' is taking place in which Christ has won the principle battle."[34] If Boersma is correct, it might explain why the emphasis on *Christus Victor* views of the atonement all but disappeared from some segments of the Reformed tradition. While he may be right of the later tradition, this difficulty would be news to Augustine and Luther. They had no trouble reconciling an all-determining God with the duping of the devil.

All these reasons reveal why the divine deception form of *Christus Victor* thinking all but disappeared from Christian history. Yet the idea, like Christ himself, would not stay dead forever.

| DECEPTION *REDIVIVUS* |

Over the past century, there have been surprising moves to resurrect the theme of trickery within atonement doctrine. As a precursor to the revival, Gustaf Aulén's (1879–1977) influential work performed a great service by recovering what he called the classical or dramatic view of Jesus's work: the idea of *Christus Victor*.[35] This retrieval of redemption as a conquest over evil came on the heels of the Great War (WWI),[36] which, along with the

---

31. For context, see G. M. Trevelyan, *England Under the Stuarts*, 17th ed. (London: Methuen, 1938), 53–54. In describing premodern England, the historian claims, perhaps with some exaggeration, that: "The fields around town and hamlet were filled, as soon as the day labourers had left them, by goblins and will-o'-the-wisps; and the woods, as soon as the forester had closed the door of his hut, became the haunt of fairies; the ghosts could be heard gibbering all night under the yew tree in the churchyard; the witch, a well-known figure in the village, was in the pay of lovers whose mistresses were hard to win, and gentlemen-farmers whose cattle had sickened. . . . The world was still a mystery, of which the wonder was not dispelled in foolish minds by a daily stream of facts and cheap explanations."

32. Luther, *Table Talk*, 197.

33. Rudolf Bultmann, "The New Testament and Mythology: The Problem of Demythologizing the New Testament Proclamation," in *The New Testament and Mythology and Other Basic Writings*, ed. Schubert Ogden (Philadelphia: Fortress, 1984), 2–4.

34. Boersma, *Violence, Hospitality, and the Cross*, 194.

35. See again, Aulén, *Christus Victor*.

36. As Philip Jenkins notes, spiritualism reached new heights during and after the First

war to follow (WWII), reacquainted optimistic and "enlightened" moderns with the reality of pervasive and seemingly inhuman evil. There was, in memorable words of Robert Jenson, the sense that there was *something* out there "laughing at us."[37]

In the same century, the stunning growth of the Charismatic movement (starting on Azusa Street in 1906) brought increased popular attention to the realm of demonic activity, spiritual warfare, and bondage to the devil.[38] In each case, the victorious solution was seen to come through the blood of Jesus and the "word of faith."[39] This movement brought a further retrieval of *Christus Victor* imagery, albeit in a less academic key. When taken together, (1) Aulén's work, (2) the aftershocks of war and holocaust, and (3) the rise of the Charismatic movement all combined to bring the theme of Christ's triumph back into focus within atonement theology. But the reclamation of trickery was left to others.

C. S. Lewis: A Narnian Atonement

Famously, C. S. Lewis (1898–1963) appeared to endorse something like the patristic account of divine deception within his fictional children's series, The Chronicles of Narnia. In *The Lion, the Witch and the Wardrobe*, the lion Aslan is presented as the rightful ruler of Narnia, despite the fact that the White Witch has gained dominion via treachery. The result is that the land is cursed, and the Witch has been granted authority by "the Deep Magic" to execute all traitors. This includes the child Edmund, who has betrayed his siblings and joined the Witch's cause.

In the tale, Aslan intervenes to rescue Edmund. Yet in response, the Witch reminds him of the ancient arrangement: "You know . . . the magic which the Emperor put into Narnia at the very beginning . . . that every traitor belongs to me as my lawful prey. . . . His blood is my property."[40]

World War, perhaps brought on by the fact that so many longed to contact their lost loved ones. See Jenkins, *The Great and Holy War: How World War I Became a Religious Crusade* (New York: HarperCollins, 2014), 16.

37. Robert Jenson, *A Theology in Outline: Can These Bones Live?* (Oxford: Oxford University Press, 2016), 60.

38. See Nigel Wright, "Charismatic Interpretations of the Demonic," in *The Unseen World: Christian Reflections on Angels, Demons, and the Heavenly Realm*, ed. Anthony N. S. Lane (Grand Rapids: Baker, 1996), ch. 8.

39. While many works ignore this popular movement because (1) it takes place (mostly) outside of academic circles, and (2) because some of its most notable proponents are deemed downright embarrassing when held up to critical scrutiny, Ben Pugh helpfully includes the "Word of Faith" phenomenon in his survey of "ransom" viewpoints. See Pugh, *Atonement Theories*, 13–16.

40. C. S. Lewis, *The Lion, the Witch and the Wardrobe* (repr., New York: HarperCollins, 2009), 130.

While Aslan does not dispute the Witch's claim, he does go on to stun onlookers by offering his life as ransom for the traitor. Edmund is released, and on the Stone Table, where such cursed justice must be carried out, the Lion is slain as devilish hordes rejoice.

But like Christ, Aslan soon rises. At the moment of his resurrection, the Stone Table splits in two, and the reader learns the reason from the lion's mouth:

> Though the Witch knew the Deep Magic, there is a magic deeper still which she did not know. Her knowledge goes back only to the dawn of time. But if she could have looked a little further back, into the stillness and the darkness before Time dawned, she would have read there a different incantation. She would have known that when a willing victim who had committed no treachery was killed in a traitor's stead, the Table would crack and Death itself would start working backwards.[41]

Because the tale is fiction, it would be unfair to claim it as the full expression of Lewis's theology. Still, it is interesting to note that this Narnian atonement model is similar to Augustine's way of fusing penal substitutionary logic with ideas of ransom and the devil's deception.[42] In line with penal substitution, Aslan offers himself "in place of" and "instead of" Edmund, to suffer the penalty of death. And like Augustine's claim, it is the Satan character who has been granted authority (by Aslan's father, the Emperor beyond the Sea) to carry out this "cursed justice." There is, in this way, a measure of "divine" sanction for the arrangement.

Yet the distance between Narnia and Hippo Regius can be seen in this: whereas Augustine placed the emphasis upon the devil's ignorance of Christ's *divinity* (we might call this the *Deus incognitus* version of the trickery motif), Lewis instead traced the Witch's ignorance to the "Deeper Magic" concerning the death of a willing and innocent victim. Aslan's divinity—though elsewhere affirmed in the saga—plays no explicit part in the Witch's deception. Still, both cases (Narnia and Augustine) feature a form of divine trickery married to a novel form of penal substitution.[43]

---

41. Lewis, *The Lion, the Witch and the Wardrobe*, 150. This logic is affirmed by Gregory Boyd in his "Christus Victor Response" to penal substitution, in *The Nature of the Atonement: Four Views*, ed. James Beilby and Paul R. Eddy (Downers Grove, IL: IVP Academic, 2006), 100–101.

42. See ch. 4.

43. It is sometimes said that Lewis rejected penal substitution as a "silly theory." Yet the reality is more complex. In *Mere Christianity*—written *prior* to the Narnia series—Lewis

Gregory Boyd: Satan's Self-Deception

In the work of Gregory Boyd, we find a theologian who endorses a version of this Narnian atonement model. For Boyd,

> God did, in a sense, deceive Satan and the powers [just as] Jesus was, in a sense, "bait." But there was nothing duplicitous or unjust in God's behavior. To the contrary, God was simply acting in an outrageously loving way, knowing all the while that his actions could not be understood by the powers whose evil blinds them to love. Like an infinitely wise military strategist, God knew how to get his enemies to use their self-inflicted blindness against themselves and thus use their self-chosen evil to his advantage.[44]

In short, Satan is deceived, but God does not act deceitfully. Rather, as Boyd argues, the devil is blind to the logic of love, therefore he cannot grasp the reason for the incarnation. The problem with later versions of the *Christus Victor* paradigm, at least in Boyd's view, is that the accounts of ransom, victory, and divine deception "became incredulous because they were pressed too vigorously for details."[45] Thus Boyd does not speculate on exactly *how* Satan was defeated by God's sacrificial love.

Boyd does believe, however, that the Bible gives enough evidence to support the notion that the devil was deceived. His reasons are threefold. First, he claims that throughout Christ's ministry, the demons seem to know *who* Jesus is (the Son of God) but not why exactly he has come. Hence their question in Mark's Gospel: "What do you want with us, Jesus of Nazareth? Have you come to destroy us?" (1:24; cf. 5:7). In this way, the demonic understanding of Christ is partial and thus prone to false assumptions.[46]

admits that penal substitution *sounds like* a silly theory "on the face of it" given our modern understandings of justice and punishment. If one considers punishment merely "in a police-court sense," then there seems no point in the condemnation of an innocent victim. Surely this is accurate. Yet in response, two points must be made: First, neither Narnia nor the biblical-covenantal narrative conceives of justice in this individualized "police-court sense." Thus, the contention that Lewis rejects all accounts of substitutionary penalty-bearing as "silly" is not supportable by a broad reading of his work. Second, as I have noted previously, it is no part of my case to claim that Lewis's Narnia typology presents a full-orbed version of his own atonement doctrine. As a work of fantasy and fiction, the Narnia series is meant to engage the imaginations of children, and to make connections with the "true myth" of the gospel, not to comprise a systematic theology. See Lewis, *Mere Christianity* (1943; repr., New York: Macmillan, 1952), 58–59. For further background, see Charles Taliaferro, "A Narnian Theory of the Atonement," *SJT* 41 (1988): 75–92.

44. Boyd, "Christus Victor View," 37.
45. Boyd, "Christus Victor View," 37n23.
46. This too may be reflected in the Witch's real but limited knowledge of Narnia's Deep Magic.

Second, Boyd also points to the secret, hidden, and mysterious nature of God's cross-shaped wisdom as a sign of Satan being fooled (Rom 16:25; 1 Cor 2:7; Eph 3:9–10; Col 1:26). While most of the above passages may be taken to reference how this understanding was hidden from *humanity*, Ephesians mentions an unveiling of God's secret wisdom to "rulers and authorities in the heavenly realms" (Eph 3:10). Likewise, 1 Corinthians 2, a passage used often in the patristic period, provides the most famous proof text for Boyd's logic. Here, Paul writes that "None of the rulers of this age understood [the wisdom of the cross], for if they had, they would not have crucified the Lord of glory" (2:8).

Third, Boyd points to the fact that "Satan and his minions were instrumental in bringing about Christ's crucifixion," for it was Satan who "entered" Judas and led him to betray the Lord (John 13:27). As true as this may be, it also raises questions. In the view of Boersma, Satan elsewhere tempts Christ to embrace the crown without the cross.[47] What is one to make of such a paradoxical devil? What sort of Satan seeks at different times to *avoid* and to *cause* the crucifixion? I will propose a possible solution to this issue momentarily, but for now I merely note how Boyd transposes Lewis's Narnian atonement into a more theological key.

Darby Kathleen Ray: Deception Demythologized

In *Deceiving the Devil*, Darby Kathleen Ray takes a different approach to redemptive trickery. By accepting resources from feminist and liberation theologians, Ray aims to "retrieve and refine" the patristic insight that "the powers of evil . . . must be creatively and cunningly subverted" rather than be forcefully overcome by unilateral force.[48] Yet in refining this notion, Ray also sets out to demythologize it, along with other traditional doctrines. In particular, she notes three major departures from the previous tradition.

First, she rejects what she calls a "dualistic framework," which seeks to make "a clear-cut metaphysical distinction between good and evil, God and the devil." In her view, this absolutism fails to recognize the subtle, complex, and pervasive nature of wickedness, while also fueling "righteous" violence against those deemed to be wrong.[49] While Ray does not explicitly reject the idea that God is wholly good, she does slide toward

---

47. The evidence for this is found especially in Matthew's Gospel, in Christ's rebuke of Peter ("Get behind me, Satan" [Matt 16:23]), and in the wilderness temptations (Matt 4). Boersma, *Violence, Hospitality, and the Cross*, 191.

48. Darby Kathleen Ray, *Deceiving the Devil: Atonement, Abuse, and Ransom* (Cleveland: Pilgrim, 1998), vii.

49. Ray, *Deceiving the Devil*, 126–27.

relativism in contending that "all definitions of good and evil are social constructs."[50] Having acknowledged this, she clarifies that her own socially constructed viewpoint is that evil is primarily an abuse of power.[51]

Second, Ray seeks to revise the patristic use of trickery by rejecting what she calls its "purely cosmic" depiction of redemption. While the church fathers viewed the great conflict as between a transcendent God and a personal devil,[52] Ray claims that the focus ought to be on "confronting human evil."[53] Satan is therefore demythologized to represent "the sum total of evil,"[54] and Christ is demythologized to function as the preeminent human example for how we should face evil with nonviolent creativity and cunning.[55]

Third, Ray also alters what she describes as the traditional portrayal of atonement as a "done deal" in which there is an "absolute and universal triumph over evil." Nearly all Christians acknowledge the continuing power of evil in the present world, but Ray goes much further by claiming that we must embrace the possibility that there may be no final victory, and that "good may not triumph." With this "sober" and admittedly "tragic" view in mind, her suggestion is that Christians learn to serve and act in the face of evil's ultimate "intractability."[56]

As should be obvious, Ray's claims represent a massive revision of traditional doctrine. However, my focus here is merely upon the theme of victory via trickery. In her view, this patristic insight holds promise for those on the underside of power, specifically because marginalized persons must often face evil by way of "cunning and creativity rather than force."[57] They must outsmart their foes, by using their oppressors' ignorance and lust for power against them. Ray also observes this approach at work in Jesus's life, insofar as he models a posture that does not seek to conquer through brute force.[58]

---

50. Ray, Deceiving the Devil, 132.
51. Ray, Deceiving the Devil, ch. 1.
52. Ray, Deceiving the Devil, 128.
53. Ray, Deceiving the Devil, 6.
54. Ray, Deceiving the Devil, 131.
55. While Ray rejects the more radical feminist claim of Rita Nakashima Brock that Jesus is "just one among many" inspiring exemplars, she nonetheless maintains that "redemption is not a thing of the past effected for us by another, but a constant challenge, a real possibility" that we must work toward. Deceiving the Devil, 145.
56. Ray, Deceiving the Devil, 129.
57. Ray, Deceiving the Devil, 140.
58. Hans Boersma critiques not only Ray's departure from traditional Christology and eschatology, but also her assumption that deceit should be seen as a form of laudable non-violence, while physical violence must be universally rejected. In his view, this distinction is

| A RESPONSE TO THE RETRIEVALS |

Having now surveyed these three retrievals of atonement by deception, a question still remains: To what extent are they viable? Indeed, while Lewis's Narnian narrative is imaginative and almost Augustinian, it remains within the realm of fiction. Likewise, Boyd's partial endorsement of Lewis's logic raises questions regarding the unspecified means of victory (on which he is silent) and the devil's apparently contradictory desires: at one point trying to keep Christ off the cross, and at another leading Judas to betray him. Finally, while Ray offers intriguing insights for the application of the paradigm in real world settings, her logic flows forth from a diminished Christ, a symbolic Satan, and a completely hypothetical victory.

In the final portion of this chapter, I will gesture toward what a more robust retrieval of the devil's deception might look like. To do so, I will draw selectively upon both patristic and contemporary sources. In keeping with the prior chapters, I will maintain that the central means (or mechanism) of Christ's victory is his recapitulative obedience and his vicarious judgment (including penal substitution) on our behalf. Those "pieces" remain. Still, my prior arguments need not necessarily exclude the idea that the principalities and powers were deceived in one way or another. Yet to show this possibility, one must first deal with the aforementioned problems.

Evil's Irrationality

A first obstacle is the apparent oddity of a biblical devil who is at one point tempting Christ to avoid the cross (Boersma) and at another helping to cause it (Boyd). While this certainly seems schizophrenic, a possible solution may be found in the work of Karl Barth and T. F. Torrance. In their own ways, both men are helpful in revealing how the realm of evil and the demonic *must* involve a kind of chaotic inconsistency at its very core.

For Torrance, evil is by its nature "contradictory and irrational." Thus "we cannot think it out into full clarity."[59] In similar fashion, Barth famously employed the concept of *das Nichtige* (the nothingness or the negative) to speak of the demonic. Lest one think that he was completely denying the reality of these powers, however, Barth also clarified: "We cannot deny their

---

all the more questionable because Ray "holds that there is no universal morality grounded in absolute foundations." Boersma, *Violence, Hospitality, and the Cross*, 198–99.

59. T. F. Torrance, *Incarnation: The Person and Life of Christ*, ed. Robert T. Walker (Downers Grove, IL: IVP Academic, 2008), 244.

existence,"[60] for *Das Nichtige ist nicht das Nichts!* ("The nothingness is not nothing").[61] In all of this, there is the idea that evil exists as a chaotic paradox, a powerful but ultimately irrational force that moves to sweep all things—perhaps itself included!—into a state of dissolution. For this reason, Thomas Noble seems right to state that "there is no logical metaphysical system which can explain evil."[62]

If this is true, then it would not be surprising that the New Testament paints Satan in a paradoxical position with regard to Christ's death. Likewise, one might also contend that the insights of Torrance and Barth fit together with the patristic imagery of a devil that cannot help himself when presented with the chance for a kill. Still, the reason for this reality need not be Satan's ignorance of Christ's hidden divinity, but the fact that—as with an addict—a rational weighing of pros, cons, and long-term repercussions simply does not describe the nature of *Das Nichtige* any more than it describes the drug user who reaches for the needle.[63] Evil is irrational; get used to it.

The God of Truth and Satan's Deception

A second issue to be overcome involves the apparent tension between deception and divine truthfulness. After all, the Lord "is not a man, that he should lie" (Num 23:19). In fact, "it is impossible for God to lie [*pseudomai*]" (Heb 6:18), for "God is true" (John 3:33) and his "word is truth" (John 17:17).

I noted previously that Gregory of Nyssa responded to these concerns with a distinction between righteous and unrighteous deceit. And perhaps, as some ethicists and theologians contend, such a case can be made. After all, few find it morally repugnant that a brave homeowner would deceive Nazi soldiers to protect the hidden Jews in the cellar. And it has been argued that the biblical notion of truth (*emet*) is more akin to faithfulness than to verifiable correspondence.[64] Likewise, there are those thorny passages that appear to speak of the Lord as involved in deception. In 1 Kings, God sends "a deceiving spirit" into the mouths of certain prophets (22:22), and in Ezekiel one reads that "I, the LORD, have deceived that prophet" (14:9 ESV;

---

60. CD III/3, 523.
61. CD III/3, 349.
62. Thomas A. Noble, "The Spirit World: A Theological Approach," in Lane, *The Unseen World*, 206.
63. A full exploration of the ontic status of the demonic must await the next chapter.
64. See Boersma, *Violence, Hospitality, and the Cross*, 193.

cf. Jer 20:7–13). Ideas of divine deception may not be as unbiblical as they initially sound—at least in certain circumstances.[65]

But there is another option with regard to Satan and "the powers." Boyd is helpful in suggesting a kind of intractable ignorance and *self-deception* at work within all depraved and nonomniscient minds. Because the fallen spiritual powers are evil, the suggestion is that they are "incapable of understanding love." And this reality leaves them unable to "fathom the possibility that the Son of God had become human out of love for this fallen race of rebels."[66] While I must refrain here from a full discussion of the ontic status of the devil, it is reasonable to claim that, whatever "Satan" is, he is both depraved and nonomniscient.[67]

This possibility gains relevance as one returns to 1 Corinthians 2. This passage asserts that the "rulers of this age" would not have crucified the Lord of glory if they had understood God's secret wisdom (2:8). The claim, however, is not that God acts deceitfully but that a sinful misunderstanding on the part of the "powers"—their ignorance and violent grasping—aids God's purposes. In this way, the demons' understanding of Christ is real but partial. They seem to know *who* he is, but not exactly *why* he has come. And within this gap, between partial and omniscient understanding, there is room for self-deceiving overreach. Nothing is more inscrutable to a liar than the truth. Just as nothing is more inscrutable to a hater than sacrificial love. In the view of Paul Fiddes, this brings one to a nugget of wisdom within the crass patristic analogies: "Evil always bites off more than it can chew."[68]

| CONCLUSION |

If all this is so, then a partial retrieval of the patristic paradigm is defensible. In this theology, one might claim that God uses the Enemy's violent momentum against him, in a mix of justice and divine jujitsu. Here, as in the Japanese martial art, victory comes not by striking back with worldly

---

65. See especially, Kevin Vanhoozer, "Ezekiel 14: 'I, the Lord, Have Deceived That Prophet': Divine Deception, Inception, and Communicative Action," in *Theological Commentary: Evangelical Perspectives*, ed. R. Michael Allen (New York: T&T Clark, 2011).

66. Gregory A. Boyd, *Crucifixion of the Warrior God: Interpreting the Old Testament's Violent Portraits of God in Light of the Cross*, vol. 2, *The Cruciform Thesis* (Minneapolis: Fortress, 2017), 802.

67. Ch. 9 will address Satan's ontic status as a potential challenge to *Christus Victor* views of the atonement.

68. Paul Fiddes, *Past Event and Present Salvation: The Christian Idea of Atonement* (Louisville: Westminster John Knox, 1989), 138.

weapons but by turning the attacker's energy, ignorance, and careless aggression back on himself.[69]

To modify Augustine only slightly, one might claim that the devil's ignorance and self-deception coexist with the idea that Christ triumphed by the "justice game" rather than the power game.[70] Once placed upon the representative *feet* of recapitulation and with the covenantal *heart* of penal substitution, this approach adds yet another facet to an integrated mosaic of atonement. It does so by giving still more insight into the way the divine triumph came about. Yet in order for this reading to gain traction, I must now deal with an objection that I have been avoiding thus far: the ontic status of the Enemy.

---

69. Since writing this chapter, I have been alerted to a similar martial arts analogy in Boyd. In his view, God's wrath and Christ's cruciform triumph come by way of "divine Aikido." This Japanese technique translates to "the way of peace" since it trains warriors to engage in "nonresistant combat" (a phrase that may seem like a blatant contradiction). While the Aikido analogy has many commonalities with my own view of the cross, I take issue with Boyd's wholesale rejection of divine violence in the Scriptures, and with his assumption that God's active personal judgment of evil automatically contradicts the cruciform love displayed in Christ. I will return to this subject in ch. 12. See Boyd, *Crucifixion of the Warrior God*, II/767.

70. Augustine, *De Trinitate*, 13.13.

CHAPTER 9

WINKING AT THE DEVIL

EXAMINING THE ONTIC STATUS OF THE SATAN

"Who's there?"

Hamlet, Line 1

Every story needs a villain. In many Christian circles that figure is unquestionably the devil. Yet if a contemporary challenge to recapitulation involves the historical Adam (ch. 2), then a crucial question hanging over *Christus Victor* is that of the historical Satan. In the words of Walter Wink, "Nothing commends Satan to the modern mind." He remains, in sophisticated circles at least, "a scandal, a stone of stumbling, a bone in the throat of modernity."[1] A recent survey indicated that even amongst American Christians around 40 percent believe that the devil is not a "living being" but merely a "symbol of evil."[2] One is not likely to bring up one's belief in the demonic at dinner parties. In many contexts, the villain has become unmentionable.

At the core of *Christus Victor* imagery stands the notion that Christ "disarmed the powers and authorities" and "made a public spectacle of them . . . by the cross" (Col 2:15). Indeed, "The reason the Son of God

---

1. Walter Wink, *Unmasking the Powers: The Invisible Forces that Determine Human Existence* (Philadelphia: Fortress, 1986), 9 and 6, respectively.

2. "Most American Christians Do Not Believe That Satan or the Holy Spirit Exist," Barna Group, December 11, 2015, as cited in Richard Beck, *Reviving Old Scratch: Demons and the Devil for Doubters and the Disenchanted* (Minneapolis: Fortress, 2016), xv.

appeared was to destroy the devil's work" (1 John 3:8). I have already explored how recapitulation and vicarious judgment function as means to Christ's victory (from *feet* to *heart* to *head*), but I have not yet explored the ontic status of the Enemy. Thus the opening question of Shakespeare's *Hamlet* echoes over the abyss: "Who's there?"

In the oft-cited words of C. S. Lewis, "There are two equal and opposite errors into which our race can fall about the devils. One is to disbelieve in their existence. The other is to believe, and to feel an excessive and unhealthy interest in them."[3] If one accepts this dictum, then it is possible to scan Christian history in order to separate persons or movements into one of two extremes: (1) excessive demythologizing or (2) excessive fascination.[4] In some cases, both poles are present in a single life. In my own past I can recall a boyhood fascination with the "spiritual warfare" novels of Frank Peretti—even setting out to write my own version at a young age. (Mercifully, that work has since been lost to history!) Yet I can also trace a later embarrassment with such vivid demonology. And the embarrassment was not unique to me.

For Stephen Noll, a "quick, sharp glance is just about all theologians of the second half of the twentieth century have allotted to the spirit world; with one exception": Walter Wink (1935–2012).[5] Through his trilogy on "the Powers,"[6] Wink managed to open new discussions on spiritual forces amongst both liberals and conservatives alike. Decades later, his project remains, in the view of N. T. Wright, "the major work" on the subject.[7] The influence stems partly from the way Wink marries lengthy study of ancient sources with vivid prose and imaginative application. He is anything but boring; and his work incorporates everything from Scripture

---

3. C. S. Lewis, *The Screwtape Letters* (1942; repr., SanFrancisco: Harper Collins, 1996), ix. Lewis spoke from experience. For while he once embraced a full-fledged naturalism, he also admitted to having dabbled in the occult at a younger age.

4. In the view of Michael Green, excessive fascination with the demonic has more often characterized the past two thousand years. Green, *I Believe in Satan's Downfall* (Grand Rapids: Eerdmans, 1981), 16.

5. Stephen F. Noll, "Thinking About Angels," in *The Unseen World: Christian Reflections on Angels, Demons, and the Heavenly Realm*, ed. Anthony N. S. Lane (Grand Rapids: Baker, 1996), 23. While Wink is certainly not the only exception to this trend, Noll's exaggeration points out his importance.

6. Walter Wink, *Naming the Powers: The Language of Power in the New Testament* (Philadelphia: Fortress, 1984); Wink, *Unmasking the Powers: The Invisible Forces That Determine Human Existence* (Philadelphia: Fortress, 1986); Wink, *Engaging the Powers: Discernment and Resistance in a World of Domination* (Minneapolis: Fortress, 1992).

7. N. T. Wright, *Paul and the Faithfulness of God*, Christian Origins and the Question of God, vol. 4 (Minneapolis: Fortress, 2013), 1285n39.

to tradition, poetry to politics, psychology to social work. It thus defies a narrow characterization.

My goal in this chapter is to examine the ontic nature of Satan with Wink's project as a primary conversation partner.[8] The matter will proceed in three movements: First, I will begin with an overview of Wink's basic claims as he traces Satan's supposed evolution from servant to Evil One. Second, I will critique some of Wink's more troubling arguments on both biblical and theological grounds. Then third, in a kind of constructive postscript, I will note some ways in which Wink's project may give positive cues toward a view of Satan that fits with what I proposed within the prior chapter. To recall, that argument built upon the old patristic notion that Christ conquered not only through recapitulative obedience and vicarious judgment, but also through the duping of the devil and his minions.

| A SURVEY OF WINK'S SATAN |

At its core, Wink's view of the powers is one of partial demythologization. In his opinion, modern persons cannot merely accept the biblical cosmology of evil spirits as personal beings that flit about the cosmos. That worldview is "beyond being salvaged."[9] At the same time, one must attempt to recover the experience that it named. "What the ancients called 'spirits' or 'angels' or 'demons' were actual entities, only they were not hovering in the air. They were incarnate in cellulose, or cement, or skin and bones, or an empire, or its mercenary armies."[10]

This "somewhat demythologized" approach is meant to find a middle ground between the ancient view of "little beings in the sky"[11] and the modern myth of atheistic naturalism. This naturalism, like modernity itself, is "terminally ill" by Wink's judgment. His hope is that whatever worldview replaces it will be able to honor the values of modern science without falling victim to its reductionism.[12]

Because power must be incarnated, Wink's central idea is that the entities described as angels or demons should be seen as the *interior spiritual*

---

8. It should be noted that the Bible's treatment of the "powers" (*dunameis*) that oppose the way of Jesus is much larger than just "Satan" or "the devil." Scripture speaks also of "authorities" (*exousias*), "elemental spirits" or "basic principles" (*stocichea*), and "principalities" (*archai*) that may align against Christ with both material or spiritual components. For sake of space, however, I must confine this chapter to (the) Satan.

9. Wink, *Unmasking the Powers*, 4.
10. Wink, *Unmasking the Powers*, 5.
11. Wink, *Unmasking the Powers*, 68.
12. Wink, *Unmasking the Powers*, 2.

expression (or "inner aspect"[13]) of material structures, communities, and persons: "Every economic system, state apparatus, and power elite [has] an intrinsic spirituality, an inner essence." While this interiority cannot be split off from the outer manifestation, it cannot be collapsed into it either. These forces, Wink insists, are real powers and not mere symbols or mental constructs.[14] In this chapter, however, my chief concern is with Satan himself.[15] With that limited focus in mind, I turn to the first stage in Wink's imaginative argument: his survey of the Old Testament.

Satan as Yahweh's Servant

In the beginning, Wink's claim is that both good and evil were ascribed to Yahweh. "I kill, and I make alive," says the LORD in Deuteronomy, "I wound, and I heal" (32:39). Within this worldview, Wink claims that "it was not inconsistent to believe that Yahweh might call Moses to deliver Israel from Egypt and then, on the way, attempt to murder him."[16] Eventually, however, the moral cost of such a deity was too high; and with this realization, Yahweh's "light" and "dark" sides were gradually differentiated.

The bright side would come to be represented by the angels, while the dark was seen in Satan and his demons. Still, "this process . . . was completed so late," says Wink, "that Satan makes only three [explicit] appearances in the Old Testament": (1) 1 Chronicles 21:1; (2) Zechariah 3:1–5; and (3) the prologue to the book of Job. In each instance, Satan appears (allegedly) not as the archetype of evil, but as God's servant and his agent provocateur.[17] I will now briefly survey each of these passages.

1 Chronicles 21:1

According to the Chronicler, "Satan rose up against Israel and incited David to take a census" (21:1).[18] In the passage, the king's action is seen as sinful, although the precise reason is not given, and it brings swift punishment in the form of a plague.[19] Yet an alternate, and probably earlier,

---

13. Wink, *Naming the Powers*, 104.
14. Wink, *Unmasking the Powers*, 25–26.
15. This limitation is primarily for sake of space. Still, since Scripture presents the devil as the "prince of demons" (Matt 9:34; 12:24; Mark 3:22–30; Luke 11:14–26) who are also pictured as his "angels" (Matt 25:41), it is perfectly reasonable to make connections between Satan and these other evil spirits.
16. Wink, *Unmasking the Powers*, 11; cf. Exod 4:24–26.
17. Wink, *Unmasking the Powers*, 11.
18. This is the only instance in the Hebrew Scriptures in which "Satan" appears without the definite article, suggesting that the word is being used as a proper name and not merely as a title ("the Accuser").
19. Because a census was often undertaken as a means of military conscription, taxation,

account of this event appears in 2 Samuel 24. In this text, it is not Satan but Yahweh (!) who in "anger" incites David to carry out a census (v. 1). The two passages have long been troubling, and not least for the New Testament notion that God tempts no one (Jas 1:13). For his own part, Wink focuses on the extent to which the Accuser acts as God's suggestive servant. In the scene from 1 Chronicles and 2 Samuel,

> The Adversary has assumed the function of the executor of God's wrath. . . . who plants oppressive ideas in a mortal's mind. He does not represent disorder, chaos, or rebellion here, but rather the imposition of a suffocating bureaucratic order (the census). Satan furthers God's will by visiting wrath on disobedient mortals, and in so doing carries out the will of God.[20]

In order for both texts to be accepted, Wink's claim is that the Adversary must be seen as acting on the orders of the LORD, like a covert agent who plants disinformation to test the faithfulness of the king. In this case, David fails the test.

Zechariah 3:1–5

In the second passage, the double agent has become the prosecutor. In Zechariah's vision, the high priest Joshua stands in filthy robes before the angel of the LORD. At his right side is "the Satan" (ha satan), who stands ready "to accuse him" (v. 1). The grimy garments represent the sin that brought forth Israel's exile, and Joshua bears the stains. Wink claims that the guilt is real and that "only God's undeserved grace causes the case to be quashed."[21] This happens when "the angel [of the LORD] said to those who were standing before him, 'Take off his filthy clothes . . . and I will put fine garments on you'" (v. 4).

Yet up until this gracious reprieve, Wink's argument is that "the Adversary merely reiterates what the accusing conscience of the people has been affirming all along."[22] He is a voice from their interior, and he echoes the judgment of God's prophets. The problem is not that the devil is lying, but that he is telling the truth: Israel's sin deserves punishment.

---

or forced labor, one possibility is that it displayed a sinful trust in human military might rather than reliance on Israel's God. See Sydney H. T. Page, *Powers of Evil: A Biblical Study of Satan and Demons* (Grand Rapids: Baker, 1995), 34–35.

20. Wink, *Unmasking the Powers*, 12.
21. Wink, *Unmasking the Powers*, 12.
22. Wink, *Unmasking the Powers*, 12.

Job 1–2

The third and final reference to Satan in the Old Testament comes in the puzzling prologue to the book of Job. Here, Satan appears as a kind of roving "district attorney, zealously seeking out lawbreakers to bring before the bar of divine justice." Yet the surprising point for later readers is that Satan appears to do so as "a fully credentialed member of the heavenly court." As the book progresses, however, Satan's activity shifts from investigation to entrapment. "Not content merely to uncover injustice, Satan is here . . . striving to coax people into crimes for which they can then be punished." And from this reality Wink draws an application: "Excessive zeal for justice always becomes satanic."[23]

While Satan's behavior may seem diabolical, Wink's point is that the LORD of Job's prologue hardly looks much better. "Have you considered my servant Job?" he suggests (2:3). And in response to this leading question, Wink adds his own: "What kind of God is this that trifles with the lives and flesh of human beings in order to win a bet?"[24] This query, like those from the whirlwind, echoes forth unanswered. While some find solace by viewing the book as a parable that guards against overreading the relation between obedience and blessing, the rough edges in the story of Job remain. Indeed, God and Satan seem to be working (or is it playing?) surprisingly well together.

In conclusion to these three passages, Wink argues that Satan is seen in every instance as a "faithful, if overzealous, servant of God, entrusted with quality control and testing." In short, he is depicted as having a positive role within the divine economy, albeit as "more a function ('the adversary') than a personality." He is "not evil, or demonic, or fallen, or God's enemy."[25] And to assume such things is, in Wink's view, to project our own prejudice upon the LORD's "light-bearer" (Lucifer).

Although it is not yet time for my full response, it bears noting that many do not share this judgment. In fact, Wink's argument mutes the tension between God and the Accuser. In Job's prologue, Satan contradicts Yahweh, he implies that the LORD was foolish to think highly of his servant, and he does not rejoice when Job proves faithful after the first test. Instead, Satan responds with impudence and a call for more torture. So while the story paints Satan as standing before the divine throne, it is hardly clear that he does so out of love and loyalty.[26]

23. Wink, *Unmasking the Powers*, 13.
24. Wink, *Unmasking the Powers*, 13.
25. Wink, *Unmasking the Powers*, 14.
26. See Page, *Powers of Evil*, 28–30.

In Zechariah, the harsh rebuke received by Satan shows that his goals are clearly contrary to those of the LORD. There is tension here as well. And while the story of David's census shows Satan acting as Yahweh's punishing provocateur, it is God alone who mercifully ends the penalty. Here, too, Satan seems interested only in guilt and punishment while Yahweh alone restores.[27] In summation of these three texts, Sydney Page offers a very different argument from that of Wink. Page's claim is that all three texts "betray an awareness of Satan's fundamental opposition to God and humanity."[28] I will return to this discussion momentarily.

Satan as Servant in the New Testament

In turning to the New Testament, Wink's portrait of Satan as God's "strange servant"[29] continues. For sake of space, I will limit the examples to three brief case studies.

The Gospels

In Luke 22, Satan is pictured as the one who has asked to sift Peter and the other disciples like wheat.[30] In response, Wink notes that Christ's prayer is not that Simon would be excused from the test but that his faith would not fail because of it (vv. 31–32). The scene, complete with the devil once more asking for permission, evokes memories of Job. The sifting functions as a kind of "stress test" for diagnostic reasons. Wink's point is that Satan's action serves an important purpose. For despite Peter's initial failure of the test, the humbling result will be important for the later building "on this rock" (cf. Matt 16:18). After all, one sometimes learns more from failures than successes.

1 Corinthians 5

Moving to Paul's letters, the devil is called to play a part in the eventual salvation of a man who is sleeping with his stepmother. Desperate times, it seems, call for desperate measures. Paul's command is to "hand this man over to Satan for the destruction of the flesh, so that his spirit may be saved on the day of the Lord" (1 Cor 5:5). While admitting that this sounds like something from the Spanish Inquisition, Wink notes the "astonishing"

---

27. As Wink rightly notes, earlier Hebrew thought tended not to differentiate between primary and secondary causes; God was sovereign over all. See Walter C. Kaiser Jr., *Hard Sayings of the Old Testament* (Downers Grove, IL: IVP, 1988), 131.
28. Page, *Powers of Evil*, 37.
29. Wink, *Unmasking the Powers*, 19.
30. While Jesus speaks only to Peter ("Simon, Simon, Satan has asked to sift you"), the "you" (*hymas*) is plural, which indicates that the other disciples will also be put to the test.

fact that Paul views Satan as the means of deliverance for the incestuous brother. The devil is therefore "to work [the man] over through the choice forced upon him by the act of ceremonial exclusion." Satan is "God's holy sifter." Had the man prioritized the sexual relationship over the church, Wink's claim is that Satan would have been "the instrument of his damnation." Hence, "Satan cannot be described here as 'good' or 'evil,'" for "it is *our choices* that cause him to crystallize as the one or the other."[31]

2 Corinthians 12

In the subsequent (canonical) letter to the church in Corinth, the redemptive role of Satan continues, albeit through the "gift" of a tormenting messenger. "In order to keep me from becoming conceited," Paul writes, "I was given a thorn in my flesh, a messenger of Satan, to torment me" (2 Cor 12:7). Although Paul's torment is excruciating, his obedient response makes the devil's messenger into an instrument of sanctification. What's more, Wink asks whether Satan's help was actually necessary for the apostle's continued ministry: "Did Paul *need* a disability in order to combat a pride too powerful for him to master?" That is what the apostle seems to think. Wink concludes his treatment of the topic with a tongue-in-cheek pronouncement of thanksgiving: "How kind of Satan to assist . . . when we cannot consciously let some part of our egos die!"[32]

In summation of these three New Testament examples, Wink wonders if perhaps Origen of Alexandria was right to say that "God has not deprived the devil of his power over the world, because his collaboration is still necessary for the perfecting of those destined to receive a crown."[33] Satan is therefore seen as "God's enforcer, prosecutor, sifter, *agent provocateur,* tester, presser of choice, catalyst of consciousness, advocate of strict justice, and guardian of the status quo."[34] For Wink, he serves a dangerous though necessary function in the divine economy. Still, he does so as the spirit-world's equivalent of Rodney Dangerfield—who "can't get no respect."

The Making of a Murderer: Satan as Evil One

Wink is willing to admit, however, that there is "another side to Satan."[35] As sometimes happens with undercover agents, the light-bearer has gone

31. Wink, *Unmasking the Powers,* 15–16, italics in original.
32. Wink, *Unmasking the Powers,* 20.
33. Origen, *Homilies on Numbers,* 13.7; cited in Wink, *Unmasking the Powers,* 177n20.
34. Wink, *Unmasking the Powers,* 23.
35. Wink, *Unmasking the Powers,* 21–22.

rogue within human consciousness. Because of this, he has overstepped his appointed mandate, and "evolved . . . into a virtually autonomous and invisible suzerain within a world ruled by God." The New Testament therefore depicts Satan not merely as Yahweh's agent provocateur, but as the "evil one" (Matt 13:19; John 17:15; 1 John 2:13–14), the "enemy" (Matt 13:25, 28, 39; Luke 10:19), the "god of this world" (2 Cor 4:4), the leader of the demons (Mark 3:22), "the Destroyer" (1 Cor 10:10 ESV), and a "murderer from the beginning" (John 8:44). For these reasons, God will ultimately chain the devil in a bottomless pit with all his demons and burn him with unquenchable fire (Matt 25:41; Rev 20:2, 7, 10). Treason carries penalties.[36]

However, Wink's anthropomorphized imagery may mask what he really claims. In his view, it "runs the risk of personifying Satan," and this would be an error, because Satan's fall—from light-bearer to the Evil One—occurs neither in time nor in the universe "but in the human psyche." For Wink, it matters not whether there is a metaphysical entity called the devil because Satan is an event experienced *within* humanity. He is "the archetypal representation of the collective weight of human fallenness."[37]

By this rather murky explanation, the claim (once more) is that our choices set Satan as either God's sifting servant or the Evil One who destroys *shalom*. In summation of this entire line of thinking, one finds a passage that is vintage Wink—imaginative, poetic, and unorthodox:

> The satanic is actualized as evil precisely by our *failure* to choose, and has no more power than we continue to give it. Hence it would be truer to say, "*We made the devil do it*"! We do not "create" Satan by our choices, however. Satan is an autonomous spirit that rises out of the depths of mystery in God. But our choices *do* determine which side Satan is on. . . . *We made Satan evil. Only we can restore him to his rightful role at God's left hand.*[38]

So much for summary.

---

36. Wink, *Unmasking the Powers*, 22–23.

37. Wink, *Unmasking the Powers*, 24. As Wink admits, his view has some commonalities here with that of Carl Jung; see Wink, *Naming the Powers*, 142. Cf. Cook's treatment of the "Christian Jungianism of Walter Wink" in Robert Cook, "Devils and Manticores: Plundering Jung for a Plausible Demonology," in Lane, *The Unseen World*, 175–77.

38. Wink, *Unmasking the Powers*, 34, italics in original.

IS IT WRITTEN? QUESTIONING WINK'S VIEW OF SATAN

My critique of Wink's work will proceed also in three parts. I will begin by addressing his controlling concept of interiority. I will then move to his view of Satan as both servant and villain, since he is constellated by human choice. Finally, I will acknowledge what might be called (with certain qualifiers) the "panentheistic Pelagianism" that results from Wink's psychologizing of the demonic. While these judgments are indeed quite negative, the chapter will nonetheless conclude with a kind of "constructive postscript" to probe the possibilities that emerge from Wink's brilliant and creative treatment of Satan and the powers.

The Insufficiency of Interiority

"Innovative inwardness" is one way to describe the seismic shift that was wrought by Shakespeare in the realm of Western drama.[39] In plays like *Hamlet*, the story's greatest battle takes place not on a bloodstained patch of Danish soil but within the psyche of a given character. *Inside* is where the action is. So too with Wink's view of Satan.

The emphasis on interiority has certain strengths. By one account, the great contribution of Wink's project is his claim that spiritual forces are not simply free spirits flapping about the cosmos and begetting mayhem. Instead, they (almost always) seem to have "a fixed attachment to the elements and structures of the world."[40] While principalities and powers have a spiritual dynamic, they are often incarnated in the form of nations, rulers, and corporations. Along these lines, Thomas Noble notes of the Synoptics and Acts that "demons are never encountered in mid-air or anywhere other than in the human psyche. They are always found, without exception, inhabiting human beings."[41] So while the King James Version was perhaps wrong to locate the kingdom of God "within you" (Luke 17:21),[42] perhaps interiority is the primary domain of devils.

To say that a concept is helpful, however, is not the same as calling it

---

39. So says Stephen Greenblatt, in introduction to Shakespeare's *Hamlet*, in *The Norton Shakespeare: Essential Plays, The Sonnets*, 3rd ed., ed. Stephen Greenblatt (New York: Norton, 2016), 1183.

40. Noll, "Thinking About Angels," in Lane, *The Unseen World*, 25.

41. Thomas A. Noble, "The Spirit World: A Theological Approach," in Lane, *The Unseen World*, 209. Noble's claim is that even where demons enter the swine, they are encountered initially in the demoniac.

42. Modern translations often opt to render the *entos humon* as "in your midst."

sufficient. In fact, Wink's *exclusive* elevation of inwardness creates certain problems. In the first place, it is not always clear what he means by identifying Satan and the powers as the "inner aspect" of persons and structures. The metaphor (to say nothing of the metaphysic) is murky, and at points the grammar verges into nonsense. To take one example, Wink also identifies heaven as the "'within' of material reality."[43] Yet so is "the exterior," for upon reaching "the interior," we find ourselves on the outside; "We find interiority outside ourselves." Alongside the nonsensical nature of such statements, there is a second concern: the suspicion that Wink uses paradox and poetry to conceal the full extent of his disbelief in the demonic realm. This is the view of Clinton Arnold, who claims that Wink "cannot bring himself to believe in the actual existence of evil spirits" since my "inner aspect" might simply be "me" at the end of the day.[44]

In truth, it would be fairer to term Wink's final position that of "open-minded agnosticism" with regard to the metaphysical status of a supernatural devil.[45] For as he tells it, his project shows a kind of "pilgrimage" away from a more dismissive demythologizing and toward a sense that beyond human evil "there was always this remainder . . . something invisible, immaterial, spiritual, and very, very real."[46] So while it is unfair to deny Wink's openness to the reality of Satan, he does seem "wrong," as Marva Dawn puts it, "to eliminate entirely a different realm of spiritual forces separate from material agents. His conflation of the two reduces the cosmic battle in which we are engaged and thereby reduces the significance of the work of Christ and the church's gospel proclamation."[47] In sum, Wink's treatment of "interiority" is both insightful and insufficient.

The Snake That Didn't Hiss

My next critique involves Wink's ingenious proposal regarding Satan's evolution from servant to Evil One. His view is that "Satan is an autonomous spirit that rises out of the depths of mystery in God."[48] Although humans did not create the devil, his fall happens "in the human psyche."[49] Through our choices, Satan vacillates from servant to villain.

43. Wink, *Naming the Powers*, 118.
44. Clinton E. Arnold, *Powers of Darkness: Principalities and Powers in Paul's Letters* (Downers Grove, IL: IVP, 1992), 198.
45. Cook, "Devils and Manticores," 176.
46. Wink, *Naming the Powers*, 5.
47. Marva J. Dawn, *Powers, Weakness, and the Tabernacling of God* (Grand Rapids: Eerdmans, 2001), 15.
48. Wink, *Unmasking the Powers*, 34.
49. Wink, *Unmasking the Powers*, 24.

While the idea is clever, one text that is conspicuously absent from Wink's Old Testament survey is Genesis 3 and its infamous snake. Indeed, the passage is almost entirely ignored through his entire trilogy.[50] One reason is straightforward: the word *satan* is never mentioned in Genesis; the text speaks only of a crafty talking serpent.

The New Testament, on the other hand, does identify this creature as "that ancient serpent called the devil, or Satan" (Rev 12:9). Perhaps the earliest example of this reading is found in the Wisdom of Solomon (Wis 2:23–24), but the view may also be discerned in John's Gospel, with the description of Satan as "a murderer from the beginning" and "the father of lies" (8:44). Likewise, Paul infers this reading when he locates the fulfillment of Genesis 3:15 (the crushing of the serpent) in God's eventual crushing of "Satan" under the believers' feet (Rom 16:20). So while Genesis does not explicitly name Satan, it is clear that the serpent of Genesis 3 is either an embodiment or an instrument of Satan when read through the lens of the New Testament.[51]

How does this point fit with Wink's portrait of Satan as God's servant? In one sense, a view of Satan as sifter and stress-tester sits well amidst the forbidden fruit of Eden's branches. One might even read Genesis 3 as an *opportunity* for humans to fulfill their calling and to progress from "little ones" to maturity. This was Irenaeus's view. But by failing the test, Wink's claim might be that humans "constellated" the serpent as the Evil One when he otherwise could have been a slithering servant of their sanctification.

The problem, however, lies not in the sifting quality of the serpent's words but in Wink's assumption that all "sifters" are "servants" until we choose unwisely. By analogy, one might say that the child molester who lures with promises of candy and puppies is "sifting" those who will heed their parents' warnings. Yet this is no defense of those who ask: "Did mom really say . . . ?" To refer to the devil as "a murderer from the beginning" seems to question seriously the claim that *only* human choices render him as evil. Why then did God curse the serpent? For all these reasons, Genesis 3 becomes "the snake that didn't hiss" (much less speak) within Wink's account of Satan. And the silence is deafening.

---

50. The passage appears nowhere in the Scripture index of *Naming the Powers*, and when it does appear (twice) in *Unmasking the Powers*, neither the serpent nor his disputed identity is ever mentioned.

51. See Page, *Powers of Evil*, 12–15. Along these lines, Kidner claims that the New Testament "unmasks" the figure of the Satan, standing behind the serpent. Derek Kidner, *Genesis: An Introduction and Commentary* (Downers Grove, IL: IVP, 1967), 71.

While two "roads" diverge in the woods of human choosing (life and death; e.g., Deut 30), this does not mean that the one tempting travelers toward ruin is ambivalent. When read with New Testament eyes, the satanic serpent presents us with three options:

1. a devil who had previously rebelled against the good Creator
2. a power that is coeternal with God
3. a dark side of the Creator-God, who is trafficking in lies and blasphemy

Wink's choice, however uncomfortable, is for some combination of the latter two options. In his view, Satan is God's "dark" side.[52] The devil is depicted (to press the metaphor) as an aspect of the Creator's interiority—"a function in the divine process."[53] And with this admission, one arrives at the most serious problem with Wink's project.

Pelagian Panentheism

In the end, Wink's theology falls into the broader category of panentheism. In panentheism, the creation is not distinct from the Creator, but God's being is not exhausted by the physical realm. In some versions of panentheism, the universe exists almost as God's body even while he retains a spiritual dimension that goes beyond the realm of matter.

Given Wink's construal of "interiority" and the inextricable interlocking of physical and spiritual realities, the embrace of panentheism should come as no surprise. When he turns to Christ and his work, however, Wink makes an even greater departure from traditional belief. His Jesus is depicted as merely a person of great integrity,[54] and the atonement is reduced to an idea that was greatly muddled by the apostle Paul.[55]

In a mixture of liberal and liberationist emphases, Wink reduces salvation to the ongoing struggle for justice through nonviolent love. He rejects the myth of redemptive violence. And since "Satan" becomes an enemy only in the interior realm of human choosing, only our choices can turn the dragon back into an angel of light. In service of this argument, Wink quotes the moving words of Rainer Maria Rilke: "How should we be able

52. Wink, *Unmasking the Powers*, 11.
53. Wink, *Unmasking the Powers*, 33.
54. Wink, *Engaging the Powers*, 136–37. This is not technically to deny Christ's divinity, since panentheism claims that all physical realities are part of the divine life.
55. Wink, *Engaging the Powers*, 139–55.

to forget those ancient myths about dragons who at the last minute turn into princesses that are only waiting to see us once beautiful and brave? Perhaps everything terrible is in its deepest being something helpless that wants help from us."[56]

As always, Wink's writing seethes with evocative imagery and provocative application. Yet his arguments surrounding Christ, creation, and salvation are far closer to a psychologized amalgam of Pelagian panentheism than anything that may be deduced from a faithful reading of Scripture or tradition. Indeed, while he remains far from the specific views of Pelagius himself (at least as they are alleged), the similarity lies in the emphasis upon the innate human ability to choose rightly and thereby to remove the necessity of a divine grace that comes *only* through the God-man and his cross.

| CONSTRUCTIVE POSTSCRIPT |

Thankfully, such criticism does not imply that Wink's entire treatment of Satan must be thrown in the abyss. In addition to reenergizing the academic discussion of spiritual powers and giving an insightful (though insufficient) metaphor of spiritual "interiority," more can be gleaned from Wink's creative reading of the biblical material.

Satan as (Unwitting) Servant

Wink's work reveals the startling extent to which Satan *does* sometimes play a positive role within God's project, regardless of the devil's intention. Whether by the pride-quashing side effect of Paul's thorny messenger or the soul-saving torture of the incestuous brother, the Bible includes Satan in the expansive category of "all things" that are made to work together for the good of those who love God (Rom 8:28).

To draw further attention to this point, Sydney Page points to the recapitulative significance of Christ's wilderness temptation. Here, the Spirit leads Jesus into the desert for the express purpose of a satanic showdown. According to Mark's Gospel, Christ "was with the wild animals" (1:13) in the desert, and in this reference some see an echo of the Adamic narrative, which Jesus recapitulates. Milton certainly thought so.[57] Even clearer is

---

56. Rainer Maria Rilke, *Letters to a Young Poet* (New York: Penguin, 2012), 8, quoted in Wink, *Unmasking the Powers*, 57. Credit goes to Cook in "Devils and Manticores," for bringing this to my attention (176).

57. *Paradise Regained* famously focused on Christ's wilderness temptation, not his cross

the fact that Christ successfully relives Israel's wilderness experience; the echoes of which are to be seen in the way that Yahweh's other firstborn son, Israel (Exod 4:22), chose food over faith, worshiped nongods, and put the LORD to the test. In the end, a recapitulation of *both* Adam and Israel may be intended in the wilderness temptation. With this in mind, Page concludes with a startling statement: in all this, Satan's efforts were "necessary to effect the salvation of humanity."[58] Or as one might picture Jesus saying, "I couldn't have done it without you."

Does this mean that the Scriptures paint a picture of a God who dupes the devil? Perhaps so. But contrary to Wink's imagery, Satan betrays no signs of knowingly serving as a covert agent of the Crown. "An enemy did this" (Matt 13:28) remains an apt description of his role within the "wheat fields" of creation. Yet his sifting service happens anyway. Likewise, in a later portion of the drama, the devil's Judas-filling presence is again utilized on the canvas of redemption. Thus, like the demons who got their wish by being cast into the swine, Satan too is plunged into the abyss by an action he himself suggested (Luke 22; John 13:2, 27). In this way, the devil functions as a more malignant version of what Vladimir Lenin called a "useful idiot."[59] For what Satan meant for evil, God used for good (cf. Gen 50:20).

A Postpersonal Devil

One objection to this colorful conjecture might be that I am treating Satan much too mythically—that is, too personally—as if he were a little creature that flaps about the sky. Yet here too one finds value in Wink's study. He seems right to locate Satan as a kind of *tertium quid*—a "third thing"—that is neither a person in the fullest sense, nor a mere symbol devoid of ontic content.[60] But to spell out the meaning of this contention, one must first define what *persons* are, and that has long been difficult.[61]

Among the most famous definitions of a person is that of Boethius (480–524): "an individual substance of a rational nature."[62] Yet with regard

or resurrection.

58. Page, *Powers of Evil*, 91.

59. *Idiot* should be read here just as Wisdom literature speaks of "the fool." In both cases, the problem is a moral deficiency rather than an intellectual one. Thus there are many brilliant fools and intelligent idiots.

60. As I will note in ch. 12, the atonement doctrine of René Girard also has unique thoughts on Satan's powerful and personal brand of "nonbeing." Yet these must wait till then.

61. See Augustine's famous confusion over the Cappadocian use of *hypostasis* to describe the particular members of the Trinity.

62. Boethius, *Contra Eutychen et Nestorium*, 2–3.

to Satan, this claim seems problematic on two counts. First, the implicit individualism seems questionable given the extent to which the demonic inhabits both persons and structures. In these cases, Wink's emphasis upon interiority is helpful in showing how the lines between the human and the suprahuman sometimes blur dramatically. "Get behind me Satan," Jesus says to Peter (Matt 16:23; Mark 8:33). Satan enters Judas (Luke 22:3–6; John 13:27) who is called "a devil" (John 6:70), and Satan fills the hearts of Ananias and Saphira (Acts 5:3).

In these statements, seeing Satan as an entirely separate individual rings hollow. Indeed, one might argue that the devil's biblical identity is somewhat closer to that of the Dark Lord Voldemort from J. K. Rowling's *Harry Potter*. In this tale, the great wizard evolves in his degree of evil, and then ultimately unites his shattered soul with physical entities (called horcruxes) as a way of preserving his parasitic existence. By these divisive unions, Voldemort's identity as a malevolent intelligence is maintained, even while his power is incarnated through a union with other objects and creatures—one of which is fittingly a snake. While the analogy is imperfect,[63] the biblical truth may be seen in the extent to which an individualistic account of Satan's "personhood" is flawed.

Second, I have noted in the last chapter that it may also be mistaken to focus on the Boethian *rationality* of the Evil One. For both Barth and Torrance, evil is irrational at its core. Even though the Scriptures depict Satan as having volition and agency, Paul's logic of the mind progressively depraved and darkened (Rom 1:28–32; Eph 4:18) may cause one to reject the "well-reasoned" nature of the devil's campaign against the Creator. At this point also, Satan falls afoul of a Boethian definition of full personhood.

A different definition of *persons* comes from modern Trinitarian theology. Here the argument has been that talk of creaturely personhood derives its meaning from the divine side of the Creator-creature distinction. For this reason, one cannot be a person without existing in a nexus of love relationships, however marred by fallenness. By this account, it is suggested that it is impossible to think of Satan and demons as true persons, regardless of their reputed intelligence and volition.[64] They are at best postpersonal, antipersonal (in a parasitic sense), or as Hans Boersma calls them, semiper-

---

63. One difference might be seen in the fact that Lord Voldemort (Tom Riddle) was never hinted to be "good" in his beginning, even while his evil surely grows over time. In contrast, the traditional Christian view of Satan is that he belongs in the category of all created beings, in that he was originally made "good" despite his later fall.

64. See Noble, "The Spirit World," 217.

sonal.[65] By both of the above definitions (Boethian and Trinitarian), Satan and his demons fail the test. In the words of Michael Green, "Counterfeiter to the last, [the devil] even counterfeits personality."[66]

Of course, these technical definitions are likely not what most Christians (and denominations) have in mind when referring to a "personal" devil. In this colloquial sense, the meaning may merely be that Satan is real, and that he has both volition and intelligence. On these points, the Bible would surely agree, as would I. To say therefore that Satan fails the test of full Boethian or Trinitarian personhood is not necessarily to question the existence of the devil or his minions.

Indeed, it seems quite odd to assume that sophisticated modern people can no longer believe in a malevolent spiritual intelligence. According to Alvin Plantinga, if one accepts the existence of at least one spiritual being (God), then it should be no great difficulty to accept the possibility of others.[67] And since belief in the divine continues to hover around 90 percent in places like the United States, it would seem strange to say that continued belief in other aspects of the unseen realm is both "mental" (in both the British and American sense) and medieval. Billions of people still believe in an unseen god at work within the world. And millions of Christians still believe that it is possible for creatures to be created good before rebelling. We are those creatures. Why then should it seem impossible for rebellion to happen in the spirit realm as well?

In fact, there is nothing (theologically) absurd about Wink's claim that the malignant intelligence known as Satan evolved over time in a progression of increasing evil.[68] If the Creator made other beings capable of change, why not this one? It has never been part of the Christian tradition to view Satan as immutable. And as Paul argued, every mind that turns away from the Creator is destined to be progressively darkened apart from a radical act of divine intervention (Rom 1).[69]

Satan may not be a "person" in the technical definitions mentioned

---

65. Hans Boersma, *Violence, Hospitality, and the Cross: Reappropriating the Atonement Tradition* (Grand Rapids: Baker Academic, 2004), 187.

66. Green, *I Believe in Satan's DownFall*, 30.

67. See J. Tomberlin and P. van Inwagen, eds., *Alvin Plantinga: Profiles* (Dordrecht: Reidel, 1985), 43.

68. To be clear, Wink sees this evolution as taking place within Hebrew tradition and within the human psyche. My claim, however odd it may sound, is that there is nothing in Scripture or tradition that would preclude the transformation from really happening (and perhaps even continuing to happen) to the satanic intelligence itself.

69. A recent evangelical argument that seems to locate Satan's fall *within* human history is found in the work of Stanley Grenz. While joining Wink in viewing the Satan of Job as one "who acts in the interest of God," Grenz nonetheless concedes that "somewhere in his

above, but the sheer enormity of earthly evil does sometimes suggest a dark agency at work within the cosmos—a suprahuman cruelty behind the curtain, a postpersonal hatred that smirks just out of sight. Many can attest to hearing the accusatory voice from within that sees only one's stains, just as all have witnessed the moral malignance that comes occasionally to inhabit rulers, nations, corporations, churches, and even particular individuals. *This* power is what Christ came to overthrow by recapitulative obedience, vicarious judgment, and perhaps even the unwitting overreach of the devil himself. And for this malevolent shadow, *Satan* is as good a name as any.

| CONCLUSION |

The goal in this chapter has been to probe the status of the satanic villain who was overcome by "Christ the victor." To quote Hamlet's question uttered toward the spirit realm, "Who's there?" To accomplish this goal, Walter Wink's creative and influential work served as a starting line for the inquiry. In the end, while rejecting the more unorthodox components that bring Wink near a brand of Pelagian panentheism, and while questioning the sufficiency of his concept of "interiority," I find great value in his innovative but biblically literate treatment of the devil and the spiritual powers.

Specifically, the Bible does teach that Satan serves a purpose in the divine economy as one of the "all things" that work together (sometimes unwittingly) for the good of those who love God. Likewise, I find reason to agree with the assessment that the devil is less than fully "personal" (in a Boethian or Trinitarian definition) even though he is still fully capable of things like diabolical intervention and self-destructive overreach. Given this last point, the modified patristic suggestion of the prior chapter remains a viable option for biblically rooted theologians—that is, that Christ overcomes sin, death, and the devil not just by recapitulative obedience (chs. 1–3) and penal substitution (chs. 4–7) but also by leveraging satanic ignorance and self-deception against the very monster that would orchestrate his plunge into the great abyss of his own choosing (ch. 8; cf. Matt 8:28–34; Mark 5:1–20; Luke 8:26–39). In the next chapter, however, I will grapple with the sense that this same defeated devil still seems very much alive and well within the world.

---

story . . . the accuser in the court of God developed a hostile intent." Grenz, *Theology for the Community of God* (Grand Rapids: Eerdmans, 2000), 226.

CHAPTER 10

O SACRED HEAD, NOW WHAT?

STAGED TRIUMPH AS THE TELOS OF ATONEMENT

*But woe to you, O earth and sea, for the
devil has come down to you in great wrath,
because he knows that his time is short!*
Revelation 12:12 ESV

Graham Greene's famous novel *The Power and the Glory* is often viewed as a modern crucifixion tale. Set in the 1930s, the story details a priest's last days as he flees an anticlerical purge in a Marxist southern state of Mexico. Yet despite being likened to Christ in his death, the martyred "whisky priest" is far from a triumphant savior. He is a faint-hearted drunkard and the father of an illegitimate child. "It was too easy to die for what was good or beautiful," he says of Christ's atoning work. The world "needed a God to die for the half-hearted and the corrupt."[1] Indeed, almost nothing in the novel—from the Mexican heat to the malarial mosquitos—seems to evidence Christ's victory.[2] And the paradox is captured in the book's title. By referencing the traditional ending to the Lord's Prayer ("thine is . . . the power, and the glory"), Greene's intention seems to be to highlight what is missing: *Where is the kingdom?* If Christ really conquered sin and Satan, why doesn't it look like it?

---

1. Graham Greene, *The Power and the Glory* (repr., New York: Penguin, 1971), 97.
2. The term *Greeneland* was famously coined to describe the dusty, dismal, and oppressive conditions that often pervade Greene's novels.

My goal in this chapter is to address this final question while simultaneously locating the *Christus Victor* motif in relation to the other pieces in my mosaic of atonement—particularly, to the yet-to-be-discussed moral influence model.[3] I will do so in two movements. The first involves the claim that triumph is the telos of atonement and the culmination of Christ's work. The triumph of the Lamb is the God-glorifying end toward which history is moving. For this reason, I have located the theme of *Christus Victor* as the crowned *head* of the mosaic Christ.

While the first part of the chapter marks triumph as the telos of atonement, the second asks, "What kind of triumph?" In response, my aim is to make *Christus Victor* strange again. For as Greene's novel illustrates, there is a painful extent to which the reign of Christ can seem absent in the here and now. Indeed, it may even seem to have been "staged" by the ecclesial powers as a way of justifying their authority. This is precisely the claim of the Communist "Lieutenant" in *The Power and the Glory*, the man who hunts down the whisky priest as an enemy of the state.[4] Despite the old smear that religion is the "opiate of the masses," my claim will be different: while Christ's paradoxical victory is not "staged" in the sense of being false or phony, it is "staged" in that it involves more than one installment. And with regard to its final chapter: "It is [not] finished."

Herein lies the link to moral influence. There is an *already* and a *not yet* to kingdom triumph. As Scripture indicates, the remaining stages of the victory involve the transformed lives of pardoned sinners who must walk and wait in the shadow of the cross, through the power of the Spirit.

The reason, as the hymns of Wesley and Watts remind us, is that the atonement is not meant merely to cancel sin's penalty in the future but to break its "power"[5] in the present—"far as the curse is found."[6] This is the paradoxical victory toward which Christ's *hands* compel his people,

---

3. I will focus specifically on the relation between *Christus Victor* and moral influence because the relation between recapitulation, penal substitution, and Christ's triumph has already been explored in prior chapters.

4. In *The Power and the Glory*, the Lieutenant's hatred of religion becomes a kind of "pious" zealotry that reveals him as the story's chief inquisitor: "[He] remembered the smell of incense in the churches of his boyhood . . . the immense demands made from the altar steps by men who didn't know the meaning of sacrifice. The old peasants knelt there before the holy images . . . tired by the long day's labour in the plantations. . . . And the priest came round with the collecting bag taking their centavos, abusing them for their small comforting sins, and sacrificing nothing at all in return—except a little sexual indulgence" (22). "They deserved nothing less than the truth—a vacant universe and a cooling world, the right to be happy in any way they chose. He was quite prepared to make a massacre for their sakes" (58).

5. Charles Wesley, "O For a Thousand Tongues." Here he writes that Christ "breaks the *power* of cancelled sin" (italics added).

6. Isaac Watts, "Joy to the World."

both beckoning and restraining us in certain ways.[7] Hence, the book of Revelation proclaims that Satan is overcome not merely "by the blood of the Lamb" but by the "testimony" of martyrs (Rev 12:11). And as Paul foresees in Romans, "The God of peace will soon crush Satan underneath *your* feet" (Rom 16:20). In light of these passages, a Spirit-driven moral influence model is essential to a kingdom that comes (for now) in quiet power and humble glory, through suffering and sometimes stumbling obedience.

| TRIUMPH AS TELOS OF ATONEMENT |

Since Aulén, it has become increasingly common to view the divine victory as the telos of atonement themes. To show this truth, I begin by turning to a trio of contemporary theologians who each make this claim, albeit in contrasting ways: Hans Boersma, Henri Blocher, and Jeremy Treat.

"Treating" Boersma and Blocher

In the view of Hans Boersma, *Christus Victor* is "in a real sense, the most significant model" of atonement even while it must not be disconnected from others. His reasoning rests on the idea that divine triumph is the goal toward which recapitulation, penal substitution, and moral influence are moving.[8] As he states, "Christ's victory over the powers of darkness . . . is the *result* of the entire process of recapitulation," just as the "subordinate" themes of moral influence and vicarious penalty-bearing are also "means toward [the victorious] end."[9]

While this argument shares obvious similarities with my own, I would take issue with the claim that *Christus Victor* necessarily describes a "model" of atonement at all, let alone the most significant one. As I have argued, models must map some answer (however partial) as to how redemption happens. Thus Kathryn Tanner rightly notes that a generic affirmation of "*Christus Victor* is not a model at all in that it fails to

---

7. As I will argue in part 4 of this book, moral influence views of the atonement may be divided into "beckoning" and "restraining" emphases. While Peter Abelard will serve as a conversation partner for the former, René Girard will represent the latter.

8. Hans Boersma often uses the language of "penal representation" as a broader category than mere substitution, although he is open to both terms. In one sense, ideas like representation or "vicarious judgment" are helpful in reminding us of the way humans are bound up *with* Christ on the cross, even though we do not experience its horrors. See Boersma, *Violence, Hospitality, and the Cross: Reappropriating the Atonement Tradition* (Grand Rapids: Baker Academic, 2004), 122n24.

9. Boersma, *Violence, Hospitality, and the Cross*, 181–82, italics in original.

address the . . . the mechanism of the atonement."[10] Though Boersma is right to note how other models function as instrumental means to divine triumph, he seems wrong to claim that this justifies the prioritizing of victory as the fairest "model" of them all.[11]

Meanwhile, in another insightful set of articles, the French evangelical Henri Blocher applies almost the same arguments as Boersma only to arrive at the opposite conclusion. For Blocher, penal substitution reigns supreme because it serves (in his view) as the ground and mechanism of Christ's victory, just as it also provides the preeminent example of sacrificial love that we must imitate (e.g., 1 Pet 2:21).[12] Unlike Boersma, however, Blocher sees the instrumentality of the penal paradigm as reason to view it as most important.[13] Hence, he claims that "Christ's punishment . . . in free and yet lawful substitution" results "in his victory over the Tempter and Accuser." For this reason, Blocher names penal substitution as "the core treasure of the deposit of Scripture truth in the church."[14]

In contrast with both Boersma and Blocher, the present study sides with Jeremy Treat in claiming that "the recognition of instrumentality should not lead to the conclusion that either penal substitution or *Christus Victor* is subordinate." Rather, "they play different roles."[15] In my view, this rejection of hierarchal or competing atonement models is exactly right. To echo Fleming Rutledge, the goal should be to "lock" Christ's substitution to his triumph rather than to make them competitive for a place of primacy.[16] Yet while Treat lends a much-needed corrective to these subtle hierarchies, his own study is limited in scope (being the published version of his doctoral dissertation), such that it does not go on to incorporate or

---

10. Kathryn Tanner, *Christ the Key* (Cambridge: Cambridge University Press, 2010), 253. I have noted previously, however, that patristic sources did often have a "mechanism" that was attached to divine triumph. That said, these assumptions are not implicit in the mere affirmation of Christ as victor. See again, ch. 8.

11. See also ch. 7; cf. McKnight's Snow White analogy in *A Community Called Atonement* (Nashville: Abingdon, 2007), 107.

12. Another example of this logic may be found in J. I. Packer, "What Did the Cross Achieve? The Logic of Penal Substitution," *Tyndale Bulletin* 25 (1974): 20.

13. Henri Blocher, "The Sacrifice of Jesus Christ: The Current Theological Situation," *EuroJTh* 8 (1999), 31; cf. Blocher, "*Agnus Victor*: The Atonement as Victory and Vicarious Punishment," in *What Does It Mean to Be Saved? Broadening Evangelical Horizons of Salvation*, ed. John G. Stackhouse Jr. (Grand Rapids: Baker Academic, 2002), 90–91.

14. Blocher, "*Agnus Victor*," 90–91; cf. Blocher, "Biblical Metaphors and the Doctrine of the Atonement," *Journal of Evangelical Theological Society* 47, no. 4 (December 2004): 644–45.

15. Jeremy R. Treat, *The Crucified King: Atonement and Kingdom in Biblical and Systematic Theology* (Grand Rapids: Zondervan, 2014), 223.

16. Fleming Rutledge, *The Crucifixion: Understanding the Death of Jesus Christ* (Grand Rapids: Eerdmans, 2015), 530.

address the themes of recapitulation and moral influence. My claim here is that these pieces need a place as well.[17]

In agreement with these three voices (Boersma, Blocher, and Treat), my own goal is to demonstrate that the divine triumph is indeed the telos of atonement. The reason, however, does not merely have to do with instrumentality. A further cause exists in the fact that, in Scripture, it is in conquering evil and restoring *shalom* that God is most glorified by his redeemed creation. In saying this, one must affirm that the atonement is ultimately about God's glory and not merely the good of humanity. It is theocentric at its blazing core. The Lord moves with overflowing and unforced love to create, redeem, and perfect creation, but this work ultimately redounds to the triumphant glorification of God as it catches creation up within the dance of victory. In this way, redemptive history concludes with worship from a multiethnic throng that gathers to sing of the *triumph* of the Lamb, victorious and enthroned, with enemies now made his footstool. In sum, the atonement is about God's glory.

God's Chief Telos in John Piper

In recent years, one of the most visible exponents of this uncompromisingly theocentric vision is the pastoral theologian John Piper (b. 1946). A Baptist with (1) conservative, (2) Calvinistic, and (3) complementarian leanings, Piper is largely responsible for inspiring the so-called "Young, Restless, and Reformed" movement that swept American evangelicalism in the early 2000s. And to put it mildly, he has a devoted following.[18] Piper's watershed work, written for a popular audience, is *Desiring God: Meditations of a Christian Hedonist*, in which he seeks to draw out points regarding the telos not only of atonement but of the divine life itself.[19]

While the Westminster catechism asks about "the chief end" of humanity, Piper follows Jonathan Edwards in asking about the chief end (or purpose) of God.[20] In Piper's words, "The chief end of God is to glorify

---

17. In fairness to the authors cited above, no study of atonement can hope to say everything. Christ's work is an ever-flowing fountain; and in response to this act of infinite love, the best we theologians can do is to catch a "cup of cool water" (Matt 10:42) that we might pour into pages.
18. For a nonacademic but informative survey of the movement, see Collin Hansen, *Young, Restless, Reformed: A Journalist's Journey with the New Calvinists* (Wheaton: Crossway, 2008).
19. John Piper, *Desiring God: Meditations of a Christian Hedonist*, rev. and expanded ed. (Colorado Springs: Multnomah, 2003).
20. See Jonathan Edwards, *The End for Which God Created the World*, in *WJE* 8.

God and enjoy him forever."[21] Against critiques that this makes the Lord seem self-absorbed and narcissistic, Piper's claim is that it is for our good that God loves his glory more than he loves us, for it is in the magnification of the divine glory that God moves to redeem (and make glad!) rebellious creatures.[22] To support this argument, Piper cites a variety of passages that speak of God moving to judge and save for *his* name's sake rather than the sake of Israel. To take just one example, God speaks through Ezekiel: "'It is not for your sake, O house of Israel, that I am about to act, but for the sake of my holy name. . . . And I will vindicate the holiness of my great name . . . and the nations will know that I am the LORD. . . . It is not for your sake that I will act, declares the Lord God; let that be known to you" (36:22–23, 32 ESV).

For Piper, such texts demonstrate that God is no idolater. He does not worship humanity in the hopes of receiving human adoration in return. Instead, God is the most God-centered being in existence, and this God-centeredness is the ground of both wrath and redemption. In Piper's words, "God is the one Being in all the universe for whom seeking His own praise is the ultimately loving act."[23]

Portions of these claims are controversial. To take just one example, the above argument sits atop a strong affirmation of divine determinism that does not shrink from crediting all manner of horrors to God's single-minded pursuit of his own glory. For this reason, Piper agrees with Charles Spurgeon that "every particle of dust that dances in the sunbeam does not move an atom more or less than God wishes."[24] If asked why God would actively determine specific and horrific instances of sin and suffering, the response seems to be that these evils are required for God's maximal glorification. In short, this is the "best" possible world, because the God-magnifying display of wrath and mercy needs sin and evil in order to go public.[25]

Although this is not the place for an in-depth discussion of divine

---

21. Piper, *Desiring God*, 31.
22. This emphasis upon the believer's joy is encapsulated in Piper's well-known dictum that is meant to encapsulate what he calls Christian Hedonism: "God is most glorified in us when we are most satisfied in him."
23. Piper, *Desiring God*, 49. Here too Piper is following Edwards, *WJE* 8:440–41.
24. Charles Haddon Spurgeon, "God's Providence," *Sermons*, vol. 54, as cited in Thomas H. McCall, "I Believe in Divine Sovereignty," *Trinity Journal* 29, no. 2 (Fall 2008): 205–26.
25. In Piper's view, "It is the glory of God and his essential nature mainly to dispense mercy (but also wrath, Ex 34:7) on whomever he pleases, apart from any constraint originating outside his will. This is the essence of what it means to be God." Piper, *The Justification of God: An Exegetical and Theological Study of Romans 9:1–23* (Grand Rapids: Baker, 1993), 219.

determinism (in various forms), Thomas McCall questions whether Piper's statements call into question not only God's goodness but also his aseity. After all, it would seem by Piper's logic that the divine life would be deficient apart from the display of attributes (specifically, wrath and mercy) that are said to be "the essence of what it means to be God." In response, one might ask: Was God therefore impoverished in his glory prior to creation? Does God *need* our sin in order to be fully glorious? Piper frankly acknowledges that his words may give these impressions but denies the charge nonetheless.[26]

Aseity aside, a deeper problem for Piper's theology may involve the implications for God's character in this glory-driven determinism. This theology appears to make God the author of evil in a misguided attempt to "justify" God's ways.[27] In response to theologies like this, David Bentley Hart contends that such evils cannot be justified or explained. Rather, they must only be grieved, opposed, and (one day) overcome. In his typical hard-charging style, Hart denounces what he terms the "unhealthy fascination with [God's] 'dread sovereignty.'" He notes, therefore, "The curious absurdity of all such doctrines is that out of a pious anxiety to defend God's transcendence against any scintilla of genuine creaturely freedom, they threaten effectively to collapse that transcendence into absolute identity—with the world, with us, with the devil."[28] In response to this tendency, Hart concludes that "it is a strange thing to seek peace in a universe rendered morally intelligible at the cost of a God rendered morally loathsome."[29]

While not all readers will find this charge convincing, the danger in Piper's determinism is, in fact, ironically similar to that witnessed in the Pelagian panentheism of Walter Wink (ch. 9).[30] Although they differ in almost every other way, both theologies appear to draw evil into the heart

---

26. John Piper, "I Believe in God's Self-Sufficiency: A Response to Thomas McCall," *Trinity Journal* 29, no. 2 (Fall 2008): 227–34. Despite deep disagreements, the exchange between Piper and McCall models the kind of careful and respectful dialogue that ought to occur between Reformed and Wesleyan-Arminian theologians.

27. Unsurprisingly, similar critiques exist against the theology of Jonathan Edwards. To take just one example, Oliver Crisp and Kyle Strobel argue that Edwards's God "appears to be morally responsible for sin." Oliver D. Crisp and Kyle C. Strobel, *Jonathan Edwards: An Introduction to His Thought* (Grand Rapids: Eerdmans, 2018), 106.

28. David Bentley Hart, *The Doors of the Sea: Where Was God in the Tsunami* (Grand Rapids: Eerdmans, 2005), 90–91.

29. Hart, *Doors of the Sea*, 99.

30. A further example of this danger may be found in the more "progressive" Reformed theology of those (like Daniel Harlow and John R. Schneider) who would replace any version of a historical fall with a world that was designed by God to be exactly as it is, even with regard to horrific evil and suffering. See again my own assessment of these claims in ch. 2.

of God, either by uniting him to the "world process" (Wink) or by making predetermined evil a necessary requirement for God's maximal glorification (Piper). Recognizing the complexities of the issues at hand, I would argue that both moves are unnecessary and unacceptable.

In Hart's view, the problem lies in denying even "a scintilla of creaturely freedom." Yet unfortunately, as soon as one begins to talk of creaturely freedom and responsibility, the charges of (semi-)Pelagianism are sure to follow. Even though I have condemned the emphasis upon innate human potential in Wink, the allegation soon bounces back on any who deny a rigid doctrine of divine determinism. Be this as it may, the fact remains that one time-honored way of avoiding the construction of a "morally loathsome" deity is to claim that evil is the result of creaturely rebellion against the Creator and that God does not traffic in such atrocities, whether for the pursuit of his glory or for any other reason.[31]

Divine grace is extended to all, but this grace may be rejected, just as those who martyred Stephen were said to "resist the Holy Spirit" continually (Acts 7:51). Likewise, within my own account of creaturely evil, salvation remains entirely by grace. No one would claim that a beggar who accepts a gift has somehow earned it. The point here is not to engage in the old polemics of, say, Calvinism and Arminianism; instead, it is to say that there are options beyond rigid determinism if a theologian desires to extol the glory of God as the chief end of redemptive history.[32] Having noted this disagreement, I now move toward a more positive appropriation of Piper's work.[33]

Appropriating Piper

While the present study rejects both the determinism and the (unintentional) erosion of divine aseity in Piper's thought (among other differences), I wish to affirm his notion that the glorification of God is the chief end of all things—atonement included. Like Barth, Piper's emphasis upon

31. For its own part, even the Westminster Confession of Faith attempts to argue similarly. For more on the discussion of libertarian freedom and divine determinism, I must await the discussion of the Holy Spirit in ch. 13.

32. While the preceding position could rightly be described as a species of Arminianism, it is important to understand what that label actually means in relation to the historical figure of Arminius. In many cases, those who use the label as a slur have never actually read Arminius. See especially Keith Stanglin and Thomas McCall, *Jacob Arminius: Theologian of Grace* (Oxford: Oxford University Press, 2012), chs. 3–4 esp.

33. In so doing, I will no doubt dissatisfy both Piper's disciples (the so-called "Piper cubs") and his detractors, especially within my own tradition of Wesleyanism. Nonetheless, my own view is that there are both serious deficiencies and weighty truths within his work.

the "God-ness" of God is helpful amidst the modern enthrallment with domesticated deities and "moralistic therapeutic deism." Gratefully, Piper's portrait is not like this. He does not, to quote Niebuhr, present us with "a God without wrath [bringing people] without sin into a kingdom without judgment through the ministrations a Christ without a cross."[34]

In the biblical storyline, the glorification of God is the telos toward which the narrative is moving. Creation is the theater of God's glory. And the satisfaction of a heart enraptured with God does, as Piper suggests, form a crossroads at which God's glory and human joy intersect. Indeed, long ago Anselm had stated that happiness is "enjoying the supreme Good, which is God."[35] Hence it seems right to say with Piper that "God is most glorified in us when we are most satisfied in Him." In the Scriptures, God is the reward, the pleasure, and the treasure that one enjoys through a life of worship. For in the famous words of Augustine: "You stir [us] to take pleasure in praising you, because you have made us for yourself, and our hearts are restless till they find their rest in you."[36]

In sum, the glorification of God is the end of creation. And this glorification shows forth most brilliantly when one considers Christ's cosmos-healing triumph over evil through recapitulative obedience and vicarious judgment on our behalf. Now to show this from the Scriptures.

Triumph as Telos in the Scriptures

On the eve of crucifixion, Christ's first prayer was that God would be glorified: "Father, the hour has come. Glorify your Son, that your Son may glorify you" (John 17:1). In the next verse, this divine glorification coincides with the giving of "eternal life" to others (v. 2). For this reason, the glorification of God should never be walled off from the salvation of humans. Rather, God's glory is made known in redeeming creation by sheer grace. Jesus therefore states, "I have brought you glory on earth by finishing the work you gave me to do" (v. 4). In this prayer, Christ's foremost request, before laying hold of his cross, was that God would be glorified. Hence the atonement is an act of worship. And Christ is no idolater.

Likewise, Piper insightfully points out that even the crucifixion was endured in the pursuit of a glorious and victorious joy. "For the *joy* set

---

34. H. Richard Niebuhr, *The Kingdom of God in America* (1937; repr., New York: Harper & Row, 1959), 193.

35. Anselm, *Cur Deus Homo*, 2.1.

36. Augustine, *Confessions*, 1.1. The familiar phrasing is here adapted slightly from the translation of Henry Chadwick (Oxford: Oxford University Press, 1991).

before him [Christ] endured the cross, scorning its shame, and sat down at the right hand of the throne of God" (Heb 12:2, italics added).[37] Here, the book of Hebrews joins with the high priestly prayer to proclaim that Jesus scorned the shame of the cross for the "joy" of finishing his work and to be exalted "with the *glory* I had . . . before the world began" (John 17:5, italics added). This too is theocentric.

Scripture likewise makes clear that this "taking a seat" in heaven is not to be confused with the exhausted sigh of a tired man who slides sleepily into his favorite chair. At the apex of ascension, Christ's session is his heavenly enthronement and the culmination of perhaps the most important messianic prophecy in Hebrew Scripture, Daniel 7. In this apocalyptic text, the imperial beasts assailing God's people are defeated, and one like a "son of man" (1) ascends on the clouds of heaven, (2) is seated next to the Ancient of Days, (3) receives eternal worship, and (4) rules an everlasting kingdom. If ever there was a text of cosmic triumph, this is it. Yet strangely, Daniel's Son of Man commits no violence in his victory. In the words of John Goldingay: "He does not fight, like Marduk. . . . He is simply invested. . . . Likewise the holy ones do not fight—at least, not successfully. It is their *defeat* that brings their attacker's downfall. One is reminded of God's disarming principalities and powers through Christ's being crucified (Col 2:15)."[38] Indeed, there is ample evidence that Christ saw himself as living out the Son of Man's vocation, right up to Daniel 9 with its final atonement for sin and its "anointed one" who is put to death (9:26).[39]

In Daniel 7, however, the triumphal session is the culmination of the Son of Man's strange victory. To cite Goldingay once more, "The affliction and the glory of Christ are not just consecutive. The affliction manifests a peculiar form of glory; the glory has the marks of the cross about it. Perhaps the same is true for the holy ones: not just affliction (v 21) then glory (v 22), but a rule exercised in a strange crosslike way."[40] Because of this nonviolent conquest, the enthroned one is praised forever. As Daniel states, "He was given glory and sovereign power; all nations and peoples of

---

37. While some have read the *anti* as referring to the way Christ endured the cross "instead of (*anti*) the joy" he had beforehand, Cockerill argues that the more familiar rendering (above) is far more likely. Gareth Lee Cockerill, *Hebrews*, NICNT (Grand Rapids: Eerdmans, 2012), 609n38.

38. John Goldingay, *Daniel*, WBC 30 (Dallas, TX: Word, 1989), 191, italics in original. In referencing Marduk, the point is to distinguish the Son of Man's strange victory from the aggressive violence of the victorious Marduk in the Babylonian myth, *Enuma Elish*.

39. See N. T. Wright, *Jesus and the Victory of God* (Minneapolis: Fortress, 1996), 513–28.

40. Goldingay, *Daniel*, 193.

every language worshiped him . . . and his kingdom is one that will never be destroyed" (7:14). While the work results in the salvation of humans, its telos is the creaturely magnification of the Lord's renown.

The same is true within the book of Revelation. In chapter five of John's vision, readers are given another glimpse into the heavenly throne room. Yet in this text, it is a sacrificial Lamb who shares the seat of divine authority. In both cases, the scene is one of worship: "Worthy is the Lamb, who was slain, to receive power and wealth and wisdom and strength and honor and glory and praise!" (v. 12). The reason for this praise is likewise given: "because you were slain, and with your blood you purchased for God persons from every tribe and language and people and nation. You have made them to be a kingdom and priests to serve our God and they will reign on the earth" (vv. 9–10). Here, too, sacrificial blood is the means to victory, yet the triumph reaches its culmination in eternal worship around a single throne. In all this, God-glorifying triumph forms the telos of atonement and of history itself.

The Final Victory

Even while the songs of victory echo back at us from the heavenly throne room, Hebrews reminds the church that there remains a *not yet* to Christ's ascended triumph. The Son of Man is still waiting for a footstool: "But when Christ had offered for all time a single sacrifice for sins, 'he sat down at the right hand of God,' and since then has been waiting 'until his enemies would be made a footstool for his feet'" (Heb 10:12–13). This has not yet happened. Although God has made all things subject to the Son of Man, "at present we do not see everything [made] subject" to him (Heb 2:6, 8).

Christ's victory has stages. The final chapter has not yet come. When it does, Jesus will return in power, the dead will be raised, evil will be judged, and the cosmos itself will experience a kind of resurrection. In this way, the followers of the Lamb will reign with him forever in a renewed creation. The point in saying this is not to delve into the myriad of eschatological theories about the nature of the millennium (Rev 20), the final state of those who oppose Christ,[41] or the specific signs of the end. The point is merely that the final victory, though guaranteed by the work of Jesus and the Spirit, is not yet fully realized.

The world sometimes seems more like "Greeneland" than God's new creation. And this painful reality must be acknowledged, especially in

---

41. See, however, my prior treatment of this issue in ch. 3, under the heading "Why Not Universalism?"

Christus Victor treatments of atonement. Nevertheless, "We do see Jesus, who was made lower than the angels for a little while, now crowned with *glory* and *honor* because he suffered death, so that . . . he might taste death for everyone" (Heb 2:6–9, italics added). Christ's "excruciating" sacrifice results in, and somehow is, his glorious triumph. The *heart* supports the *head*. Even so, it remains clear that the triumph has stages (the now and the not yet).

| WHAT KIND OF TRIUMPH? |

Having argued that the glorious victory of Christ is the telos of atonement, I must now explore the paradoxical nature of this triumph in the here and now. In terms of arrangement, I will begin by noting that, even in the life of Christ, the victory was a strange one. This is to be evidenced in the way several texts locate it not merely in his resurrection and ascended session, but in his shameful death. My second move will then be to note how Christians experience a similarly "excruciating" triumph in this fallen world. Through this consideration, I will then finally be able to address the connection between the *Christus Victor* and moral influence pieces of my Jesus-shaped mosaic.

A Peculiar Victory

While it may seem strange to speak of Christ's conquest of evil in a world that is still awash with it, one should recall that even Christ's victory was an exceedingly strange one. This fact may seem so obvious as to hardly need mentioning. But when one considers the tendency for the gospel to become amalgamated (in certain religious contexts especially) with whatever is deemed "respectable" and "traditional," it becomes clear why Christians must repeatedly reclaim the scandal of victory through a state-sponsored execution. My goal, therefore, is not merely to echo Aulén and others who have done a great service by helping to make *Christus Victor* popular once more. I also hope to make *Christus Victor* strange again, both with regard to Christ and with his people.

How might this happen? One way would be to note that while many modern theologians link Jesus's triumph to his resurrection and session, some older sources found the royal conquest *on* the cross itself.[42] This is especially so in John's Gospel. Here, Jesus speaks of his death as "the hour"

---

42. In the perceptive view of Jeremy Treat, an unfortunate chasm has opened up in systematic theology between Christ's humiliation and his exaltation. And this divide has served to

for the Son of Man to be "glorified" (12:23) and "lifted up" (12:32). Even the sign above his head proclaims his kingship. Like with his robe and staff and crown of thorns, both irony and truth are at play here. This is an odd-looking king and a strange form of exaltation.

In turning to the Synoptics, Christ's royal reign is recognized by a criminal beside him: "Remember me," he says, "when you come into your kingdom" (Luke 23:42). *This*, one learns, is why Christ dismissed the earlier entreaty of a mother for her sons to be on his left and right in his kingdom—or as Mark puts it, his "glory" (Mark 10:37). "You don't know what you are asking," Jesus says (Matt 20:21–22). Those places are reserved for criminals. The cross is not merely the height of Christ's humiliation; it is simultaneously his glorious enthronement here on earth.

This reality has been noted throughout church history. In an early example, Justin Martyr proclaimed that "the Lord hath reigned from the tree."[43] In the Middle Ages, Venantius Fortunatus (530–609) sang of "God ruling nations from a tree."[44] In the Reformation, Calvin spoke of the cross as Christ's "triumphal chariot."[45] In the modern era, Karl Barth pushed back so hard against the divide between humiliation and his exaltation that Colin Gunton summarized his view by saying, "For Barth, it is just as God-like to be lowly as to be exalted."[46] Finally, in the contemporary setting, Michael Horton writes that "Jesus embraced the cross precisely as a king embraces a scepter."[47] In each, the cross itself is viewed as a royal exaltation.

This paradoxical reality also has implications for God's people. In Matthew, it is at Jesus's death (not his resurrection) that the veil is torn, the tombs split open, and "the bodies of many holy people . . . were raised to life" (Matt 27:52).[48] While the tale of these raised corpses may seem outlandish, it is even odder to note that the bodies do not emerge from their

---

undermine the extent to which the cross itself is viewed as Jesus's glorious and royal exaltation. See Treat, *Crucified King*, 149.

43. Justin Martyr, *First Apology* 41 (*ANF* 1:176).

44. Venantius Fortunatus, "*Vexilla Regis.*"

45. *Inst.* 2.16.6.

46. For Barth, see *CD* IV/2, 250; Gunton, *The Barth Lectures*, ed. and transcribed by P. H. Brazier (London: T&T Clark, 2007).

47. Michael Horton, *Lord and Servant: A Covenant Christology* (Louisville: Westminster John Knox, 2005), 254. This quartet of voices is laid forth by Treat, *Crucified King*, 151, 153.

48. Incredibly, this text also makes an appearance in Greene's novel. After police tragically kill the child of an indigenous woman, she takes the body to the graves of several "holy people" in faint hope of a miracle. "It was like a short cut to the dark and magical heart of the faith—to the night when the graves opened and the dead walked. . . . Did she expect a miracle? and if she did, why should it not be granted her . . . ? Faith, one was told, could move mountains." (154–55).

242 | The Mosaic of Atonement

open tombs till "after Jesus' resurrection" (v. 53). In the meantime, they must wait alive in the abode of death.[49] During this interim, the evidence of their new life remains unseen by outsiders. In this sense, the strange story provides a metaphor for the Christian's present-day experience of "new creation" (2 Cor 5:17) amidst the smell of death and slowly airing grave cloths. We wait alive in the abode of death. And it was a death that brought us life.[50]

With regard to such unconventional victories, even the so-called proto-evangelium of Genesis 3:15 may be taken to point in a similar direction. Here, the lethal stomp seems to coincide with the serpent's fatal puncture: "He will crush your head, and you will strike his heel." It is a double deathblow.[51] To use a sporting analogy, it is as though one fighter's flailing knockout punch sends both men sprawling to the canvas. Yet in a twist, only the victim rises up victorious. Oddly, this winner never lashes out with fists, and his scars give testimony that the peculiar tale has not been fabricated. My point in citing all these biblical examples is straightforward: if Christ's earthly triumph was excruciating, then it should be unsurprising that his people's triumph is as well. The servant is not greater than the Master.[52]

This does not mean, however, that the sense of victory is absent. Indeed, even though overrealized eschatology (e.g., health-wealth prosperity or Constantinian triumphalism) is a danger for the church, neither should we embrace the underrealized gloom of "Greeneland." Christ's triumph continues to show itself in the present evil age. Thus, while the word *abandoned* chimes repeatedly in *The Power and the Glory*, the Christ of Scripture promised something different: "Surely, I am with you always, even to the end of the age" (Matt 28:20). Where then is the kingdom victory?

Ephesians as Test Case

To limit the inquiry, I will address the question primarily in relation to a single book: Paul's letter to the Ephesians.[53] I choose this text in part because

---

49. An "extraordinary courtesy!" in the words of Raymond Brown, *The Death of the Messiah* (New Haven, CT: Yale University Press, 2010), 2:1130. For a fuller treatment of the passage, see Charles L. Quarles, "Matthew 27:51–53: Meaning, Genre, Intertextuality, Theology and Reception History," *JETS* 59, no. 2 (2016): 274.

50. For a fuller treatment of the passage in question, see Quarles, "Matthew 27:51–53." My point here is not to delve into historicity or interpolation.

51. I credit my former Pentateuch Professor, Gordon Hugenberger, for this insight.

52. In the view of Fleming Rutledge, "The resurrection ratifies the cross as *the* way 'until he comes.'" *The Crucifixion*, 44.

53. While I affirm Paul's authorship of Ephesians, no part of my argument hinges on that fact.

the letter is often thought to have a "realized" eschatology. Ephesians is a triumphant text. In it, believers are pictured as having been *already* "raised up" and "seated in the heavenly realms in Christ Jesus" (2:6).[54]

Still, the meaning of this heavenly cosession in Ephesians may seem far from clear. Quite obviously, believers are not transported out of this world and its trials. After all, the letter was written by a "prisoner in the Lord" (4:1) and an "ambassador in chains" (6:20). Even so, the opening chapter tells the church that they have already been blessed "in the heavenly realms with every spiritual blessing in Christ" (1:3). Among these benefactions are election and a predestined calling to be "holy and blameless in love."[55] There is also adoption, forgiveness, and the grace that God lavished on his people (1:7–8). Finally, readers are told that they have received an inheritance in Christ (1:11) and as the down payment have been sealed "in [Christ] with the promised Holy Spirit" (1:13–14).

This last point is crucial. Ephesians sees the *Spirit* as the preeminent sign that the church has indeed been caught up in Christ's ascended victory. Yet while the believers have already been sealed by this Spirit, Paul's further prayer is that the Father would give this Gift all the more, so that the heart's "eyes" would be enlightened to this glorious inheritance (1:17–18). One reason believers need this enlightened vision is that the blessings of our heavenly triumph are not readily apparent from an earthly perspective. To see the victory, one must undergo a transformation of imagination.[56] However, while things like grace and forgiveness are invisible, there is one spoil of the christological conquest that is observable: a transformed moral life in a transformed earthly community. Herein lies the link to moral influence (and sanctification) toward which I have slowly been building.

The Ephesian Christians once lived by "the ways of the world," and in accordance with "the ruler of the power of the air" (2:2), but Paul claims that they do so no longer. By grace through faith (2:8), they (and we) have been fitted for "good works" (2:10). This transformation is seen in at least two ways: first, in the refusal to gratify the "cravings of our flesh" (2:3) and, second, in the tearing down of ethnic and cultural boundaries

---

54. In the words of Timothy G. Gombis, "Ephesians announces the triumph of God in Christ over the powers that rule the present evil age and then narrates how the church participates in this triumph." Gombis, *The Drama of Ephesians: Participating in the Triumph of God* (Downers Grove, IL: IVP Academic, 2010).

55. For Michael Gorman, "The church's election, like Israel's, is not to some place of privilege without responsibility but to a covenant, to a countercultural ('holy,' 'distinctive') life characterized by love." Gorman, *Apostle of the Crucified Lord: A Theological Introduction to Paul and His Letters* (Grand Rapids: Eerdmans, 2004), 506–7.

56. So says Gombis, *The Drama of Ephesians*, 61.

244 | The Mosaic of Atonement

("the dividing wall of hostility" [2:14]). This demolition results in a new community comprised of new people who do not look like they belong together. Only Jesus and his Spirit can account for this strange lot.

In the end, holiness and social reconciliation are the visible signs of heavenly triumph with Jesus. Or as the letter later argues, the mark of Christ's victory is seen in the church's response to this command: "Follow God's *example*, therefore, as dearly loved children and walk in the way of love, just as Christ loved us and gave himself up for us as a fragrant offering and sacrifice to God" (5:1–2, italics added). This statement shows the interlocking relation between sacrifice, victory, and a Spirit-driven account of moral influence.

In Ephesians, the believer's earthly life remains a battle. Yet the mode of warfare is again a strange one. In keeping with the military metaphor, believers are called to "put on the full armor of God, so that you can take your stand against the devil's schemes" (6:11). Yet even here, the way of victory bears a striking similarity to the odd example set by Christ. Christians are not called to lash out in aggressive violence but to "stand firm" (6:14) in spite of Satan's flaming arrows. The word *stand* appears no fewer than four times in four verses (6:11–14). An implication of this stationary warfare is that Christians are not called to strike out in human strength to win the final victory. After all, "Our struggle is not against flesh and blood" (v. 12).

Rather, believers are to adopt the posture of the Lamb: "standing . . . as though slain" (Rev 5:6). In so doing, we *inhabit* the victory God has already won in Christ. "Our warfare," says Timothy Gombis, "involves purpose-fully growing into communities that become more faithful corporate performances of Jesus on earth."[57] Importantly, to dispel any appearance of a growth that springs from human effort, the transformation is said to be the product of the Spirit's work.[58] In this way also, Christ's cruciform triumph—guided by the Holy Spirit—provides the model for our own victorious existence. Likewise, our Spirit-driven sanctification is one way in which the kingdom comes on earth, as it is in heaven.

I will say much more about the so-called moral influence model of atonement in the next chapter. My point here has been merely to note how the Christian's cruciform triumph is inspired by Christ's strange

---

57. Gombis, *The Drama of Ephesians*, 160.
58. It is important to note that both Christ and the Spirit are spoken of with the language of *gift* in the New Testament. For the most important recent study of such language, see John M. G. Barclay, *Paul and the Gift* (Grand Rapids: Eerdmans, 2015).

mode of conquest and enabled by his Spirit. In this way, *we* are the spoils of his victory, for "when he ascended [he] . . . took captives captive" (Eph 4:8 CSB). In addition, this triumph is all "to the praise of [Christ's] glorious grace" (Eph 1:6), so that both unmerited redemption (on the part of the church) and Spirit-driven sanctification leave Paul with a theocentric proclamation: "To him be the glory in the church and in Christ Jesus to all generations, forever and ever. Amen" (3:21).

Why Does It (Not) Look like It?

It is time to address at last the question that began the chapter. If Christ really conquered sin and Satan, why doesn't it look like it? The first reason, as Ephesians showed, is that the victory is apparent only to enlightened eyes. God's royal reign has always been a paradoxical one. One thief recognized it, but the other one did not. It involved a crown, but one of thorns. In a fallen world, God's power shows forth in weakness; hence the church's "triumphal procession" appears to onlookers as a march of the condemned (2 Cor 2:14). This is why our vision needs to be adjusted (Eph 1:18).

A second reason that the earth does not look like heaven is that Christ's victory is a "staged" one. My claim here is not that God's triumph is fake or phony, but that it consists in more than one installment. It is imperative that treatments of the *Christus Victor* motif grapple with this long-held paradox of biblical theology. While the kingdom has dawned, the final trumpet has not yet sounded. When it does, history will move into a new chapter, and it will be true that "the kingdom of the world has become the kingdom of our Lord and of his Messiah, and he will reign for ever and ever" (Rev 11:15). At this time, every tear will be wiped away (Rev 21:4). In this way, *Christus Victor* imagery has an already and a not yet.

In the meantime, a third and final reason for the delay in final victory appears to be God's loving patience with rebellious creatures. To return to Greene's novel, the world "needed a God to die for the half-hearted and the corrupt."[59] And in the same way, the world needs the Lord to be forbearing. It is to our benefit that God is slow to judge. Yet this gracious patience also means delay or, to put it differently, a "staged" victory. In response to this reality, one early Christian letter reassures us that God is "not slow in keeping his promise, as some understand slowness. Instead he is patient with you, not wanting anyone to perish, but everyone to come to

---

59. Greene, *The Power and the Glory*, 97.

repentance" (2 Pet 3:9). *This* is why the world has not been finally judged and made new: God is painfully patient.

Likewise, God is also faithful and forbearing as his people walk the circuitous and nonlinear route of sanctification. In the words of C. S. Lewis, "We shall of course be very muddy and tattered children by the time we reach home. But the bathrooms are all ready, the towels put out, and the clean clothes are in the airing cupboard. The only fatal thing is to lose one's temper and give it up. It is when we notice the dirt that God is most present to us: it is the very sign of his presence."[60] Lewis's statement should not be taken as a denial of sanctification (see ch. 13) but as an encouragement of God's patient faithfulness through life's messiness and suffering.

Despite its bleakness, even *The Power and the Glory* displays signs of a redemptive "presence" at work within the very heart of Greeneland. Despite sloth and fear and drunkenness, the whisky priest meets his martyr's death not because he cannot outrun his foes but because he chooses to reenter enemy territory to hear the confession of a dying murderer. Though he knows the invitation is a ruse to kill him, still he goes, because the dying man is real. "Even a coward has a sense of duty," he says to the murderous Lieutenant.

This stumbling obedience brings to mind another passage from Lewis—this one from *The Screwtape Letters*. In this book one has another conflict text in which Christ's unfolding victory melds with themes of moral influence. As a senior devil writes to his nephew, Wormwood:

> He [God] wants them to learn to walk. . . . He is pleased even with their stumbles. Do not be deceived. . . . Our cause is never more in danger than when a human, no longer desiring, but still intending, to do our Enemy's will, looks round upon a universe from which every trace of Him seems to have vanished, and asks why he has been forsaken, and still obeys.[61]

Like Jesus, the whisky priest stumbles toward his Calvary.

In Greene's novel, the martyrs of the anticlerical regime are rumored to face the firing squads with a triumphant cry of "*Vivo el Cristo Rey!*"

---

60. C. S. Lewis, letter to Mary Neylan, January 20, 1942, in *The Collected Letters of C. S. Lewis*, vol. 2, *Books, Broadcasts, and the War*, ed. Walter Hooper (New York: HarperOne, 2009).

61. C. S. Lewis, *The Screwtape Letters* (New York: Macmillan, 1961), 39.

Yet with the whisky priest, we read that "perhaps his mouth was too dry, because nothing came out except a word that sounded like 'Excuse'." Despite this, and despite the fact that he dies alone, hungover, and despairing, the unfolding victory of *Cristo Rey* is not absent from the story's final page. While the gospel's enemies believe that they have killed the final priest, the story ends with a soft knock upon a cottage door, and the realization that there is at least one more minister at large. "My name is Father—," he says with a frightened smile, and the door swings open. *Vivo el Cristo Rey.*

| CONCLUSION |

My claim in this chapter has been that Christ's God-glorifying triumph is the telos (or culmination) of atonement themes, even while the victory is a "staged" one. At present, believers are seated in the heavenlies with Christ and standing as though slain on the earth. While it is exceedingly common to note this "inaugurated eschatology" (both *already* and *not yet*) in biblical discussions of the kingdom of God, my claim here is that it is equally important to incorporate this "staged" triumph into discussions of atonement; and in particular, as it pertains to the interlocking relation between *Christus Victor* and moral influence themes.

Learning how to stand in a cruciform existence shows the reciprocal relation between the *head* and the *hands* of my mosaic Christ. In the words of G. B. Caird: "The transforming of sinners into righteous [humans] is the final defeat of the power."[62] To be sure, this transformation is enabled only by the Spirit, and by Christ's work on our behalf. That said, the kingdom comes on earth as Christians embody the posture of Christ's sacrificial love within the here and now. Thus moral influence is not the telos of atonement, but it is the Spirit-driven means by which more "crowns" (and not of thorns) are placed upon the Lamb. For this reason, I turn next to a moral influence model of beckoning and restraining.

---

62. G. B. Caird, *Principalities and Powers* (Oxford: Oxford University Press, 1956), 97.

PART 4

THE HANDS

Moral Influence

CHAPTER 11

BECKONING LOVE

RETHINKING ABELARD
AND MORAL INFLUENCE

What greater cause is there of the Lord's
coming than to show God's love for us?
Augustine, *On the Instruction of Beginners*

I f television dramas were inspired by the lives of medieval theologians,
none would scintillate like that of Peter Abelard (1079–1142).[1] Come to
think of it, a less scrupulous writer might break off this book right now
to begin pitching a somewhat trashier version of his biography to certain
cable channels. Parts would require no embellishment. From his youth, the
brilliant Abelard left controversy in his wake. While a student, he was said
to have challenged and defeated his own teachers in public disputation.
Then he stole their pupils and started schools of his own. In his most
famous transgression, he wooed the bright young Heloise, conceived a
child with her out of wedlock, and then married her in secret. In response,
her angry Uncle Fulbert hired thugs to break in and castrate Abelard by
force. And he succeeded.

But even after this shameful mutilation, Abelard was hardly free from
the entangling arms of love and violence. His heartfelt correspondence
with Heloise continued,[2] and he would make an ill-fated (if ironic) attempt

---

1. The following biographical sketch is indebted to Jeffrey E. Brower and Kevin Guilfoy,
eds., *The Cambridge Companion to Abelard* (Cambridge: Cambridge University Press, 2004);
herein, see especially the introduction by Brower and Guilfoy, and Abelard's "Life, Milieu,
and Intellectual Contexts" by John Marenbon (ch. 1).
2. See *The Letters of Abelard and Heloise*, trans. Betty Radice (Harmondsworth: Penguin,
1974).

to reform the sexual misdeeds at his new monastery, where monks were living with their concubines and children. The offending brothers showed their thanks by attempting to murder Abelard, and he was forced to flee again. Over the course of his life, he was condemned of heresy on not one but two occasions, and he was finally excommunicated by Pope Innocent II on the grounds of Pelagianism. For punishment, the aging Abelard was to be confined to a monastery under sentence of "perpetual silence." But Abelard was not the silent type.

In his final days, he was given shelter at a priory in Cluny (in modern France), where he lived out his life as a respected scholar and elder churchman. In time, the excommunication was lifted, and Abelard has been anything but silent ever since. In addition to his ethical writings,[3] his most influential work involves the doctrine of atonement, where he was made (for better or worse) the poster boy for an exclusively "exemplarist" interpretation of Christ's work. In full-fledged exemplarism, the efficacy is seen to reside *solely* in the transforming power of Christ's loving and ethical example, which then beckons us to imitate him.[4]

The great question, however, is whether Abelard actually was an exemplarist, or whether the sentence of "perpetual silence" has been replaced by accusations of perpetual advocacy for a position he did not hold. A great many have gotten Abelard quite wrong. Having noted the error of portraying Abelard as an exclusive exemplarist, however, this chapter will introduce the so-called moral influence model by way of its most (in)famous, and perhaps most misunderstood, "exemplar."

| THE FATEFUL PROOF TEXT |

The cause for viewing Abelard as an exemplarist can be traced largely to a single passage from his Romans commentary. In it, he reflected on Romans 3:19–26 in order to ask *how* we are reconciled to God through Christ's suffering and death. For Abelard, this violent means of redemption raised profound questions. For instance, why should God not be angrier at humanity *after* we murdered his Son than before? Was not this crime much worse than "the taste of one apple" long ago? And if Adam's sin

---

3. See Peter Abelard, *Ethical Writings: Ethics and Dialogue Between a Philosopher, a Jew, and a Christian*, trans. Paul Vincent Spade (Indianapolis: Hackett, 1995).
4. This view may be found in Albrecht Ritschl (1822–89), *The Christian Doctrine of Justification and Reconciliation* (Edinburgh: Edmonston and Douglas, 1872).

"was so great that it could not be atoned for except by the death of Christ, how shall [Christ's murder] be atoned for?"[5]

Abelard also posed uncomfortable questions to both versions of the so-called ransom argument. In the first place, he concluded that the required price for human freedom could not be paid to Satan, for this would imply that one slave had acquired rights over others simply by seducing them. And second, if the ransom was seen as being paid to God the Father, Abelard asked why "God should have accepted the death of his Son" as a means of reconciliation. Why would such an unjust death please him? At this point, it is crucial to note that Abelard did not explicitly reject the idea that some ransom has been paid ("for it is not the torturers but their lords who fix or receive ransom for captives"). Still, he admitted that this view inspired "a not insignificant question" concerning the means of our redemption.[6]

Having noted these queries, Abelard penned the infamous passage, which must be quoted at length:

> It seems to us that in this we are justified in the blood of Christ and reconciled to God, that it was through this matchless grace shown to us that his son received our nature and in that nature, teaching us both by word and by example, preserved to the death and bound us to himself even more through love, so that when we have been kindled by so great a benefit of divine grace, true charity might fear to endure nothing for his sake. . . .
>
> Therefore, our redemption is that supreme love in us through the Passion of Christ, which not only frees us from slavery to sin, but gains for us the true liberty of the sons of God, so that we may complete all things by his love rather than by fear. He showed us such great grace, than which a greater cannot be found, by his own word: "No one," he says, "has greater love than this: that he lays down his life for his friends" (John 15:13).[7]

The text touches on several topics, but later readers seized primarily upon Abelard's emphasis that Christ's "teaching by word and example . . . kindled" redeeming love in us.

---

5. *Comm. Rom.*, 166–67; this passage would be condemned by both Bernard and William of St. Thierry.
6. *Comm. Rom.*, 167.
7. *Comm. Rom.*, 167–68.

| THE ALLEGATION OF EXEMPLARISM |

The allegation, even in Abelard's own day, was that he had reduced the atonement *solely* to a moral influence upon humanity. This charge was made most famously by Bernard of Clairvaux (1090–1153), who after reading Abelard, wrote to the Pope that *this* Messiah merely "set up a standard of love" by which he taught "righteousness" but did not "bestow it." Then with notable sarcasm, Bernard suggested: "If Christ's benefit consisted only in the display of good works, [perhaps] Adam only harmed us by the display of sin."[8] The charge was meant to link Abelard with Pelagius, and it was on this ground that he was ultimately condemned.

In similar fashion, William of St. Thierry (ca. 1075–1148) accused Abelard of implying that Christ died for nothing since Abelard implied that forgiveness could have come apart from the cross.[9] The accusation (while overstated) was also traceable to the famous passage. Just prior to the claim about enkindled love, Abelard had argued that Christ's forgiveness of persons prior to the cross (e.g., Matt 9:2), proved that a ransom was not necessary in order for God to pardon sinners.[10] In fact, God could "free man from the devil by a command alone."[11] In light of this logic, Abelard came to see Christ's great travails (his "fasts, reproaches, lashes, spitting, and . . . shameful death") as necessary for another reason: they revealed how much God loves us, and this inspires our grateful obedience.[12] This too aroused the charge of an exclusive exemplarism.[13]

In the modern era, the verdict echoed on. Most famously, Hastings Rashdall (1858–1924) gloried in Abelard's exemplarism, proclaiming that "for the first time . . . the doctrine of the atonement was stated in a way which had nothing unintelligible, arbitrary, illogical, or immoral

---

8. Bernard of Clairvaux, *Tractatus ad Innocentium II Pontificem contra quaedam capitula errorum Abaelardi*, quoted in Philip L. Quinn, "Abelard on Atonement: 'Nothing Unintelligible, Arbitrary, Illogical, or Immoral about It,'" in *Reasoned Faith: Essays in Philosophical Theology in Honor of Norman Kretzmann*, ed. Eleonore Stump, (Ithaca, NY: Cornell University Press, 1993), 292.

9. William of St. Thierry, *Disputatio adversus Petrum Abaelardum*, 6; cited in Cartwright, introduction to *Comm. Rom.*, 44.

10. Cf. Athanasius, *De Incarnatione*, 44.

11. *Comm. Rom.*, 166. While this may raise questions, Abelard is joined by the likes of Augustine and Aquinas in believing that God might have redeemed humanity by other means. Nonetheless, their conclusions were that the cross must have been most "fitting." See Augustine, *De Trinitate*, 7.10; Aquinas, *Summa Theologica*, III, Q.1, A.2.

12. *Comm. Rom.*, 165–66.

13. Another medieval source for these critiques may be found in the anonymous *Capitula Haeresum*.

about it."[14] By this, he meant that "the efficacy of Christ's death" was to be seen solely in "its subjective influence upon the mind of the sinner," so that we are moved by "gratitude and answering love." Others agreed, if not with the praiseworthiness of Abelard's exemplarism, at least with its clarity. For Robert Franks, he "reduced the whole process of redemption to one single clear principle[:] the manifestation of God's love to us in Christ, which awakens an answering love in us."[15] The verdict seemed clear: Abelard was an exemplarist par excellence.[16]

| AGAINST EXCLUSIVE EXEMPLARISM |

Yet not everyone agreed with this evaluation. In the face of the consensus, a few claimed that Abelard had hardly been consulted in this sentence any more than in that of angry Uncle Fulbert. And both resulted in the maiming of his "corpus." In the late twentieth century, the tide began to turn against the older view of Abelard.[17] The main evidence for the shift was to be found in

1. his explicit support for penal substitution,
2. his robust belief in original sin, and
3. his mistranslated view of divine love.

I will now briefly examine these reasons.

Penal Substitution

Perhaps the most stunning evidence for Abelard's nonexemplarism comes in his explicit support for penal substitution. To notice this, however, one must look beyond the famous proof text. Elsewhere, Abelard claimed flatly, "The Lord bore [and] endured the punishments of our sins."[18] Hence Christ became "the price for you" as he "purchased and redeemed you with his own blood."[19] In a hymn for Good Friday, he sang

14. Hastings Rashdall, *The Idea of the Atonement in Christian Theology* (London: Macmillan, 1919), 360.
15. Robert S. Franks, *The Work of Christ* (London: Nelson, 1962), 146.
16. Cartwright includes a list of modern scholars (often in the early twentieth century) who deemed Abelard an exclusive exemplarist. Cartwright, introduction to *Comm. Rom.*, 44–45.
17. See Alister McGrath, "The Moral Theory of the Atonement: An Historical and Theological Critique," *SJT* 38, no. 2 (1985): 208.
18. *Comm. Rom.*, 216.
19. Abelard, *Letter 5*, as cited in Jaroslav Pelikan, *The Christian Tradition: A History of the Development of Doctrine*, vol. 3 (Chicago: University of Chicago Press, 1978), 128.

of how "You underwent the punishment, while we have done the wrongs"; "the offences are our own . . . [so] why do You make their punishments Your own?"[20] Discussing Romans 4:25, he clearly joined the idea of penal substitution to his famous view of love "enkindled": "We committed the sins for which he bore the punishment," and Christ died so "that by dying he might remove . . . the punishment of our sins."

Abelard was clearly espousing penal substitution, yet he married the substitutionary emphasis to his famous account of Christ's loving moral influence. In this way, Christ's sacrifice served to "draw our minds away from the will to sin and enkindle in them the highest love of himself."[21] In response, Thomas Williams concludes that Abelard viewed sin as having *both* an objective and a subjective hold on us. In assuming our nature and bearing our punishment, Christ removes the objective hold while simultaneously enkindling our subjective liberation by awakening a grateful love within us. Thus Abelard's account of moral influence sits atop an objective foundation that includes even the idea of Christ bearing our penalty.[22]

Original Sin

Alongside affirmations of penal substitution, Abelard's supposed Pelagian exemplarism is rendered doubtful by his belief in the damning effects of original sin. Even in the famous passage from his Romans commentary, Abelard refers to our "slavery to sin," which would seem to challenge the idea that a mere example could set us free.[23] Following Augustine, he believed that humans contracted original sin from Adam, that it was passed through heredity, and that it makes all humans liable to eternal punishment. Original sin was to be pardoned by the sacraments, specifically baptism, and those who died without these sacraments were condemned, including infants.[24] Though this may (rightly) sound abhorrent to modern readers, it is anything but Pelagian!

Abelard did alter Augustine's treatment of original sin at one point.

---

20. Cited in R. O. P. Taylor, "Was Abelard an Exemplarist?," *Theology* 31 (1935): 208. I have altered the translation only slightly to change "Thou" and "Thine" to more colloquial English.

21. This particular translation from Abelard's Romans commentary (regarding Rom 4:25) is that of Quinn, "Abelard on Atonement," 290; cf. *Comm. Rom.*, 204.

22. Thomas Williams, "Sin, Grace, and Redemption," in *The Cambridge Companion to Abelard*, ed. Jeffrey E. Brower and Kevin Guilfoy (Cambridge: Cambridge University Press, 2004), 266, 276.

23. *Comm. Rom.*, 168; See also Quinn, "Abelard on Atonement," 288.

24. See especially *Comm. Rom.*, 221–27.

He claimed that while we inherit the *punishment* for Adam's sin, we do not inherit the guilt. For Abelard, guilt attaches solely to a person's free actions, and as he argues, we had no say in Adam's sin. His position seems terribly unjust since we are to be punished for a crime of which we are not guilty. Nonetheless, Abelard's anomalous view still challenges the notion that a mere *example* could set us free. According to him, original sin is "that debt (*debitum*) of damnation with which we are bound, since we are made guilty of eternal punishment on account of our origin, that is, of our first parents."[25]

Mistranslating Love

A third and final argument for Abelard's nonexemplarism involves the allegation that certain modern readers (perhaps deliberately) mistranslated the crucial proof text from his Romans commentary and in so doing mischaracterized his view of God's redeeming love. In the most egregious example, Abelard's famous passage views "our redemption" as "that supreme love which is *in us* through the Passion of Christ."[26] Yet in Rashdall, God's love "in us" is translated as that which has been merely "shown to us."[27] This is not what Abelard wrote, and the mistranslation obscures Abelard's medieval view on how exactly divine love transforms us.

On this topic, many scholars now argue that, for Abelard, divine love is a mystical and powerful force that binds us to God as it is "poured out into our hearts by the Holy Spirit" (Rom 5:5) and applied through the sacraments.[28] As Weingart states, "Its exemplary quality is secondary [and] consequent upon its redemptive character." In this way, "man's responsive act of love is a direct result of Christ's gracious transformation of the sinner's person."[29] For Abelard, this love poured out within us is far more than a mere exemplar.[30]

---

25. *Comm. Rom.*, 223.
26. "Redemptio itaque nostra est illa summa in nobis per passionem Christi dilectio." Cited from Quinn, "Abelard on Atonement," 289; cf. Taylor, "Was Abelard an Exemplarist?," 213, italics added.
27. Rashdall, *The Idea of Atonement*, 358.
28. In this way, Abelard is following the favorite passage of Augustine (Rom 5:5). See *Comm. Rom.*, 206.
29. R. E. Weingart, *The Logic of Divine Love: A Critical Analysis of the Soteriology of Peter Abelard* (Oxford: Clarendon, 1970), 78–96.
30. See also Paul Fiddes, *Past Event and Present Salvation: The Christian Idea of Atonement* (Louisville: Westminster John Knox, 1989), 144.

| ABELARD THE INCONSISTENT? |

Despite this shift in thinking over Abelard's supposed exemplarism, many still argue that he was ultimately inconsistent in his various statements on how atonement happens. In a recent translation of the Romans commentary, Steven Cartwright says it this way:

> Abelard does not present an entirely consistent theology of redemption. . . . At some points he presents what seems to be a strictly exemplarist view . . . ; at other points he presents the objective views he had previously rejected; at still others he seems to mix them. This has likely contributed to the modern controversy over Abelard's views. . . .
>
> He either denies or affirms ransom and a legalistic [forensic] conception of the God-man relationship, depending on the situation. They are logically and ethically untenable on the one hand, but useful expressions of the work of Christ on the other.[31]

At the root of these alleged inconsistencies, various causes are suggested. Perhaps the objective statements were merely a façade to protect Abelard from heretical accusation (a move that apparently worked about as well as his secret marriage!).[32] Perhaps they were the product of rhetorical overstatement.[33] Or perhaps they simply demonstrate the inevitable contradictions that occur when a theologian attempts to explain the complexity of the cross with emotive analogies, biblical fidelity, and a rigid rationalism.[34]

Despite the merits of these suggestions (and especially the final one), the most charitable conclusion is slightly different. As seen previously, the best translations of Abelard's famous passage do *not* show him definitively rejecting the objective and cleansing value of Christ's sacrifice. Nor do they reveal a denunciation of the notion that Jesus paid the penalty for human sin. Instead, what Abelard rejected were two particularly crass ideas: (1) that the devil was paid a ransom because he possessed just rights over humanity, and (2) that God the Father would take perverse (salvific) pleasure in the blood of the Son.[35]

---

31. Cartwright, introduction to *Comm. Rom.*, 44, 51.
32. This is the claim of A. Victor Murray, *Abelard and St Bernard: A Study in Twelfth Century 'Modernism'* (Manchester: Manchester University Press, 1967), 126–34.
33. See D. E. Luscombe, *The School of Peter Abelard* (Cambridge: Cambridge University Press, 2008), 137–38.
34. So says M. T. Clanchy, *Abelard: A Medieval Life* (Oxford: Wiley-Blackwell, 1999), 274.
35. On these two points, I agree entirely. See chs. 5–6.

On other topics, Abelard simply raised uncomfortable questions without fully answering them. Why, for instance, would God not be angrier after the crucifixion than he was before? Why would innocent blood be justly accepted? At these points, the page was strewn with questions bereft of answers.[36] Abelard seemed sympathetic to the force of these objections, but he did not move to answer them with anything approaching comprehensive attention. For his opponents, this untidy habit was a sign of deeper problems. And it did not help that Abelard had displayed both a proof text and a personality that were easy to take issue with.[37] That said, while the unanswered questions clearly caused problems for Abelard, it is also true that questions are not the same as contradictions.[38]

Taken as a whole, Abelard was fairly consistent on five major conclusions.[39] (1) All humans are born in slavery to sin and its accompanying penalty.[40] (2) By uniting himself to our nature,[41] Christ bore that penalty on our behalf.[42] In so doing, (3) Jesus defeated Satan by removing his permission to punish the elect.[43] Because of this, (4) God offers us the opportunity to be cleansed from sin by grace and the application of the sacraments. In addition to these themes, however, Abelard also claimed that (5) Christ's act of love transforms our very motives by enkindling grateful and obedient love within us to take the place of fear-based submission. Despite unanswered questions, there are no contradictions in these five conclusions.[44] And in elevating the revelation of divine love as the chief reason for the incarnation, Abelard was in good company. It was Augustine

---

36. See again *Comm. Rom.*, 166–67.

37. See Williams, "Sin, Grace, and Redemption," 259.

38. To take another example, consider Abelard's statement about "how very cruel and unjust it seems that someone should require the blood of an innocent person as a ransom" (*Comm. Rom.*, 167). Even this does not reject the biblical idea that Christ offered his life as a ransom for many. Instead, it merely raises the honest question with which I have wrestled previously under the heading "penal nontransference."

39. I say "fairly consistent" because it is unclear why our penalty must be borne by Christ if God could have forgiven by a mere command alone (*Comm. Rom.*, 165–66). Perhaps Abelard would respond to this with the claim that a justification "by fiat alone" would not enflame the heart with love as does the realization that Christ has come personally to pay our debt.

40. See above on Abelard's doctrine of original sin.

41. See Abelard's statement on the Son having "received our nature," *Comm. Rom.*, 167.

42. See again, *Comm. Rom.*, 152, 211, and the Hymn for Good Friday, cited in Taylor, "Was Abelard an Exemplarist," 208.

43. See, for instance, *Comm. Rom.*, 154, 164–66, 264, 277, 344, 394.

44. The claim of Paul Fiddes fits well with this conclusion: "He is not inconsistent, but there is a curious untidiness about his thought." *Past Event*, 156. For two more arguments on Abelard's consistency, see Quinn, "Abelard on Atonement," and Weingart, *The Logic of Divine Love*.

of Hippo, after all, who once asked: "What greater cause is there of the Lord's coming than to show God's love for us?"[45]

This does not mean, of course, that Abelard's theology was entirely praiseworthy. His view of divine grace remained suspect to men like Bernard (and William of St. Thierry) because he argued that no additional gift of divine grace is necessary for the elect to do good works, aside from that which God had already given.[46] And when it came time to consider *why* innocent blood might be accepted as a sacrifice for sin, he did not manage to think covenantally; thus he left readers with crass questions about why a father would be happy about the death of his son. Abelard was hardly perfect. Yet on the atonement, he was not an exclusive exemplarist, nor did he make an obvious contradiction.

Abelard's is yet another voice from the tradition that managed (or at least attempted) to integrate different models of atonement with one another. Like my own account, Abelard's moral influence logic may be seen to flow forth from his more objective emphases, like that of penal substitution—an act made possible because Christ has taken up our human nature as a kind of second Adam. The exemplarist themes are clearly in Abelard's work, but they do not provide the exclusive means by which atonement happens. The task remains however to ask if this view might actually be defensible. To address this question, I turn now to a modern theologian whose ideas were "enkindled" by Abelard's example.

| ADVANCING ABELARD TODAY: PAUL FIDDES |

In *Past Event and Present Salvation* (1989), the British Baptist theologian Paul Fiddes (b. 1947) interacts appreciatively with Abelard's account of the saving power of divine love. While leaving aside the monk's occasional affirmations of themes like penal substitution, Fiddes claims that Abelard's greatest contribution is that he "grasped the power of the divine love to *create* or generate love within human beings."[47] In his view, "Abelard's great insight [is] that the revelation in Christ, when received by the human mind, is at the same time an actual infusion of love. The exhibition *is* a restoration. The manifestation *is* a transformation. This is what Abelard

---

45. Augustine, *On the Instruction of Beginners*, 4; Cf. Augustine, *De Trinitate*, 8.5.
46. Williams, "Sin, Grace, and Redemption," 272; cf. Cartwright, introduction to *Comm. Rom.*, 41.
47. Fiddes, *Past Event*, 141, italics in original.

is struggling to understand for himself and to express."[48] In sum, "Abelard believes the revelation of God's love to have redemptive impact on its own account. To say that love 'kindles' love means that it generates it within; it is no mere matter of *our* imitating Christ."[49]

Fiddes finds evidence for this argument in a sermon wherein Abelard stated: "Dispelling our shadows with light, [Christ] *showed* us, both by his words and example, the fullness of all virtues, and *repaired* our nature."[50] With the move from "showed" to "repaired," Fiddes claims that "the love disclosed is at the same time the love which recreates." Indeed, in witnessing the act of love the heart is warmed toward God. Hence this "kindling" is not the result of human initiative but the consequence of Love itself.[51]

Fiddes's aim is to challenge the usual understanding of what constitutes a "subjective" view of the atonement. In his view, Abelard's great insight was that the demonstration of divine love can be an "objective" view of the atonement. The problem, however, is that "Abelard did not altogether succeed in making clear how this might be."[52]

To address this weakness, Fiddes turns to modern psychology and to the idea that a truly compelling story can break in and shatter the diseased human ego. For help in this endeavor, he looks initially to Reinhold Niebuhr (1892–1971). For Niebuhr, to be "crucified with Christ" (Gal 2:20) means that "my ego is shattered by the crucifixion." This happens as the cross reveals both the sacrificial love of God and his verdict (both wrath and forgiveness) upon sin.[53] The self, says Fiddes, "cannot strengthen its own will to goodness. The only solution lies in a disclosure of truth breaking in from outside the self, and the cross has such power since it reveals a love which does not resort to any of the strategies for survival at which the self is so adept."[54] The point once more is that the revelation of divine love through the cross *is* itself an objective model of atonement, even as it exerts its influence upon us.

---

48. Fiddes, *Past Event*, 154, italics in original.
49. Fiddes, *Past Event*, 144, italics in original.
50. Abelard, *Sermons*, 3, cited in Fiddes, *Past Event*, 145, italics added by Fiddes.
51. Fiddes, *Past Event*, 145. If this is true, then it raises the question of why not all respond positively to Christ crucified. I will address the differing views of Fiddes and Abelard on this question momentarily.
52. Fiddes, *Past Event*, 144.
53. See Reinhold Niebuhr, *The Nature and Destiny of Man*, vol. 2 (New York: Scribner's, 1943), 113.
54. Fiddes, *Past Event*, 148.

262 | The Mosaic of Atonement

SUFFERING DIVINE FORGIVENESS

At this juncture, the question remains: How does this particular act of love—the crucifixion—both shatter and remake us? In part 2 of this book,[55] I noted how Fiddes rejects transactional views of the atonement because, in his words, "the point is not that justice has been appeased, but that the one who offers acceptance does so from the situation of knowing the whole truth about us, and being most wounded by it."[56] The idea here is that in order to forgive in the most compelling fashion, one must genuinely *suffer* wrong. By suffering injustice in the person of Christ, Fiddes claims that "God is 'enabled' to forgive through the cross; he gains the right to forgive."[57] It is therefore by God's being personally and genuinely wounded by the depth of human sin that the words "Father forgive them" carry meaning to us.

Fiddes readily acknowledges that this view of a suffering God is at odds with the classical tradition of divine impassibility, of which Abelard was a part.[58] Still, he echoes the words of Paul Tillich (1886–1965) in positing that had God not participated in our suffering and estrangement humans would not have had the courage "to accept that we are accepted."[59] Fiddes, however, does not embrace a rigid universalism. Rather, God "is humble enough to tolerate resistance to his love,"[60] even while Christians should remain hopeful, for "we cannot know over what precipices of the mind the Shepherd will travel in eternity to reach the lost." For this reason, one cannot even "limit the scope of the searching love of God to the boundary of death."[61]

Throughout this modern appropriation of Abelard, there is a mystical theology of God's creative participation in the weakness and suffering of the world. Hence, Fiddes claims that humans encounter the transforming love of Christ not merely in the sacraments or in Christian community but in the apparent godforsakenness of the so-called secular world. In this place too, God stands in solidarity with the broken. And in keeping with the prison musings of Dietrich Bonhoeffer (1906–45), Fiddes affirms that "Christ is now hidden and waiting to be found in places where God seems

---

55. See chs. 5–6.
56. Fiddes, *Past Event*, 183.
57. Fiddes, *Past Event*, 185.
58. Fiddes, *Past Event*, 157; for an entire work on this topic, see Paul Fiddes, *The Creative Suffering of God* (New York: Oxford University Press, 1988).
59. Paul Tillich, *Systematic Theology*, vol. 2 (Welwyn: Nisbet, 1968), 202; Fiddes cites the passage in *Past Event*, 160.
60. Fiddes, *Past Event*, 155.
61. Fiddes, *Past Event*, 186.

weak and powerless."[62] In these wildernesses, the Spirit blows mysteriously, and the human heart is enkindled by the objective power of divine love.

| IN FAVOR OF FIDDES |

At several points, Fiddes's Abelardian adaptations are insightful. First, he is especially helpful in noting the mysterious and powerful way in which love can generate change within the beloved. In fact, the exhibition of costly grace can be a shattering experience, as in the famous scene from Victor Hugo's *Les Misérables*. Here, after stealing the silver of a kindly bishop, Jean Valjean is apprehended by authorities. Yet when confronted with the guilty captive, the bishop only chastises the thief for carelessly leaving the candlesticks behind. In that very moment, a transformation overtakes Valjean, his heart is pricked, and in the view of the bishop his soul is purchased and given to God.[63] Exemplars like this can have transformative results.

Second, Fiddes is also helpful in noting the "humble" and mysterious way in which God allows his love to be resisted, even as he desires all to be saved (e.g., 2 Pet 3:9). This point is important, for if love generates its own response, then why do humans respond so differently to Christ? Why is one thief transformed while the other goes on hurling insults (Luke 23:42)? Without dispelling the mystery of these questions, Fiddes seems to believe that while the sparks of divine love are cast abroad in liberal fashion—and are even blown upon by the Spirit—humans retain the ability to stamp out the gracious flame.[64]

On this point, Fiddes criticizes Abelard's predestinarian tendencies, which attribute the lack of faith within the damned to the fact that the Spirit only inspires "those whom he pleases."[65] On this apparently arbitrary form of divine sovereignty, Fiddes notes that it is "very odd that a theologian who exults in the unbounded generosity of the love of God should be willing to consign little children to damnation."[66] Indeed it is; and Fiddes seems right to note that these accents within Abelard seem ill-suited for one another. Likewise, his alterations go some distance in repairing them.

---

62. Fiddes, *Past Event*, 165.
63. Victor Hugo, *Les Misérables*, ch. 12.
64. Fiddes, *Past Event*, 155. Of course, if this is so, then the supposed objectivity of impartial and transforming love might seem to be imperiled. More on this in ch. 13.
65. Abelard, *Expositio in Hexaemeron* (PL, 770d–771a); Fiddes draws upon the text in *Past Event*, 154.
66. Fiddes, *Past Event*, 154.

| POTENTIAL FLAWS IN FIDDES |

At other points, Fiddes's treatment seems less salutary. For starters, he is simply wrong to claim that Abelard denied all elements of "appeasement" or "satisfaction" in atonement.[67] On the first point, Abelard even claimed (rather unfortunately) that the Father was "made merciful" through the Son.[68] And on the next, Abelard's numerous affirmations of penal substitutionary logic illustrate that Christ's death did satisfy the penalty that humans owed: what he called our *debitum* of damnation.[69] In these ways, Fiddes fails—like many others—to account for the variety in Abelard's atonement doctrine.

A second fault in Fiddes comes in dealing with the uniqueness of the cross. Like all proponents of a predominantly moral influence view of the atonement, Fiddes must demonstrate what makes Christ's act of love distinct and saving when compared to other exemplars. After all, Jesus is not the only divine representative to offer costly forgiveness (consider again *Les Misérables*). Nor is Christ the first to lay down his life for friends. For Fiddes, the singularity of the cross lies not in the objective paying of a penalty or ransom but in the way God publicly took in human sin and suffering within his very life. In this act, God was "enabled" to forgive our sin and know our pain in a new and unique way.[70] Yet if taken in a literal and chronological sense, the claim seems tenuous. Abelard himself was quite clear that God was in the forgiveness business long before the crucifixion, and this conclusion even led him to claim that God could have pardoned us by a command alone.[71]

For Fiddes, the curious statement about God being "enabled" to forgive seems to locate the uniqueness of the atonement in the fact that it was *God* who suffered our violence. In this way, divine empathy and forgiveness are revealed in a new way that strikes our callous hearts with transformative weight. God suffers with *and* because of us. And for these reasons we find not only solidarity but also credibility in the offer of forgiveness. The Christian God is not a billionaire who forgives a small debt with untroubled detachment. Christ suffered our sin in the most personal and painful way imaginable. And it is from this place of

---

67. Fiddes, *Past Event*, 156–57.
68. *Comm. Rom.*, 107.
69. See above for a sampling of Abelard on penal substitution.
70. See again, Fiddes, *Past Event*, 185.
71. See again *Comm. Rom.*, 165–66.

woundedness that forgiveness flows like blood. By going beyond Abelard at this point, Fiddes believes that the cross can change the human attitude toward God in an even more objective fashion than the forgiveness offered in *Les Misérables*.

But is this sufficient? To his credit, Fiddes evades the critique often lodged against exclusively exemplarist perspectives. Giving voice to this charge, Scotsman James Denney (1856–1917) provides a famous illustration: "If I were sitting on the end of a pier on a summer day, enjoying the sunshine and the air, and someone came along and jumped into the water and got drowned 'to prove his love for me,' I should find it quite unintelligible." On the other hand, "if I had fallen over the pier and were drowning," the idea of a stranger jumping in and sacrificing his life to save mine would be viewed differently. In the words of Denney: "I would say, 'Greater love hath no man than this.'"[72] The illustration may be effective against strict exemplarists, but it does not touch Fiddes's argument. For Fiddes, "we" (or rather: human sin) pushed the "stranger" (Christ) off the pier. And it is while drowning that he offers transformative words: "Father, forgive them."

Of course, Fiddes's avoidance of the "Brighton Pier" critique does not change the fact that both Scripture and Abelard support more objective reasons for Christ's vicarious obedience (recapitulation) and his vicarious judgment on our behalf (including penal substitution).[73] Nor does this evasion alleviate the concerns that classical theists have with Fiddes's denial of divine impassibility.[74] Given all this, perhaps it is best to view Fiddes's Abelardian adaptation of the moral influence model as not flatly wrong but tilting (even more than Abelard himself) toward the reductionistic side of atonement doctrine.[75] Hence, when faced with the older and more blended "wine" of Abelard, one should concur with those who claim: "the old is better" (Luke 5:39).

---

72. James Denney, *The Death of Christ*, ed. R. V. G. Tasker (1903; repr., London: Tyndale, 1951), 177.

73. See ch. 5.

74. See for instance John Webster, "*Non ex aequo*: God's Relation to Creatures," in *Within the Love of God: Essays on the Doctrine of God in Honour of Paul S. Fiddes*, ed. Anthony Clarke and Andrew Moore (Oxford: Oxford University Press, 2014), ch. 6.

75. While Fiddes affirms the enduring worth of other models—via traditional appeals to sacrifice, justice, and victory—he tends to subjectivize these traditionally "objective" models, and to elevate his version of moral influence as most important. See Stephen R. Holmes, "'Who Can Count How Many Crosses?' Paul Fiddes on Salvation," in Clarke and Moore, *Within the Love of God*, ch. 8, esp. 130–32.

| CONCLUSION |

In Abelard, this initial version of the so-called moral influence model presents a "beckoning hand" that motions and inspires humans to be transformed by Christ's act of love. By his life, death, and resurrection, Christ beckons us to run *to* God and to obey him "by love rather than by fear."[76] And by the Spirit we are enabled (despite our flaws) to live out the *imitatio Christi* through the process of grace-driven sanctification.

As Abelard rightly noted, some might be driven to submit externally to God from anxiety or a sense of duty. Yet when God's love is revealed and poured out into our hearts by the Holy Spirit,[77] the redeemed are compelled to flee the far country, running with gratitude to the Father. Christ's recapitulative obedience and his vicarious judgment—I would add—make possible his status as a transforming and beckoning exemplar. But there is a second and more recent moral influence argument that must also be addressed. While Abelard presents a hand that beckons, the next "exemplar" presents a hand that restrains, unmasks, and indeed "waives off" darker and more violent impulses.

---

76. *Comm. Rom.*, 167.
77. I must delay a full treatment of the Spirit's role in moral influence until ch. 13.

CHAPTER 12

UNMASKING VIOLENCE

GIRARD AND MORAL INFLUENCE

*All our resistance is turned against the light that
threatens us. It has revealed so many things for
so long a time without revealing itself that we
are convinced it comes from within us.*

René Girard

While Abelardian atonement often focuses on igniting imitative love within us, the brilliant and creative work of René Girard (1923–2015) sought to show how Christ unmasks satanic violence in the world. Thus the first *hand* of moral influence beckons the believer toward God, and the second *hand* moves to reveal and restrain a more insidious force: the sinful human propensity to violent rivalry and scapegoating. Rarely in the past five hundred years could one point to an account of the atonement that claimed to be both biblically faithful and completely new—yet Girard purported to have uncovered exactly that. He therefore came to utter, in the enigmatic words of Jesus, *Things Hidden Since the Foundation of the World.*[1]

In the face of these grand claims, this chapter unfolds in three stages: First, I will survey Girard's novel account of Christ's work. Second, I will subject it to rigorous critique. Then, third, I will glean from it some positive

---

1. René Girard, *Things Hidden Since the Foundation of the World*, trans. Stephen Bann and Michael Metteer (Stanford: Stanford University Press, 1987); first published in French in 1976.

takeaways that will influence my own mosaic of atonement doctrine. In so doing, I will note that despite Girard's frequent talk of the cross's triumph over Satan,[2] his theory actually resides firmly within the family of exemplarist or moral influence doctrines, indeed more so than Abelard's. While some have seen Girard's system as being an "all or nothing" enterprise that must either be accepted or rejected whole,[3] my claim differs. The chapter's final argument will be that Girard's imperfect insights *do* add something to an integrated mosaic of atonement doctrine, even while they must be shorn of serious problems in order to fit with more traditional models.

| UNDERSTANDING GIRARD |

"Mine," says Girard, "is a search for the anthropology of the Cross, which turns out to rehabilitate orthodox theology."[4] This statement may sound quite traditional in terms of its conclusions, but it is worth noting that Girard was not even a Christian when he developed the basics of his grand theory. Nor was he trained in theology. His doctorate was in history (on Franco-American relations), and his earliest teaching was in literature.[5]

In 1959 he underwent a profound conversion after glimpsing how the Gospels unmask our violent machinations.[6] And for the rest of his life, Girard's ardent though anomalous Catholicism showed forth in a series of groundbreaking works. In what follows, I will draw primarily upon the most developed and digestible of these: *The Scapegoat* (1982) and *I See Satan Fall Like Lightning* (1999).[7]

Mimesis and Its Discontents

At its core, Girard's project rests upon a novel notion of human desire called "mimesis." The concept refers to the way in which humans want what we see others wanting. In essence, we borrow our desires from those

---

2. See for instance René Girard, *I See Satan Fall Like Lightning*, trans. James G. Williams (Maryknoll, NY: Orbis, 2001), ch. 11. The original French translation first appeared in 1999.

3. See Ben Pugh, *Atonement Theories: A Way through the Maze* (Eugene, OR: Cascade, 2014), 160–62.

4. René Girard, *The Girard Reader*, ed. James G. Williams (New York: Herder, 1996), 288.

5. James G. Williams, "René Girard: A Biographical Sketch," in Williams, *The Girard Reader*, 2.

6. For a personal account of Girard's conversion, see the interview that forms the epilogue to *The Girard Reader*, 262–88.

7. René Girard, *The Scapegoat*, trans. Yvonne Freccero (Baltimore: Johns Hopkins University Press, 1986 [French: 1982]); see also Girard, *Violence and the Sacred* (Baltimore: Johns Hopkins University Press, 1977 [French: 1972]). Of these, *I See Satan Fall Like Lightning* is clearly the more mature work and the one that serves as the best introduction to Girard's thought.

around us, and according to Girard, the romantic notion of spontaneous longing that springs forth from the individual is largely fiction.[8]

Unfortunately, mimetic desire leads quickly to violent conflict. The Epistle of James speaks of this when it proclaims, "You desire but do not have, so you kill. You covet but you cannot get what you want, so you quarrel and fight" (Jas 4:2). The process is evidenced by the toddler who will scream and fight for a toy that, just moments ago, she had not wanted. The transformation is triggered not by the object itself but by the mere sight of another child reaching down to grasp the trinket—or perhaps just walking near it. "As a general rule," says Girard, "quiet and untroubled possession weakens desire," and a rival enflames it. In a less childlike example, Girard points to a fictitious love triangle: My neighbor may have ceased to desire his wife, but his longing will be revived if he learns that I have feelings for her. "His desire was dead, but upon contact with mine . . . it regains life."[9] And just like the example of the toddler, this too is likely to result in violence.

In the Bible, Girard finds warnings of these dangers. The second half of the Decalogue focuses upon violence toward one's neighbor, culminating with what Girard sees as the "supreme" and longest commandment—the prohibition of covetousness (Exod 20:17).[10] "If we respected the tenth commandment," says Girard, "the four commandments that precede it would be superfluous."[11] In Girard's view, the final prohibition highlights the dangerous nature of mimetic desire, which when misdirected can even be described as "original sin."[12]

While these warnings might lead the reader to assume that mimesis is inherently bad, Girard's later work refutes this misconception.[13] "Mimetic desire is intrinsically good" for at least three reasons.[14] First, it separates humans from beasts by enabling the production of language and culture through a complex process of modeling and mimicry. Second, it opens the self to others since it is through "the other" that our desires are actualized.[15] Third, it enables a unique connection with God as we are moved

---

8. Girard, *I See Satan Fall*, 15.
9. Girard, *I See Satan Fall*, 10.
10. Girard, *I See Satan Fall*, 7–8.
11. Girard, *I See Satan Fall*, 12.
12. Girard, *The Girard Reader*, 284.
13. In *Things Hidden Since the Foundation of the World* (1976), Girard called Christians to renounce mimetic desire, but in time he became clearer in denouncing only the kind that generates mimetic rivalry. See *The Girard Reader*, ch. 5: "The Goodness of Mimetic Desire."
14. Girard, *I See Satan Fall*, 15.
15. See *The Girard Reader*, 64.

to imitate the desires of Jesus as he models the perfect love of the Father.[16] One might call this latter possibility the mimesis of love. Herein lies the paradox: "Mimetic desire . . . is responsible for the best and the worst in us, for what lowers us below the animal level and what elevates us above it. Our unending discords are the ransom of our freedom."[17]

Satan, Sacrifice, and Scapegoats

Unfortunately, human beings do not naturally imitate "the detached generosity of God,"[18] and our rivalries soon accumulate into an ever-growing mass of "violent contagion" (*mimétisme*).[19] If left unchecked, this snowballing conflict would eventually result in "the war of all against all" and the annihilation of civilization.[20] Fortunately, this conflict has a pressure relief valve. Unfortunately, the relief comes through Satan, sacrifice, and scapegoats.

Alongside Jesus, Girard views the devil as "a murderer from the beginning" (John 8:44). Still, his "Satan" is not a personal and conscious spirit but a mere "semblance of being" that is the parasitic power of violent accusation.[21] In this way, the devil is the force behind the "single victim mechanism" (*mécanisme victimaire*), which may be described as the collective channelling of communal hostility upon a "scapegoat."[22] Scapegoats are selected based on the marks (or stereotypes) of victimhood: they are *different*. Hence they come from the ranks of foreigners, minorities, drifters, the deformed, the poor, and even the very powerful.[23] By channelling the strife of the community against these innocent victims, Satan drives out Satan (cf. Mark 3:23), and a temporary calm ensues. As Girard describes it, "When the trouble caused by Satan becomes too great, Satan himself becomes his own antidote of sorts: he stirs up the mimetic snowballing and then the unanimous violence that makes everything peaceful once again."[24]

---

16. Paul even calls Christians to "imitate me as I imitate Christ" (1 Cor 11:1), *The Girard Reader*, 63.
17. Girard, *I See Satan Fall*, 16.
18. Girard, *I See Satan Fall*, 14.
19. Girard, *I See Satan Fall*, 17.
20. Girard, *I See Satan Fall*, 22.
21. Girard, *I See Satan Fall*, xii, 42.
22. Girard clarifies that his use of this term "has no direct connection with the rite of the scapegoat as described in Leviticus." *The Scapegoat*, 40.
23. See Girard, *The Scapegoat*, ch. 2; esp. 14–19. While the powerful (including members of the royal family) may seem unlikely targets, Girard points out that the son of a king is more likely to die violently at the hands of the mob than a poor peasant. The point is not mere social status but *difference* in contrast with the populace.
24. Girard, *I See Satan Fall*, 43; see also *The Scapegoat*, ch. 14.

This pacifying effect (what Girard calls the "communion of scape-goaters") is the diabolical doppelgänger of the communion of saints.[25] And in the Gospels it is witnessed in Luke's claim that Herod and Pilate became friends by their treatment of Christ, whereas "before this they had been enemies" (23:12).[26] The ensuing harmony comes through the lynching of an innocent victim since the devil maintains with Caiaphas that "it is better . . . that one man die for the people than that the whole nation perish" (John 11:50).

Because the scapegoat succeeds in delivering a measure of peace, Girard's next claim is that the victim is often elevated to the status of a god. Because the death brought harmony, the myths ascribe to the victim a divine or magical power. This move, after the initial imputation of blame, forms the second step in the process of "double transference." First we lynch our scapegoats, and then we worship them. Or in Girard's provocative assertion, "The peoples of the world do not invent their gods. They deify their victims."[27] For Rome, this is witnessed in the obvious case of Julius Caesar.[28] In the Gospels, Girard sees something like it in Herod's belief that John the Baptist had come back from the dead (Mark 6:16): "Herod murders John, divinizes him, but never repents."[29] So the cycle continues.

For Girard, animal sacrifice emerges in the aftermath of human scape-goating because the killing of these creatures is modeled after the initial act against a man or woman. Animal sacrifices were therefore meant to (1) please the god(s) and (2) maintain peace by reproducing the ritual that first brought communal healing. From this standpoint, sacrificial rites did not escalate—as anthropologists commonly thought—from animals to human victims, but in the opposite direction. They emerged when the community's "founding murder" was ritualized with other offerings.[30]

In later writings, Girard modifies this sacrificial thesis to allow for a more positive use of the concept: sacrifice as the renunciation of human scapegoats.[31] Yahweh is thus seen as graciously substituting the sacrifice of

---

25. Girard, *The Girard Reader*, 264.
26. Girard, *I See Satan Fall*, 132.
27. Girard, *I See Satan Fall*, 70.
28. Girard, *I See Satan Fall*, 99.
29. Girard, *The Girard Reader*, 265.
30. See Girard, *I See Satan Fall*, 78–81. The first kings, according to Girard, were those scapegoats whose deaths were postponed for some reason. In the intervening period, these would-be victims were shrewd enough to channel their spiritual power into a political position: kingship. See Girard, *The Girard Reader*, 270.
31. See again the interview in *The Girard Reader*, 272.

animals for firstborn sons and then later objecting to all animal sacrifices.[32] In so doing, God leads Israel patiently away from ritualized violence and toward a care for victims.[33] This is evidenced in the divine desire, even in the Old Testament, for "mercy, not sacrifice" (Hos 6:6). The New Testament then takes mercy further by encouraging a sacrificial life. Girard interprets this metaphor as an existence modeled after Jesus, who gave himself for others, though never to satisfy something so crass and pagan as the wrath of God.[34]

The Bible and Mythology

Evidence for this sweeping theory is largely drawn from the reading of ancient myths in one hand and the Bible in the other. In Girard's view, the difference between these two sources is that "in the myth, the victim is always wrong, and his persecutors are always right."[35] While in the Bible the reverse is true because Scripture "refuses to demonize or deify the victims of violent crowds."[36] The first transference perverts God's justice, and the second is idolatry. In this way, the Bible unmasks the violence of the scapegoat mechanism in order to reveal a God of self-giving love.

Mythology, by contrast, is that ancient literature that presents the sacred violence from the perspective of the persecutors. Hence "all myths"—no matter how magical—"have their roots in real acts of violence against real victims."[37] Because they were ancient people, the authors usually believed that the supernatural crimes of their demonized and deified victims were real, and for this reason, the texts must be decrypted.

One of Girard's most familiar examples of mythic decryption involves the tale of *Oedipus Rex*. While few would normally read this saga as a tale of scapegoating, Girard notes how Oedipus bears all the stereotypical marks of victimhood: he has a physical disability (a limp), he is a foreigner, and the son of king. These factors mark him out as marginal and strange—a prime target. Likewise, his supposed crimes of incest and patricide are so sensational that they have brought a divine judgment on the city in the form of a plague—a prime reason to go looking for a

---

32. Girard, *I See Satan Fall*, 119.
33. For Girard, this belief connects to "the refusal to follow Marcion" in denying that "the two testaments are united as part of one and the same revelation." *I See Satan Fall*, 123; cf. 155.
34. See *The Girard Reader*, 292–93.
35. Girard, *I See Satan Fall*, 109.
36. Girard, *I See Satan Fall*, 115.
37. Girard, *The Scapegoat*, 25.

scapegoat. Finally, Girard notes that Oedipus's punishment brings peace through violence and expulsion. He thus finds here, as in all myths, the communal scapegoating of an innocent victim (Oedipus) as a way to restore order to a fractious city.[38]

Alongside these older tales, Girard also mines medieval and modern persecution stories to reveal an altered version of the scapegoat mechanism. These include the travesty of witch hunts, the blaming of medieval Jews for the Black Death, and of course the holocaust. Because these are not ancient myths, the magical move to deify the victim does not usually occur.[39] Nonetheless, the basic process of scapegoating and communal violence persists.[40] This demonic process, says Girard, is what Jesus came to unmask and (by his Spirit) eradicate. With this claim in mind, one is finally ready to grasp the uniquely Girardian view of moral influence.

Girard on Jesus's Work

It may seem strange to say that Christ unmasked the scapegoat mechanism immediately after citing some medieval and modern scapegoats (some of whom were even murdered in Christ's name!). Girard nonetheless believes that Jesus accomplished something monumental through his work. His argument, though untraditional in many respects, turns upon two exceedingly orthodox realities: (1) the deity of Jesus Christ and (2) his resurrection from the dead.

With regard to Christ's divinity, Girard believes that "no [mere] human is able to reveal the scapegoat mechanism,"[41] for despite our best intentions we are always swept up in its wake. The proof of this reality is to be found in the denials of Peter. One might expect, says Girard, that Christ's lead disciple would "be able to imitate Christ and stand up for him. But as soon as he is immersed in a mob of scapegoaters, he surrenders to the mimetic pressure and joins them."[42] The conclusion is therefore clear: if the mechanism is to be exposed, God must do it. Even the wisest of mortals can only perpetuate the cycle of violence; the unmasking must come from one "greater than Solomon" (Matt 12:42).

---

38. For a more in-depth treatment of the myth, see Girard, *The Scapegoat*, 25–30.

39. With regard to the ridiculous medieval claim that the Jews caused the Black Death, Girard claims that "the faint traces of the sacred still [cling] to the victims." This is to be evidenced by the way that Jews were simultaneously slaughtered for causing the plague and revered for their supposed power to stop it. See Girard, *The Scapegoat*, 50; cf. 45–46.

40. See Girard, *The Scapegoat*, 50–51.

41. Girard, *The Girard Reader*, 279.

42. Girard, *The Girard Reader*, 279; cf. *The Scapegoat*, 105.

The means of exposure comes chiefly through the resurrection.[43] While Jesus indeed suffers the same fate as all the murdered prophets, he alone conquers death. And his Spirit fills his followers so they recognize the truth.[44] Although Christ's crucifixion displays the single victim mechanism in all its horror, his resurrection reveals its evil to the opened eyes of his disciples (e.g., Luke 24:13–34). For Girard, this explains why the Gospels do not cover up Christ's shameful scapegoating whereas the myths must always conceal their murders. This is also why the earliest Christians could resist the cultural currents of mimetic violence. In his words, "Only the Resurrection, because it enlightens the disciples, reveals completely the things hidden since the foundation of the world . . . the founding murder and the origin of human culture."[45]

As the references to "revealing" and "enlightening" clarify, Girard sees the efficacy of Christ's work as a version of exemplarism. Our predicament is a blindness to mimetic violence, because like those murdering Christ, we "know not what [we] do" (Luke 23:34).[46] To avoid Pelagianism, Girard is clear that our blindness with regard to scapegoating is "insurmountable" apart from Christ; still this does not change the fact that the efficacy of the cross comes solely through its "revelatory power" in unmasking mimetic rivalry and scapegoating.[47] Although this is a novel form of moral influence reasoning, it still resides quite firmly in the camp.

Signs of Triumph

As proof of Christ's successful influence, Girard turns next to the ensuing history. Beginning with the resurrection and Pentecost, he notes that Christians begin to see and reject the violent contagion like no other group before them.[48] "Wherever Christianity spreads, the mythical systems decay and sacrificial rites disappear."[49] The real benefit of this development

---

43. See, for instance, *The Girard Reader*, 280; *I See Satan Fall*, 125, 149.
44. See Girard, *I See Satan Fall*, 189; cf. *The Scapegoat*, 206.
45. Girard, *I See Satan Fall*, 125.
46. Note, therefore, the threefold emphasis upon (1) revelation, (2) understanding, and (3) moral responsibility in this synopsis of the Jesus-message: "The Gospels reveal everything that human beings need to understand their moral responsibility with regard to the whole spectrum of violence in human history and false religions." Girard, *I See Satan Fall*, 125.
47. Girard, *I See Satan Fall*, 142; throughout this discussion Girard speaks of triumph that comes by "duping" the devil. Yet one must remember that, in his view, the "devil" is actually us, since Satan is cypher for our own violent tendencies.
48. See Girard, *The Scapegoat*, 108. While Girard admits that innocent victims had been rehabilitated prior to Christianity (e.g., Socrates), still he claims that these "isolated" examples did not change society "in its totality" (199).
49. Girard, *I See Satan Fall*, 154.

however comes not in the overthrow of sacrifice but in the concern for victims that accompanies the gospel's spread: "Examine ancient sources, inquire everywhere, dig up the corners of the planet, and you will not find anything anywhere that even remotely resembles our modern concern for victims."[50] This is why both "humanism and humanitarianism develop first on Christian soil,"[51] as do hospitals (in French: *l'Hotel-Dieu*—"House of God") and other charities for the marginalized.[52] For Girard, even the bitterest of ethical debates (such as abortion) now hinge upon the interest of the "real victim"—that is, the one who most deserves our sympathy.[53] Even though some choose poorly, the very framing of the debate testifies to an unmasking of mythology.

In an ironic twist, Girard sees even the victim-fixation of postmodern secularism as unknowingly trumpeting Christ's triumph even as it scorns and scapegoats Christians for not sufficiently defending sufferers.[54] In a moving passage, he writes, "All our resistance is turned against the light that threatens us. It has revealed so many things for so long a time without revealing itself that we are convinced it comes from within us."[55] With typical boldness, he links this secular distortion—what he calls "the other totalitarianism"—to the *Antichrist's* satanic imitation of the Messiah. Though the verdict may seem harsh, the reason rests in Girard's belief that the so-called tolerance of postmodernism actually produces a return to "pagan practices" like "abortion, euthanasia, [and] sexual undifferentiation."[56] And this only multiplies the body count.

Recognizing that Christendom is hardly perfect, Girard argues that the darkest moments of the past two thousand years occurred, for example, as the Nazis followed Nietzsche in attempting to overthrow the Christian concern for victims: which Nietzsche called "the slave morality." Although these efforts may resurface, Girard is confident that, because of Christ's work, "the darkness of Satan is no longer thick enough to conceal the innocence of the victims."[57] Light has shone on the world, and the mythic night cannot dispel it.

50. Girard, *I See Satan Fall*, 161.
51. Girard, *I See Satan Fall*, 163.
52. Girard, *I See Satan Fall*, 167.
53. Girard, *I See Satan Fall*, 176.
54. Girard, *I See Satan Fall*, 180–81.
55. Girard, *The Scapegoat*, 205.
56. Girard, *I See Satan Fall*, 181.
57. Girard, *I See Satan Fall*, 185.

CRITIQUING GIRARD

After his death in 2015, Girard was heralded as an intellectual giant of the twentieth century. He has devoted followers within the ranks of theologians,[58] and the rise of a so-called "nonviolent" atonement movement is partly traceable to his influence.[59] As is often the case with seminal thinkers, however, Girard is more interesting than most "Girardians." Hence I have chosen to focus primarily on his thought, rather than that of his disciples. This is warranted because, in the somewhat exaggerated view of Gil Bailie, he "made the most significant intellectual breakthrough of the modern age."[60]

Still, not all have been enamored with Girard's inventive project. I thus move now to some critiques of his ideas under the following headings:

1. Invisible cats
2. Inadequate plight
3. Insufficient solution
4. Idiosyncratic exegesis
5. A Gnostic-sounding gospel (because not everything can start with the letter *i*!)

Not all of these charges are equally damning, but each retains at least a grain of truth as they collectively "unmask" some issues with Girard's own scapegoating of more traditional atonement models.[61]

Invisible Cats (and Unfalsifiable Hypotheses)

At points, Girard's findings are the product of rampant (albeit brilliant) speculation. And his case rests almost solely upon his own specialized

---

58. See especially, S. Mark Heim, *Saved from Sacrifice: A Theology of the Cross* (Grand Rapids: Eerdmans, 2006); Anthony W. Bartlett, *Cross Purposes: The Violent Grammar of Christian Atonement* (Harrisburg, PA: Trinity Press International, 2001).

59. As seen previously (ch. 6), the claim of the movement is not to deny that the crucifixion is a violent event, but to say that the violence comes exclusively from sinful humans, rather than resulting from the decree of a wrathful God. See especially, J. Denny Weaver, *The Nonviolent Atonement* (Grand Rapids: Eerdmans, 2011). See also many of the essays in Brad Jersak and Michael Hardin, eds., *Stricken by God? Nonviolent Identification and the Victory of Christ* (Grand Rapids: Eerdmans, 2007).

60. Gil Bailie, *Violence Unveiled: Humanity at the Crossroads* (New York: Crossroad, 1995), 4.

61. The analogy is particularly apt because Girard (like the scapegoaters he describes) seems somewhat naïve in his critique of the theological tradition. This is perhaps understandable given that his background is in anthropology and literature.

"decoding" of ancient myths. As Ben Pugh notes, "No [other] evidence is presented that might corroborate this reading of the literature."[62] What's more, when Girard lays forth the criteria by which these myths should be decoded, the theory is inconsistent and unfalsifiable.

For example, while admitting that his case "relies on nothing historical" in terms of physical evidence, Girard asks readers to decipher myths by virtue of his so-called stereotypes of persecution.[63] Yet even when *none* of these stereotypes are present in a text, we are quickly reassured that a trained eye can still spot the scapegoat deep beneath the surface.[64] The myths, it seems are like ancient Rorschach tests in which every inkblot forms a victim. The key is to "read between the lines" in order to uncover what the mythmakers have concealed from us. Though the tale claims otherwise, Oedipus was *actually* innocent of incest and patricide. And though the text says otherwise, he was *actually* scapegoated by the fractious citizens of Thebes for simply being different. He limped after all.[65]

For Girard, the absence of these details in the story only proves their presence in reality. Yet although this case is prosecuted with something approaching genius, the logic bears a striking similarity to what C. S. Lewis mockingly called "the argument for invisible cats." According to Lewis, "The very lack of evidence is thus treated as evidence; the absence of smoke proves that the fire is very carefully hidden." In talking like this, "We are arguing like a man who should say 'If there were an invisible cat in that empty chair, the chair would look empty; but the chair does look empty; therefore there is an invisible cat in it.'"[66]

To be fair, not all of Girard's mythological interpretations are so speculative. Nor does he seem wrong to note that mimetic rivalry and scapegoating exist as powerful forces within human culture. Still, he is surely mistaken to locate his grand theory beneath every stone and story in the ancient world. When confronted with the charge of unfalsifiability, he admits that much of his theory cannot be subjected to empirical

---

62. Pugh, *Atonement Theories*, 160.

63. Girard, *The Scapegoat*, 28.

64. Girard, *The Scapegoat*, 33.

65. One notes a similarity here to how counterimperial connotations have now been "discovered" in seemingly every passage in the New Testament, although rarely (we are told) "on the surface." See Scot McKnight and Joseph Modica, eds., *Jesus Is Lord, Caesar Is Not: Evaluating Empire in New Testament Studies* (Downers Grove, IL: IVP Academic, 2013).

66. C. S. Lewis, *The Four Loves* (1960: repr., New York: Harcourt Brace, 1988), 60. Interestingly, another work by Lewis would seem to corroborate several elements of Girard's theory. In *Till We Have Faces*, he recasts the ancient myth of Cupid and Psyche, wherein rivalry and plague lead to the ritual scapegoating (and subsequent divinizing) of the king's daughter.

verification.[67] Yet he remains confident that history will judge him well. After all, if falsifiability were required to decipher and destroy mythology, "We must condemn in retrospect all those who brought an end to the witch trials. They were even more dogmatic than the witch hunters and, like them, they believed they possessed the truth."[68] Despite the pithiness of the retort, less credulous readers may suspect that Girard himself is acting as the "magician of mythology"[69] that he so frequently condemns for conjuring.

An Inadequate Plight

A further weakness of Girardian atonement is an anemic reading of the human plight. While he pulls no punches in condemning the mimetic bent toward rivalry and scapegoating, he appears to think that a mere unveiling of this mechanism will stop it.[70]

Unfortunately, this rather rosy view of human nature (i.e., that we will change if only we are presented with a clear unmasking of our errors) seems at odds with, say, Paul's more pervasive view of our depravity. And if the words of Jesus are any indication, the mere reality of a *resurrected* revealer is not sufficient either. After all, "If they do not listen to Moses and the Prophets, they will not be convinced even if someone rises from the dead" (Luke 16:31). For these reasons, Girard's tendency to view our plight primarily as one of ignorance leaves him not only with an inadequate theology of sin but also with an inadequate account of the solution.[71]

A second problem is seen in the tendency to view violence as the *ultimate* consequence of our ignorance. To be sure, sinful aggression is abominable; thus it must figure prominently in the list of evils Christ comes to unmask and overthrow. But like other members of the nonviolent atonement movement, the almost exclusive focus upon the second half of the Decalogue largely leaves out the *Godward* direction of human iniquity. It is this perspective that is revealed in David's confession: "Against you [God], and you only, have I sinned" (Ps 51:4). Indeed, the claim of the Psalm is made all the more weighty as it comes (according to the superscription) after a

---

67. Girard, *The Girard Reader*, 77.
68. Girard, *The Scapegoat*, 98–99.
69. Girard, *The Scapegoat*, 73.
70. In the words of William Placher, the sense is that "once we have understood the problem, it practically fixes itself." Placher, "Christ Takes Our Place: Rethinking Atonement," *Interpretation* 53, no. 1 (1999).
71. Once more, the words of Anselm echo loud: "You have not yet considered what a great weight sin is."

case of mimetic rivalry and scapegoating. Still, the ultimate need is not merely to unmask Uriah's innocence and abjure physical violence over the coveted Bathsheba. Beneath these profound and legitimate concerns is the deeper need to be reconciled to God.

An Insufficient Solution

In atonement doctrine, inadequate plights always birth reductionist solutions. And this is also true with Girard.[72] Here, Christ came exclusively to unveil the innocence[73] of our "sacrificial" victims and to inspire (by his Spirit) a mimesis of love.[74] Given the latter emphasis, John Milbank's claim that Girard offers *only* a "negative gesture" (merely critiquing injustice) is not quite accurate—but it is close.[75] In the end, Girard becomes the reductionist extraordinaire as he moves to marginalize all other pieces in the mosaic of atonement doctrine.[76]

His disdain is most palpable when it comes to any version of penal substitution. For Girard, to view a divine sanction behind Jesus's violent and redeeming death is to fall back into the diabolical blindness of mythology. Indeed, the mere presence of penal substitution in the hallowed halls of doctrinal history is "a revealing indication of mankind's radical incapacity to understand its own violence."[77] This is because while penal substitution *is* an "effective" (if temporary) means of appeasement, it was invented by Satan.[78] It is the scapegoat mechanism dressed up for church. To espouse it is to risk "entering the passion story on the side of Jesus' murderers."[79]

---

72. In the view of George Hunsinger, Girard offers "an essentially 'Pelagian' solution to an inherently 'Augustinian' problem." Hunsinger, *Disruptive Grace: Studies in the Theology of Karl Barth* (Grand Rapids: Eerdmans, 2000), 28.

73. Another exaggeration may be seen in Girard's odd insistence that our "victims" are *always* wholly innocent because the persecutors "always . . . *hate without a cause*," *The Scapegoat*, 103, italics in original. While a welcome alternative to the victim smearing and character assassination that often occurs in, say, a sexual assault or an unjustified police shooting of an unarmed black man, this insistence that only the innocent are punished by the mob seems naïve at best.

74. In this way, Girard is far more "Abelardian" than was Abelard himself.

75. John Milbank, *Theology and Social Theory* (Malden, MA: Blackwell, 1993), 395. J. Denny Weaver is correct to note that an emphasis upon "positive mimesis" is there in some Girardians, but it does not receive enough attention. See Weaver, "The Nonviolent Atonement: Human Violence, Discipleship and God," in Jersak and Hardin, *Stricken by God?*, 346.

76. Pugh notes this tendency when he writes that Girard's atonement theory is in fact a negation of all others. This is essentially correct except for the important realization that it is clearly a novel version of exemplarism or moral influence doctrine. Pugh, *Atonement Theories*, 160.

77. Girard, *The Girard Reader*, 178.

78. See Girard, *The Girard Reader*, 270.

79. Heim, *Saved from Sacrifice*, 126.

It is to make a "fetish" of the cross,[80] a "satanic figure" of the Father,[81] and a sacred object of the violence once "divested . . . by the Gospel text."[82]

In the prior chapters, I carefully addressed these claims, even while I pushed back against the overzealous defenders of penal substitution when they either verge toward pagan notions of propitiation or attempt to make penal substitution the be-all and end-all of atonement.[83] All such reductionism should be avoided. No one benefits from the acrimonious firefights over atonement doctrine. And in some instances (as with Girard's inflated allegations), they display the very scapegoating that Girard claims elsewhere to renounce. Like in the myths he claims to decode, the visible features of the "target" (penal substitution) are exaggerated as the account is handed down by naïve (or perhaps dishonest) mythmakers.[84] The result is that one no longer sees the actual doctrine when it is set upon by a mob of angry academics. In its place, there is only a mythical monster with fangs and claws afflicting Christendom.[85] Here, as elsewhere, the scapegoating deserves to be unmasked.

Idiosyncratic Exegesis

Several problems in Girard's atonement doctrine are enabled by a reading of Scripture that is both ingenious and idiosyncratic. In particular, a handful of biblical narratives are rehearsed repeatedly while other texts, most notably those of the apostle Paul(!), are strangely silent. Snippets of the Gospels are quoted frequently, and certain stories—such as the beheading of John the Baptist, Peter's denials, and the Joseph saga of Genesis—are made to carry an interpretive weight for atonement logic that is disproportional at best.

In his use of Scripture, some accuse Girard of dancing with the ghost of Marcion as he contrasts a bloody (Old Testament?) god of war and sacrifice with the nonviolent God of Jesus Christ.[86] To his credit, Girard's later work attempts to remedy this tendency. This is seen in his rehabilitated view of

80. Girard, *The Scapegoat*, 126.

81. Girard, *The Scapegoat*, 209.

82. Girard, *The Scapegoat*, 126. In these passages, Girard does not use penal substitution by name, still it seems apparent that this doctrine is in the crosshairs.

83. See again, part 2 of this book.

84. Several examples of this "scapegoating" of penal substitution can be found in an anthology endorsed enthusiastically by Girard. See Jersak and Hardin, *Stricken by God?*

85. For Girard's own account of the monstrous distortion of scapegoats, see "The Horrible Miracle of Apollonius of Tyana," in *I See Satan Fall*, ch. 4.

86. See Hans Boersma, *Violence, Hospitality, and the Cross: Reappropriating the Atonement Tradition* (Grand Rapids: Baker Academic, 2004), 140.

Hebrew sacrifice and in his harsh critiques of Marcion's modern heirs.[87] While the shift hardly makes Girard a biblical inerrantist,[88] his spirited defense of the Bible against its modern critics does sometimes sound like that of a conservative apologist who cares little for political correctness. In his words, "When we feel like dismissing Scripture, we should watch out. Perhaps we are not, at that moment, up to what our task requires."[89]

The problem therefore involves not an outright rejection of biblical authority but a failure to wrestle with passages that may pose problems for his exemplarist account of Jesus's work. Tellingly, in the index to the voluminous *Girard Reader*, the apostle Paul appears only twice, and of these references, the first is a mere mention of his Pharisaic past as a violent scapegoater, while the second is a citation of Colossians' denunciation of satanic principalities (Col 2:13–15).[90] Notably absent is Romans 8, with its claim that God "condemned sin in the flesh [of Christ], in order that the righteous requirement of the law might be fully met in us" (v. 4). Romans 3 is also missing, alongside its notion that God presented Christ as a *hilasterion* "because in his forbearance he had left the sins committed beforehand unpunished" (vv. 25–26).[91] Tellingly Girard also ignores the book of Hebrews ("The Epistle does not succeed in defining the real singularity of the Passion"[92]).

Beyond the absence of the Bible's substitutionary imagery, Girard also fails to acknowledge the texts that deal with Christ's work as that of a second Adam who not only exposes violence but also accomplishes something positive on behalf of his people (recapitulation). And in terms of *Christus Victor* thinking, Girard does not grapple with texts that might call into question a fully demythologized account of "Satan" as a mere synonym for human violence.[93]

In addition to these parts of Scripture that do not work within Girard's canon, other prominent passages are made to fit his schema by contortion. A chief example comes in Girard's insistence that Satan always "casts out" Satan in order to *maintain* power. This view runs contrary to the more likely interpretation of the Synoptic texts that contain this quote

87. Girard, *I See Satan Fall*, 123, 129–30.
88. Girard is open to "tiny mythical infiltrations" even in the Gospels. *The Girard Reader*, 281.
89. Girard, *I See Satan Fall*, 130.
90. Girard, *The Girard Reader*, 170 and 206, respectively.
91. See again ch. 5 for an in-depth discussion of these and other passages.
92. Girard, *The Scapegoat*, 200.
93. For Girard's claim, see *I See Satan Fall*, 42.

(the so-called Beelzebul controversy). In these passages, Christ seems to ask the question in order to show its incoherence: "How can Satan cast out Satan?" (Mark 3:23). Answer: he cannot. Indeed this reading of the Markan question is confirmed by Luke's account (11:18).[94] No matter. Girard all but ignores these points because the colorful image of Satan expelling Satan fits perfectly with his theory of how rivalries are mollified through scapegoating.[95] Unfortunately, in supporting what may be a brilliant insight into human conflict and group psychology, the passage itself becomes almost irrelevant.[96]

To cite other examples, Girard informs readers that the Old Testament character of Job was *actually* scapegoated by his jealous neighbors for his prosperity. In fact, he was "followed and stoned by the inhabitants of his village."[97] With similar brevity, he also admits a sympathy for Freud's claim that Moses was *actually* killed by the grumbling Israelites as they camped at Mount Sinai.[98] These revisions do laudably recede in Girard's later works (especially *I See Satan Fall Like Lightning*), but they never fully disappear. Thus, in the end, one sees in them a similarity to the old liberal attempt to "get behind" the text in order to profess with remarkable confidence what *really* happened.

A Gnostic-Sounding Gospel

A final fault in Girard's atonement doctrine involves what sounds like a "Gnostic" emphasis upon a salvation that comes by impartation of a *secret knowledge* handed down from on high. In his view, not even the Gospel writers themselves were "capable of interpreting" this mystery, whereas he (the modern scholar) emerges like a guru to construct "the pieces of a puzzle which is the mimetic theory itself."[99] In response to this pronouncement, Placher rightly notes, "It all still sounds too much like Gnosticism to me. Our problem . . . was that we did not understand something. The solution is to realize the truth and therefore live differently."[100]

To be sure, it can be flattering for Christians—long scorned by secular

---

94. See also Sydney H. T. Page, *Powers of Evil: A Biblical Study of Satan and Demons* (Grand Rapids: Baker, 1995), 103.

95. See Girard, *I See Satan Fall*, 33–35.

96. While Girard does not dispute Christ's claim that Satan's divided kingdom will ultimately fall (see *The Scapegoat*, 185), he does ignore the fact that Christ seems to be denying that Satan *ever* casts out Satan.

97. Girard, *The Scapegoat*, 170.

98. Girard, *The Scapegoat*, 178.

99. Girard, *The Scapegoat*, 161 and 162, respectively.

100. William Placher, "Why the Cross?" *Christian Century*, December 12, 2006, 39.

academics—to receive enthusiastic endorsement from so eminent a scholar. And it is exciting to sense that one has uncovered the long lost "key" (mimesis) to unlock every door, not only in the Gospels but in human culture generally.[101] Now the origin of rivalry, religion, rulers, civilization, and sacrifice has finally been laid bare. On all these points, Girard alone emerges from the sands of time and text with answers "hidden since the foundation of the world" (Matt 13:35). Like other geniuses (whether Freud or Nietzsche), he is unflappably certain of his findings—which helps readers draw courage from his confidence. And to be fair, it can often be fantastic to read, making Girard among the most interesting voices in this volume. Yet it also draws fire for hubris.

When faced with this charge, Girard clarifies that many Christians have understood *something* of this hidden wisdom long before he wrote about it. This is to be evidenced by the many attempts to live nonviolently in Jesus's name. Still he does not shrink from the assertion that he alone has unearthed the intellectual components of this ethical posture.[102] Nor does he try to hide the Gnostic-sounding claim that "men will finally be liberated by means of this *knowledge*"—the unmasking of the scapegoat mechanism.[103]

In response to all this, I borrow (mimetically, of course) from Barth in saying, *Nein!* Redemption does not come by secret information. On this point, the work of Irenaeus remains unrivaled in battling the elitist claims of salvation *sola gnosis* (to mix Latin and Greek confusingly): falsehood and novelty are virtually synonymous in Christian doctrine. Hence one should be skeptical of those who—as Irenaeus put it—"boast loudly" of uncovering never-before-told secrets from the sacred text.

Using the previously cited metaphor of a grand mosaic, Irenaeus concluded that these men "pluck . . . sayings" from the Scriptures like "precious stones," yet "through fanciful arrangement of the jewels deceive the inexperienced who had no idea what the King's picture looked like."[104] Although Girard hardly fails to the extent of actual Gnostic heretics, his emphasis upon a secret and reductionistic wisdom (revealed only by him) serves to impoverish and deface the broader mosaic of atonement doctrine.

---

101. Despite the stunning overreach, there is something endearing about Girard's boldness: "There is always a mimetic answer to the questions posed in our text, and that answer is *always* best." *The Scapegoat*, 183, italics added.
102. Girard, *The Girard Reader*, 273.
103. Girard, *The Scapegoat*, 108, italics added.
104. *Haer.* 1.8.1. This translation is that of Behr, *Irenaeus*, 105.

| INTEGRATING GIRARD |

This does not mean, however, that Girard is without value. While some view his project as an "all or nothing" enterprise that must either be accepted or rejected whole (because it is the "negation" of "all" other models of atonement[105]), I disagree. Aspects of Girard's work may indeed be salvaged for the overall mosaic of atonement. Hence this chapter will conclude with a fresh attempt at such integration.

Anyone who spends time with small children can attest that there is something self-evidently true about Girard's brilliant insights into mimetic desire, rivalry, and the ensuing violence. Humans *do* tend to want what we see others wanting, and this *does* lead to all sorts of conflict and idolatry. Because of this, "Thou shalt not covet" is not an anticlimactic addendum to the Decalogue.[106] Likewise, the Gospels *do* reveal a kind of scapegoat mechanism at work within the world, even though Girard is gravely wrong to limit Christ's work almost exclusively to its unmasking.

Revealing and Restraining Violence

Perhaps Girard's greatest contribution to atonement doctrine comes in the way he highlights another side of moral influence logic. While Abelard revealed Christ's "beckoning hand" that motions us toward a loving God, Girard reminds us that the atonement also reveals and restrains our destructive human impulses. Christ's work does involve, as Milbank noted, a "negative" gesture that "waives off" certain violent and idolatrous tendencies. In so doing, it reveals something about how *not* to be in this world. And that is crucial.

Among the sinful proclivities (ironically) laid bare by a naked, dying Christ on a cross is humanity's pervasive and irrational bent toward violence. Girard is not wrong here. On this point, members of the peace church tradition have long argued that there is a dreadful tendency in Christian history to make something other than Jesus the norm for Christian ethics.[107] When this happens, we are more likely to relocate the

---

105. So says Pugh, *Atonement Theories*, 160.

106. Since he was a Roman Catholic, the coveting commandment may be seen as doubly climactic for Girard. This is so because Catholic (and Lutheran) tradition combines the initial words on worship and idolatry while dividing the prohibition of covetousness into two: "Thou shall not covet thy neighbor's wife" (number nine), and "Thou shalt not covet thy neighbor's ox or ass or anything else which belongs to thy neighbor" (number ten). Thanks to Jerome Van Kuiken for reminding me of this fact.

107. See especially John Howard Yoder, *The Politics of Jesus: Vicit Agnus Noster*, 2nd ed. (Grand Rapids: Eerdmans, 1994).

cross of Calvary to somewhere more like the Milvian bridge: "In this sign conquer."[108] *Nein* again!

So while Girard reduces Christ's work by failing to integrate other "precious tiles" from the tradition, many of us within the broader Christian family could stand to take more seriously the command to put away the sword (Matt 26:52) and take up the cross (Matt 16:24). For as Stanley Hauerwas once joked darkly, the one thing some Catholics, Reformed, and Lutherans could agree upon in centuries past is that it would be a good idea to kill their dissenters.[109] Lord have mercy.

At the same time, one ought not reduce atonement to a call to pacifism.[110] One reason is that it is not obvious (at least to me) that Christians must be pacifists in the absolute sense. As Hans Boersma argues, to be truly loving and hospitable within a fallen world may (regrettably) require the proper authorities to employ certain forms of violence in defense of the poor and vulnerable.[111] Biblically speaking, this may be evidenced by the much-debated power of "the sword" that God has granted to the governing authorities to justly punish wrongdoers (Rom 13:4).[112] Likewise, there is a reason that nonviolence has not traditionally been seen as a divine attribute to be placed alongside holiness and love.[113] Miroslav Volf has famously argued that the very practice of human nonviolence in many difficult situations today may actually require a belief in divine vengeance later.[114]

Of course, none of these caveats negate the point that Christ presents

---

108. According to Eusebius's *Life of Constantine*, this was the cross-shaped sign from heaven that led the emperor into victorious battle at the Milvian Bridge. For more on this contested event (and this contested figure), see Peter J. Leithart, *Defending Constantine: The Twilight of an Empire and the Dawn of Christendom* (Downers Grove, IL: IVP Academic, 2010), ch. 4.

109. For one version of this quote, see Stanley Hauerwas, "Why *The Politics of Jesus* Is Not a Classic," in *A Better Hope: Resources for a Church Confronting Capitalism, Democracy, and Postmodernity* (Grand Rapids: Brazos, 2000), 134.

110. This much is admitted, in theory, by even J. Denny Weaver, "The Nonviolent Atonement," 316.

111. See Boersma, *Violence, Hospitality, and the Cross*, 93. This logic follows the likes of Augustine, Aquinas, and Calvin in believing that, in certain settings, violence may be an ordered act of love (43). By rejecting double predestination, Boersma resists the error of drawing violence into the very "heart of God" (56). Even so, he asserts that "pure" (or completely nonviolent) hospitality in a fallen world may "end up welcoming devils" and leaving victims to their persecutors (35).

112. If one accepts this view of Rom 13 (and it is contested), then one difference between the God-ordained "power of the sword" and the "In this sign conquer" of the Milvian bridge is a refusal to use Christ as a justification for violent conquest.

113. This is in contrast with Girard's claim that "God is not violent, the true God has nothing to do with violence." *The Scapegoat*, 189. Heim has sought to modify this claim somewhat with his openness to God's apocalyptic vengeance through "the wrath of the Lamb" who will one day go to war on behalf of martyrs and victims. See Heim, *Saved from Sacrifice*, 266–67.

114. Miroslav Volf, *Exclusion and Embrace: A Theological Exploration of Identity, Otherness, and Reconciliation* (Nashville: Abingdon, 1996), 304; I quoted this passage at length in ch. 6.

us with a negative critique of so many violent human tendencies. As the Epistle to Titus states, God's grace teaches us "to say 'No' to ungodliness and worldly passions" (2:11–12)—of which sinful violence, rivalry, and scapegoating are a part. In sum, there must be a restraining and unmasking *hand* alongside the beckoning one when we speak of Jesus's moral influence.

Atonement as Praxis

Now for a potential objection. Some might argue that an emphasis on revealing and rejecting rivalry and scapegoating does not belong within atonement doctrine proper. Rather, it is the stuff of "ethics" and "sanctification," and should therefore be relegated to an appendix of Christ's saving work. To do otherwise, these critics might allege, would be to imperil the claim of salvation *sola fide* and to come dangerously close to a redemption that is linked to moral striving.[115] While these ethical concerns may, of course, be discussed by Christians, this conversation should take place only *after* the doctrine of salvation has been more or less exhausted. I beg to differ.[116]

In the provocative (but accurate) words of Scot McKnight, the "atonement is not just something done to us and for us, *it is something we participate in—in this world, in the here and now.*"[117] Atonement is praxis, both for Jesus and his people.[118] The basis for this claim resides partly in Paul's words in 2 Corinthians 5:18–21. Here we are told not only that we have been reconciled to God in Christ but also that we have also been given "the ministry of reconciliation" (v. 18): "We are therefore Christ's ambassadors, as though God were making his appeal through us. We implore you on Christ's behalf: Be reconciled to God. God made him who had no sin to be sin for us, so that in him we might become the righteousness of God" (vv. 20–21).

For sake of clarity, participation in God's reconciliation does not mean that we can atone for ourselves or for others.[119] Salvation is by Christ alone, and as McKnight makes clear, we are still "cracked eikons" of the King, holding treasure in our jars of clay.[120] The fact remains however that by

---

115. I must return to this discussion in the following chapter when examining the Spirit's role in producing "fruit" in keeping with repentance.

116. For a related critique of an excessive division between atonement, ethics, mission, and ecclesiology, see Michael J. Gorman, *The Death of the Messiah and the Birth of the New Covenant: A (Not So) New Model of Atonement* (Eugene, OR: Cascade, 2014), 20.

117. Scot McKnight, *A Community Called Atonement* (Nashville: Abingdon, 2007), 30–31, italics in original.

118. See McKnight, *Community Called Atonement*, 117.

119. McKnight, *Community Called Atonement*, 117. I will however return to this claim in the next chapter in order to complicate it further with the claims of Scripture.

120. McKnight, *Community Called Atonement*, 118.

being conformed to Christ's image by the Spirit—what Girard might call a mimesis of love—we can (and must) *share* in God's ongoing work of reconciliation. Mimesis leads to mission, and mission means participation in God's reconciling work.

The basis for this move should be clear: we participate in atonement because we participate in Christ.[121] Incorporative participation grounds salvation (as seen in my treatment recapitulation) just as it grounds our role within it. It is therefore by this real and mysterious union that Paul can say (cryptically) that he suffers "for" his congregations in order to "fill up . . . what is still lacking in regard to Christ's afflictions" (Col 1:24). This strange statement does not defame the work of Christ because it *is* the work of Christ, carried out by a member of his "body" (v. 24). It is also along these lines that Paul can claim that the "world" has been crucified to him and he to the world (Gal 6:14); this is possible only on the prior ground that he himself was "crucified with Christ" so that his individual and atomized existence is no more. Now he is inhabited by Christ and by Christ's Spirit (Gal 2:20).

| CONCLUSION |

While I must put off the full implications of the Spirit's role till next chapter, the point for now is plain: To emphasize the positive and negative gestures of moral influence thinking (as drawn and adapted selectively from both Abelard and Girard) is a crucial facet of atonement doctrine proper. This is so because God's reconciliation is both accomplished and ongoing, both past and present, both punctiliar and partly unfulfilled. There is an "already" and a "not yet" to redemption just as there is an "already" and "not yet" within the kingdom. For this reason, Christians participate rightly in Christ's ongoing reconciliation as we turn toward God with loving gratitude (Abelard) and away from violent worldly passions (Girard). In these two "hands"—beckoning and restraining, pierced but never persecuting—the two great commandments co-inhere: "You shall love the Lord your God. . . . And you shall love your neighbor as yourself" (Matt 22:37, 39).

---

121. Herein also lies the value in the patristic and Eastern emphasis upon deification or theosis. Although, I would prefer to speak of "Christification" or "Christosis" to avoid the false perception that such terms imply a blurring of the Creator-creature distinction. See Michael J. Gorman, *Inhabiting the Cruciform God: Kenosis, Justification, and Theosis in Paul's Narrative Soteriology* (Grand Rapids: Eerdmans, 2009), 37.

CHAPTER 13

PERFECTING
HAND(S)

THE SPIRIT'S PLACE IN MORAL INFLUENCE

*Where the Spirit of the Lord is,
there is moral influence.*

I will put my Spirit in you," says the God of Ezekiel, "and move you to follow my decrees" (36:27). "I will sprinkle clean water on you" (v. 25); "I will remove from you your heart of stone and give you a heart of flesh" (v. 26). The point within this passage, seething with atonement imagery, is that while human hearts can harden like the gods of wood and stone they worship,[1] the Spirit is the divine agent of softening and sanctification. The Spirit moves us to follow God's decrees; hence the Spirit is also the agent of "moral influence."

With texts like this in mind, the present chapter builds upon a controversial theme that was introduced in the previous chapter. There I claimed that Christians actually participate in God's reconciling work through the power of the Holy Spirit. Atonement is praxis, both for Jesus and his people.[2] This is so because while redemption is often spoken of as "the work of Christ," it is also a triune project that is still unfolding.[3] In this ongoing drama, God's Spirit sweeps up ransomed humans in the cause of

---

1. See the work of G. K. Beale, *We Become What We Worship: A Biblical Theology of Idolatry* (Downers Grove, IL: IVP, 2008).
2. See again Scot McKnight, *A Community Called Atonement* (Nashville: Abingdon, 2007), 117; cf. 30–31.
3. See again the treatment of the "already" and "not yet" of reconciliation in ch. 12.

making all things new (Rev 21:5). The goal of this chapter is therefore to bind together the prior treatments of moral influence (both the beckoning and restraining *hands*) through a focus on the Holy Spirit.

My argument comes in two parts: (1) pneumatology and (2) embodiment. Or if you prefer: cause and effect. It will soon be obvious however that the second part is merely an extension—rather than a cessation!—of the Spirit's work. Part one begins by selectively linking insights from Abelard and Girard to the pneumatology of Anglican theologian Sarah Coakley (b. 1951). For Coakley, the Spirit is the person of the Trinity tasked especially with *enflaming* and *purifying* human desires so that we may be conformed to the image of God in Christ. This *is* moral influence. And as will become clear, the dual function of enflaming and chastening fits quite well with the igniting and restraining emphases of the past two chapters.

In the second part of the chapter, I will connect the pneumatological argument to the notion that believers are incorporated into God's atoning work on account of union with Christ (see ch. 12). In my view, the Spirit is the ground of union between Christ and his church, and perhaps also the person who prevents our involvement from devolving into (1) Pelagian, (2) predestinarian (read: determinist), or even (3) pantheistic deficiencies. The Spirit enables, liberates, and particularizes humans so that we embody Christ within the world.

The basis for this pneumatological turn is rooted in an insight from chapter 1. As Irenaeus asserted, every act of God within creation is accomplished by his two *hands*—the Son and Holy Spirit.[4] These hands, as Colin Gunton argues, "do not act separately, like someone holding a baby in one [while] trying to bang in a nail with the other" but cooperatively.[5] Hence, if one is to use a *hand*-based image of God's work within the world, perhaps one should picture the biblical scene of the potter at the wheel, closely shaping the clay of creation without collapsing into it (Jer 18).

Alongside this picture of two-handed cooperation, one must also add the language of perichoresis, or mutual indwelling. The Spirit works in, with, and through the Son. And the Son works in, with, and through the Spirit. There is, as Michael Gorman puts it, a "reciprocal residency" in the relationship.[6] For although these *hands* are one in terms of essence (*ousia*),

---

4. *Haer.* 4.20.1. See ch. 1 for the treatment of Irenaeus.
5. Gunton, *Father, Son, and Holy Spirit: Toward a Fully Trinitarian Theology* (London: T&T Clark, 2003), 81.
6. Michael J. Gorman, *The Death of the Messiah and Birth of the New Covenant: A (Not So) New Model of the Atonement* (Eugene, OR: Cascade, 2014), 48.

they are eternally distinct as persons (*hypostases*). Such language is both technical and ineffable, yet the truth behind it is the reason we have real access to God. Because of his two hands, we are not left like orphans by a deadbeat father (e.g., John 14:18).

A further implication of this triune mystery involves the notion of inseparable operations. In the oft-cited Latin dictum, God's external action in the world is undivided (*opera trinitatis ad extra sunt indivisa*). Yet this notion need not be absolutized. If it is, then nothing specific may be said of the particular persons as they work within the story,[7] and to go down this road is to risk collapsing into modalism.[8] In keeping with this specificity of roles within God's shared work, Basil of Caesarea (330–379) argued that the Spirit is rightly called the "perfecter" of all God's work in Christ.[9] And Gregory of Nyssa (335–94) claimed that all divine action begins with the Father, goes through the Son, and is completed by the Holy Spirit.[10] Thus Colin Gunton seems right to state that "the Spirit is the one who directs the creatures to where the creator wishes them to go."[11] The Spirit is the bringer of divine futurity, or new creation.

This directedness toward new creation fits perfectly with the image of the Spirit as the brooding Dove. For today—just as with Noah long ago—the Winged-One comes with "grafted" olive branch in beak, to signal a new world coming out of watery chaos. Like Noah, we cannot see this verdant land in all its fullness, but the Dove is our "down payment"

---

7. For Stephen Holmes, "inseparability of operation can coexist with specifically, and ordered, triune action." Then in a speculative suggestion, he adds that this may make most sense if we speak of God's external action not as a multitude of discrete endeavors (actions), but as one broader work, say: salvation. See Holmes, "Trinitarian Action and Inseparable Operations: Some Historical and Dogmatic Reflections," in *Advancing Trinitarian Theology: Explorations in Constructive Dogmatics*, ed. Oliver Crisp and Fred Sanders (Grand Rapids: Zondervan, 2014), 67, 73.

8. Oliver Crisp refers to this as the "Trinitarian Appropriation Principle" (TAP), to be summarized with the longer Latin dictum that "the external works of the Trinity are indivisible, the distinction and order of the persons being preserved" (*opera trinitatis ad extra sunt indivisa servato discrimine et ordine personarum*). Crisp, *The Word Enfleshed: Exploring the Person and Work of Christ* (Grand Rapids: Baker: 2016), 153.

9. Basil says this: "When you consider creation, I advise you to first think of Him who is the first cause of everything that exists, namely, the Father, and then of the Son, who is the creator, and then the Holy Spirit, the perfecter." Basil, *On the Holy Spirit*, 16, 38. This translation is that of Stephen M. Hildebrand (New York: St. Vladimir's Seminary Press, 2011).

10. "The Holy Trinity works every activity according to the manner stated, not divided according to the number of hypostases, but one certain motion and disposition of goodwill occurs, proceeding from the Father through the Son to the Spirit." Gregory of Nyssa, *Ad Ablabium*, cited in *The Trinitarian Controversy*, trans. and ed. William G. Rusch (Philadelphia: Fortress, 1980), 155.

11. Gunton, *Father, Son, and Holy Spirit*, 81.

von the promised future.[12] Where the Spirit moves, creation is patiently crafted to become what God intends: holy and whole. Thus any talk of moral influence as a mimetic model of atonement must turn ultimately to pneumatology.

| NO "SHRINKING PIGEON": SARAH COAKLEY |

Unfortunately, while the Father and the Son receive much attention in atonement doctrine,[13] the Spirit has sometimes been diminished.[14] In the view of the Cambridge theologian Sarah Coakley, this diminished visibility extends to Trinitarian theology more broadly. In her view, Christians have often reduced the powerful brooding Dove to what looks more like a "shrinking Pigeon"—"Small, shadowy, and hard to see." This claim is argued in the fascinating first volume of her systematic theology: *God, Sexuality, and the Self: An Essay "On the Trinity."*[15]

While Coakley's volume is largely focused on the Trinity, she (like Girard) begins with a novel notion of desire. In her view, even our erotic longings to be united with another person represent a "precious clue" within "the crooked human heart" that is meant to point us to our source within the triune God.[16] Taking cues from Christian Platonism, Coakley views "yearning" (or *eros*) as a divine attribute that is nearly synonymous with *agapē*. Hence, in the view of Pseudo-Dionysius, God is "yearning on the move." In God is a longing to unite and delight with the objects of his love.[17] Freud is therefore upended; instead of God-talk really being about sex, even sexual longing is about God. These desires present to us "the potent reminder woven into our earthly existence of the divine 'unity,' 'alliance,' and 'commingling' that we seek."[18]

After this claim about desire, Coakley moves next to pneumatology. Here, the Spirit especially must be associated with the divine *eros*, for it is especially *"in and through the Spirit"* that God "stirs up, and progressively

---

12. See, in order of allusion, Gen 8:11 (cf. Gen 1:2); Rom 11; Eph 1:14.

13. See for instance the disputed posture of the Father toward the Son in penal substitution; cf. ch. 6.

14. For Robert Jenson, "The common factor in Western problems with the Spirit . . . is a tendency of the Spirit simply to disappear from theology's description of God's triune action, often just when he might be expected to have the leading role." Jenson, *Systematic Theology,* vol. 1, *The Triune God* (Oxford: Oxford University Press, 1997), 153.

15. Sarah Coakley, *God, Sexuality, and the Self: An Essay "On the Trinity"* (Cambridge: Cambridge University Press, 2013). For reference to the "shrinking pigeon," 212.

16. Coakley, *God, Sexuality, and the Self,* 59.

17. Pseudo-Dionysius, *The Divine Names,* 4.14.

18. Coakley, *God, Sexuality, and the Self,* 316.

chastens and purges the frailer and often misdirected desires of humans, and so forges them, by stages of sometimes painful growth, into the likeness of his Son."[19] This means that the Spirit is the triune person particularly responsible for both (1) enflaming and (2) purifying the desires of the crooked human heart.

The Spirit's Role in Sparking Desire

On the first count (*desire ignited*), Paul says that no one can even say, "'Jesus is Lord,' except by the Holy Spirit" (1 Cor 12:3). There is thus a sense in which the Spirit sparks our ability to respond positively to the Messiah. "The Spirit gives life" in the words of John's Gospel (6:63), and it is by the Spirit that God pours his love into our hearts (Rom 5:5). Still, Coakley's favorite text is Romans 8, in which the Spirit testifies to and with the human spirit regarding our adopted status, so that we cry out "Abba Father" (Rom 8:15–16).

The Spirit is seen as enflaming and enabling the human desire for God, both before and after conversion. Therefore, it is possible to connect Coakley's argument to my own treatment of redemption via moral influence. Namely, if Abelard was right about Christ's work enkindling our cold and fearful hearts, this ignition may be credited (at least in a special sense) to the Holy Spirit. Yet in Coakley's view, this is not a move that completely overthrows the human will by violent imposition; instead, the Spirit comes to our aid "through our own longings" (e.g., Rom 8:16) yet in a way that evades a rational dissection.

I will return to this claim momentarily when I explore how the Spirit prevents both Pelagian *and* predestinarian deficiencies (the latter being a form of divine determinism). For now, however, I merely note that Coakley sees both an experiential and a logical priority that is given to the Spirit's work as fallen humans are aroused to turn toward God in Christ.[20] Indeed, as Gregory of Nyssa argued, "It is impossible for a man, if he has not been previously enlightened by the Spirit, to arrive at a conception of the Son."[21]

Coakley also sees the Spirit as awakening the bond of love between humans. Hence the vertical sparking of desire for the divine also corresponds

---

19. Coakley, *God, Sexuality, and the Self*, 6, italics in original.
20. Coakley, *God, Sexuality, and the Self*, 112–13n14.
21. Gregory of Nyssa, *Epistle* 38 (variously called *Ad Petrum*), 1. While the letter was previously attributed to Basil of Caesarea, it is now almost universally attributed to Gregory. Coakley makes use of the passage in *God, Sexuality, and the Self*, 139.

to horizontal relationships. In this way, God's Breath births the church as diverse and divergent personalities are knit together in Christ-shaped *koinonia*. For as Augustine wrote of both the vertical and horizontal planes, "When God the Holy Spirit . . . has been given to [humanity], He inflames" not only "love for God" but also "neighbor" because "He Himself is love."[22] For Coakley, however, this awakening of love and longing also carries certain risks—especially in the realm of sexuality.

Specifically, the movement of the Spirit "with sighs too deep for words" (Rom 8:27) runs the risk of sinful confusion because the magnetizing tug toward God and others "is felt analogously also in every erotic propulsion towards union." There is a reason, therefore, that patristic and medieval Christians were drawn toward *Song of Songs*, with mixed results.[23]

This possibility of pneumatic and erotic confusion is beautifully (or perhaps tragically) captured in a work that Coakley does not cite: John Steinbeck's classic novel *The Grapes of Wrath*. In it, the simultaneously devout and degenerate Reverend John Casy (an ex–"Burning Busher" revivalist) describes the perils of his former ministry. In so doing, he recounts being vexed by the sensual temptations that seemed invariably to assail his flock when they got "all full up of Jesus" and "the Sperit" (Casy's favored pronunciation). In his "Okie" accent, Casy recounts that "the more grace a girl got in her, the quicker she wants to go out in the grass [for a sexual tryst]." "You'd think that'd be one time when the devil didn't stand a snowball's chance in hell. But there it was." Casy had long been overcome with guilt for this sinful behavior; and for leading members of his flock astray. But to no avail: "I'd feel bad, an' I'd pray an' pray, but it didn't do no good. Come nex' time, them and me was full of the Sperit, I'd do it again."[24]

Many would dismiss these sexual indiscretions as the mere product of Dionysian emotionalism (not to mention a manipulative spiritual leader), but Coakley seems open to tracing at least the *initial* ardor for both Christ and others in such circumstances to the Spirit of God. Yet these longings, like all things in a fallen world, can be bent disastrously. And for this reason, Coakley is compelled to emphasize a second facet of the Spirit's work on human longings: purgation.

---

22. Augustine, *De Trinitate*, 15.17.31; cf. Coakley, *God, Sexuality, and the Self*, 312.
23. See *God, Sexuality, and the Self*, 14, and ch. 3 more broadly.
24. For the rest of this fascinating conversation, in a charismatic dust-bowl dialect, see Steinbeck, *The Grapes of Wrath*, 75th anniv. ed. (New York: Viking, 2014), 20–25.

The Spirit's Role in Purifying Desire

Thankfully, the Spirit also interposes certain boundaries of redemptive restraint upon our human longings. While some desires are awakened and enflamed by God's Breath, others must be purged and put to death. Paul speaks of these as "fleshly" desires and quickly contrasts them with those of the "Spirit" (Gal 5:16–26). The point here is not that dark urges must be repressed under a veneer of plastic, smiling piety—but that they must be brought to light, submitted to the lordship of Christ, and redirected to the good of others. A famous example of this "moral influence" may be seen in the way Ephesians deals with thieving "hands." The command is not merely to "steal no longer" but to do "something useful" with one's hands so that "they may have something to share with those in need" (4:28).

Moving back to my own mosaic image of redemption, there is both beckoning and restraint in play. By the Spirit, we must say "No" to ungodliness, so that we may say "Yes" to something better—a life of holy love. This two-part emphasis on igniting and restraining ought to sound familiar. Indeed, it corresponds with the two sides of moral influence reasoning that I detailed in the last two chapters. It is the Spirit who "enkindles" (to cite Abelard) imitative love for Christ, just as it is the Spirit who "reveals and restrains" (with a nod to Girard) violent and idolatrous desires. Yet while Girard focuses almost exclusively on mimesis unto *violence*, Coakley reminds us that *eros* also slays when misdirected. It too is a double-edged desire, and it too must be redirected by a mimesis of the Son through the power of the Spirit.

The "missing link" between both sides of moral influence reasoning is in fact the "Link of Love." This phrase was Augustine's novel way of naming the Spirit as the Gift that binds together persons (both divine and human) in relations of holy love.[25] But if this is so, why has the Spirit sometimes been marginalized?

The "Shrinking Pigeon"

In Coakley's view, the problem emerged early with the onset of Montanism. This "New Prophecy" was a prophetic and Spirit-focused movement that spread across the empire in the second century. Its most famous convert was Tertullian (ca. 155–240), and the sect was known for

---

25. See Augustine, *De Trinitate*, 6.5. For a treatment of the somewhat exaggerated charge that the "Link of Love" language undermines the particularity and personhood of the Spirit, see my doctoral thesis, *A Free Corrector: Colin Gunton and the Legacy of Augustine* (Minneapolis: Fortress, 2015), ch. 3.

ecstatic utterances, challenges to ecclesial authority, and the release of even "wretched women" into positions of leadership.[26] The movement "gave the Spirit a bad name" within the early centuries, and the institutional church moved sharply to curb what it saw as charismatic excess by way of patriarchal power structures.[27]

In later centuries, the trend continued, and Coakley attempts to demonstrate that through a survey of Christian art and iconography. Through pages of helpful illustrations, her claim is that the powerful "perfecter" of God's work (to cite Basil)—the brooding Dove of new creation—was often replaced with what looked more like an ever-shrinking "pigeon," barely visible and functionally redundant amid the masculine dyad of the Father and the Son.[28] And while this sidelining of the Spirit succeeded in restraining charismatic excess, it also carried dreadful side effects. In Coakley's view, it hamstrung Christian understanding of the Trinity, replaced contemplative praxis with rational rigidity, and diminished the very means of our mystical incorporation into the ministry of reconciliation (2 Cor 5:18–20).

Critiquing Coakley

My goal is not to commend every part of Coakley's case.[29] To equate God's nature with eternal longing (*eros*) may seem to imply a lack within the Godhead,[30] though Coakley explicitly denies this implication.[31] Likewise, in her treatment of the "shrinking pigeon" of church history, one may detect a false antithesis between the "messy" ministry of the Spirit and the more structured realm of book and bishop. This may be true, to a point, but it also runs counter to Paul's claim that the Spirit is actually the giver of order in worship.[32]

---

26. Hippolytus (AD 170–235), *Refutation of all Heresies*, 8.12. See Coakley, *God, Sexuality, and the Self*, 121.

27. While the claim may be exaggerated by Coakley, it is perhaps no accident that some prominent proponents of cessationism (e.g., John MacArthur) are likewise opposed to women in positions of church leadership.

28. Coakley, *God, Sexuality, and the Self*, ch. 5; esp. 212.

29. For a more critical treatment of Coakley's pneumatology, see my "Shrinking Pigeon, Brooding Dove: The Holy Spirit in Recent Works by Sarah Coakley and N. T. Wright," *SJT* 69, no. 3 (2016): 295–308; likewise, for a careful treatment of Coakley's apophatic Trinitarianism, see E. Jerome Van Kuiken, "'Ye Worship Ye Know Not What'? The Apophatic Turn and the Trinity," *IJST* 19, no. 4 (Fall 2017): 401–20.

30. This is the concern of Matthew Levering, *Engaging the Doctrine of the Holy Spirit: Love and Gift in the Trinity and the Church* (Grand Rapids: Baker Academic, 2016), 38–39.

31. See Coakley, *God, Sexuality, and the Self*, 10, 333.

32. For a treatment of (1) sacrament, (2) Scripture and (3) episcopacy as gifts of the Spirit, see Kathryn Greene-McCreight, "He Spoke through the Prophets: The Prophetic Word

One could also note less insidious reasons for the Spirit's lack of a prominent place within Christian artwork. How, after all, does one paint a divine person that has been aptly described as "the Beyond who is within"?[33] In Scripture, the divine *Pneuma* is like the wind that blows but is not seen (John 3:8). Hence, like other pollinating breezes, the Spirit is witnessed by effects (love, joy, peace, etc.) rather than by ostentatious self-promotion.[34] Along similar lines, others highlight the "self-effacing" nature of the Spirit's ministry, which continually directs attention toward the Father as *seen* in God the Son. In this way, the Spirit always turns our gaze to Jesus as the perfect image of the invisible God. Like the noonday sun that cannot be gazed upon directly, the Spirit illumines and energizes the world in order "to give us the light of the knowledge of God's glory displayed in the face of Christ" (2 Cor 4:6).

Although I do not wish to extol every aspect of Coakley's brilliant and creative project, I do want to consider how her emphasis upon the igniting and restraining functions of the Spirit fit together with the igniting and restraining aspects of moral influence reasoning. And with that goal in mind, I move next to how the Spirit enables humans to embody God's message of reconciliation in this present age.

| EMBODYING ATONEMENT |

In the last chapter, I broached the claim that atonement is praxis, both for Jesus and his people.[35] Inspiration for this insight came partly from Paul's claim that being "in Christ" means receiving the "ministry of reconciliation" as "God's ambassadors" (2 Cor 5:18–20). Hence redemption (like the kingdom) is both accomplished and ongoing; both punctiliar and partly unfulfilled. This is so because while Christ has *already* taken a seat after his "single sacrifice for sin" (Heb 10:12), it remains for us to take up crosses (Matt 16:24) with his same "mindset" (Phil 2:5) and as his "body" on earth.

Made More Sure," in Christopher R. Seitz, ed., *Nicene Christianity: The Future for a New Ecumenism* (Grand Rapids: Brazos, 2001), 167–75.

33. Anthony Thiselton, *The Holy Spirit: In Biblical Teaching, through the Centuries, and Today* (Grand Rapids: Eerdmans, 2013), 21.

34. While the Father also is invisible, one can easily see how this name lends itself to a visual depiction of an old man with a long beard, with all the accompanying benefits and drawbacks thereof.

35. McKnight's claim was that the "atonement is not just something done to us and for us, *it is something we participate in—in this world, in the here and now.*" Scot McKnight, *Community Called Atonement*, 30–31, italics in original.

Yet if Christians are to embody atonement, it will require a miracle of moral influence that is perhaps better described as an act of new creation. "I will put my Spirit in you," says Yahweh, "and move you to follow my decrees" (Ezek 36:27). My claim is that only the Holy Spirit can enable these participatory effects without triggering a trio of errors, whether

1. Pelagian,
2. Predestinarian (that is, determinist), or
3. Pantheistic (homogenizing the particularity of divine and created being).

Before delving into these dangers, however, it should first be said that McKnight is not alone in his assessment of atonement as missional praxis. Pauline scholar Michael Gorman claims that the church is not merely a *"beneficiary* of Christ's atoning death, but a *participant* in it."[36] "The gift is also demand." And *"there is no cleansing without discipleship* [and] *no atonement without ethics."*[37] This is so, says Gorman, because "ethics is not a separate category! Ethics is atonement in action, not as a supplement but as constitutive of atonement itself."[38] Yet how do these statements avoid what sounds like a naïve view of human capability?

Where the Spirit Is, There Are No Pelagians

While the above claims might be taken as imperiling the status of salvation *sola gratia*, Gorman quickly renounces the Pelagian deficiency. Using John's Gospel as a case study (alongside Paul), he points out that Jesus himself refers to his death as a "new commandment" (John 13:34) that requires followers to embody a posture of self-giving love. At the same time, Christ makes clear that "apart from me you can do nothing." While fruit bearing is required, it is enabled only by remaining in the "vine" (John 15:5). The imagery is that of *empowering union*, and in John 14, Jesus identifies the Spirit as the agent of this shared and sanctified existence: "I will ask the Father, and he will give you another advocate to help you and be with you forever—the Spirit of truth. . . . You know him, for he lives with you and will be in you" (vv. 16–17).

To cite the phrase used earlier, the Spirit brings a kind of "reciprocal residency" between Jesus and his followers. "I am in my Father," says Jesus,

36. Gorman, *The Death of the Messiah*, 233, italics in original.
37. Gorman, *The Death of the Messiah*, 46, italics in original.
38. Gorman, *The Death of the Messiah*, 55.

"you are in me, and I am in you" (John 14:20). And while this in no way reduces the force of Christ's commandments as commandments, it does change the way they are fulfilled. Christians are to live out the ministry of reconciliation *sola Spiritu Christi*—by the Spirit of Christ alone. And where the Spirit is, there are no Pelagians.

Alongside Gorman, another voice in favor of atonement as missional praxis comes from the camp of conservative, though irenic, Reformed theology (yes, it does exist!). And this fact also should give pause to Pelagian critiques. Kevin Vanhoozer describes the church as a "reconciliatory theater" that is called to "perform the doctrine of atonement" for a watching world.[39] Then, in a move that resonates with the last chapter, he turns to the Girardian lexicon in order to speak of our "performance" as an act of cruciform "*mimēsis*."[40] In this act of creative imitation, Christians are performing the doctrine of atonement, though not by their own human power or brilliance. As before, this argument is rooted in Paul's claim regarding our ministry of reconciliation, with the caveat that this ministry is not so much about achieving reconciliation as it is about displaying and exhibiting the reconciliation that we received through Christ's death.[41] On these grounds, any hint of Pelagian pride is rightly quashed.

Where the Spirit Is, There Is Freedom

Alongside Pelagianism, a second danger that the Spirit helps to avoid is a form of predestinarian excess, which presents itself in the form of a divine determinism.[42] "Where the Spirit of the Lord is, there is freedom" (2 Cor 3:17). In my own view, this freedom should be seen as enabling without overpowering the human will. What's more, this freedom involves not merely the "I believe" of initial faith but also, as Nietzsche (ironically) termed it, "a long obedience in the same direction."[43] In such ways, the Spirit empowers without evaporating human agency.

---

39. Kevin J. Vanhoozer, *The Drama of Doctrine: A Canonical-Linguistic Approach to Christian Theology* (Louisville: Westminster John Knox, 2005), 426–27.

40. See Vanhoozer, *Drama of Doctrine*, 429.

41. Vanhoozer, *Drama of Doctrine*, 435.

42. This claim should not, however, be taken as denying a biblical doctrine of predestination by which God sovereignly guides history to its appointed end. The critique of "predestinarian excess" is thus directed against a determinism that would deny God's gracious empowering of a limited creaturely freedom that includes the possibility of contrary choice. More on this anon.

43. The late Eugene Peterson is responsible for redeeming Nietzsche's words in, *A Long Obedience in the Same Direction: Discipleship in an Instant Society* (Downers Grove, IL: IVP, 1980).

Michael Horton's Reformed Account of
Spirit-Enabled Human Agency

Despite the famous "I" of the Calvinist TULIP, one finds something like this argument in the ranks of traditional Reformed theology.[44] In a recent (and winsome) contribution on divine and human agency, Michael Horton identifies the Spirit as the person of the Trinity especially responsible for preventing God's effectual call from flattening human freedom. This defense of compatibilism rejects what one might call "hard determinism" in favor of the Spirit who frees but does not override the human will. In Horton's view, "The will is liberated, not violated."[45] For as John Owen wrote long before, "If it be compelled, it is destroyed."[46]

Horton's case is built upon a distinction between two types of divine decree. The first he calls the fiat of *ex nihilo* action. This is symbolized by the Genesis command of "Let there be . . ." with the accompanying answer, "And there was . . ." While these fiats still occur within a triune framework (*opera Trinitatis ad extra sunt indivisa* once again), Horton sees no hint of creaturely concursus in such cases; God simply causes. In contrast, a second type of divine decree is symbolized by the Genesis language of "Let the earth bring forth . . ." with the accompanying answer, "The *earth* brought forth . . ." (Gen 1:12, italics added). His point is that while divine sovereignty still stands behind the result, God's sovereignty is "the source rather than the antithesis of creaturely freedom."[47] The two are actually compatible.

Horton's claim is hardly new in several respects. The basic points were made long ago by the likes of Aquinas, who wrote that "when the free will moves itself, this does not exclude its being moved by another, from whom it receives the very power to move itself."[48] Likewise, even the Westminster Confession proclaims that while God ordains "whatsoever comes to pass,"

---

44. Of course, the famous "TULIP" (as a summary of Calvinist theology) is something of an annoyance to many Reformed scholars, since it does not date before the twentieth century and even then came only as a summary of the seventeenth century Canons of Dort, which were written as a response to the Arminians. See, for instance, J. Todd Billings, *Union with Christ: Reframing Theology and Ministry for the Church* (Grand Rapids: Baker Academic, 2011), 57–59.

45. Michael Horton, "'Let the Earth Bring Forth . . .': The Spirit and Human Agency in Sanctification," in *Sanctification: Explorations in Theology and Practice*, ed. Kelly M. Kapic (Downers Grove, IL: IVP Academic, 2014), 142.

46. John Owen, *The Works of John Owen*, ed. William H. Goold (Edinburgh: Banner of Truth Trust, 1965), 3:319.

47. Horton, "Let the Earth Bring Forth," 136.

48. Thomas Aquinas, *Summa Theologica*, I, q. 83, art. 1, p. 418. The passage is cited by Horton, "Let the Earth Bring Forth," 136.

he does not do so in such a way as to become either the "author of sin" or the violator of "the will of the creatures."[49] Whether successful or not, these earlier sources also attempt to maintain the compatibility of human freedom and an all-ordaining God.

But while many accounts of compatibilism culminate with logical arguments over so-called "primary" and "secondary" causes—via names like Aristotle, Malebranche, and Leibniz—Horton's approach is more *pneumatological*. In his view, the Son is the "Word" by which the Father says "Let the earth bring forth," and the Spirit is the one "at work within creaturely reality, bringing about its voluntary consent to God's word even through that word itself."[50] Instead of talking over us, "the Spirit gives us our voice back."[51] For where the Spirit is, there is creaturely freedom alongside God's sovereign will.

When it comes to biblical evidence, Horton cites the example of an overwhelmed but obedient Mary at the Annunciation (Luke 1). Here she is told, "The Holy Spirit will come on you, and the power of the Most High will overshadow you. So the holy one to be born will be called the Son of God" (v. 35). In this scene, Horton sees the triune agency of the Father speaking (through an angel), the Son as content of the message, and the Spirit as the one who brings the work to pass. Likewise, the Spirit also enables Mary's change of tone, from "How will this be . . . ?" to "Let it be to me according to your word" (vv. 34, 38).[52]

From this perspective, the Spirit brings about a voluntary "Amen" to God's foreordained plan. Instead of removing the creature's agency, the divine Breath empowers its particularity by means of preaching and sacraments. Hence while Mary is most certainly overwhelmed (in more ways than one), Horton contends that the Spirit's influence is "more like being overwhelmed by beauty than by force."[53]

A Wesleyan Alternative

There is much to love in Horton's triune telling of creaturely compatibilism, even if some (like myself) may be concerned that within a strongly

---

49. *The Westminster Confession*, III. For divergent view on whether such claims are internally inconsistent, see Oliver Crisp, *Deviant Calvinism: Broadening Reformed Theology* (Minneapolis: Fortress, 2014), ch. 3; and Jerry L. Walls, *Hell: The Logic of Damnation* (Notre Dame, IN: University of Notre Dame Press, 1993), 68.

50. Horton, "Let the Earth Bring Forth," 138.

51. Horton, "Let the Earth Bring Forth," 148

52. See Horton, "Let the Earth Bring Forth," 138.

53. Horton, "Let the Earth Bring Forth," 144.

Calvinistic account of God's exhaustive sovereignty such a Spirit remains a kind of Holy "[G]host in the machine." Horton appears to affirm an alternative to determinism in theory, but his refusal to allow for any contrary choice on the part of creatures makes it is hard to see the difference in practice. In fact, while the Spirit is pictured as the liberating hand of God within us, the image may still bear a resemblance to the hand that fills and moves a puppet.[54]

One alternative to this strongly predestinarian account appears in Wesleyan theology. For Wesley himself, humans are indeed bound in slavery to sin with no hope of self-liberation: "All men are by nature not only sick, but 'dead in trespasses,'" and "It is not possible for them to do anything well till God raises them from the dead."[55] Wesley claimed to differ from Calvin not even a hair's breadth on the subject of total depravity. And he spoke not of free will (in the Pelagian sense) but of a "freed will," for "man hath his Freedom of Will, not naturally, but by grace."[56]

The grace Wesley spoke of was "prevenient" in that it comes to humans in our state of bondage in order to elicit "the first wish to please God," and "the first slight transient conviction of having sinned against him."[57] In Brian Shelton's view, prevenient grace "makes possible the freedom component that is necessary for belief."[58] For Wesley, this grace bore a connection to what John wrote of when referencing the "true light" that has "enlightened everyone" in the world (John 1:9).[59] With this broad scope in view, Wesley claimed that "there is no man, unless he has quenched the Spirit, that is wholly void of the grace of God."[60]

As a safeguard against both Pelagian and semi-Pelagian errors (of which his successors were sometimes less careful to avoid[61]), Wesley wrote the following of God's prevenient grace:

---

54. This is, of course, a more complex discussion than I can cover here. For an accessible introduction to some of the issues at stake in questions over biblical theology, divine determinism, and human responsibility, see Thomas H. McCall, *An Introduction to Analytic Christian Theology* (Downers Grove, IL: IVP Academic, 2015), 56–81.
55. John Wesley, "On Working Out Our Salvation," in *The Works of John Wesley*, vol. 3, ed. Albert C. Outler (Nashville: Abingdon, 1986), 206–7.
56. John Wesley, "The Scripture Doctrine Concerning Predestination," *Works*, 14:421.
57. Wesley, "On Working Out Our Salvation," 203.
58. W. Brian Shelton, *Prevenient Grace: God's Provision for Fallen Humanity* (Anderson, IN: Francis Asbury, 2014), 2.
59. Wesley, "On Working Out Our Salvation," 200.
60. Wesley, "On Working Out Our Salvation," 207.
61. See, for instance, the evaluation of later Wesleyan history in T. A. Noble, *Holy Trinity: Holy People; The Theology of Christian Perfecting*, Didsbury Lecture Series (Eugene, OR: Cascade, 2013), 152–53.

Nothing can so directly tend to hide pride from man as [this] . . . we have nothing that we have not received [and] the very first motion of good is from above, as well as the power which conducts it to the end—if it is God that not only infuses every good desire, but that accompanies and follows it, else it vanishes away—then it evidently follows that "he who glorieth must glory in the Lord" (1 Cor 1:31).[62]

Despite this grace-focused emphasis, Wesley was equally insistent that prevenient grace does not override completely our power of contrary choice. It can be resisted, even while it restores a state of equilibrium, or possibility, to the fallen human will.

Unfortunately, the exegetical underpinnings of this concept may seem woefully thin. As even the Wesleyan New Testament scholar Ben Witherington writes, "Wesley's concept of prevenient grace is frankly weakly grounded if we are talking about proof texts from the Bible."[63]

On this point, many Calvinists agree.[64] The phrase itself appears nowhere in Scripture, nor does the New Testament know anything of Wesley's parsing out of differing "grace species" that attend to human beings at different points (e.g., prevenient, justifying, and sanctifying grace). This language, though hardly limited to Wesley, seems to treat grace as a kind of magic substance that is sprinkled on the soul like fertilizer to elicit faith and fruit. Thus, while Wesley's theology has the benefit of showing that salvation is by grace from start to finish, it leaves behind the biblical approach to these matters, which, as I will now show, is focused more on a prevenient work of the Spirit.[65]

---

62. Wesley, "On Working Out Our Salvation," 203.
63. Ben Witherington, *The Problem with Evangelical Theology: Testing the Exegetical Foundations of Calvinism, Dispensationalism, Wesleyanism, and Pentecostalism*, rev. and expanded ed. (Waco, TX: Baylor University Press, 2016), 213. While agreeing that there is a prevenient work of God in the believer's life, Witherington states that one "should not hang one's entire theology on what sinners can do by free choice on such an exegetically weakly supported notion" (215).
64. See Thomas R. Schreiner, "Does Scripture Teach Prevenient Grace in the Wesleyan Sense?" in *The Grace of God, the Bondage of the Will*, ed. Thomas R. Schreiner and Bruce A. Ware, vol. 2 (Grand Rapids: Baker, 1995).
65. Another variant in this discussion exists in the work of Jacob Arminius (1560–1609). Long before Wesley, he also had affirmed a grace that enables humans to accept the gift of God's salvation. And like Wesley, he also had maintained that this grace could be resisted. Yet unlike Wesley, Arminius supported his contention with a Molinist appeal to God's "middle knowledge" (*scientia media*). For an explicit endorsement of middle knowledge, see Arminius, *Disputationes publicae* (1610), IV.43; cf. IV.43. After suffering much from his interpreters (both friend and foe), Arminius's work is now undergoing a much-needed retrieval. See, especially, Keith D. Stanglin and Thomas H. McCall, *Jacob Arminius: Theologian of Grace* (Oxford: Oxford University Press, 2012).

Joining Wesley and Horton: The Prevenient Work of the Spirit

Having taken stock of Horton and Wesley, there remains some constructive work to be done on the Spirit's way of granting human freedom. To recall, my suggestion was that the Spirit guards against not only Pelagian but also "predestinarian" excess. On this point, Horton agrees. Yet his view may seem to offer distinction without much difference. Meanwhile, Wesley appealed to prevenient grace to dissolve determinism. Unfortunately, this reasoning did not adequately frame the conversation in a biblical or Trinitarian vocabulary.[66]

In the New Testament, the Spirit moves to awaken, convict, and convert those dead in sin. This work occurs within a triune framework in which the Father also "draws" (John 6:44) and the Son "calls" (John 10:3). Nevertheless, it is the Spirit, as Ezekiel shows, that blows a new wind upon dry bones. The Spirit comes to convict the world of sin (John 16:8); thus as Ben Witherington rightly notes, it would be far better to speak of the "prevenient work of the Spirit" than to speak more generally of "prevenient grace."[67] Where the Spirit is, there is possibility. Yet as Stephen's sermon in the book of Acts makes clear, it is also possible to "resist the Holy Spirit" and some may do so "always" (7:50). The Spirit enables human freedom, but the Spirit can be resisted.

This point is bolstered by other texts as well. One reads that the Spirit may be "grieved" (Eph 4:30) like a parent over a rebellious child or "quenched" like a flame that burns brightly only to be extinguished (1 Thess 5:19). In the parable of Christ, some seed falls on rocky soil, and in these cases, the initial life and growth are genuine but temporary. In the face of this withering, however, one's hope for humanity (and creation itself) resides in the reality that the Spirit is persistent, patient,

---

66. To be fair, Wesley did sometimes link prevenient grace to the work of the Spirit. As he says in a sermon on "The Spirit of Bondage and Adoption" (Rom 8:15): "By some awful providence, or by his word applied with the demonstration of his Spirit, God touches the heart of him that lay asleep in darkness and in the shadow of death" (II, 1). For indeed: "few men are so fast asleep in sin, but they are sometimes more or less awakened. As the Spirit of God does not 'wait for the call of man,' so at some times he *will* be heard" (IV, 2). Nonetheless, as Wesley makes clear, it remains possible for humans—once awakened by the Spirit's prevenient work—to "stifle the grace of God" (IV, 2). John Wesley, "The Spirit of Bondage and Adoption," in *Works*, 5:101–10.

67. Ben Witherington, "Prevenient Grace—by W. Brian Shelton," *The Bible and Culture* (blog), Patheos, October 10, 2015, http://www.patheos.com/blogs/bibleandculture/2015/10/10/prevenient-grace-by-w-brian-shelton/. Along similar lines, Kilian McDonnell (OSB) claims that after Augustine, there has been a tendency "to refer to grace in contexts where theologians of the East speak of the Spirit." McDonnell, *The Other Hand of God: The Holy Spirit as the Universal Touch and Goal* (Collegeville, MN: Liturgical, 2003), 223.

and powerful. Thus, in the words of the great theologian Yogi Berra, "It ain't over till it's over."

With regard to power, Horton is certainly right to note the occasional feeling that one has been "overwhelmed by beauty" when encountering the Spirit. But that is not always the case. Wesleyan-Arminians may go further than this metaphor. Sometimes the Spirit feels more like a violent wind of gale-force strength,[68] and in these cases, beauty is not the word that strikes us. In the Scriptures, the Spirit can be frighteningly powerful both in judgment and in courtroom conviction (John 16:7–8).[69] In instances like this, Colin Gunton seems right to note "the mysterious combination of divine determination and human free-will."[70] There is mystery here, and it must ultimately confound all accounts (both Reformed and Wesleyan!) of divine and human agency.

The issue, however, is not whether the Spirit's work is sometimes overwhelming (it most certainly is!) but what happens in the months and years that follow. As many can attest, some seed falls dramatically—like Paul from horseback—only to land in slowly growing thorns. Hence the apparent biblical warnings on the real possibility of apostasy, or falling away, must be taken seriously, even while we ought not to use them for manipulative effects.[71]

Once again, the hope for those who appear to have fallen resides not in human "perseverance" but in God's patient persistence. "All day long," God holds out his "hands [the Son and Spirit] to an obstinate and disobedient people" (Isa 65:2, italics added).[72] And like the hand of Peter after

---

68. Horton, "Let the Earth Bring Forth," 144.

69. Texts could be multiplied to show this point. The Spirit is depicted as fire, which in the Scriptures both purifies and judges. In the Old Testament, the Spirit is frequently the agent of divine punishment (e.g., 1 Sam 16:14); and in the New Testament it is Christ's "breath" (a likely reference to the Spirit) that overthrows the "man of lawlessness" (2 Thess 2:8). If, as I have argued earlier (ch. 6), God's wrath is nothing more than a mode of divine love, then the Spirit's identity as the "Love" of God (to use Augustine's language) forms a link to the Spirit's place in the outpouring of divine wrath. On this last point, I am indebted to a paper by Adam J. Johnson and Tessa McQuillan, "The Spirit of the Atonement: The Role of the Holy Spirit in Christ's Death and Resurrection" (paper presented to the Evangelical Theological Society, Denver, Colorado, November 13, 2018). See also Michael Horton, Rediscovering the Holy Spirit: God's Perfecting Presence in Creation, Redemption, and Everyday Life (Grand Rapids: Zondervan Academic, 2017), 105–19.

70. Colin Gunton, Christ and Creation, Didsbury Lectures 1990 (Eugene, OR: Wipf and Stock, 2005), 88.

71. For more on this complex and contentious issue, see Witherington, The Problem with Evangelical Theology, ch. 4; cf. I. Howard Marshall, "Election and Calling to Salvation in 1 and 2 Thessalonians," in The Thessalonian Correspondence, ed. R. F. Collins (Leuven: Leuven University Press, 1990), 259–76.

72. It is interesting that in Rom 10:21, Paul cites these bleak-sounding words of Isaiah before turning to the hopeful future of "Israel" (ch. 11)—that obstinate and disobedient

his prison break (Acts 12), Christ keeps knocking on our bolted doors, as the Spirit brings unlikely servants, like Rhoda, to alert us to the uninvited Visitor (v. 13). So while some resist with cruelty and insults ("You're out of your mind!"), the Spirit keeps "insisting" (v. 15). In this patient way, God's two hands work harmoniously both before and after conversion to awaken and restrain us, not irresistibly but powerfully, so that God receives the glory.

Where the Spirit Is, There Is Particularity

A final function of the Spirit's work also subverts not merely Pelagian and predestinarian deficiencies but also pantheistic (or homogenizing) ones. This happens through the Spirit's gifting of "particularity." In recent years, this emphasis was made most strongly by the aforementioned Colin Gunton (1941–2003), the *doctor particularis*.[73] As Gunton argued, the Spirit is, in a special sense, the particularizing person in the Trinity, and the one who simultaneously binds together and distinguishes both things and persons. To speak of particularity, or what Duns Scotus called *haecceitas* ("thisness"), was Gunton's way of referring to the uniqueness-in-relation that contrasts with atomizing individualism and bland (or pantheistic) homogeneity.[74]

For Gunton, the gifting of particularity may even be the Spirit's work within the Trinity. Hence he voiced (a rare!) agreement with Augustine in viewing the Spirit as the unifying "Link of Love" between the Father and the Son. Gunton then went further than Augustine by claiming that "it is even more necessary to add that [the Spirit] is the focus of the distinctiveness of Father and Son—of their unique particularity." Indeed,

---

people. Hence, while much emphasis is placed upon the apparently fatalistic status of "vessels of wrath" (Rom 9:22), it is sometimes missed that all of us were at one point such vessels (Eph 2:3). As Witherington argues, "The issue is where one is in the story of a particular vessel, not some act of divine predetermination of some to wrath." Ben Witherington with Darlene Hyatt, *Paul's Letter to the Romans: A Socio-Rhetorical Commentary* (Grand Rapids: Eerdmans, 2004), 259. In short, some seed gets transplanted.

73. In his eulogy for Gunton, Christoph Schwöbel claimed, "If we still followed the ancient custom of venerating the great doctors of the church by a particular title, Colin Gunton would have to be the *doctor particularis*, the teacher of the significance of the particular." Paul Cumin, "The Taste of Cake: Relation and Otherness with Colin Gunton and the Strong Second Hand of God," in *The Theology of Colin Gunton*, ed. Lincoln Harvey (London: T&T Clark, 2010), 82n39.

74. See Colin Gunton, *The One, the Three and the Many: God, Creation and the Culture of Modernity*, 1992 Bampton Lectures (Cambridge: Cambridge University Press, 1993), 194; for further reference to *haecceitas*, see Duns Scotus, *Oxford Commentary*, II. III. q. 1, in *Philosophy of the Middle Ages. The Christian, Islamic and Jewish Traditions*, ed. A. Hyman and J. J. Walsh (Indianapolis: Hackett, 1977), 582.

"The Spirit's function in the Godhead is to particularize the *hypostases*."[75] In this way, "the Spirit is the perfecting cause not only of the creation," as Basil suggested, "but also of the being of God."[76]

In recent years, such confident claims about God's inner life have been vigorously challenged with charges of rampant speculation and projectionism.[77] How, for instance, do we know that the Spirit grants the Father and Son their particularity within the triune life? Are there biblical passages that suggest this notion? Do any creeds or confessions hint in this direction? Is it logically deducible from robust prior premises? Few affirmative answers seem obvious, at least to me.[78] Thus, in the end, it may be wiser to say that one cannot know entirely the Spirit's function within the hidden life of God, as interesting as Gunton's suggestion may be.[79]

One can know something, however, about the Spirit's role within redemptive history. And on this topic, Gunton's claim regarding Spirit-driven particularity is immensely helpful as it guards against the homogenizing forces that undergird both pantheism and practical attempts to disparage or dissolve our personal differences. As Irenaeus hinted with his image of the two hands, God's personal involvement in the world by Son and Spirit allows a closeness to creation without collapsing into it. Both deism and pantheism are thus avoided by means of mediated triune action.[80]

In atonement doctrine, this insight is important given that redeemed particularity is part of God's perfecting plan for his creation. Redeemed

---

75. Gunton, *The One, the Three and the Many*, 190.

76. This is from an unpublished typescript of Colin Gunton's planned dogmatic theology, left unfinished at his death, "A Christian Dogmatic Theology. Volume One: The Triune God. A Doctrine of the Trinity as Though Jesus Makes a Difference, 2003"; cited in Cumin, "The Taste of Cake," 78. Cumin's chapter is a fantastic introduction to Gunton's pneumatology just as Harvey's edited volume is an excellent overview of Gunton's work.

77. See especially the work of Karen Kilby, "Perichoresis and Projection: Problems with Social Doctrines of the Trinity," *New Blackfriars* 81 (2000): 432–45; likewise, Kilby, "Aquinas, the Trinity and the Limits of Understanding," *IJST* 7, no. 4 (October 2005): 414–27.

78. Of course, similar questions might also be raised of Augustine's classic claim that the Spirit is the "Link of Love" between the Father and Son.

79. One route toward affirming Gunton's suggestion is through the much-debated "Rahner's Rule." The claim here is that the economic Trinity simply *is* the immanent Trinity, and vice versa. And since one might argue that the Spirit both constitutes and perfects the life of Jesus of Nazareth (e.g., through conception and guidance in obedience), this reality is seen as giving information also about the immanent Trinity. Unfortunately, such claims are not obvious, and an undue absolutizing of "Rahner's rule" has come under recent fire. One way around this impasse might be to say that economic relations are *analogous* to inner-trinitarian relations—as traditional Trinity doctrine has always claimed in dealing with the divine missions and processions. If this path is taken, then one would have further cause to find Gunton's argument intriguing, even if it is not something that can be flatly asserted.

80. See especially, Colin Gunton, *The Triune Creator: A Historical and Systematic Study* (Grand Rapids: Eerdmans, 1998).

uniqueness is a gift of the Spirit allowing ransomed humans to be "gifted" to the world for its common good. As Gunton puts it, "The Spirit enables people and things to be *themselves* through Jesus Christ."[81] There is unity but never uniformity. In Scripture this is seen in several ways. Paul reminds his readers that the Spirit does not equip the church by making everyone the same, but by making everyone uniquely who they have been called to be— some apostles, some prophets, some pastors, some teachers (Eph 4:11). These differences are by design, and they serve "to equip his people for works of *service*, so that the body of Christ may be built up until we all reach *unity* in the faith and in the knowledge of the Son of God and become mature, attaining to the whole measure of the fullness of Christ" (Eph 4:12–13, italics added). Note then that the diversity of Spirit-given callings is directed toward both service (the ministry of reconciliation) and unity amongst Christ's many members, but it is not a unity of synonymizing sameness.

Consider also the spoken tongues of Pentecost. Although Acts 2 is clearly meant as a redemptive bookend to Babel—at which point linguistic difference brought disunity (Gen 11)—the Spirit's work does not simply return humanity to monolingual sameness. Nor does the eschaton with its many nations, tribes, and tongues (Rev 7:9) around the single throne. In these ways, the redemption of the post-Pentecost world contrasts with the well-intentioned credo of the Irish rock band U2. In "I Still Haven't Found What I'm Looking For," belief in "Kingdom come" coincides with the hope that "all the colors" will eventually "bleed into one."[82]

While this is indeed a worthy hope, it is not quite the biblical one. In Scripture, it is not all who bleed into one but one (Jesus of Nazareth) who "bleeds" into all so that our particularity—our "colors"—are not "washed out" but brightened, like a renovated painting. Pentecost does not return us to a pre-Babel monochrome. Instead, it redeems diversity so that tribe, tongue, and racial contrasts remain, but without the "dividing wall" between us (Eph 2:14). The kingdom itself *is* a coat of many colors because the Spirit does not wash out but redeems particularity.

This also explains why Christ's Spirit-driven moral influence moves us away from racist, classist, sexist, and nationalist errors. These *are* gospel issues. "When [Peter] came to Antioch," writes Paul, "I opposed him to his face," for he was "not acting in line with the truth of the gospel" (Gal 2:11, 14). Peter's ethnocentrism was serious; to deny the Spirit's uniting

---

81. Gunton, "Christian Dogmatic Theology," unpublished typescript, cited in Cumin, "Taste of Cake," 67, italics added.

82. U2, "I Still Haven't Found What I'm Looking For," *The Joshua Tree*, 1987.

and particularizing work is (at least potentially) to blaspheme that same Spirit by dividing Christ's one body. Thus Peter stood "condemned."[83]

Crucial also in Spirit-driven moral influence are the many ways in which ransomed sinners are transformed in thinking and in action—ignited and restrained—on the long and winding road of sanctification. Here the Spirit prompts us toward deep and vulnerable fellowship, as we come to *know* and *be known* in ways that transcend "virtual community." This involves much more than prepackaged Bible studies and small groups; it requires the breaking of both bread and barriers in order to encounter the frightening land of Christ-shaped *koinonia*.[84]

This kind of moral influence also means a call to joyful suffering, peacemaking, and justice that coincides with gospel proclamation. When these influences comingle, we are shaped into people who are more like the Son, who was filled with "grace and truth" (John 1:14). Without the former (grace), we become the clanging cymbals epitomized by many Christian "culture warriors." Yet without the latter (truth) we are mere spineless reflections of a culture that often conflates love with full endorsement. Both grace and truth are needed. Yet to be full of them we must be filled by God's Spirit.

| CONCLUSION |

In these and many other ways, the Spirit is the engine behind moral influence—igniting and restraining our desires and preventing our response from being either Pelagian or preprogrammed. By the Spirit of Christ, our particularities are redeemed and leveraged for the ministry of reconciliation. And when this happens, new creation once again emerges out of chaos.

---

83. With regard to gender, it is important to note that baptism, unlike circumcision, is a covenantal rite (or sacrament) that is equally open to women and men, just as it is equally open to every race and tribe and tongue. So too with the Eucharist.

84. For some practical suggestions along these lines, see David E. Fitch, *Faithful Presence: Seven Disciplines that Shape the Church for Mission* (Downers Grove, IL: IVP, 2016).

CONCLUSION

THIS IS MY BODY

More can be mended than you know.
Francis Spufford[1]

Out of brokenness comes wholeness. In one sense, this simple phrase offers the perfect description both of the atoning work of Christ and of the art form of the mosaic. From the shattered remnants of common tile or pottery comes a larger image that is somehow more than broken shards. Though the marks of breaking remain (like scars etched into hands and feet and side), the beauty achieved in the incorporative reassembly far outweighs the cost of the destruction. Hence, as one turns from art to the atonement, the question is straightforward: Cannot the Potter do this even with the most sacred Vessel? The answer of the Christian gospel—echoing down the slopes of Golgotha and off the stone walls of the empty tomb—is yes. God has shown this through the body of Jesus, by the power of the Holy Spirit. Out of brokenness comes wholeness.

My claim in this book has been that the mosaic metaphor can also help the church grasp the integrated nature of certain well-known models of atonement. Unlike a photograph in which tiny pixels present a seamless blend of color and shape, a mosaic allows each piece to retain its recognizable particularity while integrating them in the service of a larger image. If one stands close, one can identify individual bits of glass or tile that compose the greater picture. And if one steps back, the whole can be admired. In the great mosaics of age-old Christian churches, the goal is

---

1. Francis Spufford, *Unapologetic: Why, Despite Everything, Christianity Can Still Make Surprising Emotional Sense* (New York: HarperOne, 2013), 148.

not for viewers to *construct* the image (as in a puzzle) but to appreciate it as a kind of icon. In short, the goal is worship.

So too with this mosaic of atonement. In this book, I have come to note some ways in which the pieces mutually support one another.

- The *feet*—recapitulation
- The *heart*—penal substitution (and vicarious judgment)[2]
- The *head*—*Christus Victor*
- The *hands*—moral influence

My claim from the beginning has been that it is high time for theologians to move past two troublesome tendencies when dealing with interpretations of Christ's work. The first is the reductionist propensity for *defensive hierarchy* when ranking models of redemption, and the second is a relativizing slide toward *disconnected plurality*.[3]

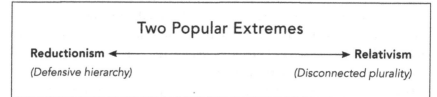

Two Popular Extremes

Reductionism ◄————————————————► Relativism

(Defensive hierarchy)   *(Disconnected plurality)*

Defensive hierarchy unduly elevates one theory of atonement as most important. "Of course," proclaims the reductionist with a veneer of diplomacy, "there are endless facets to Christ's work. But this one piece—as emphasized in *my* tradition—represents the essence of the doctrine." Although there is nothing inherently illogical about the claim, I have argued that Scripture gives no clear reason for this hierarchy, and in the worst instances, competitive and combative approaches to Christ's work have had the sad result of turning history's preeminent act of reconciliation into yet another argument. Thus Christians take up (metaphorical) arms

---

2. As I have noted throughout, penal substitution speaks to the penalty Christ endured "instead of us," while vicarious judgment speaks to the incorporative notion that we were (somehow) "crucified with Christ" (Gal 2:20), so that what happened to him has happened to us as well. Both concepts are biblical, yet my argument was that the *sense* in which each idea is true must be carefully delineated. More on this momentarily.

3. Again, the language of "reductionism" versus "relativism" is borrowed from Jeremy R. Treat, *The Crucified King: Atonement and Kingdom in Biblical and Systematic Theology* (Grand Rapids: Zondervan, 2014).

and blogging platforms to pronounce that "'I am of Anselm'; 'I am of Abelard'; 'I am of Aulén'—and this is just the 'A' list!"[4] In these instances, Paul's question to the Corinthians floats like a lament over the denuded battlefield of our atonement infighting: "Is Christ divided?" (1 Cor 1:13).[5]

On the opposite extreme from defensive hierarchy, there has been a corrective move toward relativized—or kaleidoscopic—views of the atonement.[6] The idea is that one needs many metaphors to do justice to God's saving work, and no single image should be marked out as most important. I agree. Yet the move toward a kaleidoscope of models has often failed to integrate the pieces of the doctrine in an ordered manner.[7] So while one avoids the fractious reductionism of "my model is better than yours," crucial facets of Christ's work remain scattered like Humpty Dumpty upon the ground, and "all the King's horses and all the King's men" walk away to leave Christ's work in a state of dismemberment. Here too, Paul's question echoes with insistence: Is Christ divided?

In answer to these two extremes, my mantra is as follows: Neither reductionism nor relativism; rather, reintegration. One need not rank atonement models in order to note the (theo)logical relationships between them. And one need not pit certain classic interpretations of Christ's work against each other in order to recognize their particular functions within God's masterpiece of redemption.

Like the once plastered-over artwork of the Hagia Sophia, the mosaic image of Christ's body needs some restoration. But how? How might the pieces of atonement doctrine fit together? Before summing up my argument, some qualifiers are in order. First, I make no claim that my own vision of Christ's work is the only coherent integration of atonement models. Nor do I claim that other themes may not be incorporated into the arrangement I have offered. The human body is made up of more than just feet, heart, head, and hands. Atonement doctrine echoes the feeding

---

4. Kevin J. Vanhoozer, *The Drama of Doctrine: A Canonical-Linguistic Approach to Christian Theology* (Louisville: Westminster John Knox, 2005), 381.
5. Of course, not all hierarchal arrangements of atonement models fall into the category of divisive polemic.
6. See especially Joel B. Green, "Kaleidoscopic View," in *The Nature of Atonement: Four Views*, ed. James Beilby and Paul R. Eddy (Downers Grove, IL: IVP Academic, 2006), ch. 4.
7. When speaking of "ordered but not ranked" atonement models, there is an analogy to the shape of Trinitarian doctrine. On this subject, orthodox theology has long argued that there is a certain *taxis* to the triune life of God. Hence, the Father eternally begets the Son, and not vice versa. The Spirit proceeds from the Father (and perhaps the Son), and not vice versa. Even so, this ordered arrangement of triune relations is not the same as a hierarchal "ranking" of the persons as more or less important. So too in my treatment of atonement models.

of the five thousand: there will always be baskets full of pieces left over.[8] And if this book succeeds only in encouraging others to offer a better arrangement of atonement models, I will be quite happy. Now a brief review of my conclusions.

| HOW BEAUTIFUL THE FEET: RECAPITULATION |

At the foundation of this mosaic icon, I have located the age-old notion of recapitulation. The idea here is that Christ enters the human story as both "true Adam" and "true Israel." Most importantly, he enters the story as the true image of the invisible God. And his work must not be divided from his personhood. In these foundational roles (hence: *feet*), he has the authority to act positively on behalf of all humanity. In so doing, Jesus relives the human drama faithfully on our behalf. And all other models of atonement build up from this footing.

For Irenaeus, the basis for Christ's recapitulative ability is *not* simply that "Jesus is divine" or that "God can do anything." As Colin Gunton notes, such premature appeals to omnipotence are very often signs of a bad theological argument. So too here. My claim was that the scriptural genius of Irenaeus resides largely in the way he connects Christ's recapitulative ability to a particular doctrine of the *imago Dei,* or more specifically the *imago Christi.* Because all humans have been stamped in the image of the incarnate Son, there exists an unseen (but genuine) connection between the Messiah and the masses. Jesus is the "mold" for Adam's making and the archetype of all other image bearers. Because humanity was patterned after Christ in the beginning, Jesus enters the human drama as the true head of the entire human family. And in the Scriptures, the head may act on behalf of the whole. Within this biblical logic rests a mysterious mechanism that makes Irenaean recapitulation not merely an image of atonement but a *model* with explanatory force (ch. 1).[9]

---

8. This metaphor is adapted from a beautifully written passage by Kevin J. Vanhoozer: "We struggle to understand adequately, yet we are fed the answer every Lord's Day when we take communion. . . . Then, like the five thousand, we discover that after our centuries-long banquet of atonement theology, there are still more fragments of the cross left over." Kevin J. Vanhoozer, "The Atonement in Postmodernity: Guilt, Goats, and Gifts," in *The Glory of the Atonement,* ed. Charles Hill and Frank James (Downers Grove, IL: IVP, 2004), 404.

9. See again my explanatory spectrum of atonement terminology in the introduction. In my usage, moving from left to right (from images, to models, to theories) involves stronger and stronger claims about one's ability to answer the "how" question. That is: How does Christ's work *work?* My preference for talk of "models" reflects a belief that we can provide some rationale for how Jesus saves us, but that we should not pretend that we have *the* full "theory" to elucidate atonement.

Unfortunately, the recapitulative model is hardly free from modern questions. In chapter 2, I asked whether Christians can continue to speak meaningfully of Jesus as the true Adam in a scientific age that doubts the existence of a singular man who fathered the entire human race. While taking seriously the emerging genetic evidence, my conclusion settled on a mixture of steadfast theological commitments and respectful scientific openness. In short, some version of the historical "Adam" remains important for Christian theology (specifically in accounting for evil as intruder in God's good world), but this does not mean that one's only option is to believe in a young earth and to disbelieve in modern genetic science. In fact, serious scholars in a variety of disciplines have suggested ways in which the biblical and scientific data might be held together. To take just one example, N. T. Wright suggests,

> Just as God chose Israel from the rest of humankind for a special, strange, demanding vocation, so perhaps what Genesis is telling us is that *God chose one pair from the rest of early hominids for a special, strange, demanding vocation.* This pair (call them Adam and Eve if you like) were to be the representatives of the whole human race.[10]

One need not be the father of a group in order to be their spiritual head.

Beyond the scientific questions, the most important point regarding the arrangement of recapitulation in the Christ-shaped mosaic pertained to how it may be seen to support the other pieces in a foundational respect. "The highest does not stand without the lowest."[11] And from the *feet* of Christ's recapitulative identity, one is able to draw a vertical line of causality up to the *heart* of penal substitution and on to the *head* of *Christus Victor.*

To take one example, certain recapitulative presuppositions proved essential in supporting a more coherent version of vicarious judgment and penal substitution. By addressing the problem of penal nontransference, an Irenaean account of recapitulation prevents penal notions of the atonement from running afoul of what has been called "the justice worry"—the idea that guilt or punishment cannot

---

10. N. T. Wright, "Excursus on Paul's Use of Adam," in John H. Walton, *The Lost World of Adam and Eve: Genesis 2–3 and the Human Origins Debate* (Downers Grove, IL: IVP Academic, 2015), 177, italics in original.

11. C. S. Lewis, *The Four Loves* (1960; repr., New York: Harcourt Brace, 1988), 10.

314 | The Mosaic of Atonement

be justly transferred from the guilty to the innocent. Yet if all humanity is somehow bound up *with* the Son (as our archetypal, image-granting source), then the cross presents not simply one innocent and disconnected individual bearing the punishment for other guilty ones but the judgment of the entire human race in the body of the one person who really does (somehow) "contain" and represent us all.[12] Since it is in the Son that we "live and move and have our being" (Acts 17:28), it is possible to claim that "I have been crucified with Christ" long before I ever came to profess faith in him (Gal 2:20). In short, the *feet* support the *heart* in a foundational respect.

THE BEATING HEART: PENAL SUBSTITUTION AND VICARIOUS JUDGMENT

Just as certain recapitulative presuppositions are foundational for the logic of penal substitution, so too does Christ's penalty-bearing death provide a ground for *Christus Victor* logic.[13] Despite claims that penal models of atonement are historically novel (ch. 4), biblically weak (ch. 5), and ethically repulsive (ch. 6), I claimed—quite to the contrary—that the divine victory flows forth from Christ's recapitulative fidelity (*feet*) and his penalty-absorbing death (*heart*). Once again, these three models lend themselves to order and integration even though they should not be ranked as competitors.

In all this, I have again sought to steer a middle course between two warring extremes. On the one hand, I replied with a clear "no" to those who decry penal substitution as tantamount to sadomasochistic "child abuse." Yet on the other, I have moved to chasten those (often in conservative Reformed camps) who elevate penal emphases as the apogee of all atonement models. A pox—or rather, a *pax*—on both these houses! While penal substitution forms the *heart* of the Christ-shaped icon, it is not the whole. Nor should it be singled out as most important. One way

---

12. This claim is similar to that of Oliver Crisp, who suggests that "the justice worry" of penal doctrines may be alleviated if we do away with certain individualistic presuppositions and conceive of Christ and the elect as one metaphysical entity. See, for instance, Crisp, "The Logic of Penal Substitution," 227n26. My own account (as seen previously with recapitulation) posits that the mysterious connection between Christ and all humanity has to the do with the *imago Dei* and the fact that all image bearers bear this indelible connection to their archetypal head (see ch. 3).

13. My claim throughout has been that one must hold the substitutionary and the incorporative aspects of Christ's penalty-absorbing death together, even while distinguishing the ways in which they speak of different aspects in the work of atonement.

of threading this needle involves the careful definition of what was dubbed "mere penal substitution"—a move that proves essential when one notes how many fights surrounding the model proceed with a frightful lack of terminological (not to mention Trinitarian!) clarity.

As I argued, mere penal substitution ought not pit the Father against the Son in a way that seems to sever their eternal love relationship. In place of these un-Trinitarian ideas, mere penal substitution need claim only that Christ underwent the divinely sanctioned penalty for human sin in our stead. Yet in saying this, I attempted to make a careful distinction between the incorporative and substitutionary elements of Christ's work, both of which are biblical.

Regarding sensory experience, some things were clearly suffered by Jesus that were not experienced by me. And regarding agency, I contributed nothing (except my sin) to the strange triumph at Golgotha. I was mysteriously bound up with Christ, but I was not the agent of redemptive action. Thus, incorporative participation describes things as they *really are* at some deep and unseen level,[14] while substitution describes the previously mentioned levels of agency and sensory experience.[15]

With these caveats in place, I joined a chorus of scholars who have noted that Christ's devil-defeating victory emerges not merely alongside (or in contrast to) his penalty-enduring death but precisely because of it.[16] Just as Jesus's recapitulative fidelity provides a positive ground for his emerging victory, so does his vicarious judgment on our behalf remove the Accuser's right to condemn us. In certain key respects,[17] the logic runs as follows:

Recapitulation ⟶ Penal Substitution ⟶ *Christus Victor*

In line with this thinking, Colossians states that Christ triumphed over the principalities and powers precisely by nailing our note of legal indebtedness (the *cheirographon*) to the cross (2:13–15). Likewise, Revelation glories in the fact that the Accuser has been overcome "by the blood of the Lamb" (12:10–11). Both here and elsewhere, it is not just victory and

---

14. Hence Paul can say that "all died" with Christ (2 Cor 5:14), "for in him all things were created . . . and in him all things hold together" (Col 1:16, 17).

15. In other languages the concepts may merge even further. This was witnessed, for instance, by Barth's use of *Stellvertretung*. See Editors' Preface, in *CD* IV/1, vii.

16. See again ch. 7.

17. This brief qualifier is important because I have no desire to claim that this simple flow chart fully captures the interlocking relationship of these three models. To go down this road would itself be a form of reductionism.

penal substitution but victory *by way of* penal substitution and vicarious judgment. Even the *head* must receive the cleansing lifeblood of the *heart.*

| O SACRED HEAD: *CHRISTUS VICTOR* |

Part 3 began by reexamining the popular patristic claim that trickery played a part in Jesus's triumph over Satan. While rejecting cross versions of this so-called ransom model, I moved to reclaim the place of *self-deception* in the overthrow of satanic power. Because evil is irrational (as Barth and Torrance claimed), it is by no means impossible to picture Satan and his allies in the paradoxical position of trying to keep Christ from the cross at one moment (e.g., Matt 16:23), while attempting to bring about his death about in another (John 13:27). The idea, however, is not that God acts deceitfully but that sinful misunderstanding on the part of "the powers" (both human and demonic)—their ignorance and violent grasping—comes to aid God's purposes as he uses their malevolent momentum against them (ch. 8).

Through a critical assessment of the work of Walter Wink, I sought to fill out the *Christus Victor* theme by an exploration of the ontic status of the Evil One. Although I rejected Wink's tendency toward Pelagian panentheism and excessive demythologizing, I nonetheless affirmed the idea that the devil sometimes acts as an unwitting and postpersonal servant of God's redemptive purposes.[18] Whether by the pride-quashing side effect of Paul's thorny messenger (2 Cor 12:7) or the soul-saving torture of the incestuous brother (1 Cor 5:5), the Bible shockingly includes Satan in the expansive category of "all things" that are made to work together for the good of those who love God (Rom 8:28). Nonetheless, the biblical devil betrays no signs of knowingly serving as a covert agent of the Crown (ch. 9).

The final chapter of the *Christus Victor* section addressed a more practical and gut-wrenching question: If Jesus really conquered sin and Satan, why doesn't it look like it? In dialogue with Scripture and with Graeme Greene's *The Power and the Glory*, my claim was that Christ's God-glorifying triumph is indeed the telos of atonement themes, even while it is crucial to recognize the extent to which it is a "staged" victory. To say this, however, does not imply that the conquest was false or phony but

---

18. While the "unwitting" aspect of this description points back to ch. 8's claim about the irrationality of evil, the point about Satan's "postpersonal" status marks the devil out as a kind of *tertium quid*—a "third thing"—that is neither a person in the full (Boethian or Trinitarian) sense, nor a mere symbol devoid of ontic content.

that it involves multiple installments that must not be "blurred" together or left unacknowledged. At present, believers are seated in the heavenlies with Christ, even as we "stand" as though slain on the earth. And in this paradoxical position, Christians are called to imitate the Savior in a form of cruciform triumph. In this insight resides the reciprocal relation between the *head* and the *hands* of the mosaic Christ—the model known as moral influence.

THE OUTSTRETCHED HANDS: MORAL INFLUENCE

As G. B. Caird once wrote, "The transforming of sinners into righteous [humans] is the final defeat of the power."[19] For this reason, sanctification cannot be detached from God's continuing triumph over evil through the transformed lives of his people. After all, Paul once gloried in the promise that "the God of peace will soon crush Satan under your feet" (Rom 16:20). Hence, the moral influence model is not a mere subjective afterthought to the "real" objective work of recapitulation, penal substitution, and divine triumph. Once again, there is an order and relation to such pieces.

In my mosaic of atonement doctrine, the moral influence paradigm was categorized in two ways: (1) the beckoning *hand* of divine love which calls forth grateful imitation and bold approach to God on behalf of sinners and (2) the restraining or unmasking *hand* that waives off certain idolatrous or violent tendencies. Both aspects are essential, yet the former was approached through the oft-misunderstood work of Peter Abelard (ch. 11), while the latter came to light through the bold revisionism of René Girard (ch. 12).

Contrary to popular opinion, Abelard was not an exemplarist who denied the so-called "objective" aspects of atonement. Despite his faults, he wrote approvingly of Christ's vicarious obedience (recapitulation) and even penal substitution. In Girard, however, my appropriation was more selective. Although I rejected his (1) idiosyncratic exegesis, (2) inadequate plight, (3) insufficient solution, and sometimes (4) Gnostic-sounding gospel, I found value in his brilliant and creative work. Alongside helpful insights on mimetic desire and human scapegoating, Girard reminds theologians that a crucial aspect of Christ's moral influence is the unmasking and restraining of certain destructive and idolatrous tendencies, both in individuals and

---

19. G. B. Caird, *Principalities and Powers* (Oxford: Oxford University Press, 1956), 97.

in society at large. Thus the "negative gesture" of Girardian exemplarism should complement the positive "beckoning" essayed by Abelard.

In saying this, however, my final claim was that more attention must be given to the perfecting "engine" of moral influence—that is, the Holy Spirit.[20] By linking the beckoning and restraining *hands* (of Abelard and Girard) to a more robust pneumatology, I hoped to show how ordinary, fallen humans are swept up and incorporated into God's redemptive work. Atonement is praxis, both for Jesus and his people.[21] Yet this praxis is made possible only because the Spirit makes us into the body of Jesus here on earth. In this way, believers participate in God's work of reconciliation by grace alone. Likewise, it is the Holy Spirit who helps Christians to avoid certain (1) Pelagian, (2) predestinarian, and (3) pantheist tendencies. This is so because, while atonement is often called the work of Christ, it is actualized by what Irenaeus dubbed the two hands of God—the Son and Holy Spirit (ch. 13).

SUBVERSIVE TOUR GUIDES IN THE *HAGIA SOPHIA*

There remains an order in the integration of atonement models, even though there is no need to prioritize one part of Christ's mosaic body as most important. The recapitulative presuppositions of Irenaeus ground the other images like *feet* planted in the dust of fallen Eden. Christ's penalty-bearing death pumps cleansing lifeblood like a *heart* to other members. And the triumphant *head* of *Christus Victor* rises as the telos of atonement, even as the final victory comes as the Spirit shapes sinners into saints by the beckoning and restraining *hands* of moral influence. "This is my body," Christ proclaimed, not merely broken but also mended for you.

With the summary done, it is time now to reenter the age-old Christian church that was mentioned in the introduction: the Hagia Sophia. As with the long-covered mosaic icons of this great cathedral, the task of Christian theology is not to solve the "puzzle" of atonement doctrine but to chip away the plaster that occludes the pieces of Christ's shattered but now resurrected body. The goal is not to "figure out" each aspect of his work but to "gaze upon the beauty of the LORD" and seek him in his sanctuary (Ps 27:4).

We theologians are neither editors nor inventors. Rather, we go about

---

20. This was accomplished through a critical engagement with the pneumatology of Sarah Coakley.

21. See Scot McKnight, *A Community Called Atonement* (Nashville: Abingdon, 2007), 117.

our work in the (universal) church of holy wisdom (*hagia sophia*), like subversive "tour guides" on a redemptive mission. While most guides may be content to discuss history and architecture and prevent a clumsy tourist from damaging the artwork, the theologian's aim is indeed more daring. Amid the throng from every tribe and tongue, our aim is to point toward Jesus, standing as he does amidst the minarets, the dusty relics of the past, the bustle of distracted tourists, and the political divisions that are everywhere apparent. "This is not just a museum," we say with a mixture of respect and Spirit-driven boldness. "It is a place of worship. This is Christ's body given for *you*." And though the mosaic uncovered in this book has gaps and missing pieces, the picture of atonement is clear enough: "More can be mended than you know."

ACKNOWLEDGMENTS

Someone once said that a footnote is an academic way of saying "Thank you."

I'm not sure I believe that. I have, after all, read (and written) some curmudgeonly footnotes. Nonetheless, there are people to whom I owe a special debt of gratitude that goes beyond even the numbered citations in this book.

With regard to the content of this volume, the greatest word of thanks goes to my colleague, Jerome Van Kuiken. He provided invaluable feedback on the manuscript at each stage, and he is always willing to read my drafts with a rare mix of encouragement and clear-eyed critique. While he is (of course) not responsible for my remaining errors or imbalances, the book is unquestionably better because of his input. Stephanie Leupp tracked down countless books for me through interlibrary loan, and I jokingly tell her (though with some truthfulness) that if it were not for her help, I could not produce a single publication. My PhD supervisor, Thomas A. Noble, gave encouragement and advice on aspects of the study, and I remain deeply grateful for his influence on my scholarly life. My student, Noah Storkson, was kind enough to help with the indexing.

I am also grateful for the help of all the fine folks at Zondervan Academic. A special thanks to Katya Covrett for taking an interest in the project and for improving it in countless ways. And to Matthew Estel for his encouraging feedback and for his help smoothing out the many rough edges of my writing.

An even deeper debt of thanks extends to my family. My father and mother taught me to love Jesus and his church. My wife's parents are likewise incredible, and their puzzle-crafting proclivities are mentioned in the introduction. My grandparents (on both sides) paved the way in ministry and faithful perseverance. And most importantly, my wife, Brianna, made this book possible not only by her constant encouragement but also by her willingness to give me extra time to write amid the chaos of a household overrun by four small children. To Lucy, Penelope, Ewan, and Teddy: I love you.

I hope (eventually) to dedicate a book to each of our kids. But this volume is inscribed to my oldest daughter. To Lucy Grace McNall: you are bright and brave and beautiful. My greatest hope is that you come to grasp "how wide and long and high and deep is the love of Christ" (Eph 3:18).

SUBJECT INDEX

abuse, 18, 94, 105, 114, 118, 120, 125, 149, 154, 157, 159, 161–64, 189, 190, 314

Adam, 18, 19, 23, 29, 30, 32–75, 79–83, 86, 90–95, 103, 146, 166, 171, 173–76, 182, 224, 225, 252, 254, 256, 257, 260, 281, 312, 313

Adamic guilt, 86

Adamic vocation, 92

aesthetic criterion, 34, 35

agency, 102, 103, 133, 134, 146, 173, 226, 298–300, 304, 315

Akedah, 130, 174

anakephalaiosasthai, 18

anakephalaiōsis, 38

analogies, 120, 163, 167, 258

ancient Israel, 131

angels, 213–15

animal sacrifice, 128–34, 271, 272

anthropomorphism, 154

Arianism, 114

Arminianism, 236

ascension of Christ, 24, 92, 94, 178, 182, 238

aseity, 235, 236

beauty, 34, 35, 95, 300, 304, 309, 318

Beelzebul controversy, 282

Bible, 14, 15, 20, 29, 39, 44, 48–51, 59, 60, 63, 66–68, 71, 110, 111, 127–49, 154, 163–65, 168, 170, 179, 180, 185, 199, 204, 224, 227, 228, 272

biblical literature, 63, 64

biblical narrative, 33, 38, 40, 66, 69, 154, 156, 160, 175, 204, 237, 280

biological model of original sin, 66

Calvary, 84, 93, 134, 246, 285

Calvinism, 236

canon, 20, 33, 127, 128, 138, 148, 159, 164, 167, 281

caput, 38

character of God, 16, 127, 148–59, 168, 170, 199, 235

Charismatic movement, 202, 295

cheirographon, 181, 315

chief end of God, 233, 236

Christianity Today, 19

Christ's divinity, 17, 114, 117, 141, 198, 199, 203, 208, 223, 273

Christ's vocation, 24, 45, 72, 95, 182, 185, 238

Christus Nudus, 46

Christus propitiator, 176–78, 183, 188

Christus Victor, 15–18, 23, 24, 46, 74, 88, 91–93, 95, 160, 162, 171–78, 183, 186, 191, 193–247, 281, 310, 313–16, 318

church history, 22, 29, 99–126, 165, 201, 241, 284, 295

church tradition, 33, 42, 85, 99, 100, 127, 128, 206, 284, 285

compatibilism, 299, 300

concordism, 59, 60

concupiscence, 42, 66

condemnation, 75, 76, 86, 88, 89, 109, 134, 145, 146, 177, 181, 183, 204

SCRIPTURE INDEX

AUTHOR INDEX

McConnell, T. Mark, 46, 165
McFague, Sally, 77
McGrath, Alister, 187, 255
McKnight, Scot, 20, 49, 51, 53, 57, 59,
    63, 66, 84, 134, 146, 232, 277, 286,
    288, 296, 297, 318
McLaren, Brian, 14
McNall, Joshua, 36, 42, 294
McQuillan, Tessa, 304
Michaels, J. Ramsey, 185, 186
Middleton, J. Richard, 37
Milbank, John, 279, 294
Milton, John, 91, 224
Minns, Denis, 30, 36, 42
Moberly, R. C., 103
Moo, Douglas J., 130
Morris, Henry M., 56
Morris, Leon, 110, 111
Mortimer, Richard, 63
Mouw, Richard J., 106, 162, 190
Murphy, Mark C., 76, 104
Murray, A. Victor, 258
Murray, Michael, 54
Myers, Benjamin, 116–18, 160, 179, 180,
    197
Niebuhr, Richard, 237, 261
Nietzsche, Friedrich, 62, 275, 283, 298
Noble, T. A., 43, 62, 63, 86, 88, 208,
    220, 226, 301
Noll, Mark, 56, 57
Noll, Stephen, 212, 220
Numbers, Ronald, 56
Oden, Thomas C., 87, 100, 197
Origen of Alexandria, 196, 197, 200, 218
Osborn, Eric, 34
Osborn, Ronald, 54, 68, 72
Ostling, Richard N., 19
Ovey, Michael, 83, 99, 108, 109, 114–16,
    118, 120, 121, 125, 131, 132, 135
Owen, John, 44, 83, 105, 123, 145, 177,
    178, 299
Packer, J. I., 110, 232
Page, Sydney H. T., 215–17, 222, 224,
    225, 282
Pannenberg, Wolfhart, 85

Parker, Rebecca Ann, 159, 189
Pelikan, Jaroslav, 120, 125, 255
Peterson, Brandon, 81
Peterson, David, 135
Peterson, Eugene, 298
Piper, John, 233–37
Placher, William, 278, 282
Plantinga, Alvin, 57, 68, 69, 227
Plantinga, Cornelius, 54
Porter, Stanley, 42
Pseudo-Dionysius, 291
Pugh, Ben, 83, 99, 196, 202, 268, 277,
    279, 284
Purves, Andrew, 88
Quarles, Charles L., 242
Rana, Fazale, 63
Rashdall, Hastings, 200, 254, 255, 257
Ray, Darby Kathleen, 159, 161, 205
Rigby, Paul, 43, 66
Rilke, Rainer Maria, 223, 224
Ritschl, Albrecht, 252
Robinson, Marilynne, 35
Rodes, Stanley, 88
Rosenberg, Stanley, P., 122, 198
Ross, Hugh, 63
Rutledge, Fleming, 91, 92, 126, 149,
    232, 242
Sach, Andrew, 83, 99, 108, 109, 114–16,
    118, 120, 121, 125, 131, 132, 135
Scott-Macnab, David, 121
Schendel, Joshua, 92, 93, 113
Schneider, John R., 54, 60, 62, 69, 235
Schreiner, Thomas R., 111, 132, 302
Schwöbel, Christoph, 305
Scotus, Duns, 305
Sellar, W. C., 149
Shakespeare, William, 29, 41, 212, 220
Shelton, W. Brian, 301, 303
Sherman, Robert, 129
Smail, Tom, 128, 158, 159
Smalley, Stephen, 185
Smeaton, George, 178
Smith, James K. A., 60, 66, 70
Socinus, Faustus, 78
Socrates, 152, 274

Sonderegger, Katherine, 31, 168
Southgate, Christopher, 54
Sproul, R. C., 168
Spufford, Francis, 309
Spurgeon, Charles Haddon, 234
Stanglin, Keith D., 236, 302
Stearley, Ralph, 56
Steinbeck, John, 293
Stone, William, 51, 52, 58, 62, 63
Stott, John R. W., 62, 111, 168, 169, 177
Strobel, Kyle C., 235
Stump, Eleonore, 76, 155, 164, 165, 172, 254
Swamidass, S. Joshua, 58, 63
Swete, H. B., 42
Szymborska, Wislawa, 72
Taliaferro, Charles, 204
Tanner, Kathryn, 16, 178, 231, 232
Taylor, R. O. P., 256, 257, 259
Tertullian, 30, 42, 294
Thiselton, Anthony, 296
Thomas Aquinas, 81, 184, 254, 285, 299
Tillich, Paul, 262
Tilling, Chris, 40
Torrance, Alan, 182
Torrance, T. F., 44, 45, 81, 82, 87–90, 103, 140, 141, 187, 207, 208, 226, 316
Travis, Stephen, 128
Treat, Jeremy R., 19, 21, 92, 106, 130, 153, 169, 174–78, 181–83, 185, 231–33, 240, 241, 310
Trevelyan, G. M., 201
Turretin, Francis, 123
Van Kuiken, E. Jerome, 112, 132, 143, 185, 284, 295

Vanhoozer, Kevin J., 89, 119, 141, 209, 298, 311, 312
Venantius Fortunatus, 241
Venema, Dennis, 49, 51–53, 57–59, 63, 66, 67
Volf, Miroslav, 160, 161, 285
Vidu, Adonis, 122, 123, 158
Walton, John H., 48, 49, 53, 63, 64, 66, 67, 72, 313
Weaver, J. Denny, 159, 276, 279, 285
Webster, John, 265
Weingart, R. E., 257, 259
Wenham, Gordon, 130, 131
Wesley, Charles, 123, 230
Wesley, John, 86–88, 90, 301–3
Whitcomb, John C., 56
Wilcox, David, 53
William of St. Thierry, 253, 254, 260
Williams, Garry, 80, 124, 125, 158, 159, 166, 177
Williams, James G., 268
Williams, Thomas, 256, 259, 260
Wink, Walter, 159, 160, 211–28, 235, 236, 316
Witherington, Ben, 147, 188, 189, 302–5
Wollstonecraft, Mary, 126
Wright, Christopher J. H., 61
Wright, N. T., 45, 46, 57, 58, 60, 72, 81, 111, 131, 132, 136, 155, 169, 212, 238, 295, 313
Wright, Nigel, 202
Yarbrough, Robert W., 185
Yeatman, R. J., 149
Yoder, John Howard, 190, 284
Young, Davis, 56